THE GAMBLE

GENERAL PETRAEUS AND THE AMERICAN MILITARY ADVENTURE IN IRAQ

THOMAS E. RICKS

PENGUIN BOOKS

PENGUIN BOOKS
Published by the Penguin Group
Penguin Group (USA) Inc., 375 Hudson Street, New York, New York 10014, U.S.A.
Penguin Group (Canada), 90 Eglinton Avenue East, Suite 700, Toronto,
Ontario, Canada M4P 2Y3 (a division of Pearson Penguin Canada Inc.)
Penguin Books Ltd, 80 Strand, London WC2R 0RL, England
Penguin Ireland, 25 St Stephen's Green, Dublin 2, Ireland (a division of Penguin Books Ltd)
Penguin Group (Australia), 250 Camberwell Road, Camberwell,
Victoria 3124, Australia (a division of Pearson Australia Group Pty Ltd)
Penguin Books India Pvt Ltd, 11 Community Centre, Panchsheel Park, New Delhi – 110 017, India
Penguin Group (NZ), 67 Apollo Drive, Rosedale, North Shore 0632,
New Zealand (a division of Pearson New Zealand Ltd)
Penguin Books (South Africa) (Pty) Ltd, 24 Sturdee Avenue,
Rosebank, Johannesburg 2196, South Africa

Penguin Books Ltd, Registered Offices:
80 Strand, London WC2R 0RL, England

First published in the United States of America by The Penguin Press,
a member of Penguin Group (USA) Inc. 2009
This edition with a new afterword published in Penguin Books 2010

1 3 5 7 9 10 8 6 4 2

THE LIBRARY OF CONGRESS HAS CATALOGED THE HARDCOVER EDITION AS FOLLOWS:
Ricks, Thomas E.
The gamble : General David Petraeus and the American military
adventure in Iraq, 2006–2008 / Thomas E. Ricks.
p. cm.
Includes bibliographical references and index.
ISBN 978-1-59420-197-4 (hc.)
ISBN 978-0-14-311691-2 (pbk.)
1. Iraq War, 2003– 2. Petraeus, David Howell—Military leadership. 3. Iraq War, 2003—Campaigns.
4. United States—History, Military—21st century. I. Title.
DS79.76.R537 2009
956.7044'340973—dc22
2008044510

Printed in the United States of America
DESIGNED BY AMANDA DEWEY MAPS BY GENE THORP

Praise for *The Gamble*

"In his absorbing, impressively researched new book, *The Gamble*, Ricks examines how U.S. goals in Iraq changed in late 2006. Through his impressive access to military and political leaders, Ricks demonstrates that what fueled this change was the lack of any recognizable progress in Iraq." —*The Boston Globe*

"[A] grim forecast . . . [by] the nation's best-known defense correspondent."
—Mike Allen, *Politico*

"It is Ricks' look forward that gives this book its tremendous value, not the who-did-what-when chronicle of the surge." —Tony Capaccio, Bloomberg

"Thomas E. Ricks eavesdrops on the high-ranking squabble over *The Gamble* (Penguin), General Petraeus's plan to launch the surge in Iraq." —*Vanity Fair*

"[*The Gamble*] suggests there may be a light at the end of the tunnel, but if there is, it's flickering—and a long way off." —*Time*

"If you enjoyed *Fiasco*, thrilled to have your prejudices about the clueless Bush administration confirmed, it's your responsibility to read *The Gamble*."
—Salon.com

"Rich in both vignettes and interviews." —*The Economist*

"The principle value of Mr. Ricks' book beyond being a historical chronicle is the light it may shed on the future course of events in Afghanistan."
—*The Washington Times*

"A journalistic achievement of high order." —The Second Pass.com

"Commendable." —*The Weekly Standard*

"*The Gamble* details the intriguing story of the U.S. military in Iraq from 2006 to 2008 from a fresh and credible perspective. . . . Ricks' book is a wake-up call for any neoconservative who remains too optimistic about the war's progress. . . . This book is a *must* read for any member of the U.S. military or informed American who wants to know what really took place in Iraq in the last few years."
—*Baltimore Republican Examiner*

"*The Gamble* is the most remarkable book I've read in ages." —*Macleans*

ABOUT THE AUTHOR

Thomas E. Ricks is a senior fellow at the Center for a New American Security, the only Washington think tank led by veterans of our current wars. He also writes the blog The Best Defense for *Foreign Policy* magazine. Previously he was a reporter for twenty-six years at *The Washington Post* and *The Wall Street Journal.* A member of two Pulitzer Prize–winning teams for national reporting, he has reported on U.S. military activities in Somalia, Haiti, Korea, Bosnia, Kosovo, Macedonia, Kuwait, Turkey, Afghanistan, and Iraq. He is the author of *Fiasco, Making the Corps,* and *A Soldier's Duty.*

For my wife, with love and gratitude.

Surprise and initiative . . . are infinitely more important and effective in strategy than in tactics.

—Carl Von Clausewitz, On War

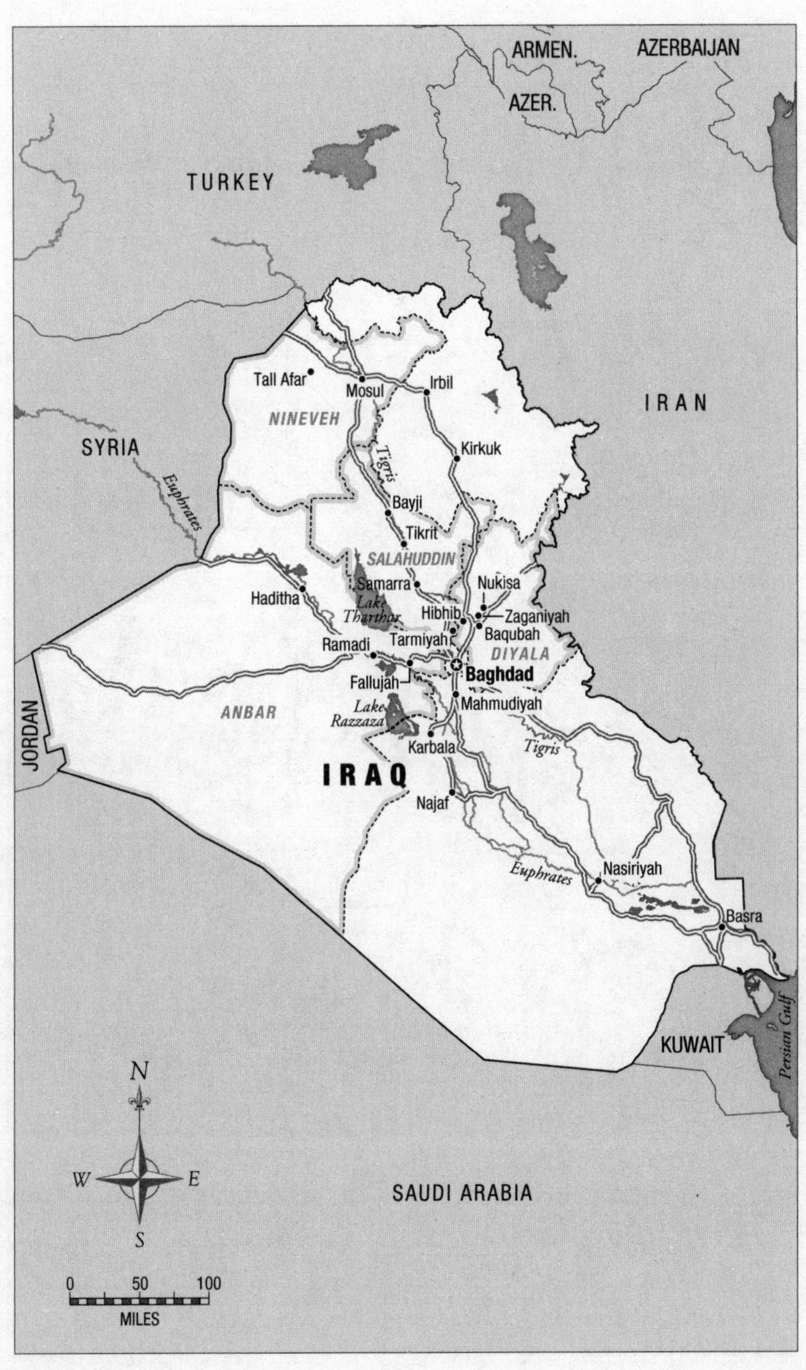
ARMEN.
AZERBAIJAN
AZER.
TURKEY
IRAN
SYRIA
Euphrates
Tall Afar
Mosul
Irbil
NINEVEH
Kirkuk
Tigris
Bayji
Tikrit
SALAHUDDIN
Samarra
Nukisa
Haditha
Lake Tharthar
Hibhib
Zaganiyah
Baqubah
Tarmiyah
Ramadi
DIYALA
Baghdad
Fallujah
Mahmudiyah
ANBAR
Lake Razzaza
Karbala
Tigris
JORDAN
IRAQ
Najaf
Nasiriyah
Euphrates
Basra
KUWAIT
Persian Gulf
N
W
E
S
SAUDI ARABIA
0
50
100
MILES

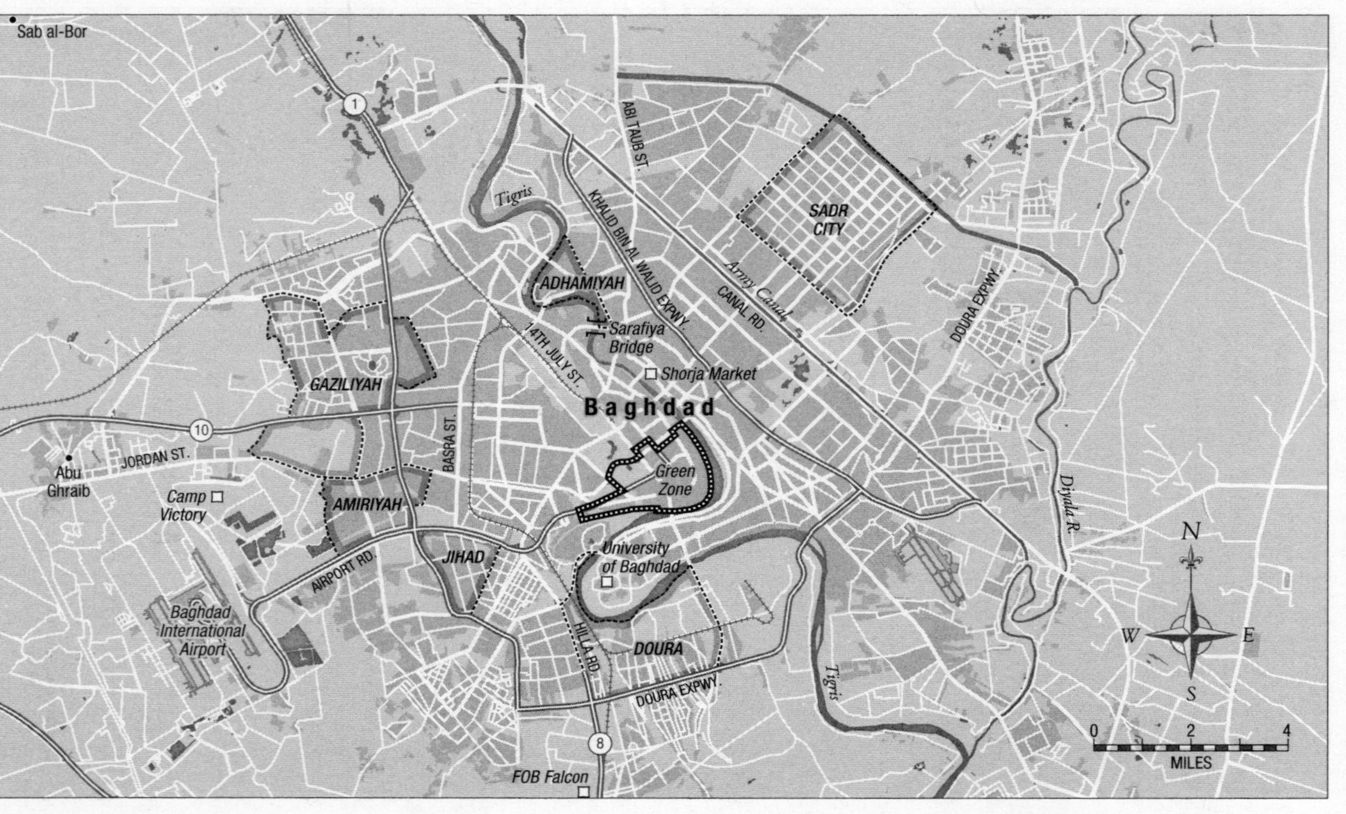
Sab al-Bor
1
Tigris
ABI TAUB ST.
KHALID BIN AL WALID EXPWY.
SADR CITY
Army Canal
CANAL RD.
ADHAMIYAH
DOURA EXPWY.
Sarafiya Bridge
14TH JULY ST.
Shorja Market
GAZILIYAH
Baghdad
10
Abu Ghraib
JORDAN ST.
BASRA ST.
Green Zone
Camp Victory
AMIRIYAH
Diyala R.
University of Baghdad
JIHAD
AIRPORT RD.
N
W
E
S
Baghdad International Airport
HILLA RD.
DOURA
Tigris
DOURA EXPWY.
0
2
4
MILES
8
FOB Falcon

CONTENTS

PART THREE
WAR WITHOUT END

CAST OF CHARACTERS

2006

Lt. Gen. David Petraeus, commander of U.S. Army educational establishment, Fort Leavenworth, Kansas

Marine Gen. Peter Pace, chairman, Joint Chiefs of Staff

Retired Gen. Jack Keane, former vice chief of staff, U.S. Army

Donald Rumsfeld, secretary of defense

Gen. John Abizaid, chief, Central Command, U.S. military headquarters for Mideast

Army Gen. George Casey, U.S. commander in Iraq

Army Col. Sean MacFarland, commander, 1st Brigade Combat Team, 1st Armored Division, operating primarily in Ramadi, Iraq

Fred Kagan, policy analyst, American Enterprise Institute

Tom Donnelly, defense expert, American Enterprise Institute

Nouri al-Maliki, prime minister of Iraq

Moqtada al-Sadr, head of the Sadr Trend and its militia, the Jaysh al-Mahdi

2007

Petraeus, promoted to full four-star general, succeeds Casey as top U.S. commander in Iraq

Robert Gates, replaces Rumsfeld

Adm. Michael Mullen, replaces Pace

Adm. William "Fox" Fallon, replaces Abizaid at Central Command and becomes Petraeus's superior officer in the chain of command

Col. Bill Rapp, head of Commander's Initiatives Group, Petraeus's internal think tank

Lt. Col. Charles Miller, deputy director of Petraeus's think tank, drafter of Petraeus's memoranda to President Bush

Capt. Elizabeth McNally, writer and editor for Petraeus

Col. Pete Mansoor, executive officer to Petraeus

Sadi Othman, interpreter and cultural and political adviser to Petraeus

David Kilcullen, counterinsurgency adviser to Petraeus

Maj. Gen. David Fastabend, director, strategic operations for Petraeus (in mid-2007, succeeded by Maj. Gen. Michael Barbero)

Lt. Gen. James Dubik, chief of mission to train and advise Iraqi army and police

Lt. Gen. Raymond Odierno, commander III Corps, oversees day-to-day operations

Brig. Gen. Joseph Anderson, chief of staff for Odierno

Emma Sky, political and cultural adviser to Odierno

Col. Martin Stanton, chief of reconciliation for Odierno

III Corps planners: Col. Martin Wilson, Lt. Col. Jeff McDougall, Maj. James Powell, Maj. Kent Strader

Brig. Gen. John Allen, deputy commander, Marine Corps in Iraq

Ryan Crocker, U.S. ambassador to Iraq

2008

Lt. Gen. Lloyd Austin, succeeds Odierno

Col. Michael Bell, succeeds Rapp as head of Petraeus's internal think tank

September: Odierno succeeds Petraeus as top American commander in Iraq

ACRONYMS AND ABBREVIATIONS

ACR—armored cavalry regiment

AO—area of operation

AOR—area of responsibility

AQI or AQIZ—Al Qaeda in Iraq; also known as "al Qaeda in Mesopotamia" or "al Qaeda in the Land of the Two Rivers" ("IZ" is U.S. military code for Iraq.)

Centcom—Central Command, the U.S. military headquarters for the Middle East

BCT—brigade combat team, or a brigade with attached units

BUA—battle update assessment, a daily overview meeting for senior commanders and staff, sometimes also called a BUB, for "battle update briefing"

CF—coalition forces; often used by American officials to refer to U.S., Iraqi, and British forces

CG—commanding general

CLC—Concerned Local Citizens, official U.S. term for local fighters, many of them former insurgents who changed sides and began to support the U.S. position, but not necessarily the Baghdad government; also known as ISVs, or Iraqi Security Volunteers; later euphemized as "Sons of Iraq"

COIN—counterinsurgency

COP—a U.S. military combat outpost

DoD—Department of Defense

EFP—explosively formed penetrator, also sometimes called explosively formed projectile; a particularly lethal kind of roadside bomb, or "IED"

FOB –forward operating base, the biggest U.S. bases in Iraq; compare COP

HMMWV—high mobility multipurpose wheeled vehicle; the modern U.S. military equivalent of the jeep; acronym usually pronounced "Humvee"

HUMINT—human intelligence

ID—infantry division

IP—Iraqi Police

IED—improvised explosive device, U.S. military term for a roadside bomb

ISF—Iraqi Security Forces (that is, Iraqi army and police)

ISR—intelligence, surveillance, and reconnaissance

IZ—International Zone, official name of the Green Zone, home of the U.S. headquarters, the Iraqi government, and many foreign embassies

JAM—Jaysh al-Mahdi, the militia of radical Shiite cleric Moqtada al-Sadr; its personnel are occasionally referred to by U.S. personnel as "JAMsters"

JSS—joint security station, similar to a COP but jointly operated with Iraqi army or police

KIA—killed in action

MI—military intelligence

MNF—Multi-National Forces, also sometimes rendered as MNF-I, for Multi-National Forces–Iraq

NCO—non-commissioned officer (that is, a sergeant or a corporal)

NSC—National Security Council

PRT—Provincial Reconstruction Team

OIF—Operation Iraqi Freedom, U.S. military name for the Iraq war

QRF—quick reaction force

RoE—rules of engagement

RPG—rocket-propelled grenade

SIGINT—signals intelligence

SOF—Special Operations Forces

SOI—"Sons of Iraq"; *see* CLC

SVTC—secure video teleconference

TCN—third country national

UAV—unmanned aerial vehicle, or drone aircraft, often referring to the missile-equipped Predator

WMD—weapons of mass destruction

PART ONE

THE OLD WAR ENDS

1.

THINGS FALL APART

(Fall 2005)

The first misbegotten phase of the American war in Iraq effectively came to an end on Saturday, November 19, 2005. "It was a mediocre morning" in the upper Euphrates River Valley town of Haditha, 150 miles northwest of Baghdad, Marine Lance Cpl. Justin Sharratt would later recall. "It wasn't too busy, and it wasn't suspiciously quiet."

Then, at about 7:15, near the corner of what they called Routes Chestnut and Viper, Sharratt's squad was hit by a roadside bomb. The Marines of 1st Squad, 3rd Platoon, Kilo Company, 3rd Battalion, 1st Marine Regiment, would do many things that long day in response to the bombing, and they later would offer much conflicting testimony about their actions. But one thing they clearly did not do was protect Iraqi civilians—and that is why the Marine killings at Haditha are key to understanding the failure of the first years of the American war in Iraq, and why it became imperative to revamp U.S. strategy, beginning by revisiting many of the basic assumptions of what the Americans were trying to achieve there and how.

As the smoke and dust cleared from the explosion, the squad realized that one of their members, Cpl. Miguel Terrazas, a well-liked twenty-year-old from El Paso, Texas, was dead. He was literally blown apart—his torso strewn on the dusty ground while his legs remained in the vehicle. Two other Marines were wounded.

A white Opel sedan rolled toward the chaotic scene. The Marines signaled it to halt. When it did, five young Iraqi men got out of the car. "They didn't even try to run away," Sgt. Asad Amer Mashoot, an Iraqi soldier, later told officials from the Naval Criminal Investigative Service. Some had their hands in the air when Staff Sgt. Frank Wuterich began to shoot them, one Marine and two Iraqi soldiers told investigators. Sgt. Sanic Dela Cruz then urinated on the head of one of the slaughtered men. Wuterich later would tell investigators that he considered them to be a threat.

The Marines began moving toward the houses along the road, "running and gunning" in Marine parlance, conducting what they would later describe as a methodical if violent sweep for insurgents. Their actions looked different from the other end of their weapons. In the second house the Marines entered, Safah Yunis Salem, thirteen years old, said she played dead to avoid being shot. She was the sole survivor in the house, with seven family members killed, including Zainab, five, and Aisha, three. "He fired and killed everybody," she told American investigators. "The American fired and killed everybody."

Lance Cpl. Stephen Tatum later said in a statement to military investigators that he knew he was shooting children. "While in the house which I identified as House #2, I did identify some targets as children before I fired my weapon killing them," he explained. "My reason for this is that House #1 was declared hostile. While in house #1 I was told that someone ran to house #2 making it hostile. . . . While in house #2 SSGT [Staff Sgt.] WUTERICH fired shots into a room. This again made me think the house was hostile. I went to assist SSGT WUTERICH and saw that children were in the room kneeling down. I don't remember the exact number but only that it was a lot. My training told me that they were hostile due to SSGT WUTERICH firing at them and the other events I mentioned leading up to this. I am trained to shoot two shots to the chest and two shots to the head and I followed my training."

One villager, Aws Fahmi, later said he watched and listened as the Americans went from house to house killing members of three families. He heard his neighbor across the street, Younis Salim Khafif, plead in English for the lives of his family. "I heard Younis speaking to the Americans, saying: 'I am a friend. I am good,'" Fahmi said. "But they killed him, and his wife and daughters." An old man in a wheelchair was shot nine times. Another of the victims was a one-year-old baby.

At 5 P.M., a call went out on a Marine radio: We need a truck to come pick up 24 bodies. Eight were deemed by the Marines to have been insurgents, including the five from the Opel. The remainder were clearly civilians.

Other Marines arriving on the scene sensed something was wrong. "The only thing I thought was, 'Hey, where are the bad guys? Why aren't there any insurgents here?'" Lt. William Kallop later testified.

Lance Cpl. Andrew Wright, sent to the site to help collect the bodies, was moved to take out his digital camera and snap a series of photographs. "Even though there was no investigation at the time, I felt that the photographs would be evidence if anything came up in the future," he later would explain to agents of the Naval Criminal Investigative Service. "In my opinion, the people that I photographed had been murdered."

Official Marine Corps statements presented a different image. The next day, Capt. Jeffrey S. Pool, a Marine spokesman in Iraq, said in a terse press release that 15 Iraqis were killed by a roadside bomb, and that "after the bombing, gunmen attacked the convoy with small-arms fire. Iraqi army soldiers and Marines returned fire, killing eight insurgents and wounding another." Almost all aspects of this statement were incorrect.

The U.S. military justice system eventually would conduct a thorough review of the Haditha incident. Charges were dismissed against six of the Marines, and a seventh was acquitted. Wuterich still faces several charges, including voluntary manslaughter, and many of the Marines involved were found not guilty of wrongdoing. But there is no getting around the fact that 24 Iraqis were killed and that some of them were women and children. The only way to sidestep the question was to persuade one's self, as Cpl. Sharratt did, that, "they were all insurgents"—including the women, children, and wheelchair-bound old man. "Personally, I think I did everything perfectly that day," he concluded. "Because of me, no one else died"—by which he meant only, no other Marines.

What happened that day in Haditha was the disturbing but logical culmination of the shortsighted and misguided approach the U.S. military took in invading and occupying Iraq from 2003 through 2006: Protect yourself at all costs, focus on attacking the enemy, and treat the Iraqi civilians as the playing field on which the contest occurs. Kalev Sepp, a counterinsurgency expert who conducted an official study of the effectiveness of U.S. military battalion, brigade, and regimental commanders in Iraq at the time, reported that the Marines were "chasing the insurgents around the Euphrates Valley while leaving the population unguarded and exposed to insurgent terrorism and coercion." This bankrupt approach was rooted in the dominant American military tradition that tends to view war only as battles between conventional forces of different states. The American tradition also tends to neglect the lesson, learned repeatedly in dozens of twentieth-century wars, that the way to defeat an insurgency campaign is not to attack the enemy but instead to protect and win over the people. "The more we focus on the enemy, the harder it is to actually get anything done with the population," noted Australian counterinsurgency theorist David Kilcullen, who would play a prominent role in fixing the way the American military fought in Iraq. The aim of a counterinsurgency campaign is to destroy the enemy—but often by isolating him and making him irrelevant rather than killing him. The best insurgent is not a dead one, who might leave behind a relative seeking vengeance, but one who is ignored by the population and perhaps is contemplating changing sides, bringing with him invaluable information.

Lt. Col. Jeff Chessani, commander of the battalion to which Kilo Company belonged, said later in a sworn statement that despite the number of civilian casualties, he didn't see that day in Haditha as particularly unusual and saw no reason to investigate what had happened. "I thought it was very sad, very unfortunate, but at the time, I did not suspect any wrongdoing from my Marines," he said. Nor did he act on a request for an investigation made a week later by the mayor and town council of Haditha.

His chain of command felt the same way. "There was nothing out of the ordinary about this, including the number of civilian dead," Col. Stephen Davis, his immediate commander, would tell investigators.

When the division commander, Maj. Gen. Richard Huck, was briefed by Chessani on the events of the day, Huck said later, "no bells and whistles went off."

The buck stopped with Army Lt. Gen. Peter Chiarelli, then newly arrived in Iraq as the commander of day-to-day U.S. military operations there. When he was told many weeks later that reporters were asking questions about what had happened in Haditha, he instructed his public affairs officer simply to brief them on the results of the military investigation. His mistake was to assume that there was such an inquiry. In fact, he was informed, there had been no such review of the killings. Chiarelli, who had been one of the most successful commanders in Iraq when he led the 1st Cavalry Division in Baghdad from early 2004 to early 2005, was puzzled, then shocked at the lack of interest expressed by the Marine chain of command. He had been trying to reorient the U.S. military to think more about protecting the people but here found an entire chain of command that seemingly lacked any interest in such an approach. On February 12, 2006, he asked Huck, the division commander, about the incident. Huck later recalled telling him, "I did not think there was a reason to initiate an investigation."

Chiarelli disagreed. He mulled the situation and two days later called Huck. "You are not going to like this, but I am going to order an investigation," the Army general told the Marine general. He assigned Army Maj. Gen. Eldon Bargewell, a much-bloodied Vietnam veteran, to look into the matter. And when Bargewell's report arrived, Chiarelli made it his top priority, clearing much of his calendar to spend most of two weeks studying the findings, the recommendations, and the appendices.

Bargewell was appalled by what he had found. He reported that the killings had been carried out "indiscriminately." Even more worrisome, he concluded that leaders in the Marine chain of command thought that was the right approach—despite having been told by Chiarelli that it wasn't. "All levels of command tended to view civilian casualties, even in significant numbers, as routine," Bargewell wrote in a report that was stamped SECRET/NOFORN and that has never been released.

The comments made by senior Marines to investigators clearly irked Bargewell. In their view, he wrote, "Iraqi civilian lives are not as important as U.S. lives, their deaths are just the cost of doing business." The general's conclusions provide a kind of epitaph for the professionally ignorant and profoundly counterproductive approach that many American commanders took during the first three years of the war. Indeed, another year would pass before the U.S. military would take the first basic step in counterinsurgency and begin to implement a strategy founded on the concept that the civilian population isn't the playing field but rather the prize, to be protected at almost all costs.

Underscoring Bargewell's findings, the Army Surgeon General's office, in a survey of the mental health and ethical outlook of soldiers and Marines in Iraq conducted the following year, found that one-third of its 1,767 respondents believed torture should be allowed if it helped gather important information about insurgents, and even more said they approved of such illegal abuse if they believed it would help save the life of a comrade. Also, about two-thirds of Marines and half the Army troops surveyed said they would not report a team member for mistreating a civilian or for destroying civilian property unnecessarily. Ten percent said they personally had mistreated non-combatants. "Less than half of soldiers and Marines believed that non-combatants should be treated with dignity and respect," the report stated.

Some Marines, especially combat veterans of earlier wars, objected to criticism of American actions at Haditha, saying that the investigators didn't understand the nature of combat. Yet Bargewell, who served as an enlisted soldier in Vietnam, in 1971 had received the Distinguished Service Cross, the Army's second-highest medal, for actions in combat while a member of a long-range reconnaissance unit operating behind enemy lines. He had also been wounded several times. Nor was he alone among military professionals in his view that something had gone very wrong that day in Haditha. Marine Col. John Ewers, taking a sworn statement from Chessani, the battalion commander, exclaimed in an aside, "God damn, 15 civilians dead, 23 or 24 total Iraqis dead—with no real indication of how it was that we arrived at the enemy KIA [killed in action] number."

"I was horrified by it," said retired Gen. Jack Keane, who had been the number two officer in the Army during the invasion of Iraq and also was a veteran of two tours in Vietnam. "I sensed that something had really gone wrong—that amount of civilians killed by direct fire? I know from my experience that to kill that number of civilians directly, you had to be in the room, pointing at them. I sensed it was a breakdown in the chain of command." His worries would intensify so much that they would propel him into a central role in the remaking of the war in the following years.

LOST AND ADRIFT

In 2005 the United States came close to losing the war in Iraq. Even now, the story of how the U.S. military reformation and counterattack came together is barely known. As the *Washington Post*'s military correspondent, I followed events as they occurred, day by day, but it was only when setting out to research and write this book that I delved deeper and found there was a hidden tale to this phase of the war. It begins with Keane, who in the following year would grow so deeply concerned by the direction of the Iraq war that he would set out to redesign its strategy, an unprecedented move for a retired officer. Despite having left active duty several years earlier, he worked behind the scenes with two former subordinates whom he trusted and admired, David Petraeus and Raymond Odierno, who partly through his efforts would become the two top U.S. commanders in Iraq.

It would take nearly 12 more months, until late in 2006, for senior officials in the Bush administration and the U.S. military to recognize that the U.S. effort was heading for defeat. Then, almost at the last minute, and over the objections of nearly all relevant leaders of the U.S. military establishment, a few insiders, led by Keane, managed to persuade President Bush to adopt a new, more effective strategy built around protecting the Iraq people.

The effect of that new approach, implemented in 2007 under Petraeus, the fourth U.S. commander in the war in Iraq, would be to reduce violence in Iraq and so revive American prospects in the war. That change likely will prolong it for at least another three years, and probably much longer. It is now quite possible that U.S. troops will still be involved in combat in Iraq in 2011, which would make the war there America's longest overseas war, if the major U.S. combat involvement in Vietnam is deemed to have lasted from 1965 to 1973.

Yet it is unclear in 2009 if he did much more than lengthen the war. In revising the U.S. approach to the Iraq war, Petraeus found tactical success—that is, improved security—but not the clear political breakthrough that would have meant unambiguous strategic success. At the end of the surge, the fundamental political problems facing Iraq were the same ones as when it began. At the end of 2008, two years into the revamped war, there was no prospect of the fighting ending anytime soon. But it was almost certain that whenever it did end, it wouldn't be with the victory that the Bush administration continued to describe, of an Iraq that was both a stable democracy and an ally of the United States. Nor was that really the goal anymore, though no one had said so publicly. Under Petraeus, the American goal of transforming Iraq had quietly been scaled down. But even his less ambitious target of sustainable security would remain elusive, with no certainty of reaching it anytime soon.

The 12 months after Haditha, from late 2005 to late 2006, were a period of agonizingly slow reassessment of the U.S. military's approach in Iraq. After that, it would take many more months for a new strategy to be implemented. During that period, no one except the president, the vice president, and the secretary of defense seemed to be happy with the direction of the war. Even war supporters were uneasy. Senator John McCain, the most prominent war hawk in the Congress, said, "There's an undeniable sense that things are slipping—more violence on the ground, declining domestic support for the war, growing incantations among Americans that there is no end in sight."

On the ground in Iraq there often was an emptiness in the U.S. military effort, a feel of going through the motions, of doing the same things over and over again without really expecting them to be effective, perhaps reflecting a fear that there really was no way out. "It sucks," said Spec. Tim Ivey. "Honestly, it feels like we're driving around waiting to get blown up."

In late 2006, Maj. Lee Williams arrived at FOB [forward operating base] Falcon on the southern edge of Baghdad to take over advising a brigade of the Iraqi National Police. He found his predecessors had all but given up. When he landed, the base was being mortared. Plus, the Iraqi unit being advised was hardly inspiring—it was, he said, "corrupt, . . . tied to being involved in extra-judicial killings, . . . definitely been known to have been connected with some of the insurgent groups with emplacing IEDs." Some of the privates on the police force were members of the extremist Shiite militias and had so intimidated their commanders that they "would even slap their faces," Williams said. Even so, he was surprised at the demoralization of the team he was relieving. Before leaving for Iraq, he explained, "We had no communication with the team we replaced. They sent one e-mail. They were just tired and they said they were busy. But when we actually got on the ground, they were only going out maybe once or twice a week. When we got there, you could tell that they were burned out."

Some in the military suspected that commanders were just trying to get through their tours in Iraq without making waves, so they could get on with their lives and careers. "The truth is that many commands in Iraq are no longer focused on winning and instead are focused on CYA"—that is, covering your ass—charged Capt. Zachary Martin, a Marine infantry officer. He continued:

> Part of this loss of focus is a lack of clear guidance on exactly what winning means and how we are to achieve it. From the highest levels, there is nothing to relate our efforts to the vague goals of "democracy in Iraq" and "the defeat of terrorism." . . . [C]ommanders in Iraq cannot win, although they can certainly lose. An aggressive commander who, in the absence of unifying guidance and in spite of inadequate cultural preparation, assesses the situation, formulates a campaign plan, and takes calculated risks in implementing it will most likely have little concrete evidence of success to show when he rotates six months later.

> The time scale of counterinsurgency is simply too long. On the other hand, a commander who takes no risks and thus keeps his casualties low can be reasonably assured of a Bronze Star with a combat "V," an article in the [Marine Corps] *Gazette* relating how well his battalion performed under his firm and dynamic leadership and, with combat command ticket punched, a decent shot at promotion.

It was a morale breaker, observed another officer, to take a city on your second tour that you thought had you had secured on your first.

In another sign of a strained force, there was a spate of legal and disciplinary issues with soldiers. These were not the usual cases of privates' abusing drugs, but of career soldiers getting into a variety of trouble. "I'd never seen it at this level before," recalled Maj. David Mendelson, a military lawyer on the staff of the top operational headquarters in Iraq in 2006. "We did over fifteen reliefs for cause and they were for senior enlisted soldiers and even battalion commanders, very senior officers. . . . We saw company commanders and battalion commanders doing the wrong things."

Gen. Keane, visiting the U.S. embassy in Baghdad, was shocked. "They had given up," he told people. "There was a sense of hopelessness and futility."

Underlying all this was a sense of drift in the war. "There was a period after that when we just didn't have an answer," recalled Tom Donnelly, a defense expert at the American Enterprise Institute who was another longtime hawk. "We knew we couldn't kill our way out of it, but we didn't want to take on the mission of protecting the people, so there was a kind of drift, and by default an emphasis on training Iraqis and transitioning to them."

Back in mid-2004, Gen. George Casey Jr., the top U.S. commander in Iraq, had inherited a mess from his predecessor, Lt. Gen. Ricardo Sanchez, who had been overmatched by the deterioration of Iraq and poorly supported by Defense Secretary Donald Rumsfeld and the rest of the military establishment. Casey made major changes, developing a formal campaign plan and focusing on the need to protect the people as the way to isolate the enemy from the people. Casey was a thoughtful man. He had been tapped immediately after the 9/11 attacks to take over as director of strategic planning for the Joint Chiefs of Staff, a position he filled so well that on the eve of the invasion of Iraq, he was promoted to be overall director of the Joint Staff, an important behind-the-scenes job at the Pentagon. Officers who do that job well tend to look over the horizon, pushing the staff below them to anticipate questions that the chairman of the Joint Chiefs might have to face in the coming months. After that Casey had become the Army's vice chief of staff, a position that tends to run the general officer corps. He was as "Army" as an officer can be, his father having been a general who was the highest-ranking American casualty of the Vietnam War. The one thing Casey lacked was combat experience. Over the previous two decades, the Army had fought in Panama, the Gulf War, Somalia, Haiti, Bosnia, Kosovo, and Iraq, but he had not been involved in any of these.

Even so, Casey's background made him far better equipped than Sanchez to know where the levers of power were in the Army and how to pull them. That helped him when he grew frustrated by the inappropriate training he saw being given to units arriving in Iraq. At one brigade, recalled Sepp, his counterinsurgency adviser, "The officers said they had been trained for 'kick in the door, two in the chest.'" To remediate such maleducation, in 2005 Casey had decided to establish a "counterinsurgency academy" at the big U.S. base at Taji, just north of Baghdad, and make attendance at its one-week immersion course a prerequisite for command under him. "Because the Army won't change itself, I'm going to change the Army here in Iraq," he told subordinates. The classes emphasized that the right answer is probably the counterintuitive one, rather than something that the Army taught officers in their 10 or 20 years of service. The school's textbook, a huge binder, offered the example of a mission that busts into a house and captures someone who mortared a U.S. base. "On the surface, a raid that captures a known insurgent or terrorist may seem like a sure victory for the coalition," it observed in red block letters. But, it continued: "The potential second- and third-order effects, however, can turn it into a long-term defeat if our actions humiliate the family, needlessly destroy property, or alienate the local population from our goals." As the Marine chain of command's reaction to Haditha demonstrated in the following months, along with similar incidents of less magnitude in the Army, many officers still didn't see those negative effects—or, if they did, they didn't seem to care.

So, concluded Francis "Bing" West, a defense expert who studied both Marine and Army operations in Iraq under Casey, counterinsurgency in 2005 and 2006 remained more a slogan than a strategy. "By and large, the battalions continued to do what they knew best: conduct sweeps and mounted patrols during the day and targeted raids at night," he wrote. Casey also undermined his own efforts, because his basic approach remained at odds with counterinsurgency theory: He was pulling his troops farther away from the population, closing dozens of bases in 2005 as he consolidated his force on big, isolated bases that the military termed "Super FOBs." That move was arguably simply a retreat in place. Casey may have been under the sway of the view popular in the military that the American public is "casualty intolerant" and that additional U.S. losses would undermine whatever political support remained for the war. He may not have been aware that a small group of political scientists had sharply questioned that view in recent years, gathering evidence that the American public actually hates losing soldiers in a losing cause but will accept higher casualties if it believes it is winning. And one of those political scientists was Peter Feaver, then a member of the staff of the National Security Council, who had been brought into the White House to work on Iraq policy.

At the same time that Haditha was occurring, an analysis done for the Pentagon's Office of Net Assessment, its internal think tank, concluded that the war was going badly and, in fact, was in far more dire a state than the Bush administration understood. "The costs of failure are likely to be high," it somberly warned, "much higher than was incurred following the U.S. withdrawal from Haiti, Somalia, Lebanon or even Vietnam."

The White House was in denial about the trend of the war. Officials around President Bush believed the problem wasn't their strategy in Iraq but a failure to adequately explain that approach. The view, said Peter Feaver, was "We've got the right strategy, but we're losing the public debate, because people don't understand our strategy." They certainly were losing the public, not entirely because of the slow downward spiral in Iraq. Hurricane Katrina hit New Orleans in late August 2005, and the Bush administration's plodding response to the catastrophic storm raised new doubts about its competence and its grasp of events on the ground. Critics of the Iraq war long had charged that the administration's handling of the war combined overoptimism with ineptitude. Now Americans were seeing that mix far closer to home. In both situations, it looked like either the U.S. government didn't care or couldn't perform. It wasn't clear which was worse.

So, to better inform the public, in November 2005—less than two weeks after the Haditha incident, as it happened—the White House issued a white paper titled "National Strategy for Victory in Iraq." In discussing it, President Bush emphasized the transition to Iraqi forces. "As Iraqi forces increasingly take the lead in the fight against the terrorists, they're also taking control of more and more Iraqi territory," he said in a speech in Annapolis, Maryland. "Our coalition has handed over roughly ninety square miles of Baghdad Province to Iraqi security forces. Iraqi battalions have taken over responsibility for areas in South-Central Iraq, sectors of Southeast Iraq, sectors of Western Iraq and sectors of North-Central Iraq. As Iraqi forces take responsibility for more of their own territory, coalition forces can concentrate on training Iraqis and hunting down high-value targets." He repeated his promise that "as the Iraqi security forces stand up, coalition forces can stand down."

When those Iraqi forces came on line, he vowed, "We will increasingly move out of Iraqi cities, reduce the number of bases from which we operate, and conduct fewer patrols and convoys." In fact, the U.S. military would decide a year later to pursue almost the opposite course: It would move into cities, establish scores of small outposts, and patrol almost incessantly, having learned that if you are present in a neighborhood for only two hours a day, the insurgents may well control it for the other twenty-two.

Despite the document's title, the Bush administration really hadn't carried out a serious strategic review that asked the basic questions: What are we trying to do—that is, what are our key goals? How are we trying to do it—that is, what course of action will we pursue? Does that course promise to achieve those goals? What sort of resources—people, time, money—are likely to be required to reach those goals? One hallmark of such a review would be to seek out dissenting views, probing differences inside the administration, especially those between civilian and military officials.

But the Bush administration's tendency was to suppress dissent and paper over differences, substituting loyalty for analysis, so the war continued to stand on a strategic foundation of sand. Nor had the president been well served by his generals, who with a few exceptions didn't seem to pose the necessary questions. "Strategy is about choices," said one of those exceptions, Maj. Gen. David Fastabend. Yet he lamented, one day in Baghdad two years later, "We don't teach it, we don't recognize it. The Army doesn't understand the difference between plans and strategy. When you ask specifically for strategy, you get aspirations."

Such incompetence can be dangerous. As Eliot Cohen, an academic who would surface repeatedly in the Iraq war as an influential behind-the-scenes figure, commented later in a different context, "Haziness about ends and means, about what to do and how to do it, is a mark of strategic ineptitude; in war it gets people killed."

By late 2005, none of the basic assumptions on which the Iraq war had been launched had been borne out, noted a senior Pentagon official as he reviewed its course years later. "If you look at the premises behind the war, they were: It will be quick, it will be easy, it will be cheap, it will be catalytic." That failure in turn led many Americans simply to advocate leaving Iraq because they saw chaos as the inevitable outcome of any course of action. "The only reason we are there now is because of the Petraeus surge, which shifted the balance so that reasonable people could say there might be a better alternative than chaos." In a Middle Eastern restaurant a few minutes' walk south of the Pentagon, the official sipped his beer. "Now, the fundamental fact about Iraq is, we're kind of stuck."

Strikingly, some of the people who would become involved in revamping the American approach to the war had disagreed with the rationale for the American invasion in the first place. Many more, probably a large majority of those who would remake the war, faulted the way the occupation had been handled. It seems that having such critical views was almost a prerequisite to grasping how to build a new foundation for the war.

GEN. DAVID PETRAEUS

The answer for what to do in Iraq would come largely through one person, Gen. David Petraeus, who over the next year would lead the way in determining how to revamp the U.S. approach to the war.

There were many experts as familiar with the tenets of counterinsurgency as Petraeus was. But he also knew how to get the Army to heed that knowledge. That is, his vision of how to change the war would become a restatement of classic counterinsurgency theory, which holds that the people are the objective, so the task is to figure out how to "win" them. This was familiar stuff to military intellectuals. In the fall of 2005, even as Petraeus was heading to his assignment at Fort Leavenworth, Kansas, where he would craft the new Army doctrine, Andrew Krepinevich, a prominent defense expert, published an essay in *Foreign Affairs* magazine that summarized the needed approach:

> . . . the United States needs a real strategy built around the principles of counterinsurgency warfare. To date, U.S. forces in Iraq have largely concentrated their efforts on hunting down and killing insurgents. . . . Instead, U.S. and Iraqi forces should adopt an "oil-spot" strategy in Iraq, which is essentially the op-

posite approach. Rather than focusing on killing insurgents, they should concentrate on providing security and opportunity to the Iraqi people.

Some 37 years earlier, Henry Kissinger, just before becoming President Nixon's national security adviser, had written in the same magazine a critique of the conduct of the Vietnam War: "To be effective, the so-called pacification program had to meet two conditions: (a) it had to provide security for the population; (b) it had to establish a political and institutional link between the villages and Saigon. Neither condition was ever met." In Iraq in 2005, the U.S. military faced a remarkably similar problem, on both counts.

As Kissinger noted, to carry out such a mission, it was necessary to put more U.S. troops into the fight. This was a point that some retired generals had been making about the Iraq war for some time. Retired Marine Lt. Gen. Gregory Newbold, who had left the military in 2002 over his concerns about the looming war, had told the Senate Armed Services Committee early in 2005 that he supported sending "additional forces . . . rather than sustain this level of effort for five more years of bleeding."

The hard part for Petraeus would be to impose his vision on the U.S. Army, one of the largest and most tradition-bound organizations in the country. Casey had tried and largely failed—but he at least had recognized that it needed a new direction. It appears that as long as Donald Rumsfeld was defense secretary, it would have been difficult to reorient the U.S. effort in Iraq. For all his talk of transforming the military, Rumsfeld appeared chary of making changes where they were most needed, in the war that was under way. Rather, his main interest in Iraq appeared to be in fending off critics. Everyone makes mistakes; Rumsfeld's tragic flaw was his inability to change course after making them.

For example, soon after Krepinevich's article appeared in *Foreign Affairs*, Rumsfeld sent a memo to subordinates saying he was hearing a lot about it and asking someone to see the author. Krepinevich, summoned to a breakfast meeting at the Pentagon, thought he was going there to provide some advice. Instead, he recalled, he was berated by Lawrence Di Rita, a Rumsfeld aide and at one point the Pentagon spokesman, who told him that he didn't understand the war. "Andy, you're misguided," Di Rita said to him. "That's what we're already doing over there."

While on active duty in the Army, Krepinevich, had earned a Ph.D. at Harvard for a courageous dissertation arguing that the Army, rather than the politicians or the media, had lost the Vietnam War. Some of his peers thought that the thesis had curtailed his Army career. He held his ground with Rumsfeld's aides. "I disagree," he responded. "When I ask for the campaign plan, the guys in J-5 [the planning office for the Joint Chiefs of Staff] give me a book of metrics"—that is, how the effort was being measured, such as the amount of money spent or the electricity produced. "If you can't explain your campaign plan, you probably don't have one."

Vice Adm. James Stavridis, a military assistant to Rumsfeld who also was at the meeting, said that Krepinevich should get out to Iraq to see for himself how well things were going. Krepinevich said he'd like to do so. At that point, Di Rita crudely joked that, yes, Krepinevich should be flown there and abandoned on the road into Baghdad from its airport, perhaps the most dangerous six miles then in the world. Hearing that unfunny threat, Krepinevich lost interest in the conversation. "After that, in terms of my active involvement—well, I gave it my best shot in the article," he recalled, turning his hands upward. (Throughout this book, accounts of conversations are based on the recollection of at least one participant, and often more than one. In this case, all three who were present contributed. Di Rita, for his part, said his recollection of the meeting was "admittedly hazy" but insisted that it was "bullshit" that he had made the joke about sending Krepinevich to the airport road. He said that he likely was referring to the fact that the road had become safer during that period. Krepinevich responded, "He does not remember such a conversation. I do, vividly.")

FORT LEAVENWORTH, KANSAS, is more than 7,000 miles from Haditha, Iraq, but like that Iraqi village, it overlooks a major river that has helped define its nation. The installation sits atop a high bluff where the Missouri, having driven nearly straight west from St. Louis to Kansas City, begins its giant swing to the northwest that carries it across the Great Plains and into the Rockies. In the nineteenth century, the wide Missouri was the river of the frontier, the pathway first for the expedition led by two Army officers, Capt. Meriwether Lewis and Lt. William Clark, and later for steamboats supplying Army units almost all the way up to Custer's last battlefield at Little Big Horn, Montana. Leavenworth also became a jumping-off point for the dragoons of the Army of the West, sending expeditions across the plains against the Apache, the Modoc, the Cheyenne, the Ute, the Nez Perce, the Comanche, the Kiowa, and the Kickapoo.

Under Petraeus's command, Leavenworth would become the starting point for a new approach in the war that would involve making peace with the tribes of Iraq. In October 2005, a month after finishing his second tour of duty in Iraq, Petraeus drove halfway across the United States to his new post at Leavenworth, where he would oversee much of the Army's training and educational establishment. He knew he would be focusing on counterinsurgency issues and would need to produce a new Army manual on the subject. Driving alone in his 2001 BMW 325i, he listened repeatedly to a series of compact discs of an exit interview done by Army historians with his predecessor, Gen. William Wallace. In mid-October, Petraeus parked at the commanding general's house at Fort Leavenworth, at the top of a grassy slope that still bears ruts carved by the wagon wheels of the Santa Fe Trail as it emerges from the river crossing.

At the time, some insiders thought that sending Petraeus to the plains of Kansas was the wrong move for a nation fighting two wars in the Middle East. "I was opposed to the assignment," said his old mentor from the 101st Airborne, retired Gen. Jack Keane. "I thought, bring him to Washington, get him close to the policy makers." Keane thought the ideal slot would be the J-3—that is, the director of operations for the Joint Staff, where his protégé could oversee and coordinate the global activities of the U.S. military, and, he said, "inform a reluctant senior leadership." Petraeus did not particularly want the Leavenworth job. He would later tell two Army historians in his own exit interview, "I have to tell you candidly, when I was told I was going to be the CAC [Combined Arms Center] commander, I thought, 'What do you do out there? Harass the students in CGSC [Leavenworth's Command and General Staff College] that day? What is this all about?' "

Petraeus found plenty to do. The first thing he did was convene a group of Army officers to consider whether the Army training establishment was doing all it could to prepare leaders and units for the wars in Iraq and Afghanistan. Then, on November 16, three days before the Haditha incident, Petraeus called Conrad Crane, an Army historian, and asked him to lead a team that would write a new manual on counterinsurgency for the Army and the Marine Corps. Eliot Cohen, a professor of strategy at Johns Hopkins University, had suggested Crane to Petraeus as a smart military expert who understood the subject and could lead a team. The perpetually bow-tied Cohen is an unusual figure in Washington, influential in several circles, with an extraordinary range of contacts inside the government, from the White House to the Congress to the military and intelligence establishments, a network created mainly because those institutions send many of the best young people to him to study strategy. He makes that study both intense and concrete, suggesting thousands of pages in readings, from Sun Tzu to Winston Churchill, but also leading his students on walks of battlefields, from Gettysburg to Italy to the Middle East, to mull campaign strategies. Cohen also was comfortable talking to journalists covering national security and foreign policy, especially if they were willing to follow up on his patient efforts to educate them. If being a Harvard-trained Jewish academic didn't make him an outsider in military eyes, his resolute dislike of spectator sports would have—despite being from the Boston area, he followed neither baseball nor football. This actually may have aided his strategic analyses, as the sports metaphors that tend to pass for strategic discourse in the American military—"we're five yards from the end zone," or "it's the fourth quarter and we're down fifty"—sailed by him. He also was the author of *Supreme Command*, an influential study of how civilian leaders have intervened in wartime to oversee strategy and steer their wars toward success. Before the invasion of Iraq, the White House made it known that President Bush had studied the book. But for all that, Cohen didn't know that David Petraeus and Conrad Crane had been friends for decades, since they sat next to each other in a West Point military history class.

Crane had gone on to a career in the Army during which he earned a doctorate in history at Stanford. After retiring he became a professor at the Army War College, where he was coauthor of a study that before the American invasion of Iraq highlighted the difficulties of occupying that country. "The possibility of the United States winning the war and losing the peace is real and serious," the study warned. "Thinking about the war now and the occupation later is not an acceptable solution." That is, of course, exactly what top Bush administration officials did, in part because many believed U.S. forces would leave Iraq quickly and so there would be no occupation.

David Lloyd George, the British prime minister for much of World War I, observed after that conflict that for officers in the British army, "to be a good average is safer than to be gifted above your fellows." This also tends to be true in the U.S. Army. Given that conformist inclination, the most surprising fact about Gen. Petraeus may be that he is a general at all.

In an Army of generals who tend to be competent company men, Petraeus is "an outlier," said Col. Peter Mansoor, who came to know him well, first in working with him on counterinsurgency doctrine at Fort Leavenworth in 2006 and then the following year as his executive officer in Iraq. "General Petraeus doesn't seem to fit the mold, because he is extremely bright, and intellectual," said Mansoor, who, like Petraeus, holds a doctorate—in his case, in military history from Ohio State University, home of a top department in the United States for that subject. "But he is a PT [physical training, or exercise] stud, and tactically and technically competent, and that matters to Army [promotion] boards."

Petraeus was an unusual figure in the Army. He was indeed a physical fitness freak, whose inclination was to run five to eight miles a day and then work out for another 45 minutes—despite having a pelvis that was smashed parachuting and a damaged lung from being shot through the chest. His physical drive was hugely in his favor, in terms of Army culture, and may have been the thing that redeemed him with his peers. He is thought to be the only officer ever to come in first in both his class at Army Ranger School and at the Army's Command and General Staff College.

Such stellar performances in mental and physical stamina were necessary because he had three strikes against him. First, he was an intellectual, holding an Ivy League doctorate in international relations. "General Petraeus was successful not because of, but almost despite, his Ph.D. from Princeton," commented Lt. Col. Suzanne Nielsen, an aide of his who herself earned a Harvard doctorate in political science. Second, Petraeus was friendly with journalists and politicians, two groups that Army generals are taught to treat with contemptuous distance. The Army ideal is the hero of the novel *Once an Eagle,* Gen. Sam Damon, a muddy-boots type who loves being in the field and grows increasingly inarticulate the closer he gets to Washington. To most Army generals, enjoying conversations with the type of people who dominate the business of the nation's capital borders on eccentricity at best and immorality at worst. In any event, it is suspicious behavior. The derogatory term for it is "standing close to the flagpole."

Most telling was the third strike: Alone among Army generals, Petraeus had posted an unquestionably successful tour as a division commander in Iraq during the invasion and the first year of the war, a conclusion confirmed in an official study by the Army War College. Commanding the 101st Airborne Division, he conducted what was generally seen as a thorough and effective campaign that balanced war fighting and nation building in Mosul, the biggest city in northern Iraq. Petraeus had laid down three rules for his subordinate commanders: We are in a race against time, give the locals you deal with a stake in the new Iraq, and don't do anything that creates more enemies than it removes.

By contrast, during that first year of the war, most U.S. commanders did what they knew how to do, not what they needed to do, noted Keane, who knew most of them well. "Our guys, . . . with the exception of Petraeus, were executing what they know, and what they knew is conventional operations—you saw that in spades."

A major difference in background between Petraeus and most of his peers in that first year in Iraq was that he came out of the "light infantry" Army. Iraq was seen at the outset by some as the star turn of the "heavy Army"—that is, units built around tanks and other armored vehicles. The invasion of Afghanistan 18 months earlier had been a "light force" war, featuring Special Forces and, a bit later, the 10th Mountain Division and some Marine units. Iraq was to be the heavy Army's turn. The early top commanders in Iraq—Tommy R. Franks and Ricardo Sanchez—were products of that mechanized force. Petraeus, by contrast, was a light infantryman, having spent much of his field time with the paratroopers of the 82nd Airborne and the helicopter-borne soldiers of the 101st Airborne. The term "light" is a bit of misnomer, because these troops carry everything they can on their backs, from ammunition to medicine, often staggering under the loads. But "light" means that such units rely very little on tanks, artillery, and other heavy weaponry. "That's significant," noted Tom Donnelly, a longtime student of the Army and its cultures. "For one thing, it makes you less obsessed with technology. The airborne community always knew that there was more to worry about than tank warfare in Europe's central front," the main focus of most of the late twentieth-century Army. While the tankers stayed in Germany, he said, "the light infantry did the Caribbean, Panama, peacekeeping in the Sinai."

That background may also illuminate the different approach Petraeus would take to the roadside bomb, the key enemy weapon in the war. The U.S. military ultimately would spend well over $10 billion on technology to counter the threat posed by IEDs, or "improvised explosive devices." While some of the new devices stymied explosions, they tended just to push the enemy to devise a more sophisticated trigger mechanism and more devastating bombs. The number of attacks would not begin to decline until 2007, when Petraeus was in command. The answer then turned out to be not technological but physical and cultural—get the troops out among the people, protect them, stay with them, and they will begin to talk to you. And even those who won't talk might help in other ways, such as anonymously spray-painting orange arrows on the asphalt to indicate where a bomb had been planted the previous night.

But even more significant than Petraeus's military background is his determination. It is the cornerstone of his personality and a characteristic that seems to strike everyone he meets. One of his favorite words is "relentless." Donnelly first encountered Petraeus in the late 1980s, when Petraeus was a young major. "He was almost identical to the guy you find today—very bright, very ambitious," Donnelly recalled. "Always ready to go for a run. Every day was a good day for him."

Some of his peers saw him as ferociously ambitious, all too willing to court congressmen and journalists. Those critics felt their suspicions were confirmed when Petraeus told a *Washington Post* reporter that his role in Mosul in 2003–4 was "a combination of being the president and the pope." Even among his admirers there churns an ambivalence about him, often provoked by his overwhelming drive. In a memoir of invading Iraq in 2003 with Petraeus, Rick Atkinson, the journalist who knows Petraeus best and has remained friendly with him, wrote, "If others found him hard to love—his intensity, his competitiveness, and serrated intellect made adoration difficult—he was nevertheless broadly respected and instantly obeyed." That is an especially striking assessment because Atkinson, according to then–Brig. Gen. Benjamin Freakley, the assistant commander to Petraeus, was "probably closer to him than anyone in the division."

Trying to explain his unease about Petraeus, an officer who has known him for years said, "I really respect his intelligence. He is very disciplined. But I'm not comfortable with his competitiveness." He said he found it difficult to get Petraeus to engage in a normal conversation. "It is all a race. Everything is a race. It's a narcissistic, exploitative way of dealing with people." This approach also has a long-term cost, he said: "Dave tends not to build teams, or think about what happens afterwards. It's the Dave Petraeus Show."

Such criticisms aren't entirely justified, because Petraeus, more than most generals, keeps an eye out for smart younger officers and helps them along in their careers. But even one of those protégés was mixed in his evaluation. "David Petraeus is the best general in the U.S. Army, bar none," said this officer, who has known him for more than a decade. But, he added, "He also isn't half as good as he thinks he is."

Another admirer, Capt. Erica Watson Borggren, graduated from West Point in 2002 and went on to become a Rhodes Scholar. When she first met Petraeus, she recalled, he asked, "What was your class ranking?" He was referring to the academy's class position, which is based on a mix of academic records, military leadership skills, and physical fitness tests. It is a key number because standing determines the order by which cadets pick their branch of the Army—infantry, armor, artillery, aviation, military intelligence, and so on.

"First academically, seventh overall," she responded.

"What dragged you down?" Petraeus asked.

She was amazed. First in academics and seventh overall was an extraordinary performance in a class of 989. She had played varsity tennis, had tutored other cadets, had become a youth minister and a parachutist. She thought to herself, "What do you mean, 'dragged down'?" But she was restrained in what she actually said to the hypercompetitive general: "Well, if you look it at that way." (Petraeus, who finished fortieth in his 1974 graduating class of 833 cadets, said he had been joking.)

"I worked with him," said David Kilcullen, the Australian counterinsurgency theorist who Petraeus would bring to Iraq as his adviser. "But I am not sure I know him."

Donnelly, a defense expert with a gimlet eye for the Army, said he felt that he has never been able to get below the surface of Petraeus. "The distinction between the mask and the man is impossible for me to distinguish. He has always been that way. I think he is doing what he always wanted to do, and it is deeply fulfilling." Indeed, under that mask may be simply many more hard laminations of talent and drive. Donnelly added that he doesn't think Petraeus's dreams extend to political office. Rather, he said, "He has an ambition to make his mark on the Army, on history. He wants to make his name as a great captain." Asked in a 2008 interview if he had ever considered being national security adviser, Petraeus appeared mildly intrigued. But when asked if he would like to be a professor of international relations at Princeton, he responded with excitement and a grin and said it would be a "thrill."

It was his extraordinary force of will that persuaded Gen. Peter Schoomaker, the chief of staff of the Army, to send Petraeus to Fort Leavenworth. "Shake it up," Schoomaker told Petraeus, who would need every ounce of his strength to change the way the Army thought about the war in Iraq.

2.

HOW TO FIGHT THIS WAR

(Fall 2005–Fall 2006)

In February 2006, Petraeus convened a meeting at Fort Leavenworth of about 135 experts on irregular warfare to discuss a new manual for the Army and Marine Corps about how to conduct counterinsurgency operations. When he called the session to order, he looked out across a tiered classroom in Tice Hall, a squat, one-story brick building in a corner of the base, not far from Leavenworth's forbidding old gray federal penitentiary. Usually used to train National Guard commanders, on this day the classroom held not just military officers but also representatives from the CIA and the State Department, academics, human rights advocates, even a select group of high-profile journalists. It was instantly clear that this wasn't going to be the standard Army manual written by two tired majors laboring in a basement somewhere in Fort Leavenworth. "I thought the most interesting thing was the range of attendees, which spoke volumes about Petraeus," said Eliot Cohen. The two had known each other since the mid-1980s, when Petraeus, then a major, was teaching at West Point, and Cohen at Harvard.

What wasn't clear was whether the manual would be produced in time to make a difference in the Iraq war, which the attendees knew was heading south fast. One of those present, Kalev Sepp, was fresh from doing his study in Iraq for Gen. Casey of how well U.S. commanders in Iraq had absorbed counterinsurgency theory. His worrisome conclusion had been that 20 percent of them got it, 60 percent were struggling, and 20 percent were trying to fight a conventional war, "oblivious to the inefficacy and counterproductivity of their operations." In other words, more than half of the U.S. war effort was wasted, and a good part of it was actually hurting the cause.

Petraeus, aware of that troubling finding, began the conference by noting a fundamental difference. In the past, he said, the Army had taught officers *what* to think. Now, he said, it needed to teach them *how* to think. Then he sat down next to Sarah Sewall, director of Harvard University's Carr Center for Human Rights Policy. Just that act in itself made it clear that this effort wasn't going to follow the usual way the Army devised doctrine.

Conrad Crane, the Army historian, kicked off the discussions by handing out more than a hundred small, hard pieces of green stones with red veins in them. It was coprolite. "They're pretty, polished, like gem stones," he told the audience. But, he explained, coprolite is actually fossilized dinosaur excrement. This, Crane warned, was what he didn't want the new counterinsurgency manual to be: a new polishing of old crap. "There has never been an Army manual created the way this one was," he said later. "It was truly a unique process."

Until Petraeus arrived at Leavenworth, its magazine, *Military Review,* had been a backwater even in the sleepy world of official military publications. Under his command, Col. Bill Darley, its editor, quickly turned it into a must-read bimonthly dispatch from the front lines. It opened its pages to the views of young officers angry over how generals were fighting the Iraq war. The magazine sometimes made news itself. One of its most controversial articles had been by a British officer, Brig. Nigel Aylwin-Foster, who accused the American military in Iraq of cultural ignorance, moralistic self-righteousness, unproductive micromanagement, and unwarranted optimism. He specifically charged that the Americans displayed such "cultural insensitivity" in the war that it "arguably amounted to institutional racism" and may have spurred the growth of the insurgency. Most relevant to Petraeus's purposes, he contended that the U.S. military's handling of Iraqis "exacerbated the task it now faces by alienating significant sections of the population." The meeting kicked off with Aylwin-Foster standing up to review and expand on his explosive charges.

The human rights specialists present were upset by a passage in an early draft of the counterinsurgency manual that was ambiguous about the use of torture in interrogations. It seemed to say that sometimes extreme measures might be deemed necessary, but they were still immoral, so any commander allowing such practices should then confess to a superior officer. Crane and his confreres already harbored doubts about that section and immediately agreed to strike it.

One purpose of the meeting was to ensure that the manual would stand up to such criticism; another was to build support for it. "I think that is always the way to go—inclusion is generally the appropriate course of action," Petraeus said later. "Frankly, if you can't convince 95 percent of the rational thinkers, perhaps the concept needs to be reexamined." He also saw it as a team-building exercise, he added, for the people who would be writing sections for Conrad Crane to get to know one another and how they thought.

Petraeus watched and listened while Crane "played ringmaster," running the discussions. "I was both physically and mentally exhausted by the end" of the two-day session, Crane said.

The manual that would be produced in the following months adhered to the classic tenets of counterinsurgency—yet in doing so it was prescribing a radical shift for the U.S. military. Historically, Americans have liked to use "overwhelming force," which under Gen. Colin Powell's influence was elevated to a first principle. But counterinsurgency, according to David Galula, the French officer who while at Harvard in 1963 wrote what is probably the best book on the subject, requires that the minimum of firepower and force be used. Galula also admonished that the people are the prize. "The population . . . becomes the objective for the counterinsurgent as it was for his enemy," he wrote, drawing on his experiences in World War II, the French war in Indochina, and the Algerian war, as well as his firsthand observations of the Greek civil war and Mao Zedong's Communist campaign in China.

If the manual were to have the desired effect, it needed to offer a sharp critique of how the U.S. Army had operated in Iraq for the previous several years. But pointing out the flaws in the American approach was delicate, because this could complicate the task of getting the Army to follow the manual. Many of the generals implicitly skewered in its analysis were still in the Army, and some were running it.

Just a month after the conference, four experts—Crane, Cohen, Lt. Col. Jan Horvath, and Lt. Col. John Nagl, who had studied under Petraeus at West Point—sent up the first flare to the Army and those watching it, signaling that the new counterinsurgency manual would be very different from the usual, small-bore stuff of Army doctrine. The heart of their article in *Military Review* was a list of the "paradoxes of counterinsurgency." (This emphasis certainly was influenced by five years of American experience in Iraq—and it is interesting to note that playing with paradox is one of the hallmarks of the classical Arab literature produced in Baghdad at its zenith under the Abbasid caliphs.)

Among the conundrums the article explored:

- "The more you protect your force, the less secure you are." In other words, it said, you need to get out among the population, because in the long run, that is the way to improve security. "If military forces stay locked up in compounds, they lose touch with the people who are the ultimate arbiters of victory."
- "The more force you use, the less effective you are." That is, you are trying to establish the rule of law, and the way to get there is through restraint, whenever possible. Aim for normalcy.
- "Sometimes doing nothing is the best reaction." This was perhaps the hardest lesson for the can-do, gung-ho U.S. military to take on board. Don't let yourself be provoked into action, because it may be counterproductive.

The article made clear that Petraeus and the people around him were seeking not only to change the way the Army was fighting in Iraq but also to change the Army itself. Its last paragraph began, "We are at a turning point in the Army's institutional history." Petraeus was out to alter how the Army thought about war—a major intellectual, cultural, and emotional shift for a huge and tradition-minded organization.

In June, Crane circulated a new draft of the manual around the Army and Marine Corps. "This was the six-hundred-thousand-editor stage," he said, referring to the combined active-duty size of the two services. There clearly was a thirst out there for a new approach, reflected in the "thousands" of comments he received.

The manual also would borrow liberally from the work being done that summer by Australian army Lt. Col. David Kilcullen, a quirky infantryman with a Ph.D. in the anthropology of Islamic extremism, a wicked wit, and experience fighting in Timor. Kilcullen came to Petraeus's attention when he wrote an essay breezily titled "Twenty-Eight Articles: Fundamentals of Company-Level

Counterinsurgency"—that is, going one better than Lawrence of Arabia's famous "Twenty-Seven Articles" on how to fight in the Middle East in 1917.

At the time, Kilcullen's principles seemed astonishing, and not just because they were articulated with a directness not often seen in public in the U.S. military. His third principle set the tone of the essay: "In counterinsurgency, killing the enemy is easy. Finding him is often nearly impossible." He also was quite willing to disregard military hierarchy if that was what was required to prevail. "Rank is nothing; talent is everything," he advised in his eighth principle. "Not everyone is good at counterinsurgency. Many people don't understand the concept, and some can't execute it. It is difficult, and in a conventional force only a few people will master it. Anyone can learn the basics, but a few naturals do exist. Learn how to spot these people, and put them into positions where they can make a difference. Rank matters far less than talent—a few good men led by a smart junior noncommissioned officer can succeed in counterinsurgency, where hundreds of well-armed soldiers under a mediocre senior officer will fail."

His tenth principle poked another stick at top U.S. commanders in Iraq. "The most fundamental rule of counterinsurgency is to be there. . . . This demands a residential approach: living in your sector, in close proximity to the population rather than raiding into the area from remote, secure bases. Movement on foot, sleeping in local villages, night patrolling—all these seem more dangerous than they are. They establish links with the locals, who see you as real people they can trust and do business with, not as aliens who descend from an armored box. Driving around in an armored convoy, day-tripping like a tourist in hell, degrades situational awareness, makes you a target, and is ultimately more dangerous."

Also, he counseled in rule 26, don't obsess on fighting your foe. "Only attack the enemy when he gets in the way. Try not to be distracted or forced into a series of reactive moves by a desire to kill or capture the insurgents."

Petraeus read the cheeky essay and sent it rocketing around the Army via e-mail. Even before the manual appeared, it would begin to affect how some officers thought, perhaps reflecting the pent-up eagerness for change among younger soldiers. One young officer with the 1st Cavalry Division, Lt. Rory McGovern, later recalled that while he was preparing in the fall of 2006 to deploy to Iraq, he was told to read Kilcullen's "Twenty-Eight Articles." It changed the way he thought about intelligence operations, he said.

A year later, Petraeus would bring Kilcullen to Baghdad as his adviser on counterinsurgency. There the Australian would explain his role with the memorable comment, "Just because you invade a country stupidly doesn't mean you have to leave it stupidly," a comment that Barack Obama adopted in somewhat modified form for his stump speech during the 2008 primaries.

As the writing of the counterinsurgency manual neared completion, Petraeus began editing key portions word by word—and not just once. He made, he remembered, some "twenty or thirty edits."

Again, this was not the way that the Army usually worked. "I can't think of a precedent for a commanding general to be so involved in writing doctrine," said Keane. "It is usually driven by bright young majors." The hands-on approach helped Petraeus move the product along quickly, and also would make it far more readable—and influential—than most Army manuals.

Published at the end of 2006, just 11 months after the meeting at Leavenworth, the new manual had two striking aspects: It was both a devastating critique of the conduct of the Iraq war and an outline of the approach Petraeus might take there if ever given the chance. In political terms, it amounted to a party platform, the party in this case being the dissidents who thought the Army was on the path to defeat in Iraq if it didn't change its approach.

- Think twice before launching a raid, it recommended, and consider its consequences. "An operation that kills five insurgents is counterproductive if collateral damage leads to the recruitment of fifty more insurgents." This was a calculation that had eluded many commanders in Iraq.
- Don't hole up in big bases, as the U.S. military increasingly was doing in Iraq. "If military forces remain in their compounds, they lose touch with the people, appear to be running scared, and cede the initiative to the insurgents."
- Don't let yourself be provoked, as President Bush and other U.S. officials were by the killing of four Blackwater contractors in Fallujah in March 2004. "Often insurgents carry out a terrorist act or guerrilla raid with the primary purpose of enticing counterinsurgents to overreact."
- Don't abuse your prisoners, as had happened with the 2004 Abu Ghraib detainee scandal and in many other instances in the war. "Treat detainees professionally and publicize their treatment."

- Don't take relatives of suspected insurgents hostage, because it is both illegal and unethical. "At no time can Soldiers and Marines detain family members or close associates to compel suspected insurgents to surrender or provide information."
- Don't waste time and money attempting to build a local replica of the U.S. military. "Have local forces mirror the enemy, not U.S. forces."
- And don't concentrate on big, capital-intensive reconstruction projects. "Remember, small is beautiful."

Even discussions that didn't appear to be about the Iraq war carried clear messages about it. The first "vignette" in the manual—a box inserted in the text that tells an instructive story—is about Marine Gen. Anthony Zinni, who had been a fierce critic of the war and by 2006 was seen by the Bush administration as a political foe. Even more remote, but at the same time even more pointed, is a discussion of Napoleon's mishandling of his campaign in Spain in 1808. "Little thought was given to the potential challenges of subduing the Spanish populace. . . . Napoleon believed the conquest of Spain would be little more than a 'military promenade.' . . . The French failed to analyze the Spanish people, their history, culture, motivations. . . . Napoleon's cultural miscalculation resulted in a protracted occupation struggle that lasted nearly six years." All these missteps, of course, were also ones the U.S. military had been committing in Iraq.

The manual also pointed toward the very different approach Petraeus might take:

- "Remain alert for signs of divisions within an insurgent movement." By the time Petraeus arrived to take command in Iraq, Sunni insurgents were willing to talk to Americans about cease-fires, and he would seek ways to expand on that trend. "Encourage insurgents to change sides." Sitting down to talk with the evil-doers, as President Bush tended to portray them, would be a radical departure for the American effort in Iraq.
- "At the strategic level, gaining and maintaining U.S. public support for a protracted deployment is critical." Petraeus would devote much of his time and energy in the coming years to what he called "putting more time on the clock," especially in his 2007 and 2008 appearances

before Congress, which would be the highest-profile occasions of military testimony in decades.

- Most important, "The cornerstone of any COIN [counterinsurgency] effort is establishing security for the civilian populace." In 2007 this insight would become the starting point for U.S. strategy in Iraq.

Ambassador Ryan Crocker, a veteran diplomat, would read the manual early in 2007 as he prepared to go to Iraq as Petraeus's civilian counterpart. "If only that had been published in 2002," he thought to himself.

"A C-130 INTO HELL"

While the counterinsurgency manual was coming together, Iraq was falling apart. When Iraq's parliamentary elections were held at the end of 2005, they seemed to many to mark a major turning point. Bush administration officials, buoyed by the photographs of smiling Iraqis holding up fingers inked with the purple of the ballot booth, eagerly greeted the election as a major victory. Vice President Cheney, who 10 months earlier had declared the insurgency to be in its "last throes," used the occasion to make his first postinvasion visit to Iraq. "I think we've turned the corner, if you will," he told a group of Marines. "I think when we look back ten years hence, we'll see that the year '05 was in fact a watershed year here in Iraq." Gen. Casey, the top U.S. commander in Iraq, said it looked to him as though American troop levels could begin coming down in the following months.

In hindsight, the December 2005 elections were part of the problem, not the solution. "We needed elections in the worst kind of way in 2005—and we got them," Maj. Gen. David Fastabend, who would become Petraeus's chief of strategy in Iraq, wrote in a memo to his boss. Most notably, because Sunnis largely boycotted the vote, they planted Shiite-dominated governments in majority Sunni areas—and it would be those areas that would become most resistant to the Baghdad government. Also, less noticed, the elections encouraged U.S. commanders and planners to become overly optimistic. They began formulating plans for major drawdowns in 2006. Most significantly, by holding national elections without any other political structures in place, the U.S. government inadvertently herded Iraqis toward sectarian identification. In the 9 primarily Shiite provinces, the leading Shiite party, the United Iraqi Alliance, won 70 of 81 seats.

The Kurds swept the 35 seats in their region, and Sunni parties won 15 of 17 seats in al Anbar and Salahuddin provinces. The election results in Baghdad, Nineveh, Diyala, and Kirkuk also resembled the sectarian makeup of each province. This may have helped light the fuse of the small civil war that exploded in Baghdad months after. As Petraeus himself would put it much later, "The elections hardened sectarian positions as Iraqis voted largely based on ethnic and sectarian group identity."

Neither Cheney nor anyone else knew it, but 2006 would, in fact, prove to be the crucial year for the war—but not in the way that American officials had hoped or wanted. Rather, 2006 would be the year that American policy ground to a halt, the Bush administration finally conceded that it was on a path to defeat, the American civilian and military leadership in the war was jettisoned, and a new set of commanders—Petraeus and Odierno—installed to execute a radically different strategy. "Iraq came pretty close, I think, to just unraveling in the course of that year," Ambassador Crocker said.

It would take agonizing months—indeed, the whole of 2006—for that process of assessment and adjustment to occur. Many observers, both Iraqi and American, think the key event was the bombing on February 22, 2006, of the Golden Dome Mosque in Samarra, one of the most important Shia shrines in Iraq, and, indeed, in the world. Maj. Jeremy Lewis happened to be in Samarra, 65 miles north of Baghdad, at 6:44 that morning. He was preparing to go on patrol with some Iraqi National Police when

> . . . we heard an explosion. All eyes turn toward the explosion. You see this plume of smoke going up, and the plume of smoke was right next to the mosque. I guess that was an initial charge, one of the minarets they had blown up or something like that. . . . Then all of a sudden, the mosque just explodes. You blink and shudder and hunch down. You're thinking, "What the heck happened there?" . . . It was kind of a cloudy day, overcast. Now there's this huge plume of smoke, a monstrous cloud, and it's kind of yellowish and black. My gunner says, "Sir, it's fucking gone! It's gone!" I'm like, "No, it's not gone, it's not gone." But then the wind carried the plume of smoke away and you just saw the rebar and everything from the mosque.

Lewis and his comrades battened the hatches. "Every last one of us said this was the beginning of the civil war in Iraq," he recounted.

Hundreds of Iraqis would die in sectarian fighting in the following weeks, and many American commanders came to see the mosque bombing as a major turning point. But some officers and many observers argue that the incident simply was the culmination of a worsening trend that top officials weren't grasping, in part because of their focus on developing Iraqi security forces rather than on the situation of Iraqi civilians, and also because they didn't have troops living among the people. As James Miller, a former Pentagon war planner, put it, "The mosque bombing was just gasoline on a fire that already was burning pretty well." Indeed, according to the U.S. military's database of "significant acts," violence had increased at a steady pace since March 2005 and would continue to increase at about the same pace after the mosque bombing until peaking in June 2007. In 2005 and the following year, hundreds of thousands of Iraqis had fled the country. Many of them were doctors, lawyers, teachers, and journalists, the professionals who are part of the glue of a modern civil society. Because they had both money and education, they were targeted for kidnappings and murders by criminal gangs and political extremists alike. "The situation in the last six months has gotten so bad, we couldn't continue," Dr. Omar Kubasi told the *Washington Post*'s Doug Struck as the flow of refugees increased.

The mosque bombing "wasn't a trigger, it was an indicator," concluded Col. Christopher Holshek, a civil affairs veteran of Iraq. "All that did was expose some of the weaknesses in our approach."

The real effect of the bombing, added Jeffrey White, a former analyst of Middle Eastern affairs, was that it compelled U.S. commanders to deal with reality. After that day, it would become harder for them to argue that there were enough troops, because they had been given the additional mission of containing Shiite militias, on top of the existing tasks of countering the Sunni insurgency and training Iraqi security forces.

One Army officer who recalled buying into the optimism of late 2005 and early 2006, when he was a commander in Iraq, reluctantly agreed. In retrospect, he said, the situation had been far worse than he and his peers had understood it to be. It was the Samarra bombing that led him to believe that Iraq was indeed caught in a civil war: "What Samarra came to mean for me was a defining point in time, almost like a teaching point, where the real face of the Iraq war became clear."

Kilcullen, the Australian counterinsurgency theorist, was at Petraeus's conference at Fort Leavenworth when the Samarra bomb exploded. He immediately left for Baghdad, catching an Air Force cargo plane for the last leg. As he landed two days later, he said, "I felt like I was riding a C-130 into Hell. I mean, everything was burning."

OUT OF SIGHT, OUT OF MIND

One of the questions raised by the bloodshed of 2006 was whether it was a revealing preview of what would happen if the U.S. military withdrew altogether. Gen. John Abizaid, at the time the chief of the U.S. Central Command, had argued for years that the U.S. military presence was an irritant to the Iraqi population. Yet as U.S. forces had pulled back from Baghdad in 2005, as part of a consolidation effort, violence actually had increased. There were 130,000 U.S. troops in Iraq, but they were becoming increasingly irrelevant as fighting swirled around the tall walls of their bases. To a surprising degree, they were offstage and ill informed. U.S. military intelligence gathering tended to focus on two sorts of events: anything that affected American troops and the killing of Iraqis. Other actions affecting Iraqi civilians—kidnappings, rape, robberies, acts of extortion, and other forms of intimidation—didn't appear to be on the U.S. military's radar. As one soldier in the 4th Infantry Division dismissively put it, all that was "background noise."

As 2006 opened, there were almost no U.S. troops present on the streets of Baghdad, which U.S. commanders were trying to turn over to Iraqi forces. "We have become reactive," warned Capt. Zachary Martin. "With our fortified bases and our few secured major supply routes linking them, we have immobilized ourselves and cut ourselves off from the battlefield—the populace of Iraq." Many commanders, he charged, seemed more concerned with "force protection" than with winning.

American officials believed they were turning security over to Iraqi forces. But those Iraqi troops and police weren't able to control the streets, which meant that the American commanders really were abdicating responsibility and letting the streets become a battleground for sectarian groups. The Americans wouldn't enforce order and the Iraqis couldn't—even if they wanted to. As one Army major put it early in 2006, the capital resembled the pure Hobbesian state where all are at war against all others and any security is self-provided. Iraq appeared to be slipping steadily toward chaos. On one day, 22 civilians would die in a car bombing in Baghdad. On another, 17 policemen would be slain. By the third anniversary of the war, on March 19, it was clear that Iraq—or at least greater Baghdad, home to about a quarter of the nation's population—was on the edge of a civil war.

Enemy attacks were growing in both number and sophistication. In March, 17 policemen and security guards were killed in a dawn raid on a police station in Muqdadiyah that also released 33 prisoners. The attackers, numbering about 100, also set fire to a courthouse, destroyed 12 police cars, and held off an outnumbered U.S.-led counterattack. A month later, the enemy double-bombed an American outpost in the same province. The attack began with a truck exploding against a wall, clearing an opening for a second truck to barrel into the base and detonate against a security wall, which, improperly placed, fell over onto a building, killing 9 American troops inside.

In some U.S. Army units, commanders seemed simply to be keeping their heads down and plodding forward. "It is like we are on a combat patrol and what we see are all the indicators of an ambush—and yet we continue forward as if we had not been trained to detect, avoid, or take preemptive measures," said one Army colonel in Iraq who was versed in counterinsurgency theory.

Despite Gen. Casey's efforts with his new Counterinsurgency Academy, abuses by American soldiers, while less common than in 2003–4, still occurred. Even Petraeus's old division, the 101st Airborne, which had posted a nearly spotless record while under his command in northern Iraq in 2003–4, ran into ugly trouble in 2006. In March, two of the division's soldiers raped and murdered a fourteen-year-old Iraqi girl and killed her parents and sister to cover their crimes. In May, other 101st soldiers killed three detainees they had captured and handcuffed. Ultimately, four of them would be charged. One of their comrades, Pfc. Bradley Mason, would later testify that they had threatened to kill him if he reported their action.

The court-martial took an illuminating turn: The accused cited the aggressive tone set by their brigade commander, Col. Michael Steele, whose ham-fisted approach long had raised eyebrows in the Army. Retired Army Col. James Hallums, one of his predecessors in commanding the same unit, and himself a veteran of much combat, commented, "The supermacho image that Steele projected permeated his unit, and in my opinion, led directly to atrocities." When the brigade deployed, Steele, whose role in the fighting in Somalia in 1993 was captured in the book and film *Black Hawk Down*, had given a speech that was captured on videotape by documentarians following the unit. "Anytime you fight, you always kill the other sonofabitch," he had told his soldiers. "Do not let him live today so he will fight you tomorrow. Kill him today." When you go to Iraq, he added, "You're the predator."

The fight would be won, Steele told his men, by those who "get violent the fastest." The counterinsurgency manual then being written advised almost the opposite: "Sometimes, the more force is used, the less effective it is." The manual also would recommend that prisoners be treated kindly, the better to obtain information from them and perhaps even get them to change sides. Steele was from the old school, telling his soldiers that ensuring that prisoners were shaded from the sun and given water was "bullshit."

The documentary, made by John Laurence, a veteran war correspondent, captured how one of Steele's sergeants interpreted that approach. Speaking to his soldiers before a raid, the sergeant instructed them, "We are not bringing anyone back alive."

By mid-2006 insurgents were detonating about 1,000 roadside bombs every week, according to the U.S. Central Command. Much of the U.S. effort was focused on countering those attacks. Meanwhile, large numbers of Iraqis were being slaughtered almost daily. Insurgents who later changed sides would report that during 2006, primacy in their movement shifted from former members of Saddam Hussein's regime, some of whom were running low on cash, to al Qaeda, which "came in with a lot of money and bought away the young men," reported Maj. Joel Rayburn, an intelligence officer who would later work for Petraeus.

On May 7, car bombs killed about 30 people in the Shiite Muslim holy city of Karbala, 60 miles southwest of Baghdad. One of the car bombs was heading to a major mosque when it exploded in traffic—an echo of the Samarra attack 10 weeks earlier. On the same day, 51 bodies were found in Baghdad, handcuffed, blindfolded, and shot. A week later, 9 bombs detonated in the capital, killing 37. Six days later, a pickup truck loaded with explosives blew up in a crowd of day laborers in Sadr City, the huge slum on the eastern side of Baghdad. Called "Saddam City" until the American invasion, it was almost immediately renamed for the father of Moqtada al-Sadr, the radical Shiite cleric. It became the heart of the son's growing power. The bomb that day killed or wounded 99 people. Also, 6 policemen were killed by a bomb in the town of Qaim, and police found 40 bodies.

The slide into anarchy accelerated at the end of May after Nouri al-Maliki, a second-tier Shiite politician who was the grandson of a pre-Saddam minister of education, became the compromise pick for prime minister, ending months of stalemate between Shiite leaders. Gen. Chiarelli, the number two 2 U.S. commander in Iraq at the time, argued later that the U.S. effort went off track not because of February's Golden Dome Mosque bombing but because of the six months of drift that occurred when the elections didn't quickly lead to the selection of a prime minister. During that time, he said, Americans kept saying that the government, when it formed, would be a force for reconciliation. "We had said it so long, we believed it," he said, the regret evident in his voice. Instead, he explained, the selection of Maliki may have been the starting gun for a small civil war because the Shiites no longer felt they needed to be on their best behavior with the Americans. They finally held power, and also had the Americans backing them up. So why hold back?

"All hell broke loose," Chiarelli recalled. On May 30, another 51 people were killed in bombings. Inexplicably, American officials blithely continued to talk about drawing down the U.S. troop presence and turning over control of security to Iraqi forces. Such talk begged the question: If well-equipped and well-trained American troops couldn't control the situation, why would a new, divided, and distrusted Iraqi police and army be able to do any better?

In the following 12 months, the Army's 24th Transportation Battalion sent over 400 convoys north from Kuwait and across Iraq, and was hit 170 times. "Every time you left the gate, it was a greater than one-in-three chance that you were going to get hit," said Maj. Dan Williamson, the battalion's executive officer.

The U.S. intelligence community warned at this time that a cycle of "self-sustaining violence" had begun in Iraq, recalled Feaver, the NSC aide. As criticism of the U.S. strategy mounted, he added, "I was finding it harder to answer these critiques."

What was happening was that the "strategic edifice" of the American effort in Iraq was collapsing, Col. Peter Mansoor, Petraeus's executive officer, later observed. But, soft-spoken in his steel-rimmed glasses and short graying hair, he added with dry underestimation, "It took a few months longer to realize it."

RETIRED GENERALS VS. "THE DECIDER"

Back in Washington, the feeling of deterioration in the war was intensifying. One Pentagon official recalled the dysfunctional dynamic of the Bush administration that spring. "The president would say, 'Get this done,' and leave the room," he recalled. "And then Rumsfeld would start squabbling with Condi—'We're not gonna secure your PRTs!'"—a reference to the State Department–led Provincial Reconstruction Teams that were at the heart of the strategy of rebuilding the economy of Iraq from the bottom up in order to improve security and so eventually reduce the American military presence. His thought on Rumsfeld at that point, he said, was, "Well, you fucking idiot, that's your ticket out of Iraq."

Officially, all was going well. "Iraq is making steady progress in meeting the president's short-term and medium-term security goals," said a bizarrely cheerful assessment of Iraq released by the Bush administration in April. The elections and subsequent security operations had led to "a political process that now includes all of Iraq's major communities for the first time."

But behind the scenes, a rift was developing between senior commanders in Baghdad and their bosses back in Washington about how to see the war. "It was clear to me that it had shifted from an insurgency against us to a struggle for power, that it wasn't any longer totally about us, it was about them," Gen. Casey said in 2008 as he looked back at that time. He was sitting in his Pentagon office under a portrait of Gen. Ulysses S. Grant, the Old Testament patriarch of today's Army. When he sought to convey that sense of an altered war to officials at the Pentagon and White House, he got blank stares. "We tried until we were blue in the face to get folks [in Washington] to understand that the struggle had fundamentally changed. . . . I always felt I wasn't conveying it in a way that people could grasp it."

Officials at the White House were likewise beginning to lose faith in their military interlocutors. "We could just see the Samarra thing spiraling, and no progress on getting a government," recalled Feaver, who had become one of the key NSC staffers working on Iraq issues. "As we see the situation eroding, there's a growing question: Do we have the right strategy, is it going to work? And is it time for Rumsfeld to go? This is at the White House staff level—this is people talking at the water cooler. The nub of this is, who can replace him?"

The continuing lack of realism in official statements was one of the factors that precipitated the "revolt of the generals," which really was just a few retired officers going public with concerns, albeit ones that had grown fairly widespread in their peer group. The wave of criticism began on March 19, when retired Maj. Gen. Paul Eaton, who had been the first overseer of the Iraqi military training effort, wrote an opinion piece for the *New York Times* that essentially made the

Army's case against Rumsfeld. More troops were needed in Iraq, the senior military officers around Rumsfeld were too pliant, and the defense secretary was "incompetent strategically, operationally and tactically," he wrote. There wasn't much new in these assertions. Their significance was that they were made by a general who had been on active duty in Iraq. If Bush was simply heeding the advice of his generals, as he had so often asserted, then why was this one calling for his defense secretary to be fired?

The next officer to jump Rumsfeld's ship was retired Lt. Gen. Gregory Newbold, who went public with a similar critique in *Time* magazine. Like Eaton, he had been on active duty during the run-up to the war, serving in the key position of operations director for the Joint Chiefs of Staff. Arguing that the Iraq war was a mistake, he took aim at the entire Bush administration, which he blamed for a series of failures. Among them were distorting intelligence, micromanaging the war, alienating allies, failing to retain the Iraqi army, and denying that an insurgency existed. Again, this came not from any one of a thousand retired officers, but from someone who had seen Rumsfeld up close.

Other retired generals decided it was time to speak out. The third blow came from another officer with credibility gained from firsthand experience, both in the Pentagon and in Iraq. Retired Maj. Gen. John Batiste had been the senior military assistant to Paul Wolfowitz, who as deputy secretary of defense had been one of the leaders of the drive to war. Batiste then had become commander of the 1st Infantry Division, leading it to fight in Iraq in 2004–5. It also was widely known that he had been offered a promotion to lieutenant general to return to Iraq as the number two officer there but had declined because he no longer wished to serve under Rumsfeld. "I think we need a fresh start" at the top of the Pentagon, Batiste said. "We need leadership up there that respects the military as they expect the military to respect them. And that leadership needs to understand teamwork."

Reporters soon found more generals willing to criticize the administration. Retired Maj. Gen. Charles Swannack, who had commanded the 82nd Airborne Division in Iraq, laid responsibility for the Abu Ghraib scandal at Rumsfeld's feet, saying it was the result of top-level pressure to step up interrogations. Retired Gen. Anthony Zinni and retired Maj. Gen. John Riggs, who previously had questioned the handling of the war, now were recast as members of a growing group of dissident officers. Riggs made the point that three years into a war that was intended to end in weeks or months, it was growing increasingly difficult to believe the Bush administration's explanations of events. "I think they've made fools of themselves, and totally underestimated what would be needed for a sustained conflict," he said.

Rumsfeld's response was to sidestep the substance of the criticism and instead belittle the critics. Rather than respond to the fact that people who had seen him operate firsthand were offering heartfelt—if angry and tardy—commentary, he acted as if they were a few inevitable if inexplicable malcontents. "I don't know how many generals there have been in the last five years that have served on the United States armed services—hundreds and hundreds and hundreds. And there are several who have opinions. And there's nothing wrong with people having opinions. And I think one ought to expect that. When you're involved in something that's controversial, as certainly this war is, one ought to expect that." That anodyne comment was fundamentally dishonest because it didn't answer the nagging question. Nor did Rumsfeld's dismissiveness serve his president well. Bush had been saying since the start of the war that he relied on the judgment of his generals, and these were generals whose opinions mattered because of their personal experience in Iraq or with Rumsfeld. To swipe aside their collective judgment could only deepen the public's lack of faith in Bush and those around him.

The generals' revolt may have been most significant for the irritated response it provoked from a peeved President Bush a few days later. At the end of a press conference to announce the appointment of a new director of the Office of Management and Budget, Bush was asked about talk that Rumsfeld might be forced out by the officers' criticism. "I don't appreciate the speculation about Don Rumsfeld," Bush said. "He's doing a fine job." As for the generals, he said, "I listen to all voices, but mine's the final decision. . . . I hear the voices, and I read the front page, and I know the speculation. But I'm the decider, and I decide what is best. And what's best is for Don Rumsfeld to remain as the secretary of defense." With that awkwardly put comment, Bush gave Rumsfeld another seven months in office.

Just as the generals' revolt was simmering down, the killings at Haditha the previous November erupted into a major news story. Investigations had been under way since February and had intensified after *Time* magazine ran a thorough article in March that cast doubt on official accounts. But the incident jumped onto page one because of comments made during a press conference by Representative John Murtha, a Pennsylvania Democrat and a Marine veteran of

Vietnam who had turned strongly against the Iraq war. Midway through the conference, he blurted out that the incident was "much worse" than was understood. "Our troops overreacted because of pressure on them, and they killed innocent civilians in cold blood," he said. In the following days, amid talk of another Abu Ghraib scandal that would inflict a strategic wound on the war effort, other members of Congress used less inflammatory language but expressed grave concern. The commandant of the Marine Corps, Gen. Michael Hagee, flew to Iraq to address his troops.

Andrew Krepinevich, who had written the *Foreign Affairs* article that laid out much of the strategy that the United States eventually would adopt, but much later, observed that the center of gravity in Iraq was the Iraqi population. The task is to convince the population that you will protect them, and also that you will win. So, he concluded, allowing an incident such as Haditha to occur, and then dismissing it as routine, as the Marine chain of command had done, was tantamount to "losing a major battle."

Oddly, the revelations and allegations about the killings provoked less reaction in Iraq—but not for reasons that were good for the American cause. Some Iraqis said they hadn't heard the news because they lacked electricity. "We live in darkness," said Muhanned Jasim, an antiques seller in Baghdad. At any rate, he added, "What's the big news about Iraqis getting killed? We're powerless to change the situation."

As Ghasan Jayih, a pharmacist, ruefully and correctly observed, "It's normal now to hear twenty-five Iraqis are killed in one day."

Feaver, whose official title on the staff of the National Security Council was Special Advisor for Strategic Planning and Institutional Reform, thought it was time to confront the president with the bad news. The cheerful son of a Lehigh University classics professor, Feaver himself was a political scientist with a full professorship waiting for him back at Duke University, which gave him a bit of freedom. He was in no position to oust Rumsfeld, but he could and did write memos to the national security adviser, Stephen Hadley, urging that the president hear from some sympathetic but worried outsiders. Feaver and a fellow staffer put that meeting together for a day in June at Camp David, the presidential retreat in the hills of Maryland. One of those on his list was his old friend Eliot Cohen, whom he had known since both were at Harvard in the early 1980s.

But then Feaver's plan was undercut by an unexpected stream of good news arriving from Iraq. It all had started weeks earlier with the arrest in Jordan of

Ziad Khalaf al-Kerbouly, a Jordanian customs worker, who confessed that he had helped smuggle cash and supplies to Abel Rahman, who was believed to be the spiritual adviser to Abu Musab al-Zarqawi, the head of al Qaeda in Iraq. Rahman also was thought to be the liaison between the Iraqi Sunni religious leadership and Zarqawi. U.S. Special Operations teams then began using his contact information to find Rahman and monitor his movements. After three weeks of watching, in the late afternoon of June 7, the spiritual adviser was tracked to a farmhouse in a palm grove in the village of Hibhib, about 35 miles north of Baghdad. U.S. forces went on high alert because Rahman had performed certain tasks—the specifics were never disclosed by the U.S. government—that he usually did before meeting with the terrorist leader. An F-16 jet that had been refueling was dispatched to the area. At 6:12 P.M., its pilot released two 500-pound laser-guided bombs that obliterated the hideout. American troops came upon Zarqawi as he lay near the rubble. He was suffocating as his lungs, torn and bruised by the bombs' blast waves, ceased to function. He died at 7:04. It was a surprisingly swift and merciful end for the man who was believed to have been behind much of the car bombing of Iraqi civilians in the preceding weeks and months, attacks that had killed and maimed hundreds of innocent men, women, and children. Soldiers from a military intelligence unit found not only Islamic religious material, as they had expected, but also a copy of the May 2nd issue of the Arabic edition of *Newsweek*.

A MISSED CHANCE AT CAMP DAVID

In June 2006, the presidential meeting with those sympathetic war critics came together at Camp David, atop a ridge in the Maryland foothills just southwest of the Gettysburg battlefield. Eliot Cohen, Michael Vickers, Fred Kagan, and Robert Kaplan—the first three men, smart national security experts; the last, an influential journalist—were generally supportive of the war but critical of its conduct. They were invited to tell the president how it might be better run.

Kagan went to the meeting hoping that it would be "a major turning point." He had believed for years that the war was being mishandled. "Doing the right thing the wrong way" was the phrase that came to characterize the views of his faction of hawks who thought that the decision to invade Iraq had been correct but who were troubled by the U.S. performance since the fall of Baghdad. "Do we have enough troops?" he asked at the meeting.

Cohen, who on the advice of Feaver had given up his customary bow tie for the meeting, agreed that this wasn't the time to discuss troop cuts, as the generals were doing, but thought Kagan was fiddling too much with the tactical level of operations and wanted the president instead to focus on strategy. "You probably need more people, but the real question is what you do with them," he said. He also urged the president to get the rest of the U.S. government beyond the military more seriously engaged in the effort in Iraq. Cohen knew that Bush had read his *Supreme Command.* He wanted to make Bush think about how to deal with his generals—and consider replacing some. For him, the heart of the matter was "different commanders and a different approach." After the meeting, he would lash himself for not hitting this point as hard as he should have. Also, he said, "You know, the Army is in worse shape than you think." Bush didn't respond. Defense Secretary Rumsfeld and Gen. Pace, the chairman of the Joint Chiefs, also listening, squirmed a bit. Pace had proven a weak chairman, seemingly unwilling to stand up to Rumsfeld when other generals thought he should and instead trying to simply ease the discord at the Pentagon between uniformed military and its civilian overseers. He had a reputation for being a good and decent man, but too pliant. His accomplishment may have been of another sort—keeping the Joint Chiefs from going off the reservation when they split with the president later in the year over whether to change the strategy in the war.

Nor had Pace been much of a presence in discussions of that strategy. It was the major war on his watch, but he tended to defer to Casey and Abizaid, the two four-star officers directly involved in its prosecution. The irony of all this was that policy formulation was following the prescribed method, with the hierarchy being observed and all the correct bureaucratic players involved, but the system wasn't really working. That is, it looked good, but it wasn't leading to a robust discussion by top officials of the necessary strategic questions. Nor were leaders held accountable and quizzed on their failures. It was only months later, when the prescribed system was subverted and the chain of command bypassed, that a rigorous examination of American strategy in the Iraq war would get under way.

Kaplan used his time to talk about counterinsurgency practices. "Get rid of periodic presence patrols and provide twenty-four/seven security, get out of big bases and deploy smaller units in neighborhoods," he said. He was ambivalent about increasing the number of troops because he believed that those already in Iraq were being used incorrectly.

Vickers, a former CIA officer, had played a key role in outfitting the Afghan mujahadeen in the 1980s in their struggle against the Soviet occupation, a role later immortalized in the book and movie *Charlie Wilson's War.* Reaching back to his time then, he emphasized what strategists call the indirect approach—that is, helping a local ally fight rather than having Americans carry the combat load. Draw down your conventional forces and rely more on elite Special Operators, he said. "You're on borrowed time with the direct approach," said Vickers, according to people who attended the meeting.

The conversation flowed freely, and the president enjoyed the brisk dialogue, said Feaver, the NSC aide who helped conceive and arrange the meeting. But it didn't work as he had intended, which was to confront the president and his key advisers with the worried critiques of loyalists. Bush was riding on good news. Not only had a new government been seated, but just a few days earlier, Zarqawi had been found and killed. And as Bush was listening, he knew something his four visitors didn't—that he would be slipping away from Camp David just minutes later to make a secret trip to Baghdad, his first since Thanksgiving 2003. ("He was almost a little bouncy," Kagan said. "I now recognize that he was very excited about the trip he was about to pull.") So rather than lead to a much-needed review of strategy, the three events effectively combined to reenergize the president's commitment to the existing one, Feaver said.

Kagan agreed with that assessment. "I think it [the meeting] had no effect. It certainly didn't change the minds of the principals. It didn't generate any follow-up." Rather than a radical change in strategy, he said, "we continued to drift."

Returning from Baghdad, Bush gave a tempered but upbeat assessment. "I sense something different happening in Iraq," he said in a Rose Garden press conference. "The progress will be steady toward a goal that has clearly been defined. In other words, I hope there's not an expectation from people that, all of a sudden, there's going to be zero violence—in other words, it's just not going to be the case. On the other hand, I do think we'll be able to measure progress."

In fact, the Camp David meeting would have a far greater long-term effect than anyone could know at the time. In the following months, three of the four worried loyalists who had trekked to the presidential retreat would become deeply involved in revamping Iraq strategy. Cohen took the position of counselor at the State Department, where he became a major strategic voice in the government, not just advising the secretary of state but also officials at the Pentagon and at the White House. Vickers, another of Cohen's former students, became chief of overseeing Special Operations and strategy at the Pentagon. Bush, still taken with Vickers's role in arming the Afghan rebels, pinged the Pentagon twice to hurry the clearance process for him. Kagan wouldn't go into the government but would help redesign U.S. strategy in Iraq, both figuring out what to do and then helping sell the new approach to top White House officials.

THE BATTLE OF BAGHDAD BEGINS

After the Camp David meeting the situation in Iraq turned sharply worse. The period from mid-2006 to mid-2007 would prove to be the bloodiest 12 months that American troops had seen thus far in the war, with 1,105 killed. Iraqi civilian deaths are harder to determine but were clearly a multiple of that figure. In the summer and fall of 2006, Shiite militias carried out a concerted campaign that pushed Sunnis out of much of Baghdad, which until then had been a mixed city, with Sunnis predominating west of the Tigris River and Shiites to its east.

The battle of Baghdad effectively began at sunrise on Sunday, July 9, when Shiite militiamen, some of them masked, appeared in the Sunni neighborhood of Jihad, near the Baghdad airport. They set up checkpoints on main streets and killed those passersby whose identity cards indicated they probably were Sunni. They shot up a vegetable market. They also went into homes they believed were occupied by Sunnis. All told, about 50 people were slaughtered. "This is a new step. A red line has been crossed," said Alaa Makky, a Sunni member of parliament. "People have been killed in the streets; now they are killed inside their homes."

The next day, Monday, Saleh Muhammed, a resident of the Sunni neighborhood of Amiriyah in far western Baghdad, called the police emergency line to report that the leading Shiite militia, the Mahdi Army, was attacking the quarter's Malouki mosque. He was surprised by the dispatcher's response: "The Mahdi Army are not terrorists like you. They are people doing their duty. And how could you know that they are the Mahdi Army—is it written on their foreheads?"

A wave of Sunni retaliation followed. Two car bombs exploded in Sadr City, the city's biggest Shiite neighborhood, home to about 2 million people, killing or wounding nearly 30. On Wednesday, gunmen kidnapped a group of people, apparently Shiites, at a bus station in Muqdadiyah, and murdered 22 of them.

The following Sunday, a café filled with Shiites was blown up north of Baghdad, killing 26. On Monday morning, death squads assaulted the marketplace in the mostly Shiite southern Baghdad suburb of Mahmudiyah. They fired heavy machine guns, burned cars, threw grenades, and entered a café to shoot 7 elderly men in the head. At least 40 people were killed. On Tuesday, a minibus loaded with explosives blew up near a Shiite mosque in Kufa, killing 53 day laborers and wounding at least 130 more. Hundreds more Iraqis were dying in smaller incidents. Police in the tough southern Baghdad neighborhood of Doura said 425 people were killed in that area alone during the week after the Jihad marketplace massacre. Altogether, more than 3,000 Iraqis were slain during July, the United Nations estimated. It was the deadliest month in three years.

Army Capt. Don Makay, who fought in southwest Baghdad, recalled that during his tour, every Sunni mosque in his area was attacked, in one case, he thought, with the involvement of the local commander of the National Police. From July through October, the number of murdered bodies dumped near Sunni districts "rose considerably," wrote another Army captain, Michael Comstock, in his study of the ethnic-cleansing operation. Other Iraqis were luckier, receiving "night letters" that contained a bullet and an order to vacate their homes within a day or two.

The core of the Iraqi state was rotten. The Iraqi army was heavily Shiite, and even worse, the National Police were thoroughly infiltrated by Shiite militias. These forces didn't have to carry out the cleansing themselves. All they had to do was go into a Sunni neighborhood and demand in the name of pacification that all heavy weapons be relinquished. After that was accomplished, they could tip off the Shiite militias, who might arrive that night or the next morning, ready to take on the newly defenseless population. As one foreign diplomat in Baghdad summarized the legitimate complaint of Sunnis, "You come and denude us of weapons, and the next day the militias visit."

Nor did the gunmen need to kill everyone—just enough to intimidate the rest. This is how Capt. Eric Haas summarized the tactics of Jaysh al-Mahdi, Moqtada al-Sadr's radical Shiite militia: "JAM/Shia militia group kidnaps a Sunni male from a mixed-sect market; takes Sunni male to the edge of Sunni-dominated neighborhood; takes Sunni male from the vehicle shot in the back of a head with a pistol; Shia militia drives off."

Crueler tactics, such as using power tools to drill holes in the kneecaps or heads of victims, also became common. "People are killed here every day, and you don't hear about it," Capt. Lee Showman told the *Washington Post*'s Josh Partlow. "People are kidnapped here every day, and you don't hear about it." As the ethnic-cleansing campaign intensified, the number of Iraqis seeking refuge in neighboring nations spiraled, with an estimated 2 million leaving the country. An equal number were classified as internally displaced, with much of that movement occurring in 2006.

But the militias' work was hardly done once the Sunnis had been driven out. The next step was to turn the neighborhood into a paying concern. First the vacated houses would be rented to Shias. Then kidnapping and extortion rings would raise money from shop owners and other holders of wealth. Shiite party banners would festoon the altered area. Local police would be intimidated, co-opted, or replaced with Shiite militia members who would cooperate. The explicit support and assistance of all civilians in the area was demanded. "Leave, join or die" was the summary offered by Army Capt. Josh Francis. At this point the area might become less violent, but that wasn't necessarily a positive sign. Instead, it might just mean that the job was done and that the newly quiet neighborhood then could be used as a base from which to begin launching attacks on adjacent Sunni areas.

Sgt. Victor Alarcon watched as his battalion in the 1st Infantry Division lost 20 troops in an unsuccessful effort in 2006 to prevent the destruction of what had been a bustling middle-class Sunni neighborhood. "I don't think this place is worth another soldier's life," he said near the end of his tour.

Maj. Mark Gilmore gave this dismal summary of his time in one Baghdad neighborhood: "When we got there, it was mixed Sunni and Shia. When we left, it was Shia. . . . When we left, it wasn't even worth counting the Sunnis because there weren't that many left."

THE FIGHTING in Iraq wasn't just sectarian. Two other major players in the tragedy of Iraq were also escalating their activities at this time: al Qaeda in Iraq, and Iran.

In August, Col. Peter Devlin, the senior Marine intelligence officer in Iraq, filed a secret report concluding that the U.S. military had lost al Anbar, in western Iraq, and that al Qaeda was now the dominant factor in the province. "The social and political situation has deteriorated to a point that MNF [Multi-National Forces] and ISF [Iraqi Security Forces] are no longer capable of militarily defeating the insurgency in al Anbar. . . . Underlying this decline in stability is the near complete collapse of social order in al Anbar." What's more, al Qaeda in Iraq, which was mainly made up of nihilistic Iraqi religious extremists but also included some foreign fighters, who frequently were used in car bombings, had elbowed aside other centers of power in the province and made itself Anbar's "dominant organization of influence." (Devlin's assessment is reprinted in full as the first document in the appendix.)

To the north of Baghdad, al Qaeda in Iraq, sometimes referred to by the U.S. military as "AQIZ," launched a swift and viciously effective campaign. "Using a small, localized cell of hardcore believers, AQIZ successfully coerced and intimidated the local populace over time through a four phased plan: clandestine organization, psychological preparation of the people, expansion of control, and consolidation of power," Army Capt. James Few wrote in a study of the terrorist takeover of the town of Zaganiyah.

A *mukthar,* or town elder, sought an audience with al Qaeda leaders in the town of Nukisa to complain about the behavior of the organization's recruits. He was beaten in public, the humiliation intended to demonstrate that there was a new sheriff in town. In November 2006, while American forces were focused on the deterioration of security in Baghdad, al Qaeda members in the town made their move, launching a complex attack on the local Iraqi police station, with a car bomb followed by an assault by fighters. "Over the next two weeks, ISF stopped patrolling the area, and CF [coalition forces] designated Zaganiyah as 'No-Go' terrain," Few wrote. The al Qaeda cell then consolidated its hold, destroying the home of an Iraqi working as an interpreter for the Americans and beheading a captured Iraqi soldier and a local Shiite. They also dug fighting positions around the town and deeply buried more than 160 bombs, establishing a defensive belt.

Meanwhile, Iran, capitalizing on the cover provided by violence and counting on the Americans to be distracted, quietly launched its own offensive in Iraq. Devastating "explosively formed projectiles," the most lethal type of roadside bomb, began appearing in great numbers in late 2006. These high-tech bombs operate by melting a disk of metal into a spray of high-velocity drops that cut through armored vehicles, frequently killing three or four soldiers in one blast. U.S. intelligence officials said all the devices were imported from Iran. During 2007 they would become the greatest threat to U.S. troops, inflicting 73 percent of all American casualties.

Asked what he would do differently in 2006 if he could, Abizaid, the top American commander for the Middle East, said, "We didn't react quickly enough to Shia and Sunni violence," or, he said, to the misdeeds of the Iraqi police.

"FORWARD" INTO FAILURE

Finally, in the summer of 2006, the U.S. military and its Iraqi allies launched a major counteroffensive aimed at improving security in the capital. Dubbed "Together Forward," the operation involved some 42,500 Iraqi police and army personnel backed up by 7,200 U.S. troops. The Iraqi forces were instructed to erect new checkpoints, enforce extended dusk-to-dawn curfews and new restrictions on carrying weapons, and step up the frequency of their foot patrols. Posters were distributed showing an Iraqi soldier in tan battle fatigues holding the hand of a smiling Iraqi boy. But the Americans were operating more and more from big bases, removing themselves from the population and from the civil war being waged beyond the tall cement walls of their isolated bastions. They also continued to judge their actions all too often by input, such as the number of patrols conducted, rather than by output, such as the reduction in violence.

The offensive never really got off the ground. "They were dead in the water by midsummer," said Krepinevich, the counterinsurgency expert.

For Brett McGurk, a staffer on the National Security Council who was in Baghdad that summer, the failure was a turning point in his view of the approach the U.S. military was taking. "Gaziliyah was probably the best example of a clearly failing strategy," he recalled. "We go in, MNF-I reports its metrics (buildings cleared, violence reduced), we leave, and violence in Gaziliyah hits all-time highs." His conclusion was that "it was clearly a failed recipe—the question was whether we could do anything about it."

Fred Kagan, the defense analyst who had been at Camp David as the summer began, later said the offensive was doomed from the start, because it relied excessively on Iraqi police forces, which he said were part of the problem, not the solution. "They were not and could not be effective bulwarks on their own against sectarian violence of which they were a part," he wrote.

American commanders would, in fact, blame Iraqi units for the failure. "The loyalty of the Iraqi security forces, particularly the police, was the overriding issue that kept this from being a success," Gen. Casey said in an interview. A secondary flaw, he said was the slowness with which the Iraqi government moved to conduct follow-on economic aid projects. "It was never clear whether it was incompetence or sectarian bias."

Chiarelli, the number two U.S. commander in Iraq, added," I was under the impression that we would get two additional Iraqi brigades, and they didn't show up." In addition, Abizaid said, the American liaison connection to Iraqi forces needed to be strengthened.

Some in Iraq said that Chiarelli and Casey should have known that the Americans couldn't rely on Iraqi forces to carry a large part of the burden. "They ordered these Kurdish units to come down," recalled Maj. Matt Whitney, who at the time was an adviser to the Iraqi Ground Forces Command, a top headquarters. "One of them mutinied. They look for troops in the south and they wouldn't come either. They looked for two more units from the north and they didn't come." He wasn't surprised by this, because many Iraqi units thought they were supposed to defend the area where they were based. They had neither the training nor the equipment to pack up and move around the country. "General Casey was frustrated because he couldn't get Iraqi units to deploy, although we never built that army to deploy. Somehow he was surprised by this."

Together Forward not only didn't work, it backfired on Gen. Casey, because it undercut the confidence of Bush administration officials in his ability to deliver. "In July, when Baghdad Security Plan One tanked, they said, 'We didn't have enough reliable Iraqi units, they didn't show up,'" recalled Feaver, one of the National Security Council staffers working on Iraq. "Over the summer, doubts began to grow among White House officials working on Iraq. By September the NSC staff initiated a quiet but thorough review of strategy with an eye to developing a new way forward."

McGurk, the NSC staffer, returned to the White House with doubts not just about the approach but about the people implementing it. He "had lost all faith in our security strategy. MNF-I and the embassy were locked in a corrosive cycle of finger-pointing . . . with nobody asking serious questions about what to do differently."

A new iteration, Together Forward II, was launched on August 8. It did nothing to stop the big bombings. Casey called in additional troops from his theater reserve and sent those reinforcements to help clear the city, block by block. The notion was that Iraqi forces then would hold those areas. "Clear, hold, and build" was a phrase that grew out of Col. H. R. McMaster's successful campaign in the northern Iraqi city of Tall Afar, one of the few bright spots in the war that year. A visiting State Department official picked up the phrase and passed it along to Secretary of State Condoleezza Rice, who used it in congressional testimony. Rumsfeld resisted the phrase, even after the White House adopted it. He argued that it was the job of the Iraqis or the State Department to oversee holding and building, but grudgingly seemed to accept the idea as at least a rhetorical necessity.

There was little reason to believe that the plan to clear, hold, and build in Baghdad would work any better the second time around. Brig. Gen. John Campbell started in Baghdad as the assistant commander of the 1st Cavalry Division on the day Operation Together Forward II began. He watched as attacks rose steadily despite U.S. efforts. "They went through and cleared, and tried to hold that with Iraqi forces," Campbell said. "The issue was, we didn't have enough ISF, both in quantity and quality."

The failure to hold meant that the U.S. military was simply repeating the pattern of 2003–5 that Kilcullen, the Australian counterinsurgency analyst, had labeled "kiss of death" operations, in which American forces moved into an area, found cooperative locals, and then, after some improvement of security, pulled out of the area. "Then," Kilcullen grimly concluded, "insurgents kill those who cooperated with us."

White House officials were also concluding that the government of Prime Minister Nouri al-Maliki was impeding success, especially because it wouldn't allow actions to be taken against Shiite militias, Feaver said. Indeed, after U.S. Army units launched a raid into Sadr City in early August, resulting in a two-hour-long firefight, Maliki angrily appeared on television to apologize for the operation. "This won't happen again," he promised. Chiarelli said that Maliki constantly impeded U.S. operations during the summer and fall of 2006. Near the end of the year, for example, U.S. Special Operators would pick up in Baghdad one of the most senior leaders of the Iranian Revolutionary Guard's Quds Force, the guard's wing for foreign Islamic revolutionary operations. He was believed to be involved in planning attacks on U.S. forces and was found at the compound of Abdul Aziz al-Hakim, head of an influential Shiite political party that was a big part of Maliki's ruling coalition and one of the most prominent politicians in Iraq. U.S. officials were furious when a few days later, Maliki's government sent the Quds man back to Iran.

August ended with two days of ferocious bombings, with 27 people killed in the Shorja market, Baghdad's largest bazaar, on the thirtieth, and then 66 killed the next day as a huge explosion flattened an apartment building in a Shiite neighborhood. Meanwhile, Shiite militiamen battled U.S. troops both in Sadr City and in the southern city of Diwaniyah. The same month saw a 33-day Israeli war with Hezbollah in southern Lebanon end in what was widely seen as a military and political setback for Israel, an outcome that only further worried analysts assessing the American position in Iraq.

Despite the growing violence, Casey continued to insist on a policy that emphasized transition to Iraqi forces. Late in August, he predicted that Iraqi forces would be able to provide security in the country pretty much on their own by late 2007 or early 2008. "I can see—over the next twelve to eighteen months—I can see the Iraqi security forces progressing to a point where they can take on the security responsibilities for the country with very little coalition support," he said.

Chiarelli, the number two officer in Iraq, and so commander of day-to-day operations, occupies an ambiguous position in this tale. As the commander of the 1st Cavalry Division in Baghdad during his previous tour, he had done a far better job than most in understanding the principles of counterinsurgency. There were rumors of disagreement between Casey and him over the way forward. Publicly he was entirely supportive of Casey, reiterating in mid-September the view that sending additional U.S. troops was not the answer. "I feel that given the conditions we've got in Baghdad, we've got the force posture exactly where it needs to be," he said. On the face of it, there would appear to be little else that he could do, given his subordinate position. Yet just a few months later, Lt. Gen. Odierno would arrive to take over from Chiarelli in that number two slot and effectively challenge Casey as Chiarelli had never done, conducting his own strategic review that ultimately would reverse almost every tenet of American strategy in Iraq. Chiarelli struggled with the number two position; Odierno would redefine it.

Sadi Othman, who would become one of Petraeus's closest advisers in Iraq, said that in retrospect, neither American officials nor Iraqi leaders understood just how dangerous the situation was in 2006. "I think people knew the situation was bad, but they didn't know it was very, very bad," he said in 2008. "The Americans didn't get out of the Green Zone. The government of Iraq didn't get out. And we didn't have troops on the streets. So when people said things were okay, they weren't lying. They were innocent."

Chiarelli, in a 2008 interview, disputed Othman's assertion. In fact, he said, he had gone to Maliki in July "to tell him how bad it was." The prime minister's chilling response, he recalled, had been "It was a lot worse in Saddam's time." American officers interpreted this to mean that Maliki didn't intend to do anything to curtail the violence, which was Shiite payback against Sunnis for what had happened before.

Meanwhile, political pressure was building for a radical shift away from Casey's approach. In September the Iraq Study Group, which had been appointed by Congress to review policy in the war and to make recommendations to improve it, arrived in Baghdad to check its views against the thinking in the Green Zone, the heavily guarded enclave in the center of Baghdad that housed the headquarters of the American effort in Iraq. Many of the study group's members, such as former congressman Lee Hamilton and former secretary of state James Baker—its two chairs—were more familiar with politics and diplomacy than warfare. Another member, Robert Gates, was destined to become defense secretary just four months later, but nobody knew that then. At the time, there were just two members of the group who knew the military establishment well: former defense secretary William Perry and former senator Charles Robb, a Marine veteran of the Vietnam War and a longtime member of the Senate Armed Services Committee. Both Perry and Robb had come to think that current U.S. strategy couldn't continue and were mulling advocating a troop escalation.

Before heading to Baghdad, Perry had distributed a memorandum to the group making an argument for such a "surge" in troops in Iraq. "We thought we couldn't get enough troops to surge the whole country, but we could maybe have an effect in Baghdad," he recalled. (President Bush said in 2008 that when he interviewed Robert Gates in November 2006 about becoming defense secretary, Gates told him that he also had favored such an increase.)

When the group met with Casey and Chiarelli, the generals threw cold water on the idea of a troop increase. "They were very explicit," Perry said. "Both Casey and Chiarelli said this would not be useful, as they saw the problems in Iraq." The officers offered three arguments: First, it would give the Iraqi government the impression that the Americans would solve their problems. Second, it would decrease the leverage the Americans had. Third, whatever improvement it provided wouldn't last. "They made the point that wherever you put American troops, it would stabilize the situation—but when they left, it would destabilize the situation."

Perry worried that the group was being given what he called a "party line," so he asked for separate one-on-one meetings to get the generals' personal views. In those private sessions, he said, "Both stuck to their guns."

Faced with the opposition of the top U.S. military leadership on the ground, Perry withdrew the idea. When he wrote the first draft of the military section of the group's report, he left out the idea of a surge. "It would have been in there if they had responded differently," he said. Ultimately, the group's report straddled the idea, rejecting a major increase but conditionally supporting "a short-term redeployment or surge of American combat forces to stabilize Baghdad . . . if the U.S. commander in Iraq determines that such steps would be effective."

Chiarelli said later that he wasn't against getting additional forces. "In fact, I already knew where I would put a brigade," he said in an interview at the Pentagon in 2008 shortly before he pinned on a fourth star and became the vice chief of staff of the Army. But, he added, he knew that it would take time to bring in additional troops. "I thought we could push violence down a lot faster if we went to Maliki" and delivered a strong message: Your policies, such as not delivering services to Sunnis, are exacerbating sectarian tensions. "We need to use our leverage with Maliki," was his recommendation. At any rate, he remembered, when he arrived in Iraq at the beginning of 2006, he had been told that during that year, the U.S. combat presence would be nearly halved, from 108 bases to 50, and from 15 brigades to as few as 8.

In sum, Casey and Chiarelli were sticking to their approach, even though there was little evidence of it working. The U.S. strategy, concluded Anthony Cordesman, a defense analyst at the Center for Strategic and International Studies, was "deeply flawed in timing and resources. It was based on a grossly exaggerated estimate of political success, an almost deliberately false exaggeration of the success of the economic aid effort and progress in developing the ISF."

Francis "Bing" West, a former Marine and Pentagon official who had a son fighting in Iraq, put it even more bluntly: "The strategy was a hope posing as a plan."

By late 2006, agreed Philip Zelikow, who at the time was counselor at the State Department, there was essentially "a strategic void" in Iraq.

Oddly, the White House also decided that this was a good time to attack critics of the war as appeasers and worse. Rumsfeld said they were morally and intellectually confused, not unlike those who had opposed confronting Hitler in the late 1930s. Cheney said those who disagreed with his administration's approach were abetting terrorists. Bush, a mite more generously, conceded that the detractors were "sincere" and "patriotic," but said "they could . . . not be more wrong."

That White House move was an inept political tactic, because it made it appear that the president was divorced from the realities of Iraq and dismissing the legitimate worries of those who believed—with ample evidence—that the war was being mishandled and that it, in fact, was rapidly spinning out of control. During the winter of 2005–6, there had been about 500 attacks a week on U.S. and allied forces. By late in the summer of 2006, there were almost 800. Some 1,200 roadside bombs were detonated in August. The number of roadside bombs was at an "all time high," conceded Maj. Gen. William Caldwell IV, the U.S. military spokesman in Iraq. The bombings continued like a daily drumbeat, contributing to the capital's monthly civilian death toll of about 1,000.

In one of the most horrific incidents, on September 23, a bomb exploded as people waited in line to buy gasoline, sending women engulfed in flames running through the streets. Witnesses reported that two young girls embraced each other as they stood in the inferno burning to death. "This deployment, every patrol you're finding dead people," Staff Sgt. Ian Newland told *Army Times*. "It's like one to 12 a patrol. Their eyes are gouged out. Their arms are broken. We saw a kid who had been shot 10 to 15 times." Newland's company arrived in Baghdad in August, and over the next 15 months it would lose 14 men, the most of any Army company to fight in Iraq. In the first week of October 2006, some 24 soldiers and Marines were killed, most of them in Baghdad, and nearly 300 more were wounded. The violence was also spreading, with Shiite militias fighting Iraqi police to the south of the capital and confronting Sunni militias to the north.

Internal Army surveys of the morale of soldiers underscored the feeling of loss. In both 2004 and 2005, studies by an official Mental Health Advisory Team had reported that morale was improving among troops involved in combat. But a September 2006 assessment found a sharp decline.

On October 19, Gen. Caldwell, the U.S. military spokesman, acknowledged that the renewed security effort in the capital was failing. "Operation Together Forward has made a difference in the focus areas, but has not met our overall expectations of sustaining a reduction in the levels of violence," Caldwell said. "We find the insurgent elements, the extremists, are in fact punching back hard. They're trying to get back into those areas. We're constantly going back in and doing clearing operations again."

Caldwell's admission might have been the worst point of the entire war, at least so far. The U.S. military had played its ace in the hole—"the sole superpower" had asserted itself in Iraq's most important city—yet had not been able to reverse the deteriorating security of the capital. What's more, not only had U.S. commanders taken their best shot and failed, they apparently were going to continue on the same unpromising course of handing off control to Iraqis who didn't seem competent or much interested in the stability the Americans wanted.

In the midst of all this, in the fall of 2006, Iraqi army and police forces finally hit their targeted size of about 325,000 total—but the U.S. wasn't able to stand down as they stood up, as the president for years had said would happen, repeating the phrase as late as June of the year. Paradoxically, as the number of Iraqi soldiers and police grew, so did the violence in the streets of the capital. From August through October 2006, the number of attacks in Iraq grew by 22 percent, according to the U.S. military database, which almost certainly undercounted the total but probably was accurate in tracking the direction of the trend.

The Americans seemed to have run out of both troops and ideas. The one possible bright spot in that bankrupt approach was that it created the conditions for the strategic surprise that Petraeus and Odierno would launch a few months later, as they showed both new flexibility and determination. Given the track record of the previous four years, no one in Iraq saw that one coming.

The downward trend continued. In October 2006 an American soldier was kidnapped. American intelligence officials suspected he was being held in Sadr City, the stronghold of Moqtada al-Sadr's militia, the Jaysh al-Mahdi, or JAM. The U.S. Army, searching desperately for the missing soldier, erected a series of checkpoints along the Canal Road, the broad boulevard that parallels the south side of a densely packed neighborhood slum. Maliki told Casey to lift the checkpoints. "If that's your order, we'll do it," Casey responded. "But people will say you don't care about American soldiers, and that you kowtowed to Sadr. Third, the Sunnis will read this as a pro-JAM action. Can you accept that?" Maliki said he could.

Casey was reading a history of the Vietnam War at the time and thought of the weak and chaotic governments that American officials had dealt with in Saigon back then. "How do you save a head of state when he is diametrically opposed to the policy you are trying to save him with?" he thought to himself.

Then he called his deputy, Chiarelli, and told him to lift the checkpoints. "This was going on all the time with Maliki," Chiarelli recalled. "We had certain things we could do in Sadr City, but not what we needed to do."

Maj. Gen. David Fastabend, hearing about the order to remove the checkpoints, called another general and said, "This is the singular moment of defeat. If you want to know when we lost, this was it." The ethnic cleansing continued as Shiite militias pushed Sunnis westward. "You'd find dumped bodies every day," recalled Maj. David Voorhies, who was advising an Iraqi army unit that he believed was infiltrated by Shiite militias. "You'd see murders, a lot of extra-judicial killings, a lot of kidnappings, a lot of demonstrations would arise. Eventually those areas would collapse . . . on Amiriyah and Gaziliyah, which were really the last two big Sunni neighborhoods in west Baghdad."

The failures of the summer and fall of 2006 may have given the U.S. military establishment the push it needed to realize that everything it had tried over several years wasn't working, and that—despite the assurances of commanders in Iraq—a very different approach was needed. A major split was developing inside the military about what the next step in Iraq should be. Some called for an accelerated transition to Iraqi control, but others said that would just lead to an intensified civil war. Others called for backing out of Iraq and letting the Iraqis sort it out, and others responded that that move could lead to regional war. And a few, here and there, were thinking about increasing the number of troops and using them differently. One of the significant consequences of this split was that, really for the first time in the war, the Bush administration could no longer blandly state that it was following the advice of the military. By late 2006, there simply no longer was a consensus view to follow. "We may need more resources, but first we need a strategy," Eliot Cohen and Francis "Bing" West would write a few months later.

Even more significantly, the doubts White House staffers had held about the top American general in Iraq had reached the president. Bush usually was affable in his conversations, but in mid-November, "the president was noticeably cold," Casey recalled. So, after three years of war, Bush and his aides would be forced into a serious review of their strategy in Iraq. Finally, they would begin to ask some of the basic questions that they had neglected to address before the invasion.

WASHINGTON WINCES

Back in Washington, Jack Keane, the old general who was more influential in retirement than most officers are while on active duty, was growing increasingly concerned as he watched the two Baghdad security operations sputter to a halt. "We had two bites of this apple in Baghdad, and we failed both times," he said. "I knew that our chances to succeed in Iraq were just slipping by us." He decided it was time to share his worries with the Bush administration.

The White House was ready to listen to him. Gen. Casey may not have known it, but the failures of the Together Forward operations were the beginning of the end for his command in Iraq. Behind closed doors, the outlook appeared even worse. "Even in the military, there's a concern right now that wasn't previously," said one worried Marine colonel. "Folks that took things at face value in the past are asking more questions."

Pressure was clearly building for an overhaul of American strategy in Iraq, but a major obstacle stood in the way at the top of the Pentagon. Not long before he was fired, Defense Secretary Rumsfeld insisted that the strategy of passing responsibility to the Iraqi forces was working and needed no change. "The biggest mistake would be to not pass things over to the Iraqis, create a dependency on their part, and instead of developing strength and capacity and competence," he said at a press conference the day after Caldwell spoke in Baghdad. "It's their country. They're going to have to govern it, they're going to have to provide security for it, and they're going to have to do it sooner rather than later. And that means they've got to take pieces of it as we go along, even though someone may inaccurately characterize it as a strategic mistake, which it wouldn't be at all."

Bush would back up Rumsfeld, saying he was flexible about tactics but wasn't contemplating a change in strategy or goals. "Are we winning?" asked a reporter at an East Room news conference a few days later.

"Absolutely, we're winning," Bush insisted. At the same time, he said, "I know many Americans are not satisfied with the situation in Iraq. I'm not satisfied either. And that is why we're taking new steps to help secure Baghdad and constantly adjusting our tactics across the country to meet the changing threat."

Feaver, the White House aide, cringed at Bush's "winning" comment. "That wasn't the way it felt from where I sat." He recalled that at this time, Karl Rove, the president's political adviser, was also speaking up, telling others, "We need a new face on Iraq"—by which he apparently meant that Rumsfeld should leave.

Support for the war was eroding rapidly among the Republican Party faithful. Back in February, John Warner, the courtly Virginia Republican who was chairman of the Senate Armed Services Committee, had expressed "a high degree of confidence" that a new government would take charge and that by the end of the year the conflict "won't be the same." But as October opened, Warner returned from Iraq with a far grimmer assessment: "The situation is simply drifting sideways."

Something had to give, said Senator Olympia Snowe, a centrist Maine Republican. "I don't believe we can continue based on an open-ended, unconditional presence."

Senator Lindsey Graham, a conservative South Carolina Republican and a close friend of John McCain's, was mulling a different strategy. "The American people are beginning to wonder if the Iraqi people can get this right," he said. "People have begun to wonder about the basic premise, that the Iraqi people are capable of solving their problems politically. We're at a real crossroads. The level of violence in October just shows you we don't have enough security to ensure long-term success."

Others argued that the situation was even more dire than that. "Basically, the bottom has fallen out of support with the general public," former Republican congressman Vin Weber said later that October, just before the election. "The public is on the verge of throwing up its hands over Iraq. They are right on the edge of believing that success isn't possible."

A LIGHT IN RAMADI

Near the end of Gen. Caldwell's press conference on October 19, a few minutes after the spokesman had announced the failure of the Baghdad security plan, one reporter had inquired about some odd reports coming out of Ramadi, 60 miles to the west of Baghdad. Specifically, inquired the man from Reuters news agency, why were armed civilians marching in the streets? What was going on out there? Caldwell responded that he hadn't heard about that and would look into it.

It was a good question, because Ramadi had been one of Iraq's most dangerous cities for years. This time, to the astonishment of anyone focused on Baghdad, the armed men were not members of al Qaeda in Iraq but allies of the Americans, albeit tentative ones. Ramadi, the capital of turbulent al Anbar Province, had begun to provide a counterexample to Baghdad. That turnaround, led by Col. Sean MacFarland, would take place even as the senior Marine intelligence officer in the country pronounced the province lost. Ramadi in 2006 would become the link between the first successful large-scale U.S. counterinsurgency campaign in Iraq, in Tall Afar in 2005, and the "surge" counteroffensive in Baghdad in 2007.

By chance, MacFarland's unit first had been assigned to replace the 3rd Armored Cavalry Regiment in Tall Afar, in the far northwest of Iraq, and had spent several months there before moving south to Ramadi. What MacFarland and his subordinates had seen there was very different from how the U.S. military had operated in Iraq for several years. The new approach made sense to him. Under Col. H. R. McMaster, an innovative officer unafraid to chart a different course, the 3rd Armored Cavalry Regiment had slowly and patiently approached Tall Afar, a medieval feeling town of about 250,000. After the U.S. military reduced its presence in northern Iraq in 2004, Islamic extremists had begun to seep in from Syria and make contact with local allies. By mid-2005 they had intimidated the locals with terror tactics and made the town a base from which to send suicide bombers and other attackers 40 miles easy to Mosul, the most important city in northern Iraq. "Give the enemy credit," said Maj. Chris Kennedy. "As soon as we started pulling back, the enemy identified that as a weak point."

McMaster, who is both a rugby player and a Ph.D. in history, began by telling his soldiers to treat Iraqis with dignity and respect. "Every time you treat an Iraqi disrespectfully, you are working for the enemy," he instructed them—neatly summarizing counterinsurgency theory in a way that any nineteen-year-old infantryman could grasp. In a marked contrast to the attitude found in some other units, his standing orders required his soldiers to "Treat detainees professionally; do not tolerate abusive behavior." He met with sheikhs and clerics who had ties to the insurgency and apologized for past American mistakes: "When the Americans first came to Iraq, we were in a dark room, stumbling around, breaking china. But now Iraqi leaders are turning on the lights." And, he added, the time for honorable resistance had ended.

Then, after months of preparatory moves in the desert around the city, cutting off lines of retreat and safe havens, McMaster attacked Tall Afar. Rather than just stage patrols from his big base outside the city, he moved his people into it, establishing 29 outposts in its neighborhoods. In sum, it was a model of a counterinsurgency campaign, the first large-scale one conducted in the war. It was an example the U.S. military needed badly. In far northwest Iraq, a Marine battalion commanded by Lt. Col. Dale Alford carried out a similar campaign, establishing outposts in the area of al Qaim and cutting deals with local sheikhs. However, these examples weren't imitated by other commanders, probably because they were at odds with the strategy set by Gen. Casey and his boss at Central Command, Gen. John Abizaid. Working on the theory that the U.S. military presence was an irritant to Iraqi society, the generals were trying to oversee a transition to Iraqi forces and so wanted an ever-shrinking American "footprint." By contrast, McMaster injected thousands of U.S. troops into the middle of a city, implicitly saying that they were not the problem but part of the solution, that American troops weren't the sand irritating Iraqi society, but could be the glue that held it together.

McMaster's organization also began to grasp the significance of Iraqi tribal power. One of MacFarland's officers, Capt. Travis Patriquin, a bright, bushy-haired, Special Forces veteran who spoke Arabic, Spanish, and Portuguese, was particularly intrigued by this. Lt. Col. Paul Yingling, his counterpart in the 3rd Armored Cavalry Regiment, told him about an officer's encounter with a sheikh of the Shammar tribe. "Sheikh, why do you smuggle sheep and benzine in from Syria?" the officer asked.

The sheikh had responded, "Why did you put the Syrian border in the middle of my sheep? We were here first."

Yingling told Patriquin about the Shammar tribe's view of the world. "He understood it very well, and got a good laugh out of the story," he recalled.

A few months later MacFarland was ordered to move his unit, the 1st brigade of the Army's 1st Armored Division, to Ramadi. A soft-spoken officer from an Irish Catholic neighborhood in Albany, New York, MacFarland knew that every brigade assigned to that violent provincial capital had lost about 100 soldiers during its tour of duty, even as the city steadily declined into chaos. "I'll be goddamned if I lose one hundred soldiers here and have nothing to show for it," the brown-haired cavalryman, a 1981 graduate of West Point, vowed to himself.

His orders were to "fix Ramadi but don't do a Fallujah"—a reference to the intense battles for that city just to the southeast in 2004. "But I really wasn't sure how I was going to 'fix Ramadi.' "

All the conventional responses had been tried and none had worked, so three years into the war, MacFarland was willing to take a gamble on something different. Anbar Province had at first been all but ignored in the planning for the 2003 invasion, then treated as an "economy of force" operation, and then saw two bruising battles for control of Fallujah in 2004. In a low point just before MacFarland's brigade arrived, a protest broke out at a graduation ceremony for 978 Iraqi soldiers, most of them Sunnis, at nearby Camp Habbaniyah. Provoked by word that they would be ordered to deploy outside their home province of al Anbar, some soldiers began tearing off their uniforms before the astonished eyes of the Iraqi and American officials in attendance for the event, which they had hailed in speeches as a major step in the formation of the Iraqi army. At the time, U.S. military spokesmen attempted to minimize the significance of the event. "It was actually a very small number of graduates," claimed one, Army Lt. Col. Michael Negard. But Carter Malkasian, a counterinsurgency adviser to the Marine Corps in Anbar, later disclosed that a full two-thirds of the soldiers refused to deploy, and more than that ultimately deserted.

On top of that, the Iraqi battalion that MacFarland was counting on for help had mutinied upon being informed that it would be deployed to Ramadi. Of several hundred men in the Iraqi unit, only about 140 showed up, he recalled—and most of them refused to leave the base to go on patrol. "We basically just sent them home," he said.

MacFarland's audaciously different approach to Ramadi ultimately would become an out-of-town tryout for the surge that came eight months later in Baghdad, not so much in troop numbers, but—far more important—in the strategy of moving into the population and the tactics of how to do that successfully. The two major differences are that Ramadi is overwhelmingly Sunni, and so didn't have sectarian fighting, and also is a fraction of the size of the capital.

In 2005 al Qaeda in Iraq had mounted a ferocious campaign against about 12 tribal leaders who competed with the terrorist group for the loyalty of al Anbar's population by forming the Anbar People's Council. "This was the first broadly based opposition to al Qaeda," recalled Marine Brig. Gen. John Allen. "Al Qaeda recognized the threat and attacked almost immediately," conducting a focused and efficient assassination campaign. In one month, half the sheikhs in the council were dead, with the remainder fleeing the country. The Americans really hadn't come to the aid of the sheikhs, who had multiple ties to the Sunni insurgency.

"There was a large safe haven there. . . . Al Qaeda was calling the shots," MacFarland said. "Zarqawi was known to go out there, for instance. I mean, this was where al Qaeda went when they got pushed out of Fallujah." In retrospect, he estimated that he faced perhaps 5,000 fighters in the city.

When MacFarland's unit arrived in Ramadi, it was hit by bombs, grenades, mortars, and rifle fire an average of 25 times a day. It was replacing a unit from the Pennsylvania National Guard that had retreated from parts of the city. "My predecessor was just trading artillery fire with the rocket and mortar fire," he remembered. "Al Qaeda had the run of the town. . . . The enemy basically controlled the center part of the city." Every night, insurgents were planting an average of eight roadside bombs in and around the town. The National Guardsmen had stopped patrolling in areas where they had been hit hard, he said, leaving parts of the city map that, he joked, were labeled, HERE BE MONSTERS.

The city wasn't even on life support. "There was no mayor, there was no city council, and there were no communications like we had in Tall Afar," he said. "Basically, all services had stopped."

Sheikhs were telling reporters that they no longer felt safe being around Americans. "Today, there is no tribal sheikh or a citizen who dares to go to the city hall or the U.S. base, because Zarqawi issued a statement ordering his men to kill anyone seen leaving the base or city hall," said the head of one tribe, Bashir Abdul Qadir al-Kubaisat. The U.S. military assessed that of the 21 tribes in the area, only 6 would cooperate with it.

Desperation may be one of the stepmothers of invention. "There was really no place to go but up," MacFarland recalled. "I was willing to try whatever made sense." Other units were moving away from the cities, concentrating their forces on big bases. He decided to go in the opposite direction. His commanders, who were Marines, were skeptical, having seen dialogues with tribal leaders start up and then peter out before, but they let him take a flyer. "I had the backing of my bosses, but not a lot of guidance. I felt like if it failed, it would be my failure."

Sterling Jensen, who was working as an interpreter for MacFarland's brigade and had become deeply involved in tribal issues, recalled the Marines' being even more negative. "They'd say, you guys don't know what you're doing. You're way too arrogant. You're going to get yourselves killed." The Marines had tried several times to reach out to tribes, only to see al Qaeda assassinate sheikhs who turned. Senior Marines also thought that MacFarland was dealing with third-rate sheikhs who didn't hold real power. What MacFarland wasn't seeing was that some Marine generals had noticed that there was a quiet, almost secret war under way in Anbar between some tribes and al Qaeda. The Marines were reaching out to some of the harder hit sheikhs, offering them help.

On the upside, MacFarland's superiors were willing to give him what he needed—a Marine infantry battalion, snipers from two Navy SEAL platoons (dubbed "Task Force Bruiser"), and even four 40-foot-long armored Marine riverine boats to cut off the enemy crossing points on the Euphrates River and stealthily insert patrols. "They were fast, they were quiet, they were heavily armed, and they could carry a squad and put them ashore," he said. "They could kind of run up on the beach, dump them off, back off, and then provide fire support."

Interestingly, among the Marines deployed to Ramadi was Cpl. Jimmy Webb, son of James Webb, the novelist (*Fields of Fire*) and former Navy secretary who in 2006 was running a long-shot campaign to become a U.S. senator from Virginia. While home on leave, the corporal asked his father why his opponent, Senator George Allen, made cowboy boots the symbol of his campaign "when Virginia doesn't have any cowboys." Webb was intrigued. His son also pointed out that he and his father both had worn combat boots in wartime. He gave his father his own boots, which he had worn in the streets of Ramadi. Webb would wear them throughout his campaign.

MacFarland and his staff began by thinking about the "metrics" they should use. If the goal was to protect the population, as they had seen in Tall Afar, then that is what should be tracked somehow. They also knew they would have to confront the skepticism of local leaders, who had seen Americans come and go for more than three years, making promises that often weren't met or were forgotten by successor units. MacFarland began to spread the word that the Americans weren't leaving anytime soon.

Knowing that Americans had put in office a generation of leaders, and then seemed unable to keep alive those police chiefs, mayors, and governors, MacFarland made protection of local leaders a top priority. He stationed tanks at key intersections near their houses and put drone aircraft circling over their homes to keep an eye out for attacks. He also asked sheikhs for advice on where to place new police stations and outposts, calculating that they would put them near their homes.

He named the Arabic-speaking Capt. Patriquin as his liaison to the sheikhs. Together they tried to sort out who was a real sheikh, with big *wasta*, or influence, and who was a lightweight. They also realized that years of fighting had created an opening: Not only had some sheikhs been killed, many others had moved to Jordan—and so a new generation of tribal leaders was emerging. "It was like going into Don Corleone's house—you can tell who has *wasta*," especially by following who moderated the discussion, he observed. The first sheikh with whom he began to work closely was Abu Ali Jassim, whose tribe was based out in the desert.

Following the example of the 3rd Armored Cavalry Regiment in Tall Afar,

MacFarland began to establish small bases in the city. In the past, U.S. units had operated from a large FOB, or forward operating base, outside it. "They exited the FOB, drove to an objective or patrolled, were attacked, exchanged fire, and returned to base," he wrote later.

The first step under the new approach was to send Special Operations sniper teams to sneak into the building he wanted to occupy. Then he would have a "route clearance" team work its way through the roadside bombs to the building, followed immediately by a company of Army troops or Marines to occupy the building. Upon arrival they would begin building a new combat outpost. The snipers would move out to the surrounding area to disrupt counterattacks. Overnight, the outpost would appear, with living spaces and walls and barriers to limit the damage from car bombs. They even figured out how to use a crane to immediately deposit a steel "crow's nest" on top of a building, so they could begin with a well-protected observation post without having to divert troops into filling and carrying sandbags to the roof. (Learning that filling sandbags between patrols was wearing out the troops in the outposts, MacFarland instituted a new policy on his base. Everyone had to fill two sandbags before every meal. "No work, no food," he said. "We could generate ten thousand to twelve thousand sandbags a day on Camp Ramadi and push them out to the combat outposts.") Quick steps to establish combat readiness in the outposts were necessary because new outposts were almost always assaulted within two or three days.

Four benefits, much of them unexpected, flowed from the redisposition of troops into the small new bases, which eventually would total 18. In the most successful ones, Americans and Iraqi soldiers lived and ate side by side. This meant Iraqis and Americans could learn from each other—about Iraqi culture, about weapons maintenance, about leadership. Also, Iraqi soldiers living on American rations began to show more energy. "You'd be surprised at how much work you can get out of an Iraqi if he has had enough calories to eat," he said. Another immediate benefit of this redeployment, he found, was that his soldiers became less predictable. No longer could Iraqi fighters simply watch the front gates of an American base to know when a patrol was coming. "Because we now maintained a constant presence in disputed neighborhoods, the insurgents could no longer accurately trace and predict our actions."

Most important was the political effect of the new outposts. MacFarland laid down a rule that once one was established, they wouldn't let themselves be driven from it. "You never give it up," he said. "More than anything else, that was what persuaded the sheikhs we were there to stay." In the past, he said, American commanders had said, "Don't worry, we're leaving." He decided to say the opposite: "We're staying until we win this fight." It helped that once he had an outlying base, he would begin spending reconstruction funds in the surrounding neighborhood. All told, he estimated, he would dispense more than $2 million in 2006 and early 2007.

He sought to keep up the pressure, so that the enemy, once knocked off balance, couldn't regain the initiative. "What can I do to make life miserable for al Qaeda today?" he would ask himself. "We tried to have an operation every few days. Can I put up another combat outpost? Should I start an adult literacy class? Can I throw in the kitchen sink?" Figuring that the local al Qaeda fighters might move to the outskirts, he set up Iraqi police stations in the rural tribal areas. Police were always recruited locally, which gave them extra incentive to stand up to the terrorists, he noted. "The IPs [Iraqi police] refused to be intimidated because they were defending their own homes," he said.

By the end of July 2006, he was beginning to sense that the new approach was working, even though it brought new risks. The commander of the Marine battalion attached to MacFarland's Army brigade told him that west Ramadi was quieting down. Top Marine commanders began to be convinced that what was happening in Ramadi was different from previous sheikh-led pushes against al Qaeda. Even so, there were days when MacFarland had his doubts, especially as the enemy launched a counteroffensive. At the end of the first week of August, he thought to himself, "My God, I've lost ten guys." Two weeks later, on August 21, Sheikh Jassim, his first ally in the tribes, was assassinated. "I couldn't have protected him if I wanted to," MacFarland said. The sheikh's killers hid his body for four days, a pointed violation of the Muslim custom of quick burial. On the same day, a new Iraqi police station, in the Jazeera neighborhood, and manned mainly by members of Sheikh Jassim's tribe, was bombed. All told, MacFarland lost two dozen vehicles—a few tanks, but mainly trucks—as he moved into the city.

But, he said, the local reaction to the August attacks indicated that al Qaeda might have overplayed its hand: They drove some fence-sitters into the American camp. One sheikh, Sittar albu-Risha, was particularly angry. "Sittar has lost enough family members that he was ready to throw away caution." This sheikh, a minor tribal leader who had a reputation for running a thriving cross-border smuggling business, called a meeting for September 9. More than 50 sheikhs and other notables showed up. They created what they proposed calling "The Awakening Council." They had a platform with 11 planks. "Ten of them I would have written for them almost exactly the same way they wrote them," MacFarland recalled. The last one was problematic, in that it implied they might have to kill the governor of al Anbar Province. He suggested they modify it.

As MacFarland parleyed with sheikhs, the energetic Capt. Patriquin worked the other people in the room. "He was very extroverted and friendly and was very popular among the tribes because he was the officer who identified little things we could do for them, like attention for a sick child." Sheikh Sittar eventually gave the captain the honorary tribal name Neshan Abu Risha, which some Iraqis say means "a warrior of the Albu Risha," the sheikh's tribe.

That day was a turning point for MacFarland—and as it would develop, for al Anbar Province and Iraq. "To me, it was the first real clear vindication of the strategy we were pursuing, that we were beginning to turn the tide." The meeting encouraged more sheikhs to come in and work with the Americans, and with them came a "snowball effect" on recruiting of local police and other tasks, MacFarland said. "Whenever a tribe flipped and joined the Awakening, all the attacks on coalition forces in that area would stop, and all the caches of ammunition would come up out of the ground. If there was ever an attack on us, the sheikh would basically take responsibility for it and find whoever was responsible, and this happened time and again. So it was incredibly effective and they were as good as their word."

MacFarland had come to terms with the fact that some of those newly forthcoming sheikhs had participated in attacks on Americans. "I'm a product of Catholic schools," he said, "and I was taught that every saint has a past and every sinner can have a future." Sittar reported that he had several thousand volunteers who didn't qualify for the police, because they were illiterate, underage, or overweight, so he was allowed to create three "emergency battalions" to employ them. MacFarland armed them with captured weapons and had his SEAL teams give them a one-week training course. The prevailing American theory for years had been that improvements in security would lead to progress in politics. This was the opposite—political change leading to improvements in security.

That decision also took the United States into the dangerous and complex new territory of supporting an armed group that was opposed to the government in Baghdad that the United States also supported. As Carter Malkasian, the counterinsurgency adviser to the Marine Corps in al Anbar, put it, "For all intents and purposes, the government was permitting Sittar and his movement to have their own militia." But, as Petraeus and Odierno would do the following year, MacFarland had decided it was time to take some risks, especially given that the alternative appeared to be failure.

The Shiite-dominated Iraqi government, in the midst of a small civil war in Baghdad between Shiites and Sunnis, wasn't happy with what it was hearing out of Ramadi about the Americans cutting local cease-fire deals with Sunni sheikhs. Here again, MacFarland found that American experience on the ground in Iraq helped. His deputy commander, Lt. Col. James Lechner, had spent time as an adviser to the Iraqi military and "knew how to work the system to get guys paid." Among other things, MacFarland noted, "That built up my *wasta* with the sheikhs."

Faced with skepticism from his superiors, and from journalists who were being told by Iraqi officials in Baghdad that he was arming Iraqis to fight the Iraqi army and police, MacFarland had Patriquin create a briefing to explain what he was trying to do. Far from the usual razzle-dazzle of U.S. military PowerPoints, the briefing was written breezily, almost in the style of a children's book, with stick figures. It was titled "How to Win the War in Al Anbar, By CPT Trav."

Capt. Travis Patriquin's briefing was both perhaps the most informal one given by the U.S. military in Iraq and the most important one. "This is an American Soldier," it began. "We'll call him Joe. Joe wants to win in Al Anbar. But sometimes it seems like other people don't share that idea." This made Joe sad. Then the briefing posed the key question: "How can Joe win in Al Anbar? By fighting the insurgents?" The briefing didn't say so, but the answer the U.S. military had given for three years had been: Well, of course, yes.

A subsequent slide identified the problem with that approach: "Poor Joe can't tell the terrorist from the good Iraqis." The smiling stick figures look all the same to him. The solution, the brief said, was to talk to the sheikhs about making local militiamen members of the police force. "The Iraqi Policeman can tell the difference. And the insurgent knows that. See, that's why he's sad." This makes everyone else happy. "The sheikh brings more sheikhs, more sheikhs bring more men. Joe realizes that if he'd done this three years ago, maybe his wife would be happier."

The theory was working, but the fighting continued. On September 29, Michael Monsoor of Garden Grove, California, a twenty-five-year-old member of a Navy SEAL team, threw himself on a hand grenade while his team was being attacked, an act of valor for which he was posthumously recognized with the Medal of Honor. He already had received a Silver Star for rescuing a wounded comrade under fire four months earlier.

On November 25, about three dozen al Qaeda men with weapons drove into Sufia, home of the Albu Soda tribe, just east of Ramadi. The small tribe, which had only about thirty men of military age in that area, had rebuffed MacFarland's recruiting efforts, he said, because it wanted to be neutral. But as part of that effort, it had established checkpoints to keep out al Qaeda, which antagonized the terrorist group, because the tribe lived along the main corridor from Fallujah to Ramadi. After the gunmen opened fire, some tribal members escaped in boats across the Euphrates and ran to an Iraqi army base. Soldiers there called an Iraqi interpreter for an American officer, who called MacFarland's headquarters. Capt. Patriquin and Sterling Jensen, the interpreter, began gathering information. "We're being wiped out," the tribe's beleaguered sheikh told Jensen. "People are killing us." The sheikh's sister had been killed, and al Qaeda men were dragging the body by ropes behind a pickup truck. MacFarland postponed another operation and sent the units involved in that to the aid of the tribe, even though it had held him at arm's length. A drone reconnaissance aircraft was sent to circle over the fight. Patriquin called the sheikh of the tribe. "Hey, look," he said. "We can't tell who is who. Could you have your guys wave towels over their heads so we can identify friend from foe?" That done, Marine F-18 warplanes rolled into bomb those without towels, and then arriving U.S. Army tanks began to fire on fleeing al Qaeda automobiles.

After the fight, MacFarland went to talk to Albu Soda's bloodied, combat-shocked leaders. "They were kind of battle-fatigued, had lost a lot of family members. At the same time, it was like a switch had been flipped. Guys who had been reluctant to talk to us were saying, 'Would you please build a combat outpost near our home?' and telling us where al Qaeda was in their area." That day was the tipping point, he said. After that, he was flooded with tips and recruits. "After that tribe flipped, the kids were running around, it was like liberated France, it was like Rumsfeld imagined it would be in 2003." Also, a major insurgent route into the city had been cut.

One of MacFarland's enlisted men studied street life and concluded that people in Ramadi didn't read newspapers or even listen to the radio much, but that they did pay attention to the messages from loudspeakers on the minarets of mosques. So, beginning at one platoon-sized base, Combat Outpost Firecracker, MacFarland's soldiers put up loudspeakers to broadcast, every day but Friday, the Muslim sabbath, sports news and weather reports—and occasionally slip in information about al Qaeda attacks. "The news was pulled from places like Al Jazeera and Al Iraqia and news sources that people would know were not ours," he said. Some of it was just helpful tips: "The UN warehouse has a new shipment of rice." Occasionally another message would slip in: "Last night al Qaeda killed a family of five in their home."

But even as late as December 6, 2006, MacFarland would be thrown for a loss. On that day, Spec. Nicholas Gibbs, a twenty-five-year-old from Stokesdale, North Carolina, was killed by small-arms fire. "Part of me died along with him," his mother told a reporter. "I will never be the same."

The same day, Sgt. Yevgeniy Ryndych, a 1998 émigré from Ukraine to Brooklyn, was killed by a roadside bomb. His fiancée received her engagement ring in the mail from him the same day. "He was one of those people who not a lot of people liked because he sat home the whole day and read books," said his brother Ivan. "He was like a genius kid."

And Marine Cpl. Dustin Libby, from Presque Isle, Maine, was manning a machine gun on a roof in Ramadi when he was shot.

Three other soldiers died that day when their Humvee was hit by a bomb. The first, Spec. Vincent Pomante, was from Westerville, Ohio. The second, Marine Maj. Megan McClung, became the highest-ranking female to die in combat in Iraq. A triathelete, McClung had organized a marathon for troops in Iraq. A journalist in North Carolina remembered that when a police officer pulled over McClung, she proved she was sober by doing a backflip on the side of the road. A graduate of the Naval Academy, McClung had left the Marine Corps but went back on active duty in order to serve in Iraq. Her name would become the first woman's to be added to the marble tablet at the academy that memorializes graduates killed in action. "Please don't portray this as a tragedy," her mother requested of a reporter. "It is for us, but Megan died doing what she believed in."

The sixth loss that day perhaps hit MacFarland hardest: Capt. Patriquin, the soldier who had reached out to the tribes, had been sitting next to McClung.

The next morning MacFarland found his staff and commanders downcast. "Everybody was kind of looking at their feet." He told them about how Gen. Ulysses S. Grant handled that first terrible day at Shiloh in April 1862. The Confederates had pushed the Union troops back to the Tennessee River, where thousands huddled terrified below the bank. Thousands more lay dead and wounded on the battlefield above them. That night Grant met with his commanders next to a log house being used as a hospital, reviewing the day's losses as men under the surgeon's knife screamed and died nearby—probably not the best place to locate a command post. At midnight, Grant went out to smoke a cigar, taking refuge from the driving rain under a tree. There, MacFarland told his soldiers, Gen. William T. Sherman found him. "Well, Grant, we've had the devil's own day, haven't we?" Sherman said to his dripping friend.

MacFarland reminded them of Grant's laconic response: "Yes. Lick 'em tomorrow, though."

The stoic, taciturn Grant was an inspiration to MacFarland throughout the year. "I felt I was fighting my way through the Wilderness Campaign," he said, referring to Grant's running battle through rough ground in northern Virginia against Robert E. Lee in May 1864. "I was taking a lot of casualties." MacFarland was hardly alone. In recent years, as the Army has come to grips with Iraq, Grant seems to be enjoying a resurgence in popularity with today's officers, probably because he is its patron saint of the long, hard slog.

By the onset of winter it was becoming clear that something fundamental had changed in Ramadi. "In the latter half of December, it was like the fever broke," MacFarland said. "Up until then, when we threw a punch, they threw a punch." The death rate for U.S. forces began to decline after that incident. By the end of that month, 12 of the tribes in the area were deemed cooperative, and 6 neutral, leaving just 3 classified as "uncooperative." By mid-2007 it wasn't uncommon for a month to go by with no U.S. losses. Al Qaeda, meanwhile, was reeling. As David Kilcullen, Petraeus's counterinsurgency adviser, later put it, "In Anbar, we've got the tribal vengeance structure working in our favor." That is, where Armericans once had been the target of Iraqis seeking revenge, now they were helping direct that impulse against al Qaeda and its allies in the insurgency.

Not only were the roadside bombs less numerous, they were becoming less sophisticated. "They went away from the remote-controlled IEDs to subsurface command wires to just hastily throwing out IEDs with pressure plates because that was all they could do," MacFarland said. "Because we were keeping such pressure on them, they just weren't able to get the big IEDs and get them all set up. So, we knew we had them on the run when we started to see those kinds of things evolve and their attacks became smaller and smaller and less and less effective."

The attacks would continue, though. All told, MacFarland lost 83 soldiers in Iraq—but he had something to show for it. In February 2007, Gen. Petraeus, newly arrived in Iraq, would come to see him and ask some questions about his methods and metrics. "Sean had obviously done something extraordinarily important," Petraeus said later. "What you had there was the first really significant example of the concept of reconcilables and irreconcilables." Petraeus already knew that he wanted his troops to go out and protect the population. In Ramadi, he learned that "a key way of implementing that is not just living with them, it is also . . . literally separating them, protecting the population from the irreconcilables. That means you have to know who the reconcilables are and who the bad guys are, and then of course try to achieve some separation and protect the one from the other."

Chiarelli, the number two U.S. commander in Iraq in 2006, said that MacFarland's operation marked the first time in the Iraq war that a counterinsurgency campaign had been conducted and then had been sustained by the succeeding unit. "Sean was the first guy who did it and it stuck for the guy who followed," he said.

Upon arriving in Iraq, Odierno would seek to build on what MacFarland had started. "He's the guy who put this together"—that is, how to operate differently and more effectively in Iraq, Odierno said later. "Once they cleared Ramadi, and they stayed in Ramadi with a significant amount of force, that was the tipping point. The whole province seemed to turn over."

But Baghdad would be more complicated. Not only was it at least 10 times larger, it also had both the Shiite militias that weren't active in Ramadi, which was homogeneously Sunni. Tribes were less significant in the cities and among Shiites. Securing Baghdad in 2007 would make MacFarland's experience in Ramadi in 2006 look relatively simple.

A RUN IN OCTOBER

In October 2006, Petraeus was in Washington, partly to lay the groundwork for rolling out his counterinsurgency manual a few months later, but also because Gen. Pace, the chairman of the Joint Chiefs of Staff, had sent word that Defense Secretary Rumsfeld wanted to see him.

Petraeus didn't know what the meeting would be about. But he could see his time at Leavenworth coming to an end, and he was eager to get back into the fight in Iraq. Every indication was that a radical change in the handling of the war there was urgently required. He felt ready to lead that charge.

As he prepared, he contacted Lt. Col. Charlie Miller, whom he had known since he himself was a lieutenant colonel and Miller was a green officer in his battalion in the 101st Airborne, to ask him to go for a morning run. In 2006 Miller was a strategic planner on the Joint Chiefs of Staff, and like many of his peers, was anxious about the state of the war. The next day the two met at Petraeus's hotel. It quickly became clear that Petraeus wanted to talk about Iraq. "He was very spun up on the war, knew what was happening," Miller recalled.

As they ran along the sandy paths of Washington's mall toward the Capitol, Petraeus posed a series of questions. "The nation has to decide what it is going to do—is it going to do what it takes, or is it going to get out?" he began.

After the run, Petraeus said to Miller, "What are we trying to accomplish there? And what resources do we need to do it?"

This was magic to Miller, a native of Virginia's Shenandoah Valley who was trained in strategic thinking and who had believed for years that more troops needed to be sent to Iraq. "This had been a major frustration for me," he said. "We have undertaken a major national project and put it on the backs of a small group of volunteers."

These also were the basic questions any strategist would ask about a war—especially if he suspected he might about to be put in charge of that war.

When Petraeus went to see Defense Secretary Rumsfeld, he thought that perhaps he would be offered command in Iraq. But as he was walking up the Pentagon stairs with Pace to Rumsfeld's office, the Joint Chiefs chairman turned to him and said, "Don't be surprised if this is about the Afghanistan job." That was not a bad command, but it was still a relative backwater compared to Iraq. As it happened, Rumsfeld, who could be extremely noncommittal, didn't offer Petraeus anything.

3.

KEANE TAKES COMMAND

(Fall 2006)

The turning point in the war was the American midterm elections of November 2006, which transferred control of both houses of Congress to the Democrats. Without that "thumping," as President Bush termed it, the administration might never have contemplated the major revisions in strategy and leadership that it would make in the following two months. Until the election, Bush seemed satisfied with blather. After it, he began to speak about the war seriously. The sweeping changes that followed ultimately would reverse the steady downward course of the war—and perversely for Democrats, thus likely extend the conflict for many more years. "I think that without the '06 elections, there might not have been a change" in U.S. strategy, said Tom Donnelly, one of the original Iraq hawks who in the wake of the November elections would help plan the escalation that would become known as "the surge."

The precise moment of the shift in both congressional majorities came two days after the election, when Senator George Allen of Virginia conceded to James Webb, a pugnacious Marine veteran and former Republican who had trailed him by a wide margin during most of the race. Webb's win tipped the Senate into Democratic hands, giving the party control of the entire new Congress. Webb, celebrating his extraordinarily narrow victory, stood outside the Arlington County Courthouse, just outside Washington, D.C., and held in the air the Marine combat boots that his son had first worn in Iraq and that the senator then had worn while campaigning.

Webb said in an interview that he displayed the boots at the rally not as a reference to the war, but as a symbol that the campaign was over. Yet those boots that had trod the bloody streets of Ramadi gave Webb's opinions on the war an added gravitas: Not only had he served in Vietnam, his son was in the fight now. He knew what it was like to stand in combat boots. After he waved those boots, he delivered a speech unusual for any politician, but especially for a Democrat. He began not by thanking the people of Virginia or his family or his campaign staff, but instead by saluting the Marines. "The first thing I'd like to say is tomorrow is the most special day for the United States Marine Corps—they celebrate their birthday. You almost have to be a Marine to understand that, but I want to say 'Happy Birthday' to all our Marines. There are a lot of them in harm's way today. We are going to remember them tomorrow." Next he cited those who had served in the military in earlier days. "The day after that is Veterans Day, and we remember all of those who have served our country and who are serving it, wherever they are, we all have them in our hearts and prayers." Then he turned to the politics of the situation and, among things, predicted that the shift in congressional power meant that there would "result soon . . . a diplomatic solution in Iraq."

His main emotion at the time, he said later, was one of relief. Webb had proven an energetic but awkward candidate, at first walking down the center of the street in parades, rather than shaking the hands of spectators. He seemed most at ease among the coal miners of southwest Virginia, home of his Scots-Irish ancestors. The Virginia Senate campaign had been contentious but not exceptionally so. Yet Webb emerged from it furious, later declaring it "one of the nastiest campaigns in American history." He said that at the time of his victory speech, "I literally felt like I was stepping out of a sewer."

Webb had been molded by his experience as a young Marine officer in the Vietnam War. Back then, his Appalachian tenacity and populist distrust of centralized power made him a fierce critic of anti-war activists. He ended *Fields of Fire* with a scene in which a Vietnam vet challenges a crowd of Harvard protestors: "How many of you are going to get hurt in Vietnam? I didn't see any of you in Vietnam." Yet those same deep-running character traits had made Webb an opponent of the Iraq war, where he thinks elites once again are recklessly sending someone else's children to die while their own stay home and tend their careers.

For decades Webb had nursed a cold contempt for such people who took from their country more than they gave.

One of those who had evaded service in Vietnam was George W. Bush. In mid-November, Webb went to a postelection function at the White House for newly elected members of Congress. He avoided the reception line, but Bush sought him out. "How's your boy?" the president asked.

"I'd like to get them out of Iraq, Mr. President," Webb responded.

"That's not what I asked you," Bush persisted. "How's your boy?"

"That's between me and my boy," Webb said. It was an abrupt, ungracious response that proved to be controversial. Seven months later, in a gesture of reconciliation, Webb would bring his Marine son, wearing his dress blues, to a White House meeting and introduce him to the president.

Even as the ghosts of Vietnam flitted over Washington, there was a growing sense among defense experts that the strategic consequences of the Iraq war could be far worse than that earlier war. The United States could walk away from Vietnam, a relatively isolated country with few resources, and six years later, with the election of Ronald Reagan, declare it "morning in America." (Of course, it didn't feel like that in Cambodia, or in the reeducation camps of Vietnam where former allies of the United States were held.) It was unlikely to be morning in Iraq anytime soon. The Iraq war "makes Vietnam look like a cakewalk," said retired Air Force Gen. Charles Wald, a Vietnam veteran. The domino theory that nations across Southeast Asia would go Communist was not fulfilled, he noted, but with Iraq, he said, the "worst-case scenarios are the most likely thing to happen," such as a spreading war in the Middle East, which likely would cause a spike in oil prices that would shock the global company.

THE TRIUMPH OF THE DEMOCRATS

The day after the election, the president announced that he was removing Defense Secretary Rumsfeld. Uncharacteristically, Rumsfeld was subdued, brief, and inarticulate. His verdict on Iraq that day was that it was "a little understood, unfamiliar war, the first war of the twenty-first century—it is not well known, it was not well understood, it is complex for people to comprehend." He seemed to be saying that the American people just didn't get it and had demonstrated their lack of understanding in the previous day's vote.

There was little unhappiness in the U.S. government about his departure.

"Rumsfeld appeared to draw from the commissar school of management, leading with a pistol from the back, because he would tell folks to advance, not offering his own vision of where to go, instead waiting to watch their choices and then questioning or potentially penalizing them," said Philip Zelikow, who was then counselor at the State Department. "The style can be praised as one of delegation and prodding, but it is also designed to allow the chief to keep his own preferences obscure as long as possible."

There was abundant evidence that Rumsfeld was an inept leader. For all his willingness to chew out subordinates, he consistently seemed unable to address major problems and make adjustments in personnel, policy, or command structures. On top of that, his leadership of the U.S. military establishment was eroded by the Abu Ghraib prisoner abuse scandal, which became public in the spring of 2004. It was a major setback for the U.S. war effort, and indeed a strategic loss for the United States globally. But only underlings took the hit for it. "From May of 2004 onward, he was damaged goods," military commentator Francis "Bing" West later observed. "He had lost the moral authority to lead."

After his last day in office, Rumsfeld took his family to Buck's Fishing & Camping, which, despite its rustic name, is an upscale Washington restaurant. Underscoring the loathing Rumsfeld had generated in many Americans, the chef-owner there, Carole Greenwood, told her coowner, James Alefantis, to kick him out. "I'm not serving a war criminal in my restaurant," she declared. Alefantis pointed out that her business was to serve people and that Rumsfeld was with his family. Greenwood eventually relented but only on the condition that someone else cook Rumsfeld's meal. To Alefantis's chagrin, he heard that Rumsfeld soon was telling people that Buck's was his favorite restaurant in the area. Greenwood likely would go ballistic if Rumsfeld returned with his buddy Dick Cheney.

In both art and strategy, personality plays a large but murky role. The personality of Robert Gates was the strongest asset he would bring to the Pentagon as Rumsfeld's successor. Where Rumsfeld was blustery, Gates was quiet, even stealthy. He was a career intelligence officer, spending most of his life serving his country in the federal government, an organization that people like Rumsfeld and Bush tended to denigrate. Gates did share with them a strong sense of loyalty—but in his case, to his longtime best friend, Brent Scowcroft, who had been close to the first President Bush but had become persona non grata with the second because of his public opposition to the invasion of Iraq. Gates also had been a member of the Iraq Study Group, which had introduced him to the principal players in policy and steeped him in the current debate.

"Bob Gates will bring a fresh perspective," President Bush said with unusual understatement. And while a few weeks earlier Bush had said that tactics might change but that the strategy would remain the same, he now pronounced himself open to change in both. "Stay the course means let's get the job done, but it doesn't mean, you know, staying stuck on a strategy or tactics that may not be working," he said.

Despite the change at the Pentagon, everything seemed to be going the way of the anti-war Democrats. In early December, Senator Gordon Smith, a low-key Republican from Oregon, made his way to the Senate floor to break dramatically with the president on Iraq. He had been reading John Keegan's somber history of World War I, which had led him to meditate on the sins of the British generals who sent a generation head-on into the slaughter of German machine guns, despite growing evidence that their frontal approach wasn't working. It had made him think, he said, about "how we kept doing the same thing over and over again at the cost of our soldiers' lives with no improvement in the political environment in Iraq." He also had been reading books critical of the Iraq war. One Thursday in December, he awoke to news on his clock radio that another ten soldiers had been killed in Iraq. (Six of the ten were those Col. MacFarland lost in Ramadi, including Maj. McClung and Capt. Patriquin.) He decided that he had heard and seen enough. "I went from steamed to boiled," he recalled.

"I have tried to be a good soldier," Smith began in his very personal statement to the Senate that evening. "I have tried to support our president." But he said he could no longer. He remembered back to 2003, when it seemed as though the fall of Baghdad had brought a swift victory. "Now all of those memories seem much like ashes to me," he said. He no longer would be able to stand with the president, he continued. "He is not guilty of perfidy, but I do believe he is guilty of believing bad intelligence and giving us the same." So, he said, the time had come to speak out. "I, for one, am at the end of my rope when it comes to supporting a policy that has our soldiers patrolling the same streets in the same way, being blown up by the same bombs day after day," he said. "That is absurd. It may even be criminal. I cannot support that anymore." It was a stunning statement.

It began to look like 15 or more similarly upset Republicans might during the course of 2007 go into opposition on the war—a shift that promised to give the Democrats a veto-proof majority. The Democrats also knew that soon they would take over the committees where much of the substantial business of Congress is done. No longer would the panels on Appropriations, Armed Services, Foreign Affairs, and Intelligence be chaired by diehard supporters of the administration. Instead, starting in January 2007, skeptics of the Iraq war would be setting the agendas, directing the committee staffs, initiating investigations, and calling the hearings.

In their moment of triumph, some Democrats began to sense the dilemma that was about to ensnare them: How to bring an end to the war without being blamed for how it ended? Their evasive answer, unfortunately, would be to appear to do something without really doing anything. They liked having the Iraq conflict be "Bush's war" and most certainly didn't intend to take possession. "Like it or not, George Bush is still the commander in chief, and this is his war," Harry Reid of Nevada would say in 2007, months after becoming Senate majority leader.

This result would be a prolonging of the war, because it meant that the Democrats ultimately would shy away from any confrontation with the Bush administration—and the White House knew it. So, for example, by the end of December, Senator Joseph Biden, the incoming chairman of the Senate Foreign Relations Committee, and two years later Barack Obama's running mate, would emphatically oppose an increase in troop levels. "I totally oppose the surging of additional troops into Baghdad, and I think it is contrary to the overwhelming body of informed opinion, both people inside the administration and outside the administration," he said. Neither he nor other Democrats, despite controlling both houses of Congress, would take any serious steps to block it.

BIG JACK KEANE INTERVENES

In the fall of 2006, Jack Keane effectively became chairman of the Joint Chiefs of Staff, stepping in to redirect U.S. strategy in a war, to coordinate the thinking of the White House and the Pentagon, and even to pick the commanders who would lead the change in the fight. It was an unprecedented and astonishing development for a retired general to drive policy making and indeed bypass the entire chain of command in remaking war strategy. "Retired four-stars can be very influential, but this was really an order of magnitude beyond that," commented Tom Donnelly, who worked with Keane on developing the idea of "the surge." "He is almost the keystone in the whole thing. The window was almost closed. He kept it open."

Keane was given his opening by the failure of the chairman of the Joint Chiefs, Gen. Peter Pace, who was proving unable to deal with the Iraq war. With no official backing, and nothing but his credibility and persuasive abilities to go on, Keane helped one general in Iraq and some civilians in a think tank formulate "the surge" as a new strategy for Iraq, pitched it to the president, and then, with a green light from Bush, told top officials at the Pentagon about how to proceed. He continued to work with that general in Iraq, Raymond Odierno, behind the back of Gen. Casey, the senior commander there, who told Keane not to visit Iraq.

Maj. Gen. Michael Barbero, who at the time was the J-33, the director of current operations for the staff of the Joint Chiefs, recalled that during the fall of 2006, Keane "was the one driving the planning." Asked if Keane effectively was acting as director of the Joint Staff—that is, a crucial but low-profile slot—Barbero responded quickly that Keane was playing a far more elevated role. "No, like the chairman" of the Joint Chiefs, he said—meaning the highest military officer of the land. "He was a key player, and he was saying, 'We've got to win this thing.' "

Keane's unusual journey to the center of American military policy making commenced on August 3, 2006, a hot, sticky day typical of the Washington summer. Keane was at home in McLean, a pleasant Virginia suburb. That evening, while the temperature was still in the nineties, he went downstairs to his easy chair in his basement den, put his feet up on the ottoman in front of his big-screen television, and keyed in C-SPAN, which was carrying a hearing on the Iraq war that been held earlier in the day by the Senate Armed Services Committee. Keane had come to believe that "it was obvious that we had serious problems, that the strategy wasn't working." He wanted to see if Rumsfeld, Pace, and Abizaid, the three witnesses at the hearing, had anything new or different to offer.

Keane had been worrying about Iraq since his first visit there, in the summer of 2003. Then the vice chief of staff of the Army, he had left the country feeling deeply concerned and a bit guilty. "When I flew out, I was really troubled," he recalled. "I knew the Army collectively was not prepared to deal with irregular warfare. I said to my guys, we simply are not prepared to do this." He began to think about how to make amends.

Of the hundreds of thousands of soldiers then on active duty, he was one of the handful with firsthand knowledge of what the Army had done wrong in Vietnam, where he had been a platoon leader and a company commander in the 101st Airborne. When he left Vietnam and got back to Fort Benning, Georgia, he began reading history to figure out what he should have been doing. "I and others came to the conclusion that we had been conducting a conventional war against an irregular enemy."

By the end of that war, he said, the Army had learned how to conduct a counterinsurgency campaign. "We'd studied the history, we'd learned the doctrine, and some of us had the experience," he remembered. After the war, the Army "purged" that knowledge, he said. But "I kept the memory, especially the idea that you must protect the population." That idea would become the core of Keane's 2006 campaign to change the American approach to the war in Iraq.

Big Jack Keane talks like the native New Yorker he is, with a working-class tone that he brought with him from the Lower East Side and Washington Heights, the two neighborhoods where he was raised. "I think New York is such a magical city because it is a place where, truly, immigrants get started, and then immigrants come and go, and different cultures are there, so it all transitions," he said in an interview. With his accent, big hands, square face, and hair combed straight back, Keane could easily be mistaken for an old-style member of the New York City Police Department. Indeed, he bears a passing resemblance to the corrupt police captain shot by Michael Corleone in an Italian restaurant in *The Godfather.* Underneath that old-school appearance, Keane is crackerjack smart, and extremely articulate, often in a concise, blunt way. Most importantly, and unusually, he is an independent and clear thinker.

He didn't go public with his concerns in 2003, but after he retired he began to share them privately with others. He had gotten to know Henry Kissinger, an adopted son of Washington Heights, when both served on the Defense Policy Board, and in 2005, he began a series of conversations with the former secretary of state. One day that year, Kissinger, preparing to visit President Bush, asked Keane, "What is the military strategy to defeat the insurgency?"

Keane paused, then said, "We don't have a military strategy to defeat the insurgency."

"Jack, we will lose," Kissinger replied. As Keane remembered it, Kissinger meant that there would have to be a political solution, but it would come about only if enabled by an effective military strategy. So, Keane said, "if we don't have a military strategy to defeat them—and by defeat we meant change the behavior and attitude of the insurgent—then we would lose."

As Iraq grew bloodier, Keane watched and worried more. "I knew that the violence was worse in '04 than it was in '03, worse in '05 than it was in '04. And now the wheels were coming off and it was going off the charts." Yet American strategy, inexplicably, wasn't changing—"I also knew at the time that we are still on a mission to transition to the Iraqis despite this." His worry was that the American strategy didn't protect the people and instead remained focused on transitioning to Iraqi forces, who could not protect the population either, so staying the course really meant riding a losing strategy into defeat.

Other insiders were also becoming persuaded that the course in Iraq was a loser. In May 2006, after five months of wrangling, a new Iraqi government was finally assembled, to be led by a compromise candidate, Maliki, to the relief of American officials in Baghdad and Washington. But in the following weeks, it became clear that this political movement wasn't leading to a lessening of violence—which was the keystone of the Bush administration's strategy in Iraq—but rather increasing it. "At this point, the strategy couldn't explain what was happening," said Fred Kagan, the American Enterprise Institute analyst who was a member of the group that met with the president at Camp David in June. "I think it [the strategy] became visibly bankrupt" at that point.

One day in the summer, Keane got a phone call from Adm. William "Fox" Fallon, the U.S. commander for the Pacific. As Keane remembers it, Fallon began by saying, "Jack, I just came out of Iraq. Could you help me to understand what the fuck is going on? . . . Casey is up to his ears in quicksand and he doesn't even know it. This thing is going down around him."

For Keane, the final straw came on that August night as he settled before the television and watched that tape of Rumsfeld, Pace, and Abizaid appearing before the Senate Armed Services panel earlier that day.

"Despite the many challenges, progress does continue to be made in Iraq," Abizaid had reassured the senators. That could be understood as code for: Get off my back, we are going to stay on the same path of passing the mission of providing security to Iraqi forces. Indeed, he said he could "imagine" additional U.S. troop reductions later in the year.

Abizaid, a bright, witty officer who spoke Arabic, had been the great hope of the Army when he replaced Tommy R. Franks as chief of Central Command in 2003. Not only did he understand the region, he also had shown a willingness to stand up to Rumsfeld. But by 2006 he appeared burned out, as did many who worked closely with the defense secretary. In 2003–4, Abizaid had left in place as his top general in Iraq Lt. Gen. Ricardo Sanchez, seen by many inside the Army, especially those in Iraq, as an overwhelmed and perhaps incompetent general. Abizaid had failed to get the Army to send out enough specialists to staff Sanchez's headquarters. He had stood by as persistent differences poisoned the relationship between the U.S. military and U.S. civilian officials in Iraq, with Sanchez and L. Paul Bremer III, the civilian occupation chief, barely civil to each other by the end of their 12 months together. He had not been able to get other parts of the federal government to engage enthusiastically in Iraq. Most of all, he had failed to stand up to the Bush administration's blandishments of "steady progress" in Iraq, and instead, over time, seemed to join in them.

Rumsfeld said at the hearing that ending the sectarian violence was a job for Iraqis, not American troops. As Keane watched, he knew that wasn't happening, and he worried that such false hopes would lead to defeat. "I liked these guys," he said. "What was bothering me most, it seemed blatantly obvious that our strategy had failed. It had blown up in our face. We were on the precipice of the new Iraqi government fracturing. That's where we're heading, a humiliating defeat for the United States, and all the security problems that would ensue from that."

The hearing climaxed with Senator Hillary Clinton's rebuke of the defense secretary. "We hear a lot of happy talk and rosy scenarios, but because of the administration's strategic blunders and, frankly, the record of incompetence in executing, you are presiding over a failed policy," the New York Democrat asserted. "Given your track record, Secretary Rumsfeld, why should we believe your assurances now?"

Rumsfeld's response made it even clearer to Keane that the administration was digging in its heels. "My goodness," Rumsfeld began in his anachronistic fashion as he launched into a passionate defense of his past deeds and of current policy. "History will make a judgment" on past decisions about troop numbers, he announced, as if to tell her that coming to such conclusions was above her pay grade.

As for an increase in troop levels, the prospect that Keane was mulling, Rumsfeld rejected the idea. "The balance between having too many and contributing to an insurgency by the feeling of occupation, and the risk of having too few and having the security situation not be sufficient for the political progress to go forward, is a complicated set of decisions. And I don't know there's any guide book that tells you how to do it. There's no rule book, there's no history for this." In fact, as Keane knew, there was ample history on just that point. The experiences of the British in Malaya, the French in Algeria, the Americans in Vietnam, and in a dozen other smaller counterinsurgency campaigns all taught the same lesson: You must protect the people and separate them from the insurgents, and to do so you had to live among the population. And doing all that required a lot of troops. Indeed, the manual on counterinsurgency that Gen. Petraeus was drafting out at Leavenworth as Rumsfeld spoke would make just that point.

But Rumsfeld was sticking to the existing plan, despite the multiple setbacks it had encountered. "The goal is to not have U.S. forces do the heavy lifting in Baghdad. There are many, many more Iraqi forces in Baghdad. The role of the U.S. forces is to help them." As Keane knew, there was growing evidence by this point that this transitional approach wasn't working.

The defense secretary concluded by lapsing into his trademark rhetorical device of posing a question and then answering it himself. He didn't seem to grasp how condescending this could be, especially with people like United States senators who tend to have a strong sense of the importance of their positions. He did so some ten times. Three of them were, "Are there setbacks? Yes. Are there things that people can't anticipate? Yes. Does the enemy have a brain and continue to make adjustments on the ground requiring our forces to continue to make adjustments? You bet."

Abizaid supported Rumsfeld. Going above the current level of 140,000 troops in Iraq, he said, would place "a tremendous strain" on the Army.

Gen. Pace, never particularly impressive as the chairman of the Joint Chiefs, had even less to offer that day. "Shia and Sunni are going to have to love their children more than they hate each other," he said. It was an almost despairing phrase, pointing toward no discernible strategy for the U.S. government. He apparently so liked the thought that he repeated it later in the hearing.

As Keane watched, the doubts he had been gathering for months coalesced and solidified. "My God, if we don't do something different, we're going over a cliff," he thought that night. He was not a man who came to a conclusion like that idly.

The next afternoon he sat in his living room, meditating on what to do and how to do it. He was there for so long that evening fell. Lost in thought, he didn't turn on any lights, and his wife came into the room to find him sitting in darkness. She asked what he was doing. "Iraq," he responded. "Our strategy there is failing. We need a new strategy, and new people, 'cause the guys doing it don't think it's failed."

"What are you going to do about it?" she asked. It was an unusual question to pose. She knew that many Americans had similar concerns, but that her husband was uniquely positioned to do something about it. After decades of service, he was an Army insider. In particular, he had been a mentor to two rising Army generals, David Petraeus and Raymond Odierno, and he thought they could be key to making the changes, even though neither was in Iraq at the time.

"I think I am going to try to change it," he told her. It wasn't an idle response. He began to write some notes, outlining the problem.

Since retiring from the Army, he also had come to know influential strategic experts such as Kissinger and Eliot Cohen, other members of the Defense Policy Board who were growing increasingly worried about the direction of the war. In May 2004, Cohen had gone to Iraq for the board and come back to deliver a grim assessment. "There is no sense of a common vision or direction, a real operational or strategic level plan," he reported. A senior officer had told him that mid-2003 to mid-2004 was "a lost year." In addition, Cohen had concluded that Army and Marine doctrine for conducting a counterinsurgency campaign was badly outdated—an observation that may have encouraged the Army to send Petraeus to Leavenworth.

Keane agreed with many of Cohen's worries. And while many active-duty officers shared his deepening concerns, he possessed an option they didn't: If he felt he didn't get a thorough and serious hearing, he could take his concerns public. He knew how to do it—he was a retired four-star general who maintained cordial relations with several defense reporters.

"DAVE, YOU'RE SHOT"

Perhaps most important, Keane had known Petraeus for years. An advocate of realistic training, Keane loathed seeing soldiers toss grenades as if they were outfielders hurling metal baseballs, instead of in the context of how they would be used in combat, where people who want to survive don't stand up in view of the enemy. So he had pushed for "live-fire" exercises, in which soldiers used real bullets while training and moved as if they were on a battlefield. One day in 1991 at Fort Campbell, Kentucky, Keane and Petraeus were observing just such an exercise, in which a squad was practicing taking down a machine gun bunker. Some soldiers provided suppressive fire while one of their comrades crawled forward from one side and, leaning to one side while still prone, lobbed a hand grenade into the bunker.

Under the cover of the explosion, the grenade thrower turned and ran as fast as he could back to his fellow squad members. He hit the dirt using the butt of his M-16 rifle to break his fall, as he had been taught to do in order to get down quickly. But the soldier, probably distracted by his grenade throwing, had made two mistakes: He had his kept his finger on the trigger of his weapon, and the safety was off.

Petraeus, observing from 40 yards away, grunted and stepped back, but didn't fall. Keane, standing next to Petraeus, looked over. "Dave, you're shot," he said. The bullet from the soldier's weapon had pierced Petraeus in the right side of his chest, just above the *A* in PETRAEUS on his fatigues, and clipped both a lung and an artery. Keane laid Petraeus on the ground, then reached around him and felt for the exit wound. It was about the size of a half-dollar coin. He called for a medic. Then he looked down at Petraeus and said, "Dave, you know what's going on here, we've got to stop the bleeding. . . . Then we have got to make sure you don't go into shock."

Characteristically, while waiting for a medical evacuation helicopter, Keane took aside the commander of the company training that day and told him to continue the exercise. "What I was trying to teach them," he recalled, is that "in combat it's going to be much worse than this, we are going to get our guys shot and get our guys killed and, one, we go on with the mission, two, we find out what the mistakes were after it's over so we can fix it for the next time."

Keane held Petraeus's hand on the short helicopter hop to Fort Campbell's Blanchfield Army Community Hospital. A doctor there picked up a suction tube to clean the entry wound of strands of Petraeus's uniform and dirt. "Colonel Petraeus," he said to his new patient, who was supine but still conscious, "I've got to clean this wound out, because when the bullet goes in there it takes all of that with it. I've got to get as much out of there as I can so it doesn't start to get into your bloodstream." Not waiting to administer an anesthetic, he worried: "This is going to hurt like hell"—and told some orderlies to hold him down. Then he jammed the tube into the bloody hole in Petraeus's chest.

Usually, the doctor later told Keane in the hallway, the procedure inflicts so much pain that the body jumps up on the operating table and the patient "screams like hell."

Petraeus just grunted. "That really is one tough soldier in there," the doctor said.

"Yeah, I know that," Keane replied. The chest operation that Petraeus would need required a second flight, this time by an Army Black Hawk helicopter to a hospital in Nashville, where he was met by Dr. Bill Frist, who had yet to enter politics but who would later become Senate majority leader. Frist, still in his golfing outfit, saw the small entry wound and wondered what all the fuss was about. Turning Petraeus over, he saw the exit wound and understood. Keane told him that the exit injury was typical of a high-velocity weapon, which was outside Frist's usual cases of wounds made by cheap pistols and knives. Frist operated for more than five hours.

Less than a week later, Petraeus was back recuperating at the Fort Campbell hospital and growing impatient with it. "Dave was raising all sorts of ruckus because he wanted to get out of there and go home," Keane recalled.

A senior doctor went to see this troublesome patient. "Hey, Dave, you're not going home so just leave my staff alone," he ordered. "You're just out of surgery, you're not going to be able to get out of here for a few more days."

Everybody heals differently, Petraeus argued. "I believe that I'm recovered enough to be able to go home," he said.

"That's impossible—you're not going home," the doctor said.

"Can I demonstrate to you the degree of my recovery?" asked Petraeus.

The doctor asked what he meant. "Just undo my tubes here," Petraeus said. "Don't worry, I'm not going to do anything to hurt myself, just undo my tubes." He got down on the floor and counted out 50 push-ups for the doctor, who then allowed him to leave the hospital.

The life of a light infantryman is tough for soldiers in their twenties, requiring both strength and stamina. The weight, the rain, the stress, can combine to break the health of soldiers in their thirties. Petraeus left the hospital worried about regaining his strength. "What was really eating at me at the time was how well I was going to be able to run again," he recalled. He went to the base gym to work out on a stationary bicycle, "gently, just to keep the legs moving." But there was a running track just outside the gym. And the watch on his wrist had a stopwatch function. "One thing led to another," he said a bit sheepishly, explaining how he happened to find himself jogging on the track, trying to see if he could still breathe deeply. "It wasn't the gunshot wound alone, I had thoracic surgery where they cut you, I have a scar that goes from here all the way around to there," he said, tracing a line from his chest, under his arm, and to his back. "There is a lot of scarring so the lung doesn't glide in your chest the way it used to, so it feels like you are permanently taped up. I just wanted to get a sense of what it was going to feel like." The next round of X-rays revealed that that spontaneous bout of exercise had begun to fill the injured lung with fluid. The doctors told him to knock off running.

KEANE ON THE WARPATH

On September 19, 2006, Keane was ready to make his case to Defense Secretary Rumsfeld. The two old bulls had had some differences in the past, but Keane felt there was mutual respect. "We could talk to each other," he said.

Gen. Pace showed up at the meeting, a bit to Keane's surprise, because Pace's reputation was that he was taking a hands-off approach to Iraq, on the grounds that his plate was full with the rest of the world and that two other four-star generals, Abizaid and Casey, were on the case. Keane worried that Rumsfeld would play to Pace, as was his wont. But the chairman remained quiet, just taking notes, and Rumsfeld stayed focused on Keane's grim message. "We are edging toward strategic failure," Keane warned the defense secretary. "Despite capturing Saddam Hussein, killing his two sons, holding three elections, writing a constitution, installing a permanent government, beginning to develop a capable ISF, killing Zarqawi—the level of violence has increased every year in the contested areas. Security and stability is worse today than it has been since the insurgency started. It threatens the survival of the government and the success of our mission."

So, Keane asked rhetorically, what is wrong with our strategy? His answer: "It is not designed to defeat the insurgency and therefore the insurgency thrives, and the violence is growing. It begs the question, how can you defeat it?"

Continuing to borrow Rumsfeld's approach, he posed another question and then answered it: "How can we possibly obtain victory out of all that is happening?" First, Keane said, "you have to admit that you cannot defeat the insurgency by destroying their forces or simply transitioning to Iraqi security forces. You have to come to grips with that." Next, he said, start employing classic counterinsurgency practice: "The only way to do this is the way that it's been done in the past, using proven COIN [counterinsurgency] practices—and that is by protecting the people and permanently isolating the insurgents from the population." So, he told Rumsfeld, the U.S. Army needed to stop conducting mindless Humvee patrols out of big bases and instead start living among the people and patrolling small areas on foot. Set up traffic-control points, conduct a census, and issue identity cards—all classic measures to channel and track the movements of a population. His most controversial recommendation was that Rumsfeld order everyone to stop talking about drawing down troop levels in Iraq. Get some new generals in there, hold them accountable, and match your policies to your resources. To live among the people, and dry up the sea in which the insurgents swam, you are going to need more troops. And focus them on Baghdad. What Keane was saying was hardly novel. He had captured the core lesson of David Galula, the great French theorist of counterinsurgency, who argued in his influential *Counterinsurgency: Theory and Practice* that to defeat an insurgency, military units must live among the population. Indeed, Keane recommended that book to Rumsfeld. The defense secretary was "uncomfortable" during the meeting and opposed increasing the troop levels without offering a reasoning, Keane said as he read aloud from his extensive notes of the meeting.

GRADING THE CHAIRMAN

Pace followed up by asking Keane to come see him. Two days later, Pace began that meeting by asking Keane with a smile what grade he would give him as chairman of the Joint Chiefs.

"F," Keane replied. He wasn't smiling.

Gen. Pace was taken aback. People didn't usually talk to a top officer in the U.S. military that way, not even retired four-star generals. What do you mean? he asked.

"Well, Pete, the number one national security priority we have is Iraq, and it's the number one priority in the Pentagon," Keane told him. But, he added, "you're absorbed in so many other things." And, he continued, why the hell are you, the chairman of the Joint Chiefs of Staff, asking a retired general about the situation in Iraq? How is it possible that you, with all the far-flung resources of the global U.S. military establishment at your fingertips, know less about the war than one guy who goes out there and asks a few questions? "You've got to get into this full time," Keane admonished. (One of Pace's subordinates would later recall that at about the same time, Adm. Mike Mullen, then the chief of the Navy, sent a similar message, to the effect, "This is going down on your watch. You need to do something.")

Keane also told Pace to put new people in charge: Replace Abizaid at Central Command with Fox Fallon, who as an experienced regional commander could step into the job quickly, Keane said. And replace Casey with Dave Petraeus.

Pace responded with alacrity, Keane recalled, canceling a planned trip to South America and instead starting up a group of officers to review Iraq policy. This new panel, dubbed "the council of colonels," was tasked first to look at the entire war on terror, but then decided that the first question had to be whether the strategy of the Iraq war was working. It first met on September 27, not long after Keane rang Pace's bell. It began asking a series of questions that in the following weeks would make Pace and the Joint Staff reexamine the deteriorating situation in Iraq.

In November, Raymond Odierno, another Keane protégé, headed out to Iraq to take over the number two position in the war from Lt. Gen. Pete Chiarelli. On November 20, a macabre note was struck when a leading Iraqi comedian was assassinated. It wasn't clear what the point of the killing was, because Walid Hassan had specialized in mocking the difficulties of life in occupied Iraq in a nonsectarian fashion. Three days later, a barrage of car bombs, mortars, and missiles hit Sadr City, killing more than 200 people. It was the single deadliest attack in years. The next day, Shiite fighters retaliated with a citywide attack on Sunni mosques crowded for Friday prayers. Bombs, rocket-propelled grenades, and automatic-weapons fire hit crowds of worshippers.

As he did Petraeus, Keane knew Odierno well. (It is an interesting coincidence that all three men are from the greater New York area, which generally isn't seen in American culture as a hotbed of generalship. Keane is from Manhattan; Petraeus from Cornwall, just up the Hudson; and Odierno from just across that river, in northern New Jersey.) In the summer of 2001, Keane, then the vice chief of staff of the Army, had gone to a meeting with Rumsfeld at which 40 slides were presented on various recommendations the defense secretary had planned to make. This was before the 9/11 attacks, and long before there was any serious thought of invading Iraq. Tucked among the slides, to Keane's surprise, was a plan to reduce the active-duty Army to eight divisions from ten, and on top of that to cut four divisions from the National Guard. This represented a major reduction in the ground combat strength of the United States, and Keane, the number two officer in the Army, had received no advance notice that it was coming. He was stunned—that just wasn't how a superpower was supposed to work. "Mister Secretary, I disagree with this strongly," Keane had said. He asked for 24 hours to develop a response. Back in his office, he summoned Odierno, then a bright young one-star general on his staff, and told him to brief Deputy Defense Secretary Wolfowitz on how the Army had arrived at its current force structure and how that related to the size of the Army that actually fights. He picked Odierno, he said, in part because "he had this intellect, this grasp, this power of persuasion." Also, he said, "a lot of guys become afraid to fail. You want them to push the envelope, and Odierno was doing that."

The next day, Odierno gave a presentation to Wolfowitz and others on why the Army's numbers shouldn't be cut. At the end of the briefing, Wolfowitz, who had been given the lead on the issue by Rumsfeld, said, "I'm convinced." He said he would take the recommendation to the secretary, who concurred.

Even so, Keane wasn't entirely approving of Odierno. He had some issues with how he had led the 4th Infantry Division in 2003–4, during his first tour in Iraq. Nevertheless, Keane thought Odierno was a tough, intelligent officer who, unlike some of his peers, was willing to take risks for what he thought was right.

KEANE AND ODIERNO VS. THE WORLD

Between Keane and Odierno, a kind of guerrilla campaign was launched inside the U.S. military establishment. Keane was in Washington and Odierno was in Baghdad, but they talked by telephone almost every day.

"We don't easily jump the chain of command," retired Col. John Martin, a friend and adviser to Petraeus, said in another context. Making one of the most audacious moves of the entire war, Odierno did exactly that, bypassing two levels of command above him to talk to officials at the White House and aides to the Joint Chiefs of Staff. He was about to become the sole senior official in the active-duty military speaking out for an increase in troops, recalled a senior U.S. intelligence officer who privately supported such a full, five-brigade counteroffensive. "He was the only one in the chain of command—not MNF-I, not Central Command, not the Joint Staff," this intelligence official recalled. (Adm. Mike Mullen, who was then the chief of the Navy and in 2007 would become chairman of the Joint Chiefs, would later insist that he had supported the surge, but apparently meant that he had endorsed the smaller, two-brigade option that Pace would take to President Bush just after Christmas 2006.)

"Odierno and I are having a continuous dialogue" at this time, Keane recalled. "He knows he needs more troops, he knows the strategy has got to change. His problem is General Casey."

Just as Odierno was beginning his epic end run around Casey and the rest of the senior leaders of the U.S. military establishment, the president asserted in an interview with the *Washington Post,* "It's important to trust the judgment of the military when they're making military plans. . . . I'm a strict adherer to the command structure."

Ironically, it was only after Odierno stepped outside that structure, rejecting the views of his superiors and lobbying the White House on his own, that policy formulation began to work effectively, producing a workable strategy. Arguably, his actions amounted to insubordination. Casey seemed puzzled when told in a 2008 inverview that Odierno had grave doubts about the direction of the war back in December 2006. "Ray never came to me and said, 'Look, I think you've got to do something fundamentally different here,'" Casey said.

"Courage takes two forms in war," observed Hew Strachan, the British military historian and interpreter of Clausewitz. "Courage in the face of personal danger, whose effects are felt in the tactical sphere, and the courage to take responsibility, a requirement of strategic success." By taking on his new boss, Odierno displayed that second, more elusive form of bravery. He was laying his career on the line. If the surge went wrong, he would be the first blamed by many inside the military who had made clear their profound concerns and objections.

Lined up against Odierno were the collective powers at the top of the U.S. military. Abizaid, the chief of the Central Command, told Senators John McCain and Lindsey Graham in a Senate Armed Services Committee hearing on November 15 that he and every general he had asked opposed sending more troops to Iraq. "I do not believe that more American troops right now is the solution to the problem," Abizaid emphasized. "I believe that troop levels need to stay where they are now."

Gen. Chiarelli, who was about to leave Iraq, was also questioning a troop escalation. He said at the time, "I happen to believe we have done everything militarily we possibly can." Asked about that in 2008, he said his concern had been "How are we going to source them? And I still thought, troops alone are not going to stop this problem, that we need to get the Iraqi government to act differently."

In early December, Pace, the chairman of the Joint Chiefs, was privately telling his colleagues that he didn't see that 160,000 U.S. troops in Iraq could do anything that 140,000 weren't doing. He agreed with the other members of the Joint Chiefs: What was needed, he griped, wasn't a troop surge, but a new commitment by the rest of the U.S. government. In this view, the military was doing its part but had been left high and dry by the civilians. Like the rest of the Joint Chiefs, Pace believed there was no military answer to the situation in Iraq. "In the military sense, you'd only commit the reserves if you were exploiting success or salvaging failure," said one general involved in the discussions, explaining that he didn't seen anything happening from a relatively small troop increase. "It isn't that we're opposed to doing it, it's just that we don't see the payoff." This was a rational calculation, because at the time no one could predict that the Sunni insurgency would largely come over to the American side, or at least to the American payroll, or that Moqtada al-Sadr would order his Shiite militia to stand down.

Even Colin Powell, who though retired from active duty for more than a decade remained the best known military figure in the country, spoke out against the notion. Gen. Casey already had tried a surge in Baghdad in the summer of 2006, the former chairman of the Joint Chiefs of Staff argued in a December appearance on CBS's *Face the Nation.* So, Powell said, "I am not persuaded that another surge of troops into Baghdad for the purpose of suppressing this communitarian violence, this civil war, will work." At any rate, he added, "There really are no additional troops."

By mid-December, the notion of some sort of troop escalation, or "surge," was a major topic of conversation in both Washington and Baghdad. Yet Maliki's government seemed lukewarm at best on the idea. After Gates met with Iraqi officials in a house in the Green Zone at this time, I buttonholed Abdul Qadir Muhammed Jassim, the Iraqi defense minister, as he was leaving and asked him in the driveway if he had told the Americans that he supported the surge. Somewhat inscrutably, he responded, "I didn't say no." Maliki was said to favor a "donut" approach—that is, put more U.S. troops outside the capital and leave the city to him, perhaps so the ethnic cleansing of Sunnis in several Baghdad neighborhoods could be finished. "I think they wanted to present us with a fait accompli of a Shiia Baghdad," Kilcullen suspected.

One of the very few voices in American public life supporting an increase in troops was that of Senator John McCain, who was in the difficult position of arguing that the war had been poorly executed but that more troops would improve the situation. "Without additional combat forces, we will not win this war," he said in mid-November.

On the morning of Thursday, December 7, President Bush sparred with reporters over Iraq. One asked if he were in denial about the state of the war. "It's bad in Iraq," he replied with a glare. "Does that help?"

Actually, it may have. Finally, and years later than he should have, the president was beginning to grapple with the ugly facts on the ground in Iraq.

ONE WEEKEND AT AEI CHANGES THE WAR

The 2003 invasion of Iraq arguably was conceived at the American Enterprise Institute, the right-wing think tank that is the mecca of American neoconservativism. Its boxy building across from the National Geographic Society's headquarters in downtown Washington, D.C., was the roost of a variety of prominent hawks—Fred Kagan, Richard Perle, Gary Schmitt, Tom Donnelly, William Kristol. In the fall of 2006, they saw their war going down the tubes. The same building also houses the *Weekly Standard,* the torchbearer publication of neoconservativism, and the Project for the New American Century, an advocacy group for an aggressive interventionist foreign policy that was an early and persistent advocate of ousting Saddam Hussein.

For years, the American right had been far more conflicted over the war than liberals generally perceive. Kagan, who had met with Bush at Camp David in June, long had thought that the war was mishandled. He was especially wary of Rumsfeld, who he thought was overly absorbed with restricting troop numbers in Iraq and insufficiently focused on providing the troops and other resources needed to prevail. After the Abu Ghraib scandal broke in 2004, Kagan and others called for the defense secretary to step down—an action that he believed had made him persona non grata at the Pentagon. Like Keane, he had grown increasingly concerned during the course of 2006, especially after a new Iraqi government was seated and violence increased rather than tapered off, as the Bush administration had predicted.

Bob Woodward's thorough but White House-centric *The War Within* reports that the president was settling on a surge by November 2006. There is little on the public record to support that assertion. On the other hand, there is strong evidence that Bush's meeting with outside experts early in December had a strong effect on his thinking.

The road to that meeting began on Friday, December 8, when Kagan gathered a handful of like-minded analysts and military planners on the top floor of the American Enterprise Institute's 12-story building. The most important person invited to the conference was Gen. Keane. Kagan had heard about his dissent on the conduct of the war, which was becoming the talk of conservative Washington, but had no inkling that Keane was talking regularly to Odierno and Petraeus, who were about to take command of the war.

The three-day exercise wasn't intended to change the course of the war, or even to add more troops, which Kagan didn't think was possible. Rather, it was to see if it was possible to devise an alternative military approach for Iraq. At any event, Kagan thought, it was quite possible that the exercise would be purely academic, because the word from the White House was that the president would be giving a major speech on Iraq within just a few days. "We were disappointed with the quality of the debate over the military aspects of the war," Kagan said. "Baghdad is burning, Iraq is about to explode, and we are moving toward a primitive civil war. This is about to head off the cliff. So, the mandate was: Stop the bleeding in Baghdad."

An untold aspect of the exercise at the think tank was the involvement of some active-duty Army officers. These weren't just any random military planners. Rather, the ones attending had served with the 3rd Armored Cavalry Regiment in Iraq under Col. H. R. McMaster. That's meaningful for two reasons. First, they had participated in McMaster's maverick 2005 campaign in Tall Afar, the first place in the Iraq war where the U.S. military conducted a successful large-scale counterinsurgency effort. They had shown how to use more troops effectively. Their example had not been embraced by top commanders, probably in part because it wasn't consistent with stated U.S. strategy, and perhaps also because the Army didn't see how to replicate the effort in larger cities: The McMaster approach worked in relatively small Tall Afar, but to many seemed inapplicable to the larger, more important ones, such as Mosul, Kirkuk, and, most of all, Baghdad, home to around 6 million souls. At any rate, the Army seems never to have taken a serious look at the feasibility of following the Tall Afar example elsewhere.

On top of that, at the time the American Enterprise Institute exercise was being held, McMaster was playing a significant role across the river at the Pentagon as a member of the council of colonels reviewing Iraq policy for Gen. Pace, the chairman of the Joint Chiefs. He had been suggested for service on that panel by Gen. Petraeus. In the course of working on the study, he met Gen. Keane, and the two hit it off. Tying all these connections in a neat package, McMaster had shared an office with Kagan when both taught at West Point, and the former thanks the latter in the acknowledgments to his influential book *Dereliction of Duty*, about the failures of the Joint Chiefs of Staff during the Vietnam War.

Another officer helping Kagan was Maj. Joel Rayburn, also a veteran of West Point. His involvement wasn't official, he said, but rather grew out of months of "writing and talking and arguing" with Kagan about the war. "It became sharper as we went along—and became urgent in the fall of '06."

Not all the officers attending bought into the American Enterprise Institute's hawks' view of the world. "They completely blew it," said retired Army Col. Joel Armstrong, the former executive officer of McMaster's regiment. "All the assumptions [about Iraq] were wrong." But when Kagan, spurred by McMaster, asked Armstrong to fly in from Spokane, Washington, for the weekend exercise, he agreed because he thought the United States was sputtering toward defeat in Iraq. "We were basically heading for a loss, and I couldn't see anything changing without something dramatic," Armstrong said. It felt odd, he added, to advocate a course of action that the generals leading the war opposed. "I felt kind of strange going against the chain of command, but I felt I had to."

The basic concept was to figure out how to redeploy American troops in Iraq so that they might protect the population, which had become a major theme of Gen. Keane's. Establishing outposts with that mission was an issue Armstrong had thought about since early 2005, when he had suggested putting a small, company-sized base in Salman Pak, southeast of Baghdad. "I was told by division I was out of my mind," he recalled. Donnelly and others from AEI sat with Armstrong and retired Maj. Dan Dwyer, another officer who had served in Tall Afar. "We'd look at a neighborhood, and use the 3rd Armored Cav's experience to say, 'Yeah, we could do that,'" Donnelly said. The military officers unrolled maps and Google images of Baghdad and began discussing what sort of troop numbers might be needed in its neighborhoods. There were company-sized problems, they would decide, and there were battalion-sized problems.

Armstrong's role was to make the participants loosely adhere to the military-planning process, which is basically to pose a problem, figure out a solution, decide which tasks are the logical steps toward reaching that solution, and then calculate what troops and other resources are needed to execute those tasks. Ultimately, they concluded that to improve security in Baghdad and neighboring al Anbar Province, nearly seven brigades would be needed—five from the Army, almost two from the Marine Corps. The next question was how to find those extra troops. On midafternoon Saturday, AEI's Donnelly and Armstrong, the retired colonel, had a quick discussion about the actual number of troops they thought doable. Looking at the Army's planned rotation schedule, which he had found posted on the Internet, Donnelly quickly figured out how many combat brigades the Army could send. "The five-brigade answer was immediately obvious, in terms of the max that could be done in a timely fashion based upon the current force generation model," he said. (The calculations would prove to be so accurate that when Keane and Kagan went to brief Gen. Richard Cody, the Army's vice chief of staff, on their recommendations, he offered only one tweak, which was that they were three weeks off in their estimate of the availability of one of the surge brigades.)

The next major step was for an active-duty officer who was attending to "red team" the planning—that is, to look at the proposed operation from the enemy's point of view. He discussed how al Qaeda might react, what the Shiite militias would do, the steps other fighters might take to counter the American moves. This was the moment "when I really came to believe this could work," Kagan said. "He persuaded me that we had a pretty good feel for the operational patterns of the enemy."

Keane mainly sat and watched, absorbing their thinking. "He was pretty quiet," said Armstrong.

Keane said later that he was impressed by the quality of the information and analysis the group presented. "I was amazed by the intel they got from open sources," he said. "I was very current but they understand pretty clearly what was happening among the factions; the level of detail that they understood was amazing to me." Much of what they told him, he noted, he would use a few days later in a meeting with President Bush. By coincidence, the White House had called Keane on Friday and asked him to come by on Monday to talk to the president about Iraq. He already had an appointment that day with Vice President Cheney, who also had gotten wind of Keane's concerns, so Cheney's office said the two meetings would somehow be combined.

One major assumption of the exercise was that improved security would lead to a political breakthrough. At first, this kind of slipped in as an afterthought. Donnelly said he wasn't focused so much on what the surge might produce as he was on just getting one. "It was more a sense of, if you don't turn the security issue around, you're about to lose," he said. He was just trying to figure out a way to keep the United States in the war.

But Keane had what he needed to take to the White House the next day: an informed look not just at why more troops were needed, but how they might be used differently. This what was the White House had wanted to know, but the Pentagon hadn't bothered to look into. It wasn't a subject that seemed to interest the Joint Chiefs of Staff—a lapse that, to borrow McMaster's title, amounted to dereliction of duty.

BUSH GETS BOTH BARRELS

On Monday, December 11, President Bush hit a new low in his ratings, with only 36 percent of respondents approving even "somewhat" of his performance and a stunning 62 percent disapproving.

At a White House meeting that began at 3:20 that afternoon, Keane listened as Professor Eliot Cohen began on a frank note. About a dozen high-level note-takers—Karl Rove, National Security Adviser Stephen Hadley, and some of his staffers—sat in the outer circle. Cohen, the sole attendee from the Camp David meeting the previous June to be asked to this session, remembers it as being far harder edged than the desultory discussion six months earlier. "There was something in the air—more tension," he recalled.

Stephen Biddle, a defense expert at the Council on Foreign Relations, later said that going in, he had half-expected the session to be a photo opportunity, intended to demonstrate that the president did indeed talk to smart outsiders. Instead he found the tone of the hour-long meeting to be open, even confrontational. "It was obvious that the president and Cheney were taking this seriously," he said. "The president had a drawn face, was very subdued, looked depressed."

Cohen was determined to be clearer and more emphatic than he had been the previous June at Camp David. "Mister President, I'm going to be very blunt," he began. "I don't mean to cause offense, but this is wartime, and I feel I owe it to you." He also owed it to his own family and friends: Not only were many of his former students at Johns Hopkins University's School of Advanced International Studies military officers on duty in Iraq, so was his own son, a recent Harvard graduate who deployed there as an Army lieutenant specializing in military intelligence.

This time Cohen hit the issue of generalship squarely. It was high time to get a new team and a new strategy in Iraq, he advised. "It's not enough to say these are good guys—of course they are good guys. The question is, are they the *right* guys?" He said he didn't think so. He urged the president to hold them accountable.

He also talked about how presidents need to push their military advisers. "Generals disagree, sometimes profoundly," he said, citing a lesson he knew both from his academic work and from his time assessing Iraq for the Defense Policy Board. "Civilian leaders need to discover these disagreements, force them to the surface, and probe them. This is what Lincoln and Roosevelt did. LBJ's failure in Vietnam was not micromanagement, but failure to force serious strategic debate." Cohen, who is steeped in military history, was on solid ground in rejecting the conventional wisdom that President Johnson's error had been to meddle too much. Retired Army Brig. Gen. Douglas Kinnard, who surveyed Army generals who served in Vietnam for his study *The War Managers,* wrote that it is possible to argue that "there was not enough civilian participation in terms of asking the big questions about what we were really doing in Vietnam." As Cohen himself had pointed out in *Supreme Command,* during World War II, Winston Churchill also injected himself into the smallest of issues, but while doing so he never lost hold of the big strategic picture.

Cohen, whom retired Gen. Barry McCaffrey, also at the meeting, sometimes called "Mr. Bow Tie," also questioned the nature of advice Casey was providing, in which the general sought to balance his needs in Iraq with the state of the Army. That wasn't Casey's job, Cohen said. There were plenty of people at the Pentagon paid to take care of the Army. Casey's mission was very different, he said. His job was to win the war. "Not all generals are up to the task," he advised, knowing, for example, that well over a dozen division commanders had been relieved during World War II. Yet the Bush administration handled its generals as though they were all equally successful, interchangeable parts. "Not a single general has been removed for ineffectiveness during the course of this war." The Army needed a push here, he noted. "The current promotion system does not take into account actual effectiveness in counterinsurgency. We need not great guys but *effective* guys. Routine promotion and assignment systems for generals in wartime is a disaster."

Keane, speaking second, was also emphatic. "Mister President, to my mind, this is a major crisis," he began. "Time is running out." We need more troops, he said. And more important, he continued, we need to use them differently. "For the first time, we will secure the population, which is the proven way to defeat an insurgency," he explained. "In time the troops will be more secure, but I can't hide from you that the casualties will initially go up. In any counteroffensive operation that we have ever done, from Normandy to the island-hopping campaign in the Pacific, Inchon in Korea, multiple ones in Vietnam, casualties always go up, because you are bringing more troops and more firepower to bear on the problem."

To Keane's surprise, the two other retired generals at the meeting, McCaffrey and Wayne Downing, disagreed with his call for an escalation, while the two academics there, Cohen and Stephen Biddle, supported it.

"No more U.S. forces," argued Downing.

McCaffrey explained why. "Sir, I have known Jack Keane since we were young officers," he began. "I have great admiration for him. But this so-called surge is a fool's errand. Yes, it will have a short-term impact. But it isn't sustainable. The solution is Iraqi forces." But even as he spoke, McCaffrey began to suspect that the president really wasn't listening to his view and had already made up his mind. Indeed, a study of personnel-mobilization issues associated with the surge done by William Luti, a staffer on the National Security Council, already had concluded that a surge was doable both in terms of the effect it would have on readiness and on how long the troops would stay. "I think it went in one ear and went out the other," McCaffrey said later. "I don't think the president was listening. Cheney was—he was taking extensive notes."

Bush asked them what to do with the advice, especially about selecting generals. "All well and good, but how am I supposed to know, and who I am supposed to pick?" Bush responded, according to Biddle, who spoke last.

"David Petraeus," said Cohen. His thinking, he recalled was that "all armies get it wrong at the beginning, as [the great British military historian] Michael Howard says—the question is who adapts fastest." Cohen believed that Petraeus was the general who while serving in Iraq had best shown the ability to adapt. Keane and McCaffrey seconded the idea. (McCaffrey believes he was first to mention the name, but others disagree.) All the invitees were in accord that Petraeus was the only serious candidate for the job.

Then why is he disliked by some people at the Pentagon? Bush asked, apparently referring to some supposed friction between Petraeus and Rumsfeld, who liked to be the smartest person in the room.

Don't worry about that, the participants said. "You got to go with this guy," McCaffrey responded, with Keane supporting him.

Cheney asked only one question during the session. As it ended, McCaffrey watched as the vice president took Keane down the hall with him, which he thought confirmed his hunch that "the fix was in." Asked about this, Keane said that he was just going to his existing appointment with Cheney to go through the details of how a new counterinsurgency strategy might be implemented in Iraq.

Not long after, Keane got a call from a White House official telling him that the meeting had had a decisive impact on the president's thinking. A small group of NSC staffers had been pushing for a troop surge for weeks, pointing to the examples of Tall Afar and Ramadi. Now this group, which dubbed itself "the surgios," had been given ammunition by a respected group of outsiders.

Despite that, Bush continued to hold his cards close. He would say later in the month, "I haven't made up my mind yet about more troops."

THE COUNCIL OF COLONELS UNLOADS

Two days later, on Wednesday, December 13, Bush traveled to the Pentagon, where Gen. Pace briefed him on the ominous findings of the council of colonels.

Despite general discouragement, the group had been unable to find a consensus on the war, especially on whether to escalate. "The Air Force and Navy guys were clearly anti-surge. But Mansoor, H. R. McMaster, and the Marine, Colonel Greenwood, were for it," said one Pentagon official who worked with the council. These were the three most influential members of the council. After commanding a brigade in Baghdad, Peter Mansoor had become a counterinsurgency adviser to Petraeus at Fort Leavenworth. Tom Greenwood had served several years on the staff of the National Security Council and then done two tours commanding units in Iraq. H. R. McMaster was probably the most prominent colonel in the Army at this point. All three agreed with Keane: Put more troops into Iraq even if it means breaking the Army. That's what you do in war, this official said: "You serve the national interest."

Nor did Pace, the chairman of Joint Chiefs, who had ordered the study, settle the argument. "Passive Peter Pace, he was looking for the path of least resistance," this Pentagon official continued. "He brought no strategic vision, and no determined leadership—and the nation was at war. He is an honorable, genuinely nice man, but a tool for others."

The council ultimately recommended a small increase in forces, but nothing like the surge that eventually would occur. Yet the group's minority view in favor of a bigger escalation, although put aside at the time, ultimately would have more staying power and impact, because its leading advocates, Mansoor and McMaster, would be asked by Petraeus to come to Iraq. The colonels' group, along with the barrage of pointed criticism being gathered for the development of the counterinsurgency manual, played a little noticed but helpful role in civil-military relations: Together they quashed the growing view among officers that the U.S. military had performed marvelously in Iraq but had been let down by the rest of the government, the Congress, the media, and the American people. "There had been a 'stab in the back' school emerging, but then there was a point at which the Army turned introspective and said, 'You know, we can do this better,'" said Lt. Col. Paul Yingling, a veteran of three tours in Iraq.

It wasn't quite put to Bush in such blunt terms at the Pentagon meeting, but the council of colonels had concluded that the United States had invaded Iraq on the basis of a series of flawed assumptions—that Bush and others wrongly assumed that it would be a war of liberation, that Iraqis would take over power quickly, and that the country would remain more or less orderly, with a functioning police force. Likewise, the Bush administration was operating on some assumptions that badly needed to be examined. Can the Iraqi government survive? Is it under the control of Iran? Does it have staying power? Are Iraqi Security Forces truly a national institution? Will they crack if the civil war spreads and deepens? Will neighboring powers, especially Iran, become more involved in Iraq? And, most important of all, are we past the point of no return? If so, how do we reposition ourselves to minimize the damage? If not, what do we do next? Does anybody in Iraq believe we will stick around? The point was that until these questions were thought through, the United States wouldn't have a strategy; it would have only aspirations.

Those sharp questions weren't put to Bush, but the group's findings were. Even those conclusions were a sharp departure from Bush administration policy. Iraq was indeed in a "low-grade" civil war, the colonels said, and on the path to a bigger one. "We are losing because we are not winning and time is not on our side," they flatly stated, according to the document summarizing their work. Their warning that Iraq was experiencing "an intensifying civil war" was a finding that both the Pentagon and the White House had long resisted. (The slide containing these key findings on the Iraq war appears in this book's photo insert.)

The colonels also pointed to a basic problem with the approach then in place: "Current . . . troop strength was inadequate to secure the population (cannot execute 'clear, hold and build')." In other words, the Americans were trying to implement a strategy for which they hadn't devoted enough people. The point of that finding, recalled Greenwood, the Marine colonel who was a member of the council, was that, "unless troop levels were increased dramatically, the U.S. strategy would remain bankrupt."

The report amounted to a blinking red light for the U.S. effort in Iraq. Either the strategy had to change or more resources had to be devoted to making the current strategy more plausible. In any event, the colonels were saying, we should not try to stay the course. "In every measurable category we were failing, and in fact we were on the path to defeat," summarized Mansoor, another member of the group.

The colonels had split over the way forward. Mansoor advocated sending more troops as part of a plan to eventually have a long-term but smaller U.S. military presence in Iraq, an approach he called "Go Long." But the majority of the group, and especially its members from the Air Force and Navy, opposed the idea of a broad escalation—that is, a troop surge. "What the group said was, if we spike, it should be for a specified purpose, in order to, say, take down the Jaysh al-Mahdi in Sadr City," Mansoor said, referring to Moqtada al-Sadr's Shiite extremist militia, also known as "JAM." "They would have opposed just an increase in counterinsurgency forces." Even more broadly, there were doubts in the group about whether the U.S. military really had enough troops available to escalate sufficiently to make a difference.

The council had laid three choices before the Joint Chiefs of Staff. "The options we had were 'Go Big,' 'Go Long,' and 'Go Home,'" said Mansoor, who was one of the group's most influential members. His "Go Long" approach eventually would become U.S. policy.

The next day, Thursday, December 14, Keane and Kagan went to give a more detailed briefing to Cheney. Being a former defense secretary, Cheney asked questions that were informed and precise. But being Cheney, he gave away very little. "I didn't get any feedback," Kagan shrugged.

Military resistance was still running high after the pair's two White House meetings. Underscoring that, the next day Keane and Kagan were scheduled to fly down to Central Command's rear headquarters in Tampa, Florida. At the last minute, with their tickets in hand, they were told that their visit was canceled. They were offered no explanation. Treating a respected four-star general such as Keane in that backhanded way was a strong indication of how the military chain of command felt about having its thinking second-guessed by White House staffers, think tankers, and a retired general.

Indeed, Casey, still in place as the top American commander in Iraq, would argue for another two weeks against a big troop increase. He didn't know that he already had lost both the debate and his job. He had been planning to leave Iraq in the spring, but was told in December that he was being moved out in just a few weeks. "I left not really understanding what the hell had happened." Even in 2008, he added, "The whole process with the surge and how that came to be" remained murky to him. Bush told others that he didn't want to appear to be blaming Casey for executing a strategy that the president had approved, so Casey was to be given a "soft landing." The general would be named Army chief of staff—ironically, the same position given Gen. William Westmoreland upon his removal from command of a failing war in Vietnam in 1968.

A few days later, Vice President Cheney called Keane and asked if he would consider coming back on active duty and taking command in Iraq. Keane declined but said he was close to Petraeus, and knew and liked Odierno, and was willing to travel to Iraq as needed to advise both generals. This outcome was a victory for Keane, but it raised troubling questions about the ability of the chairman of the Joint Chiefs of Staff and his peers at the Pentagon to carry out their mission of figuring out how to fight and win. "Why did the American military establishment so fail to come up with a war-winning strategy that it was up to a retired general and a civilian think tank, AEI, to do their job?" asked retired Army Col. Bob Killebrew. "This is a stunning indictment of the American military's top leadership."

SADDAM IN THE AIR

Before dawn on the morning of Saturday, December 30, Saddam Hussein was taken to the former headquarters of the Iraqi military intelligence service. As an official read aloud his death sentence, he interrupted, "Long live the people, long live jihad, and long live the nation." He added, "Down with the Persians and the Americans." The hangman arrived, and Saddam met with a Muslim cleric.

His bizarre ending was illicitly captured by someone in the room using a cellular phone camera. The condemned man, wearing a white shirt, black pants, and newly shined shoes, stepped to the gallows platform, his hands cuffed behind his back and his legs tied together. He appeared stone-faced, trying in his last act on earth to salvage whatever dignity he could from the day. A yellow noose was placed around his neck. It was Saddam's turn to be interrupted. Someone yelled, "Moqtada, Moqtada, Moqtada"—a shout of triumph invoking Moqtada al-Sadr, the radical Shiite cleric who rose to great power in the wake of the American invasion.

Saddam, who had never been free to witness the rise of Shiite power in post-Saddam Iraq, responded sarcastically: "Moqtada?"

"Go to hell," someone shouted.

"Long live Muhammed Bakr Sadr," someone else shouted, referring to Moqtada al-Sadr's uncle, a founder of the Dawa Party.

"The man is facing execution," pleaded Saddam's prosecutor, Munqith al-Faroun, who was also present. "Please don't."

Saddam dropped through the scaffold's trapdoor as more than one thousand pounds of torque snapped his neck. A few minutes later he was pronounced dead. In both its lethality and unruliness, the event was, somehow, a fitting end to 2006 in Iraq. (Two weeks later, when Saddam's half brother was hanged, his head came off, provoking more disapproval.)

But that worst year of the war had one more ugly day left in it. On New Year's Eve, two soldiers were killed by a roadside bomb while on patrol in Baqubah and a third was killed in Baghdad, eerily bringing the U.S. military death toll in the war to precisely 3,000.

4.

A STRATEGY IS BORN

(Winter 2006–7)

When he left Iraq at the end of his first tour of duty early in 2004, Raymond Odierno, then a major general, had believed the war in Iraq was going well. "I thought we had beaten this thing," he said several years later, as he began his second tour. "I could walk down the streets of Kirkuk, Tikrit, Baqubah, Samarra. I can't do that now." Returning in the fall of 2006 on a preliminary trip as a lieutenant general, a corps commander preparing to take command of the day-to-day operations of the war, he was stunned by how much worse Iraq felt. In the two big operations to improve security in Baghdad, "They had cleared areas but were unable to hold them."

He also began to worry that he was being set up to suffer defeat on his watch. "I felt like we were in the process of leaving, no matter what the consequence," he said in one of a series of candid interviews. "I felt very disconcerted about that, because I had no control over that."

Oiderno's strongest trait is determination. After that preliminary visit, he returned to his base at Fort Hood, Texas, thinking about how not to lose the war. On November 28, 2006, he and his key staff began the long flight from Texas to Iraq. Maj. James Powell, whose longish shock of hair combed sideways lent him a resemblance to a 1940s W. H. Auden, was exhausted and went to sleep. Somewhere over the Atlantic, Powell opened his eyes to see his boss, Col. Martin Wilson, the head of the corps' planning office, standing before him and staring at him. Wilson had come to Powell directly from a conversation with Odierno, who had given him and his other key staff officers these orders: Come up with a plan to retake Baghdad.

"When I got here, the situation was fairly desperate, frankly," Odierno said. "The only thing I thought would decisively change it was doing something in Baghdad, and the only way to do that was to increase forces. I didn't know if it would work."

If Jack Keane was the spiritual godfather of the surge, Odierno was its biological parent. Petraeus, arriving in Baghdad two months later, would become its adoptive father. In order to position the U.S. for a new strategy—that is, get additional brigades and use them differently—Odierno had to take on his direct superior, Gen. Casey, who in turn was backed by the entire chain of command. It is extraordinary to consider that the new strategy that would be implemented by the U.S. military in Iraq in 2007 was opposed by the U.S. military in both Baghdad and Washington. With the exception of Odierno, it came from outside the military establishment.

LT. GEN. RAYMOND ODIERNO

Odierno was an unlikely savior to appear in the midst of the Iraq war. There was little in his past to indicate that he would buck his entire chain of command and push the U.S. military in Iraq in a radically new direction. After growing up in New Jersey, he attended West Point and played varsity baseball there, most notably pitching against Ed Kranepool and Dave Kingman of the New York Mets in an exhibition game. He graduated in 1976 and became an artillery officer. He gained a reputation as the best of the conventional thinkers—intelligent, industrious, ambitious, and focused on using the tools the Army provided him, rather than discovering new and different ones. He deployed for the 1991 Gulf War and again for the Kosovo campaign eight years later.

During his first tour in Iraq, commanding the 4th Infantry Division in the middle of the Sunni Triangle in 2003–4, he and his subordinates earned a reputation as heavy-handed, kicking in doors and rounding up tens of thousands of "MAMs"—military-aged males. As I wrote in my book *Fiasco,* about the first three years of the Iraq war, when Brig. Gen. Barbara Fast, the top Army intelligence officer in Iraq, questioned the 4th ID's indiscriminate approach, she was told by its intelligence officer, according to a subsequent Army report, that Odierno didn't care. "The division commander did not concur with the release of detainees for fear that a bad one may be released along with the good ones," Maj. Gen. George Fay wrote.

Fast said in a statement to investigators that Odierno's attitude was "We wouldn't have detained them if we wanted them released." She asked retired Army Col. Stuart Herrington, a veteran intelligence officer specializing in interrogation, to review the way intelligence was gathered from detainees. Herrington concluded that some U.S. commanders, in seeking to shut down the insurgency in their areas of operations, were using tactics that effectively made them recruiting sergeants for it. Herrington was especially bothered by the actions of Odierno's division. "Principally due to sweep operations by some line units—the 4th ID was consistently singled out as the major offender—the number of detainees" was rising steadily, he wrote in his report to Fast. He emphasized that point five pages later: "Some divisions are conducting operations with rigorous detention criteria, while some—the 4th ID is the negative example—are sweeping up large numbers of people and dumping them at the door of Abu Ghraib."

"Odierno, he hammered everyone," said retired Army Lt. Gen. Joseph Kellogg Jr., who was serving with the U.S. occupation authority in Baghdad.

"The 4th ID was bad," said an Army intelligence officer who worked with them. "These guys are looking for a fight," he remembered thinking. "I saw so many instances of abuses of civilians, intimidating civilians, our jaws dropped."

Lt. Col. David Poirier, who commanded a military police battalion attached to the 4th ID, said he found the division's approach to be indiscriminate. "It became a philosophy, 'Round up all the military-age males, because we won't know who's good or bad.' "

Col. Alan King had a similar view that the division helped the insurgency. "Every male from sixteen to sixty" that the division caught was detained, he said, "and when they got out, they were supporters of the insurgency."

A subsequent review by the Army inspector general said interrogators reported "detainees arriving at the cage badly beaten. Many beatings occurred after the detainees were zip-tied by some units in 4ID. Some units wouldn't take THTs [Tactical Human-Intelligence Teams] on raids because they didn't want oversight of activities that might cross the line during capture."

The most striking instance of abuse in Odierno's division occurred in January 2004, when some 4th ID soldiers forced two handcuffed detainees to jump into the Tigris River. One reportedly drowned. Lt. Col. Nathan Sassaman, their battalion commander, believed, as he put it later, that "we had to convince the Iraqi people that they should fear us more than they feared the insurgents." He obstructed Army investigators trying to determine what happened with the detainees at the Tigris. Lt. Jack Saville would testify at his court-martial that he had discussed with Sassaman how to mislead those investigators. Despite that, Sassaman received only a written admonishment from his commanding general. "On 7 January 2004, you were briefed . . . that soldiers of the 1st platoon pushed two Iraqi men into the Tigris River causing one of them to drown," Odierno wrote. "You ordered them to deny that the men were pushed into the river and to say that they were dropped off at the side of the road. Your conduct was wrongful, criminal and will not be tolerated."

Despite that conclusion, Odierno let Sassaman remain in command of the battalion for months, an outcome that shocked Poirier. "When you have a battalion commander who leads his staff in rehearsing a story about a murder—and he's still in command?" Poirier said. "That's not right."

It isn't clear what led Odierno to reconsider his approach. He spoke at Basin Harbor, an academic conference on counterinsurgency run by Eliot Cohen in June 2005, and left the experts on the subject there distinctly unimpressed. He began by congratulating those present for holding such a conference because, he said, according to several participants, "we in the Army don't think that much about counterinsurgency"—a comment that provoked some eye rolling. "He indicated he knew there were different ways of dealing with insurgency but also showed he was not certain that population-centered COIN was the way to do it," said retired Marine Col. T. X. Hammes, one of the specialists who attended the meeting. In comments the following morning, some said they found him utterly conventional and so not really focused on the task at hand in Iraq.

Between his first and second tours in Iraq, Odierno served as assistant to the chairman of the Joint Chiefs of Staff, a position that has evolved into being the role of the U.S. military's ambassadorship to the rest of the national security establishment. For example, the general holding the job frequently accompanies the secretary of state on overseas travel, in order to provide a military perspective as needed and also to keep the Pentagon attuned to U.S. diplomacy. This may have been the work that best prepared Odierno for the role he would play later in Iraq, as it broadened his view and acquainted him with the personalities and levers of power at State, CIA, and the White House. Notably, this was during a period when a schism was developing inside the government about the trend in

Iraq, with State and CIA being far more pessimistic than the military or the White House. Odierno would return to Iraq fully aware that many well-informed officials thought the war was going badly, far worse than the White House, or even the generals in Baghdad, seemed to understand.

Odierno was prepared, even determined, to operate differently on his second tour of duty in Iraq. "I think that before, he thought that through force you could achieve anything in the world," said Emma Sky, a pacificistic British woman who would have an important role on his staff the following year. "I think he now has a much more sophisticated understanding of how society works," she said. "I think he's learned a tremendous amount." Still she said she didn't agree with how his time commanding the 4th ID was portrayed in *Fiasco.* She didn't believe, she said, "that he somehow has turned from an ogre into a good man."

He didn't much want to talk about how his transformation occurred, brushing aside the question. "I think everyone's changed," he said. "We've all learned. We came in here not thinking about counterinsurgency." He didn't like to dwell on those old errors, but sometimes in discussing details of current operations, he would refer to them. "One of the mistakes we made early on—and one of the mistakes I made—was not understanding the importance of the tribes." He also pointedly and ruefully remembered being told by one of his superior officers in May 2003 that the fighting likely would last as long as 45 days. Odierno gives the impression that he doesn't much care what reporters and politicians think about him, but very much what his peers in the Army do.

Part of the change may stem from his knowledge that he most likely would be reporting to Petraeus, who had been steeped in counterinsurgency theory. Odierno is "a good leader, charismatic, and a tactically competent soldier," said Donnelly, the defense expert at the American Enterprise Institute. "I think that intellectually, he has learned from his mistakes. And I think that working for Petraeus makes all the difference in the world. It is very different from working for [Lt. Gen.] Sanchez and getting no education."

Another impetus to change, Odierno agreed in an interview, was the severe wounding of his son in August 2004. Lt. Anthony Odierno, then in the 1st Cavalry Division, had been leading a patrol near Baghdad's airport when a rocket-propelled grenade punched through the door of his Humvee, severed his left arm, and then mortally wounded his driver. "It didn't affect me as a military officer, I mean that," Odierno said one evening in Baghdad much later. "It affected me as a person. I hold no grudges. My son and I talked a lot about this. He was doing what he wanted to do, and liked what he was doing." But he said it did deepen his determination. "I was going to see this through—I felt an obligation to see this through. That drives me, frankly. I feel an obligation to mothers and fathers. Maybe I understand it better because it happened to me."

But the most important part of it was likely the growing recognition in the fall of 2006, as he prepared to redeploy, that the war was heading toward defeat, and it might occur on his watch. He didn't want to lose and realized that meant taking on his new boss, Casey. On a predeployment trip to Iraq in August, he had been told that the plan was to cut combat troop levels by as much as one-third in 2007. On December 4, he was briefed on the plan he would be implementing, called the Bridging Strategy, which of course was referred to in U.S. military circles as "TBS."

This was an all-important briefing for Odierno, because it amounted to his overarching orders for the next year. Officially, his job was not to assess and challenge these goals, but to figure out how to achieve them. The key points were:

- "Move outside all major cities" and establish a handful of even bigger bases along key roads leading into Iraq,
- deploy U.S. forces to Iraq's borders in order to limit outside influence,
- speed up the transition to Iraqi security forces, and
- let Iraqis handle fighting in the cities.

Together this plan (the briefing is reprinted in the appendix) amounted to a half withdrawal, not leaving Iraq but hanging on its periphery. The more Odierno and his planners considered this plan, they less they liked it. They feared that it got ahead of the ability of the Iraqis to do the job, and so, in keeping with the American pattern in Iraq from 2003 on, would likely amount to one more rush to failure. He was, he recalled, "very nervous" about the course of U.S. strategy. He decided he would formally oppose any additional troop cuts. He wasn't even thinking about a surge, because, he said, "I didn't think I could get more."

After taking command in December, Odierno and a small group of advisers met almost every night for several weeks, trying to figure a way out of the jam. Ultimately, they would decide on a course almost the opposite of the plan given them. Instead of moving out of the cities, they would deploy more into them.

Instead of consolidating their base structure, they would establish scores of smaller outposts. Nor would they withdraw to the borders. And most emphatically, they would slow the transition to Iraqi forces. He realized that to take all those steps he would need more troops—something Keane had been telling him in telephone calls. "Odierno was standing up to Casey, and he deserves a lot of credit for it," said Keane, who was trying to get to Iraq. "I was trying to go see him, but Casey wouldn't let me come in." Keane called Casey directly, but the general put him off, saying, "It's a really bad time."

Petraeus also was talking to Odierno about the notion of a major increase in troops. When Casey got wind of it, he had his executive officer call Petraeus with a message: "Hey, man, don't be calling Ray." Petraeus responded that he had been asked by the chairman of the Joint Chiefs to look at Iraq and so needed to talk to senior officers there.

By mid-December it was clear to subordinates that Casey and Odierno were at odds. "Casey fought it all the way," recalled Brig. Gen. Joe Anderson, Odierno's chief of staff. Planners were beginning to scratch their heads. Odierno was telling them to figure out how they might employ several brigades. "We would backbrief one general and get one set of guidances, and then brief the other and get a different set," remembered one senior Army planner in Iraq.

Keane, who was talking to Odierno once or twice a week by telephone, told Odierno that he should ask for five brigades. But when Odierno raised that number with Casey, his commander threw cold water on the notion. "He said, 'You can do it with two brigades,'" Odierno recalled. "I said, 'I don't know.'" Casey eventually said that they could deploy only one brigade a month anyway, so he would commit to two brigades, and then make a decision about each additional one. Casey's notion, coming off the disappointment of the Together Forward operations the previous summer, was to stiffen the backbone of Iraqi forces operating in Baghdad by putting them in some joint outposts with American troops. He figured it would take about two U.S. brigades—perhaps 7,500 soldiers—to do that. He wasn't particularly interested in the other three brigades.

Hearing about the two-plus-three compromise, Keane first hit the roof and then called the White House. Odierno "started with one brigade, and Casey was fighting him over the first brigade," Keane recalled, "and then he finally gave him one. And then he fought for a second one and then they came up with this godforsaken strategy of having three on hold in the U.S. and advancing them one at a time as needed, advance to Kuwait and then go from Kuwait to Baghdad. I knew what was going on here. Its pretty obvious—Casey doesn't want his strategy dramatically changed."

Keane, believing that Casey's incremental approach was unsound both militarily and politically, warned Hadley, the national security adviser, that having three units on hold would mean that there would be a separate debate about each one being sent. "Just think about what's going to happen," he told Hadley. "You are not going to be effective in bringing down the violence with only two additional brigades, therefore you will call for an additional brigade three separate times, each time because we do not have sufficient troops. The media will be all over you for failing three more times. Meanwhile, the president is going to bite this bullet; he should only bite it once. He shouldn't bite it one time and then three more times."

Hadley agreed: "Yeah, this makes no sense."

Keane told White House officials that "there was a huge struggle going on inside the command." He also broke the news to Hadley that the surge wouldn't conclude by midsummer. "Can we get that wrapped up in, what, five or six months?" he recalled Hadley asking him. "That'll be the summer and we can hold on to the wobbly Republicans because we've made some progress."

Hell no, Keane responded. "It will take all that time to get them in there.... It's going to take twelve to eighteen months before we can realistically start reducing these forces."

Odierno told his planners to think about how they would use five additional brigades of combat troops. The planners were puzzled—they didn't think he would ever be given that many. They didn't know how he had come up with that number. "That stuff just kind of shows up," said Lt. Col. Jeff McDougall, one of his top planners. "You don't know, sitting in our little dungeon, where that stuff comes from."

One day in December, Odierno told his planners, "We have to secure the population, first thing. We have to get back out into Baghdad." They and Odierno thought that they really needed about eight brigades but knew that no more than five were available, and that it would take months to get them all to Iraq. Odierno thought that the shortfall could be made up somewhat by adding other, smaller units, such as Marine battalions, a helicopter squadron, and some Special Operations troops.

Casey's resistance was being supported by the chief of the Army and other members of the Joint Chiefs of Staff. The notion of escalation had been floating around, and most of the chain of command was against the idea. "I was not supportive at the time because of several concerns that I had," said Gen. Pete Schoomaker, the then chief of staff of the Army. "First, that no one had articulated or had established a clear purpose for the surge, including how to know when that purpose had been achieved." Also, he thought it would hurt the readiness of the Army without any clear payoff.

Casey finally agreed to an increase of two Army brigades and two Marine battalions, plus one more brigade on tap in Kuwait, recalled Maj. Gen. Barbero, who at the time was watching from the Pentagon as the J-33, or deputy director for current operations, for the staff of the Joint Chiefs. (A brigade has about 3,500 soldiers, while a Marine infantry battalion has about 750.) This was more or less where the council of colonels had come out. Barbero thought it was exactly the wrong answer and said so at Pentagon meetings. "This is the worst course of action we could do," he argued, "enough to put a strain on the force, but not enough to do anything."

Barbero had once commanded a battalion in the 101st Airborne, and he also was talking to his old division commander, Jack Keane. "He was the first person I heard the number five brigades from," he said. And, typical of the web of personal connections that every military career produces, he also had been the assistant commander of the 4th Infantry Division from 2003–4—serving under Raymond Odierno.

As Odierno's planners worked on a big surge, the political context of the war began to change—and that tipped the balance in their favor. Back in Washington, the Iraq Study Group recommended accelerating the American turnover to Iraqis. This was far different than what Odierno was advocating but was pretty much what Casey had told him to do, except faster—that is, get U.S. forces out of combat and speed the transition to Iraqi security forces. The biggest difference was that the group recommended a tighter deadline, of getting U.S. combat forces out by early 2008.

But, coming just a month after the November 2006 elections, the political effect of the Iraq Study Group may have been more significant. "The situation in Iraq is grave and deteriorating," began its report, released on December 6. This grim finding, the consensus view of political and military experts from across the spectrum, ultimately was the real contribution of the group. "It stopped all the happy talk about how well things were going and how the press was reporting it wrong," noted former defense secretary Perry, one of its members.

Just before the elections, the president had said, "Absolutely, we're winning." On December 6, the same day that the Iraq Study Group released its report, a new defense secretary, Robert Gates, who had been a member until his nomination, was confirmed by the Senate. He was sworn in December 18. The next day, Gates's first full one at the Pentagon, President Bush said for the first time, "We're not winning, we're not losing in Iraq"—a striking turnaround from his formulation the previous month. (He also said that he was planning even before the election to replace Rumsfeld.) A month later, the president would go another step and say that the course he was on in 2006 was "maybe a slow failure."

Gates is a surprising man. The white-haired former CIA director is calm, quiet, and soft-voiced, reserved almost to the point of seeming humble—a presentation that blurs his tough-minded nature. One key to his nature is an observation he offers in his 1996 memoir, *From the Shadows,* that some of the most effective U.S. officials he had seen were Henry Kissinger, Zbigniew Brzezinski, and George Shultz. The commonality among them, he concluded, was that they were "basically hawks who drew extensively on the ideas and initiatives of the doves."

In office Gates would prove both less windy and more decisive than his predecessor. "The interesting thing about Rumsfeld is that he didn't make decisions," defense expert Anthony Cordesman said after Rumsfeld's firing. Referring to the defense secretary during the Vietnam War to whom Rumsfeld was often likened, he added, "McNamara at least made decisions. Rumsfeld micromanaged, but he didn't make decisions." Gates also would bring a skeptical view of the Iraq war shaped by his time on the Iraq Study Group. He had been at the Pentagon just two days when Gen. Abizaid, the head of Central Command, announced that he planned to retire a few months later. "He was told, 'It's time to go, we need some fresh air here,'" recalled an officer who was at Centcom at the time. Abizaid disputes that, saying that he had submitted his request to retire months earlier, and that it had been approved by Rumsfeld.

In any event, it would soon become evident that behind the new defense secretary's slight smile lurked a very sharp set of teeth. In the spring of 2007, he would fire Army secretary Francis Harvey and the Army surgeon general over their sluggish handling of a scandal about the poor treatment of recuperating soldiers at the Walter Reed Army Medical Center. That June, he would ease out the chairman of the Joint Chiefs, Gen. Pace, who at that point was the last senior military figure associated with the botched handling of the first three years of the war who was still in office. In March 2008, he would throw overboard Adm. William "Fox" Fallon, Abizaid's successor. Three months later he would simultaneously oust the Air Force chief of staff and the Air Force secretary over lapses in that service's handling of nuclear weapons. He executed these decisions in a soft-spoken way, showing no emotion. It was the opposite of Rumsfeld, who barked but appeared to have no bite.

Indeed, Gates was greeted as a liberator at the Pentagon simply because he wasn't Rumsfeld. "You can already feel the stability," said retired Air Force Gen. Charles Wald, formerly the deputy U.S. commander in Europe, who deemed the appointment of Gates to be the Bush administration's best move in years.

In the following months, he would be greeted with similar relief in Baghdad. "He seems to be just about everything you want in a sec def," said Charlie Miller, an aide to Petraeus in 2007 who would sit in on several video-teleconferences with Gates. "It's too bad we didn't have him from the get-go, instead of the other guy."

The day after Gates took office, he asked Petraeus to come talk to him about Iraq. "I'm going to Iraq in two hours," the new defense secretary said. "What should I look for?"

Petraeus had been thinking for months about the war and about how to change it. He had been talking to staff members on the National Security Council, among others, and also had "reviewed very carefully the AEI findings" from the exercise that Kagan and Keane had done. So when Gates asked, he was ready. Both men understood that the context of the conversation was that Petraeus was being considered for top command in Iraq, and at a crucial time. "You should focus on whether or not the approach is working," Petraeus said. "Get a sense of whether the emphasis on transition to ISF [Iraqi Security Forces] is working or not," and also on whether that emphasis is "appropriate, given the level of violence."

Another thing that emerged in the conversation was that the two men shared a preference for candid, even blunt assessments that would lead to strategic clarity. Both understood the need for more precision about the U.S. mission in Iraq.

Gates had another question. Zalmay Khalilzad, then the U.S. ambassador in Iraq, had concurred with an intelligence assessment that the U.S. effort was failing. What, Gates asked, did Petraeus think of that? I haven't been in Iraq for a while, Petraeus responded, but from what I can tell, it is correct.

Then Gates left for Iraq, bringing with him Gen. Pace. In Baghdad he met with Abizaid, Casey, and Odierno. The first two generals were at loggerheads with Odierno, the newer, younger, and junior officer pushing hard for more troops. Gates was soft-voiced and guarded. He listened but gave no indication of which way was he was leaning. Anderson, Odierno's chief of staff, recalled that Pace offered the whiff of a possibility of meeting Odierno's request. "What if we gave you more?" he asked in a meeting. "What if we gave you five brigade combat teams?" He seemed to be asking if they really had anything to show: What makes you guys smarter than Casey, Abizaid, and the Joint Chiefs of Staff?

Gates, to his credit, also breakfasted with a group of young soldiers and found far more agreement there on the need for more manpower. "Never mind all the generals standing around," he began, according to a tape recording of the meeting, which reporters didn't attend. While Odierno and Pace listened, Spec. Jason Glenn, a drone aircraft operator for the 1st Infantry Division, told him that when he flew his aircraft over insurgents, they would just look up at it, "so I really think we need more troops here, with more presence on the ground. More troops might hold them off long enough to where we can get the Iraqi army trained up."

Pfc. Cassandra Wallace seconded that view. "I think we do need more troops over here," the Texan said. "More troops would help us integrate the Iraqi army into patrols more."

On the long flight home to Washington in a C-17 military cargo jet, Gates disappeared into his mobile home in the jet's belly with Gen. Pace and a bottle of California cabernet sauvignon. A few days later, Odierno got the word: Gates wants you to have all five brigades. "The surge really began the day that Gates visited," Odierno later concluded.

But the issue was still in the air. While Gates and Pace were traveling, Bush gave an interview to the *Washington Post* in which he began by emphasizing his intention to increase the size of the Army and Marine Corps. "The reason why is, it is an accurate reflection that this ideological war we're in is going to last for a while, and that we're going to need a military that's capable of being able to sustain our efforts," Bush explained. It was an odd statement to make, coming more than five years after the 9/11 attack. Yet it hinted at the major strategic shift the president was contemplating: dropping the pattern of overoptimistic assumptions and instead moving to a strategy for long wars in Iraq and Afghanistan.

When Pace got back to the Pentagon, he sent down word to analyze how to get two to five additional brigades into Iraq, in terms of both transportation and troop availability. Barbero, on the Joint Staff, received the assignment. He liked the idea. "We're finally going to try to do something more than just hold on until the Iraqis can take over," he thought.

Lt. Col. Charlie Miller, then working under Barbero, was surprised. Two weeks earlier, he recalled, neither the Pentagon nor the U.S. headquarters in Iraq had been particularly interested in a surge. In fact, when Casey's command had been asked, he said, its response had been indifferent: "Sure, you can send an extra brigade or two, if you want." The new order was "interesting," he said, because the impetus clearly "didn't come from inside the building. And it didn't come from Iraq."

Even as Odierno's planners were fleshing out the plan in late December, they secretly thought there was no way they were going to get five brigade combat teams, or BCTs. There was good reason to doubt it. Pace, who as the top U.S. military officer was the president's direct adviser of military affairs, still wasn't signed on to a full surge. Just after Christmas he flew to Texas to see the president at his ranch in Crawford and proposed the compromise of sending two brigades, plus keeping three more on tap ready to go.

Keane had gotten wind of this odd "minisurge." He also heard that Pace was telling officers on the Joint Staff who thought that two brigades was insufficient, "Don't tell me what is wrong with this plan, tell me how to sell it at Crawford." Keane called John Hannah, who had replaced the disgraced Scooter Libby as Cheney's national security adviser, and told him that "the force level you are going to see presented at Crawford is inadequate and destined to fail." He asked Hannah to give this question to Cheney or Bush to pose to Pace: "Is this a decisive force to succeed?" Privately, Keane thought that Odierno and Pace really needed eight to ten brigades, but he knew that only five could be made available.

After the Crawford meeting, Keane got a call from a White House official: You'll get the five Army brigades, plus two Marine battalions. It would amount to about 20,000 additional combat soldiers and eventually would include another 8,000 support troops.

Pace returned to the Pentagon with a new urgency. Rather than the cool response he heard weeks earlier in discussions of the surge, Miller, the Joint Staff officer, recalled, it was, "Hey, we need to do this *today*."

The planners in Baghdad suddenly found themselves hit by an avalanche of RFIs—requests for information. Officials at the White House, the office of the Secretary of Defense, and the staff of the Joint Chiefs were bypassing several echelons in the chain of command to call Odierno's headquarters directly and ask colonels there a question they now considered crucial: What would you do if you had more troops? Frequently those officers in Baghdad would zip back a quick e-mail—and only later realized how much influence they were having. "We would get a ping," said Maj. Kent Strader, "we'd respond, and twenty-four to forty-eight hours later, it would show up in the national debate."

They also were getting questions for which they had no answers. "They would ask, you'll get one brigade a month, where will it go?" said Maj. Powell, one of Odierno's planners. "We didn't know. It would depend on the evolving situation on the ground."

WWSHD?

Once it was decided that the surge would have five brigades, the question was what to do with them. The plan devised at the American Enterprise Institute under Kagan's purview had been simply to flood Baghdad with troops. "The Kagan plan had four brigades going into the city, two or three into Anbar, and none into the 'belts,'" or the areas surrounding Baghdad, said Powell, the planner. The plan as ultimately implemented would be more nuanced. The seed had been planted with Odierno by his next-door neighbor back at Fort Hood, Maj. Gen. James Thurman, who had commanded the U.S. troops in Baghdad in 2005–6. In a series of conversations, Thurman had passed along two lessons: Don't give up any ground and do something about the car bombs coming into the capital from the surrounding countryside.

Odierno laid down several new principles to his planners:

- This wouldn't be just Baghdad. He told the planners to figure out how to cut the roads, dirt paths, and riverways the bombers used to move into the city, what the military calls the "lines of communication." His decision was influenced not just by Thurman, but also by heeding the revelations of generals who worked for Saddam Hussein. American analysts, studying the deployment of Republican Guard troops in 2002–3 outside the capital to the areas west and south of it, had assumed that this was done to reduce the ability of commanders to launch a coup. No, they were told: The elite troops were kept there, rather than in Baghdad, because that was where the trouble was.

"I looked back: What would Saddam Hussein do?" Odierno said. "He would use Republican Guards to control those areas." So Odierno decided that, as much as possible, he would deal with the Baghdad belts as much as the city itself. As every one of the five surge brigades arrived, he would ask himself whether to use it in the city or in the belts. The first two went into the capital. The next three went mainly into areas around the city. Ultimately, the 21 battalions (five brigades plus some Marine units) that came in as part of the surge would be divided about evenly between Baghdad and its outskirts.

- Don't make a move unless your presence is sustainable, and once you take an area, don't leave it uncovered. "Don't give up terrain," he ordered his commanders. "Don't try to do too much." This emphasis on tactical patience was consistent with Petraeus's counterinsurgency manual, which had just been published in December but was new to the U.S. military in Iraq. "One principle I went by was that we would never give up anything we'd gained," Odierno said. "So when I wanted to move a unit [out of an area], I'd ask, Can the Iraqis hold it?" If the answer was probably not, the unit would stay put. This also meant that the counteroffensive would take much longer than the American Enterprise Institute planners had thought or Bush administration officials believed.
- In order to really protect the population, Odierno would have to go after more than just al Qaeda, because Shiite militias were intimidating Sunni civilians. Donnelly, a member of the AEI group, applauded the changes to the Kagan approach. "I don't think we thought beyond making the Baghdad security situation better and establishing a rationale for keeping the United States in the war."

In December, Odierno also went to visit Col. MacFarland to check out what he had heard about strange doings in Ramadi. He also looked up Sheikh Sittar, who was leading the turning of the tribes in al Anbar province away from al Qaeda and toward the Americans. "I spent quite a long time speaking with him, and he told me how his mind-set changed," he recalled. There was a lot of that going around.

PETRAEUS, MOVING AROUND Washington and the Army to explain his new manual, was also quietly looking at a new way to operate in Iraq. Lt. Col. Douglas Ollivant had coauthored an article the previous summer for the Army's *Military Review* advocating moving troops out into the population. Titled "Producing Victory: Re-thinking Conventional Forces in COIN Operations," it stated as a principle:

> For the local people to feel secure and provide intelligence, they must have 24-hour access to the counterinsurgent force. Units with control over an AOR [area of responsibility] should live in that neighborhood. . . . Having a fortress mentality simply isolates the counterinsurgent from the fight.

On January 9, Petraeus e-mailed Ollivant to ask two questions: "Do you still believe what you wrote in 'Producing Victory'? And can MND-B [the American headquarters for Baghdad] do it?"

Ollivant wrote back: "Yes, with caveats." He was in a position to know, having been for the previous 45 days the chief planner for the American division in Baghdad. Now he had top-level backing for the idea of putting outposts in the city.

In January 2007, Keane flew out to Baghdad and met with Odierno's planners for three hours. They were joined by some intelligence officers and H. R. McMaster. The purpose was to persuade Keane that it was crucial for the surge plan to deal with Baghdad belts, where they told him a fierce fight continued between Shiite expansionists and al Qaeda, which was casting itself as the defender of local Sunnis. They succeeded. At the end of the session there was a pause, recalled Wilson, Odierno's chief planner. Then Keane spoke. "He kind of got a glowing look in his face and said, 'You know, you folks get it.'" Keane's six-month fight to mount a counteroffensive was over. After this point, his role in the conduct of the war became smaller. As he put it, "They were in the execution phase." His job was done.

On the evening of January 10, Odierno's chief planner, Col. Wilson, went to his room in Camp Victory's military version of a trailer park and set his alarm for 5 A.M. As it rang, he rolled over in his bunk and reached out to switch on his small television. Half asleep, he watched President Bush tell the world about what Wilson and his office had written.

BUSH RISES TO THE OCCASION

As Col. Wilson watched in his aluminum hootch, George W. Bush delivered what may be remembered as the most impressive speech of his presidency. There was no dodging, no divisiveness, none of the brusque claims of extraordinary success that Vice President Cheney tended to fling about. Rather, as he stood awkwardly alone at a lectern in the White House library, Bush somberly accepted responsibility for a badly handled war, confessed that the course he had pursued hadn't worked, and laid out a clear new plan, differentiating it from past efforts.

He had looked, finally, into the abyss. "The situation in Iraq is unacceptable to the American people, and it is unacceptable to me," he said early on. "Our troops in Iraq have fought bravely. They have done everything we have asked them to do. Where mistakes have been made, the responsibility rests with me." This was exactly the right way to begin, setting the tone for everything that would follow. "It is clear that we need to change our strategy in Iraq," he continued, logically. He laid out with some precision how he envisioned it working, with a new Iraqi command structure for Baghdad and new Iraqi troops injected to conduct patrols and operate checkpoints.

Then he got to the news: To make this work, he said, he would send "more than twenty thousand additional troops to Iraq." It was only at this point that Col. Wilson and Odierno's planners really began to believe that they would get all five brigades. In fact, they would get more, as a helicopter brigade and support troops were added three months later, eventually pushing the total addition to nearly 30,000. The mission of those new forces, Bush continued, would be "to help Iraqis clear and secure neighborhoods, to help them protect the local population, and to help ensure that the Iraqi forces left behind are capable of providing the security that Baghdad needs." In other words, after more than four years of fighting, the "kill and capture" mind-set that had led to Haditha and to a losing effort was being replaced with classic counterinsurgency theory: The people are the prize.

Immediately, he addressed those who doubted his plan—the majority of his audience, according to polls taken after the speech. "Many listening tonight will ask why this effort will succeed when previous operations to secure Baghdad did not," he said. Using the word "listening" was a good touch, evoking the radio days of President Franklin Roosevelt's World War II "fireside chats," as when he confessed during the dismal days of February 1942, "We Americans have been compelled to yield ground, but we will regain it." The difference, unfortunately, was that FDR faced the hard facts three months into World War II, while it took Bush more than three years to reach a similar point in his strategic thinking.

Bush then laid out what he thought the difference was between the new effort and the failed Together Forward operations of 2006: "In earlier operations, Iraqi and American forces cleared many neighborhoods of terrorists and insurgents, but when our forces moved on to other targets, the killers returned." Also, he said, the Iraqi government had blocked some operations—a reference to putting Sadr City generally off limits, along with some other key targets across Baghdad. This time, Bush said, "Prime Minister Maliki has pledged that political or sectarian influence will not be tolerated."

He then turned to the political goals he envisioned: passing a law to share oil revenues, stepping up Iraqi spending on reconstruction, and holding provincial elections later in 2007. The assumption here was that improved security would lead to such political breakthroughs. This would prove to be the weakest part of a strong speech.

Turning back to security operations, he did the right thing in warning that "the year ahead [will be] bloody and violent."

He concluded with two other departures from the Bush administration's habitual approaches. Bush pledged to be flexible: "If circumstances change, we will adjust." And rather than question the integrity and patriotism of his opponents, labeling them as "cut and runners," Bush said that, "Honorable people have different views, and they will voice their criticisms."

At the end he said, "We go forward with trust that the Author of Liberty will guide us through these trying hours." That unusual reference to God resonated with evangelical Christians, who sometimes use the phrase, while the "trying hours" again subtly evoked FDR.

Bush effectively had turned over the fate of his presidency to Petraeus and Odierno. Over the next six months, he would mention Petraeus in speeches and press conferences at least 150 times. But he was at ease about the move. "At least from my perspective, the hardest part of making a big decision is the run-up to the decision," Bush would tell Bob Woodward. "But once you make up your mind, it's a liberating moment."

The moment felt different to others involved. In Baghdad, Odierno's planners felt as if they were in a twilight zone. "We were on the other side of history," said Powell. He explained that, "When you read history, you're on that side of it. When you realize you've contributed to history, you're on the other side of it."

Neither Keane nor Fred Kagan felt much joy. For Kagan, back in the United States, watching the speech on television at home with his wife, it was a similarly eerie moment. For a think tank analyst, he had achieved nirvana: An academic exercise he had held a month earlier had helped alter the American approach to a war, and the president was announcing that on national television. But he felt no elation. "We felt a burden," he said. "We felt very nervous." Also, he worried that the president was handling the changes the wrong way. He thought the speech went into too much tactical detail and also should have been postponed until Casey's replacement, Petraeus, was in place and had had a chance to review the plans.

The lack of clarity intensified the next day as Gates told the House Armed Services Committee that he thought the surge would be relatively short, "not eighteen months or two years." As it happened, he was incorrect—and many of those involved in planning the surge already knew it. Kagan's unease grew a few days later after Gen. Casey had taken one final pop at the plan, telling reporters that the surge might be over by "late summer," just six or so months later. "We were wigging out over that," Kagan said. "If you actually understood the nature of the task, you knew there was no way you could start bringing troops home in the summer."

In fact, the surge would last for eighteen months, with the last of the five additional brigades leaving Iraq only in the summer of 2008. What some insiders understood, but the president hadn't said and Gates didn't seem to grasp, was that the new strategy was a plan for a "long war." First would come increased security. Then would come political progress, and with it, the building of a reliable army and police force. And all that—if it worked—would take many, many years. In sum, the short war approach that the United States had followed for years had been abandoned. The U.S. military had arrived in Baghdad in April 2003 with the expectation of largely leaving by that September. For three years after that, commanders had planned variations on that swift exit.

Now the long war was about to begin.

Part Two

A NEW WAR BEGINS

5.

IF YOU'RE SO SMART . . .

(Spring 2007)

In early January 2007, David Petraeus was north of Los Angeles, riding in a rental car on Interstate 5 to see his aged father, Sixtus, a one-time Dutch sea captain who took refuge in New York when World War II broke out. Petraeus's wife, Holly, was driving while the general answered his e-mail, using an air card on his laptop. His son was in the backseat. As if on signal, every cell phone people in the car were carrying began to ring. An aide to the chairman of the Joint Chiefs got through to Petraeus's son with the message that Defense Secretary Gates was looking for Petraeus. One of Petraeus's own subordinates called Holly with the same message. Petraeus looked down at his laptop screen and saw that the e-mail inbox was filling up with notes from colleagues who were hearing the same rumor: He was about to be offered command of the war in Iraq.

Gates came on the line on one of the phones. Holly exited off the freeway and drove into a parking lot in a rundown neighborhood to ensure that the cell signal wasn't lost. "I just want to confirm that you're willing to take this one," the defense secretary said to Petraeus.

Petraeus assured Gates that he was. But in return he wanted some clarity from Gates. "Sir, with respect, I just want to talk a bit about my thoughts on what a commander in that position should do," he said. "That is, that he should have a very clear understanding with you of what the mission is." For years the mission had been conflicted between creating a stable Iraq and getting out of the country quickly, and trying to do both at the same time wasn't working. Petraeus thought that the policy of "standing down as they stand up" wasn't realistic then because "the situation had reached the point where they couldn't stand up—in fact, some of them were flat on their face, if not helping the enemy."

The top priority in the mission should be to secure the Iraqi people, Petraeus said. Turning control over to Iraqi security forces would have to take a backseat. "Transition is a task we all want to perform but it is a task that can only come when the conditions exist to make that possible, and those conditions are of course a level of violence that Iraqi forces can handle."

Petraeus also wanted his direct line to Gates to stay open, in order to maintain clarity in policy. "That dialogue should be fairly continuous; it should be based on updates of the situation. This should be a very forthright, brutally honest discussion." Gates agreed.

Gates also was looking for someone to take over Central Command. What did Petraeus think of "Fox" Fallon, the crusty chief of the Pacific Command? In his heart, Petraeus would have liked to have seen Gen. Keane picked for the job. He didn't say that, but instead said he didn't know Fallon but said he had heard Jack Keane speak highly of him. It was an exchange that he later would remember a bit ruefully.

On January 5, the White House announced that Petraeus would take command in Iraq. With that selection, the Bush administration was turning the war over to the opposition inside the U.S. military. Casey was kicked upstairs; Abizaid would follow Rumsfeld out the door. In their place, the president and his aides selected pragmatists and skeptics, especially the experts whose advice had been disregarded and even denounced during the run-up to the war. Some had been opponents of the war. Most were critics of current policy, and disillusioned, in the best sense of that word, that they had been stripped of the false assumptions that had hamstrung the U.S. war effort for years. What they all tended to have in common was an eagerness, even an insistence, that the war should be approached in new and different ways, from how troops would be used to how the Iraqi government would be handled to how prisoners would be treated.

INTO THE "GHOST TOWN"

The long journeys on aging chartered airliners from the United States to Iraq are frequently a time of reflection for soldiers, especially those going back for a second or third or fourth tour. As Petraeus was flying into Iraq in February 2007, Col. Pete Mansoor, his new executive officer, knelt alongside his seat. "You know, sir, the hardest thing for you, if it comes to it, will be to tell the American people and the president that this isn't working."

Petraeus didn't say anything. "But he heard it," Mansoor said. And he nodded.

They were stunned at just how bad the situation was. The first thing that struck them was the extent of damage inflicted on Baghdad during the municipal civil war of 2006. Then, in briefings, Petraeus learned how widespread Iranian operations were inside Iraq—and how effective, with the sophisticated bombs they provided becoming a major killer of American troops. A few days after landing, he took a tour of two Baghdad neighborhoods, Gaziliyah and Doura. "That was an 'Oh my God' moment—the damage done by sectarian violence," he said. "I mean, they were just ghost towns. When I left in '05, these were prosperous, fairly high-rent areas. Now there were no shops open. There were weeds and trash and bombed-out hulks." Amiriyah was arguably worse, he remembered: "We reached a point where you were not allowed to drive in Amiriyah unless you were in a tracked vehicle—a tank or a Bradley."

Mansoor, who accompanied him on the grim tour, simply described Doura as "lifeless." As they drove in convoys of Humvees, the two men talked. "We remarked how these neighborhoods, which seemed largely depopulated, had a tense, frightened feel to them," Mansoor said. "It was clear to us that the AQI terrorists and Shia militias had intimidated the population into submission. We had a lot of work to do to reverse this downward spiral, and time was not on our side."

THE ODD COUPLE

"There are three enormous tasks that strategic leaders have to get right," Petraeus said one day in Baghdad. "The first is to get the big ideas right. The second is to communicate the big ideas throughout the organization. The third is ensure proper execution of the big ideas."

The accuracy of that view is borne out by a comment by Maj. Roy Myers, a chaplain in the detention operation. All chaplains are especially sensitive to morale issues, but one ministering to soldiers handling detainees must be especially so, because low morale can quickly lead to abuses. "We have to be able to develop a sense of identity and a sense of purpose, even in an environment where the people above us are just baffled," Myers commented later. "That's probably why General Petraeus comes off as such a breath of fresh air. . . . [H]e has brought a sense of purpose: 'What are we going to do in Iraq?' Otherwise, the tactics overwhelm it: 'Well, we're going to go kill bad guys.' At least now there's a larger operational/strategic sense of purpose."

On his first day in command, Petraeus issued a one-page letter to his troops, letting them know he understood how tough a road they were on. "The truth is, at the strategic level, all you can do is convey a handful of ideas—a handful," he said later. "Then you do oversight, take the organizational actions that institutionalize the ideas." That was the point of this letter, which set the scene for following ones. "We serve in Iraq at a critical time," he began. "A decisive moment approaches." The enemy, he said, included mass murderers. It wouldn't be easy taking them on, he said, "but hard is not hopeless."

The first question facing Petraeus was how well he would mesh with his new deputy, Odierno, who would oversee day-to-day operations, managing downward, while Petraeus focused upward on the Iraqi and American governments. The two made an odd physical pair: Odierno, at 6 foot 5 inches, and 245 pounds, is 8 inches taller and 90 pounds heavier than Petraeus. Odierno's most noticeable physical trait is his bulk topped by his hairless, bulletlike head. Petraeus is both small and slightly buck-toothed, sometimes giving him, as he hunches over intently to make a point, a bit of a chipmunklike aspect. The small, nimble Petraeus is as much a diplomat as a soldier, while the hulking Odierno always seemed inclined to use firepower. But Odierno knew that in 2007 he would always do so with Petraeus, the Army's counterinsurgency expert, looking over his shoulder.

Odierno is big and emotional, the type of general who will bear-hug a colonel having a hard day. Petraeus generally is cool to the point of being remote. Brig. Gen. "Smokin' Joe" Anderson—he earned the nickname as a welterweight boxer at West Point—knew both men well, having been a brigade commander for Petraeus in combat in northern Iraq and then becoming Odierno's chief of staff in 2007. "Odierno is more loyal to his people," he concluded. "Sometimes if you move on from Petraeus, he will forget you. . . . It's a little bit more about Dave than it is about Ray." He also thought Odierno better suited for combat. "Odierno is a better war fighter than Petraeus. Petraeus is more the statesman. Odierno understands the big picture, but his default mode is make sure the enemy knows he can shwack them."

Odierno and Petraeus were peers during their first tours, in 2003–4. They had commanded divisions in adjacent areas—Odierno with the 4th Infantry Division headquartered in Tikrit, and Petraeus with the 101st Airborne north of him in Mosul. They had been two of the hottest generals in the Army, quiet allies against the blustery incompetence of their commander, Lt. Gen. Sanchez, and also against the clumsy micromanagement of L. Paul Bremer III, the civilian overseer of the occupation authority. At meetings with top officials, the two tended to support each other. On November 4, 2003, Petraeus complained that he was "astonished" that Bremer and his staff were developing plans without talking to affected U.S. commanders, according to verbatim notes taken by one of Bremer's subordinates. "It's a mistake to have planning isolated in Baghdad," he added.

Odierno backed him up. "Yes, the campaign plan has to be worked out at all levels," he said. "Frankly, my sense is you want to cut us out."

But they had run their divisions very differently, with Odierno inclined to use the closed fist and Petraeus the open hand. "I see Petraeus up in Mosul," recalled one general who visited both commanders in the summer of 2003. "He completely understands that he has an urban insurgency on his hands. Therefore, he is spending a considerable amount of time on political and social development. He doesn't permit indiscriminate major sweeps." Odierno's 4th Infantry Division felt unnecessarily aggressive to this general, as if it came in looking for a fight, finally found one, and began overreacting. "He's conducting one operation after another. They are going through neighborhoods, kicking in doors at two in the morning, without actionable intelligence. That's how you create new insurgents."

The two generals also experienced a bit of friction during Petraeus's second tour, when he was overseeing the training of Iraqi army and police forces from June 2004 to September 2005. Odierno was part of a small Pentagon delegation sent to Iraq to look at ways to improve Washington's support of the operation—but perhaps also to assess who was slowing things down in Baghdad. When the group met with Petraeus, he seemed defensive. "There is enormous impatience" back home, Odierno warned him. "You've got to get on with this."

Petraeus didn't have a lot of time for pressure from Bush administration officials who had rushed into invading Iraq. "If folks were so impatient," he snapped, "they might have thought about that before they kicked this whole thing off."

Some members of the group found Petraeus guarded to the point of being opaque. One of them was Odierno, who finally asked, "Are you telling me you have everything you need, there's nothing you want from us in D.C.?"

Now Petraeus outranked Odierno, and the larger man would have to follow the lead of the smaller, less conventional one. "Everyone knows that Petraeus and Odierno really didn't get along before," said Kilcullen, the Australian infantryman and anthropologist who became Petraeus's adviser on counterinsurgency. But as they worked together in Baghdad in 2007, he noted, there was almost no discernible friction.

Ambassador Ryan Crocker, who saw them together often, said, "I have noticed when we are doing a campaign review or something like that the quality relationship between the two is such that Ray has no hesitation saying, 'Let me give you a different take on that,' and Dave has no problem saying, 'Good point.' "

This time, subordinates were struck by how well they worked together. "That dynamic has been like hand in glove," said one senior intelligence official, who had been unsure about how the two would mesh. "Odierno is extremely good at using the force to execute what Petraeus wants to do. It's a beautiful thing to watch." Odierno, this officer said, "understood intelligence, and the geometry of the battlespace—how does what I do *here* affect what I do *there,* and what I'll do *next.* That's an art. It's seeing things multidimensionally, in terms of time, space, and human terrain."

For all their differences, Petraeus and Odierno brought a key similarity to Iraq in 2007. Col. H. R. McMaster, analyzing American errors in Iraq in the first years of the war, commented that "flexibility as applied to military leadership might be defined as being open to change as an opportunity and having a tolerance for ambiguity; adjusting rapidly to new or evolving situations; applying different methods to meet changing priorities." That captures well the approach the two generals would take in Iraq as they mounted the counteroffensive of 2007.

Almost the first thing Odierno did after Petraeus arrived in Baghdad on February 7 was lay out his plans for the surge, which he called "Security Now." (This briefing is the third document in the appendix.) One new brigade, from the 82nd Airborne, had come in, and a second one, from the 1st Infantry Division, was arriving. Three more would land in the following months. The plan was to use U.S. forces in a radically different way, moving them off the big bases and into small outposts among the population. While the top priority of U.S. forces for years had been handing off to Iraqi forces, the mission was changed to protecting the Iraqi population. "I think he bought it whole," Odierno recalled.

The top priority Odierno listed in this first brief to Petraeus was to "secure the Iraqi people, with a focus on Baghdad." By contrast, making the transition to Iraqi security forces, formerly the top goal of the U.S. mission for years, had been downgraded to the seventh priority on Odierno's list. Raising the ante a bit, he also warned Petraeus, "Time is not on our side."

Early on, Petraeus made what Lt. Gen. James Dubik, another Army three-star general in the country, called "the blood pact" with his top generals. "It was, we're gonna do this, or we're gonna go down trying," Dubik recalled. "But we're not going to operate so that the next generation of Americans are going to have to go to war to finish this thing. And we're going to have our integrity when we're done." The message: Act like this is your last tour of duty, and don't worry about what comes next for you.

Petraeus also sought to make his commanders more flexible and open in dealing with the media. On his fourth day in Iraq, February 10, Petraeus took command and sat down with his generals. "We are in an information war," he told them. "Sixty percent of this thing is information." He told them he wanted them to talk more with reporters. "Don't worry about getting out there too much—I will tell you if you are." That order reversed the standard approach of Army officers of dealing with the media only as much as was absolutely necessary, in the correct belief that little credit could be gained but that a mistake could damage one's career. "It was culture shock," recalled his adviser on communications, Col. Steve Boylan. "They hadn't been taught to engage." Boylan, a veteran Apache attack helicopter pilot, argued that the American effort had lost so much credibility that official pronouncements of progress had become meaningless. "We couldn't tell the American people anything anymore. We had to show them. They had heard enough."

THE PETRAEUS BRAIN TRUST

Two anomalies characterized the team Petraeus brought together in Baghdad. First, it was one of the most selective clubs in the world, dominated by military officers who possessed doctorates from top-flight universities as well as combat experience in Iraq. "I cannot think of another case of so many highly educated officers advising a general," said Carter Malkasian, who has advised Marine Corps commanders in Iraq on counterinsurgency and himself holds an Oxford doctorate in the history of war. Second, to a surprising degree, it was a minority organization, in the sense that the surge had been supported by only a small group inside the military and would be implemented by a group of dissidents, skeptics, and outsiders, some of them foreigners. "Their role is crucial if we are to reverse the effects of four years of conventional mind-set fighting an unconventional war," said a Special Forces colonel who knew some of the officers.

Foremost among the doubters was Petraeus, who during the 2003 invasion of Iraq had skeptically said several times to a reporter, "Tell me how this ends." It was clear back then that he hadn't joined Gen. Tommy Franks and other top commanders in believing that toppling a statue or two in Baghdad was the answer.

After years of inclining toward anodyne pronouncements about steady progress, which always begged the question of whether there was enough progress, or whether the speaker actually knew what was happening, the new team could be refreshingly blunt. "We have done some stupid shit," Maj. Gen. Dave Fastabend, who moved out to become Petraeus's chief of strategy, said at the beginning of one interview about the conduct of the war, as he put his feet on the table behind his desk and stared eastward out the window, toward the part of Baghdad where rockets and mortars are launched into the Green Zone.

There also surfaced occasionally a tone of resentment, of being sent out to clean up a mess created by Rumsfeld, Wolfowitz, Franks, and others, and who resented the criticisms being leveled by the new crew. "People were like, 'Fuck you, you think you're smarter than us,' " recalled David Kilcullen, whom Petraeus recruited to be a kind of counterinsurgency coach for his commanders. "A lot of them were waiting for us to fail."

Interestingly, that antipathy didn't extend to the ringleader of the mess, President Bush, even in private conversations. Lt. Col. Charlie Miller, who prepared Petraeus for his weekly video-teleconference with Bush, and sometimes sat in on them, said the president actually surprised him in the first meeting. "He was very different from the president you see on TV, that sideways smile of his. He was very informed, questioning, engaged." But Miller was peeved by the Pentagon officials who launched the war and then left the government: "What bothers me is Martha Stewart went to jail for the little stuff, but people who fundamentally misunderstood the situation are teaching at Georgetown," he said over dinner one day at Camp Victory, referring to Douglas Feith, who was under secretary of defense for policy during the invasion and occupation of Iraq and went on to become a professor at Georgetown University and publish a soporific memoir.

Lt. Col. Suzanne Nielsen, a Harvard Ph.D. who was a strategist for Petraeus, said that five years after the event, "I still find it kind of unforgivable" how the war was commenced in 2003.

At a planning office at Central Command, the headquarters to which Petraeus officially reported, someone pinned up a photo of Gen. Anthony Zinni, the Marine who preceded Tommy Franks at the command. He had gone into opposition against the Bush administration during the run-up to the invasion and had been something of an outcast since then. Posting his photo spoke volumes. This wasn't Franks's headquarters anymore, where Zinni's "Desert Crossing" plan for invading Iraq if it collapsed, drawn up in 1999 after some new intelligence on the shakiness of Saddam's regime, had been neglected and even disparaged as outmoded.

The team Petraeus assembled included Col. Michael Meese, son of the former attorney general, and himself a Princeton Ph.D. in economics; Lt. Col. Douglas Ollivant, a veteran of battles in Najaf and Fallujah, who did a Ph.D. dissertation on Thomas Jefferson's political theories; Lt. Col Miller, a Columbia University Ph.D. in political science; and Col. H. R. McMaster, former commander of the 3rd Armored Cavalry Regiment.

The last officer on that list, McMaster, seems to pop up repeatedly at key points in the Iraq war, like the military equivalent of Eliot Cohen, the ubiquitous bow-tied academic. McMaster was well known in the Army from his leading role in a key tank attack in the 1991 Gulf War. The Army's official history of that war, *Certain Victory,* opens with him as a cavalry captain leading a charge of nine tanks. He became even better known for his nervy doctoral dissertation in history, written at the University of North Carolina at Chapel Hill, about the failures of the Joint Chiefs of Staff during the Vietnam War. Published in book form as *Dereliction of Duty,* it was widely read in the military in the 1990s, and in 1998 even made required reading for four-star commanders by the chairman of the Joint Chiefs of Staff, Gen. Hugh Shelton. Early in the Iraq war he was a skeptical adviser to Abizaid at Central Command. Then, after taking command of the 3rd Armored Cavalry Regiment, he posted what was arguably the first genuine success in the postinvasion war, his counterinsurgency campaign in the city of Tall Afar, in 2005–6. Later he was an influential member of the council of colonels at the Pentagon that informed the chairman of the Joint Chiefs that the U.S. military was on a path to defeat in Iraq. He arrived to advise Petraeus in Iraq just after finishing a paper sharply critical of how the wars in Iraq and Afghanistan had been fought. "A short-term approach to long-term problems generated multiple short-term plans that often confused activity with progress," he charged.

For his intelligence adviser, Petraeus tapped Derek Harvey, a retired Army colonel who had become a dissident inside the Pentagon, going to top officials in 2004 and telling them the situation in Iraq was more dangerous than they understood. Gen. Keane took him under his wing and insisted that Rumsfeld give him a hearing. He did, and then was sent to do the same with Bush—but was never invited back to give an update on his darkly pessimistic view of the war.

Even the junior officers around Petraeus seemed to have a maverick streak to them. One of his aides, Capt. Elizabeth McNally, looked like a future general, having been first in her class at West Point and then a Rhodes Scholar. But in 2007 she decided to quit the Army when she got home from Iraq, partly to become a mother, but also, she said, because "I'm kind of disillusioned with the government now." One of her successors would be Capt. Erica Watson Borggren, who had used her own Rhodes scholarship to study social policy and theology at Oxford, the latter subject because she was contemplating eventually leaving the military to become a missionary, perhaps in India. Her best friend at Oxford displayed on the wall of her room a photograph of a burning American flag.

Stephen Biddle, the Council of Foreign Relations defense expert who had participated in the crucial White House meeting with Bush in December 2006, was surprised to be asked to join Petraeus in Baghdad because he had published an analysis of the Iraq war and had been told that Petraeus "disagreed heartily" with it. Another invitee was Toby Dodge, a British academic who "was fundamentally against the decision to invade. I thought it was badly planned and badly executed, and led Iraq into a civil war." Nonetheless, he accepted the invitation because he also opposed the idea of the United States simply leaving as fast as possible.

Petraeus also handpicked Lt. Gen. Dubik to take over the effort to train and advise Iraqi forces. It was known as MNSTC-I, which the military, in a Freudian moment, began pronouncing "min-sticky," as if it were the ministry of intractable problems, which it effectively was. It wasn't known publicly, but Dubik had long been an internal critic of the handling of the war, sending three memos to the leaders of Army from 2004 to early 2007, warning them that the United States was losing it. Dubik saw the entrance of Petraeus also as a cultural shift for the Army in Iraq, the ascendancy of the light Army, comprised nowadays of three divisions, the 82nd Airborne, the 101st Airborne, and the 10th Mountain. Those light-infantry units, lacking tanks and much other armor, had been easier to deploy, and so were assigned the odd jobs of the Cold War, from peacekeeping in the Sinai and Somalia to hurricane relief in Florida. The heavy Army, with its tanks, armored personnel carriers, self-propelled artillery pieces, and thousands of other pieces of gear, remained focused on the plains of Central Europe, where its mission was to be prepared to blunt the onslaught of a Red Army. "We were the window-doers throughout the Cold War," said Dubik, smiling with both his mouth and his warm brown eyes. "The 'real Army' didn't do windows," he said, until forced to do so in Bosnia in 1995. The heavy Army also led the invasion of Iraq in 2003, perhaps feeling it was its turn, after the Special Operators and light infantry had invaded Afghanistan two years earlier. The initial headquarters for the occupation was V Corps, which was based in Europe. In 2007 Petraeus led the light Army into Iraq.

The two most important advisers to Petraeus were two colonels, Bill Rapp and Pete Mansoor.

Col. Rapp became the head of Petraeus's unusual internal think tank, the Commander's Initiatives Group, which the general established to ask the hard questions and push the envelope. It was intended to keep him one step ahead of events, escaping the traps that had snared earlier American commanders in Iraq of being reactive, or of acting on assumptions unthinkingly inherited from the Army's culture, or of trying to follow White House rhetoric. That is, the president may call the insurgents evildoers—but why not cut deals with the enemy? And what about amnesties? Where did the French go wrong in Algeria as they thought they had won in the late 1950s, and how can we avoid repeating their errors? Is the task of the Army to destroy the nation's enemies or to bring the war to a successful conclusion? It was not an office present in most U.S. military headquarters. Rapp, a big, slim, intense, earnest man, with close-cropped hair, graying at the temples, tends to look angry while thinking but is really just deep in thought.

He had written a Ph.D. at Stanford on the reliability of democracies in war-fighting alliances.

Rapp had arrived home from his previous tour in Iraq in October 2006, only to receive a call three months later from Petraeus, who wanted him to come to Baghdad.

"Sir, I just left," Rapp said, at a loss for words.

"Yeah," Petraeus replied. Rapp knew that meant: *So what?*

"Sir, I'm still in command of my brigade," Rapp added.

"Let me make a phone call," Petraeus said. Rapp knew what that meant as well: *That obstacle soon would be gone.*

Two days later the Army chief of staff's office notified Rapp that his command had been curtailed. "Give it up and go to Baghdad," Rapp told himself. He arrived in Iraq in mid-February. He would become an extra set of eyes and ears for Petraeus, accompanying him to almost every meeting, observing, taking notes, offering the general another view on what he was hearing and seeing, and what the next steps might be.

Mansoor, who commanded a brigade of the 1st Armored Division in Baghdad in 2003–4, received a Ph.D. at Ohio State for a dissertation on how U.S. Army infantry divisions were developed during World War II. He became Petraeus's executive officer in Baghdad, a key figure in implementing the general's decisions. Unusually in the U.S. Army, Mansoor was of Palestinian background. His father, born in Ramallah, emigrated to New Ulm, Minnesota, in 1938. "It was ten thousand people of German descent and one Arab family," Mansoor recalled. They moved to Sacramento, where he proudly remembers that his mother, a schoolteacher, won awards for designing an "open classroom" approach. His father was a traveling salesman. In high school, Mansoor was valedictorian, student body president, and head of the math club. He also would graduate first in his class at West Point in 1982.

In late March, Ryan Crocker flew to Baghdad to become the U.S. ambassador, succeeding Zalmay Khalilzad. His arrival completed the most sweeping personnel turnover of the entire war, surpassing even the changes that came after the invasion when Franks and the chief of the Army, Gen. Eric Shinseki, stepped down. Now, as then, there was a new U.S. commander, who was working with a new deputy and a new ambassador, and, like then, they would have above them a new Army chief of staff and a new chief of the Central Command. But surpassing the changes of 2004, there also was in place a new Iraq director on the staff of the National Security Council and, most important, a new defense secretary. Also, they would be overseen by a new, Democrat-controlled Congress.

Crocker and Petraeus would become close partners in 2007, creating almost the reverse of the dysfunctional relationship that had existed between the first permanent postinvasion U.S. envoy, Ambassador Bremer, and his military counterpart, Gen. Sanchez. They were determined to get along, to achieve the "unity of effort" whose lack had so plagued the American effort. Where Bremer had been a control freak, Crocker could be self-effacing. Where Sanchez dove into minutiae, Petraeus strove constantly to keep his head above water, to focus on the big picture. Neither Crocker nor Petraeus seemed to think invading Iraq had been a wise choice. On election night in November 2002, as the Bush administration was running up toward invading Iraq, Crocker had worked late in his Washington office and then gone home with a sinking feeling. "It was clear where it was going," he recalled. "I told my wife, 'We have just voted to have us a big old war.'"

He hadn't opposed the invasion wholeheartedly, he said one day in his Baghdad office, a few steps from Petraeus's. "I was against it, but not happily," he said. "This was a truly evil regime. I had spent two years here. I had seen it firsthand, just truly evil, and we are supposed to stand for something as the United States. It was a truly evil and active regime that was wearing us down." So, he thought to himself, if you are against the invasion, what do you do, especially if you believe, as he did, that "sanctions weren't going to last—they were already falling away." Plus, he recalled, "I had to take seriously the WMD thing. So if you've got a guy who is as evil as he is, as violent as he is, armed as he was said to be—and I had no reason to doubt it—and we are losing our international containment, what are you going to do?" At the same time, "What kept me up at night wasn't what I knew but what I didn't know. And I knew full well we weren't prepared to handle it. As a regionalist, my feeling was, *Don't do it.*"

Crocker would oversee an embassy stocked with similar skeptics. Retired ambassador Timothy Carney, for example, had served under Bremer early in the occupation, only to quit after two months, angry and frustrated with the sloppiness of American planning and its even worse implementation. In January 2007 he was asked to go back to oversee reconstruction efforts. Talking to State Department officials, he picked up a new "sense of reality," and added, "It's been a long time coming." He accepted.

LISTENING TO FOREIGNERS

Underscoring how much the U.S. Army had been changed by Iraq, three of the most influential advisers added to the U.S. effort in Iraq were foreigners. One was David Kilcullen, the Australian counterinsurgency specialist. Another was Sadi Othman, the lanky, pacifistic Arab turned New Yorker. The third was Emma Sky, a small, fiercely anti-war British expert on the Middle East. None of them were particular supporters of President Bush's decision to invade Iraq or of the way the occupation had been handled.

Kilcullen was perhaps the most outspoken and articulate of Petraeus's advisers. Sandy-haired, apple-cheeked, and boyish, he enjoyed semimythical status as the man that Petraeus, the Army's new king of counterinsurgency, had asked to be his counterinsurgency adviser. Also, as an Australian far from his own chain of command, Kilcullen, who had opposed the invasion of Iraq, could say in his Crocodile Dundee accent what American officials only thought privately. "In '03, we confused entry with victory," he said. "What we have to do now is not confuse departure with defeat."

He loathed his time in the cocoon of the Green Zone, where he felt he was just a sitting duck for incoming mortars. It was better to be out and about, embedding with brigade and battalion commanders, helping them seize the initiative whenever possible. Sitting in his closet-sized office in the old presidential palace, just around the corner from Petraeus's, Kilcullen, the son of an Australian medievalist, exclaimed one day, "There's a line in Joseph Conrad's *Heart of Darkness* about the smell of defeat seeping out of the walls. I feel that being in this palace—the bureaucratic inertia, the feel of defeat, seeping out of the walls." He came to hate the insularity of the place: "The system in the Green Zone is built to protect you from realizing there's a war on."

His job was to help change the way American officers in Iraq thought about how to fight the war. Kilcullen briefed each group of incoming commanders how to operate. His prescriptions were almost the complete reverse of how most U.S. forces had operated in the first years of the war. Among his top ten rules were:

- "Secure the people where they sleep."
- "Never leave home without an Iraqi."
- "Look beyond the IED: get the network that placed it."

- "Give the people justice and honor. . . . We talk about democracy and human rights. Iraqis talk about justice and honor."
- "Get out and walk"—that is, "patrol on foot."

Kilcullen found that last dictum, about literally putting boots on the ground, to be one of the hardest to get some units to adopt, especially those who were already in Iraq as command shifted from Casey to Petraeus. He concluded that American soldiers simply had grown accustomed to driving around Iraq, three or four to a Humvee. But that separated them from the Iraqi people, he argued. "In the eyes of the population, we ceased to be human beings," he told commanders on his trips around Iraq to advise them on counterinsurgency techniques. "We were just big moving metal boxes from which Imperial Storm Troopers would occasionally emerge. When an IED blew off, it didn't kill anyone they'd ever seen before."

He also told commanders that these "dismounted" operations ultimately would reduce casualties, because the insurgents wouldn't waste a bomb just to kill one or two soldiers in a spread-out patrol. This promise came back to haunt him on one of the first days of major foot patrols, when four soldiers from the 10th Mountain Division were blown up while walking. He found himself unable to sleep and paced the marbled hallways near Petraeus's office, mournfully wondering whether to recommend dropping the idea. He decided to helicopter down to observe the operations of that 10th Mountain unit. "It turned out they were so used to working in Humvees that they patrolled in clumps of four," he said. He gave them a talk.

A few months later, he was pleasantly surprised in an observation of the patrolling methods of another unit. "No one is doing 'pure' vehicle patrols anymore," he reported. Some units were running foot patrols on one block, with Humvees operating in parallel a block away, available to move quickly to help them. Others left behind their vehicles altogether and conducted double patrols, with one squad on the street and another moving in tandem with it across the rooftops. "There's a lot of night work happening too," he said. This wasn't just raids but also meeting people. "The locals are much more willing to talk freely at night."

Show Iraqis respect, he admonished commanders, but also hold your counterparts to standard. For example, he said, he was with an American patrol commander who approached an Iraqi checkpoint. The Iraqi soldiers had been instructed to stop and inspect every vehicle. "The Iraqi officer was urgently waving us to stop, but our patrol rolled through it at ten miles per hour. The company commander said, 'We don't stop for you people.' I thought, 'You've just lost that guy.'"

One American battalion commander told Kilcullen that he planned to sever relations with a Shiite-dominated Iraqi army unit in his area that, he had learned, was detaining any Sunni it deemed capable of paying a ransom. Kilcullen recommended a different method: Hold the Iraqi commander to standard. Ask him to show you the evidence behind the detentions. If he fails to do so, require that he release the Sunnis, pay them compensation, and formally apologize. "If he doesn't do that, you withdraw support," Kilcullen said.

"Can I do that?" the American officer asked.

"Fuck yeah," Kilcullen said. "That's what you're here for."

He also argued at high levels that the Americans had been putting the cart before the horse in terms of communications. "We use information to explain what we're doing on the ground." The enemy, he said, "does the opposite—they decide what message they want to send, and then design an operation to send that message." He called that more effective approach "armed propaganda." The American equivalent would be putting American troops out into the neighborhoods to protect the population: Don't say it, do it.

Most controversially of all, Kilcullen and some others were thinking about how to "target" their allies in the Baghdad government—not to kill them, but to alter their behavior. Petraeus recalled that his initial set of talks with Maliki in February and March were "really tough," with "voices raised." One of the issues was that Maliki "had made Casey take the checkpoints off Sadr City." Petraeus said he would accede if absolutely necessary—but made it clear that he would have to be pushed hard to do so.

"The weaker partner is always dominant, because we are always trying to prevent them from tipping over, while they can pretty much do what they want," advised Kilcullen. For example, the Finance Ministry, he said, was quietly contributing to "soft ethnic cleansing" by refusing to allow banks to operate in Sunni areas. That meant Sunnis either needed to keep a lot of cash in their homes, where it might be stolen, or drive it to a bank through Shiite checkpoints, where it might well be taken from them. This Hobson's choice forced many Sunnis simply to leave Baghdad, which of course achieved the aim of the Shiite death squads. Likewise, he said, the government was supplying electricity twenty-two hours a day to Shia areas, but just one or two to Sunni neighborhoods. "You have no refrigeration, so you have to go to market every day, and the big food markets are in mixed or Shia neighborhoods." In both cases, he said, "the purpose is to encourage people to leave."

Not everyone was a Kilcullen fan. "He didn't know a thing about Iraq," sneered a senior U.S. intelligence officer, who also noted that Kilcullen was only in Iraq for a few months early in 2007, as Petraeus settled in. "He took just enough pictures so he has a great slide show."

That said, Kilcullen's influence on how the U.S. military thought about counterinsurgency campaigning cannot be overstated. "For a staff guy, he had an extraordinary feel for what was happening," said Col. Michael Galloucis, who commanded a military police brigade in Baghdad in 2007.

SADI OTHMAN

Of the three foreigners who became key advisers to new American commanders, the most unusual was also the one closest to Petraeus. Of them, Sadi Othman probably also had taken the longest journey, both physical and psychological, to becoming part of the American war effort.

Othman was a Palestinian born in Brazil but raised in Jordan, where he attended a boarding school run by Mennonites, the pacifist Protestant sect related to the Amish. While he is ethnically Sunni, he said that decades later, he feels "more Mennonite than anything else." How does he reconcile that with being the political and cultural adviser to the top U.S. general in a war? "I am here for peace, not for war."

At the University of Amman, he grew to 6 foot 7 inches, and soon achieved a bit of local celebrity as the first Jordanian ever to dunk a basketball. Even today, he seems all legs and arms, with the fingers of a pianist, which tend to always be holding a cigarette. Sitting in the bright winter sunlight by the pool behind the U.S. embassy, he seemed almost haloed by his thin white hair and the curling smoke of his Marlboro Lights. He carried two cell phones, which rang every few minutes. On this day he was answering them with a visible sag—he was fatigued from nonstop telephone calls he had been making to help free eight Turkish soldiers being held hostage in the north by Kurdish guerrillas. Othman also became Petraeus's envoy to emissaries from Moqtada al-Sadr, the firebrand Shiite cleric who has been a big winner in post-Saddam Iraq. Could Sadr's people be brought into a working relationship with the Americans? He also was sent frequently to talk to senior members of the Iraqi government.

At age nineteen he transferred to Hesston College, a Mennonite institution in Kansas, and later became an American citizen. On 9/11, he was a taxi driver in New York City. He found the day's terrorist attacks devastating in three ways. "As an American, I was attacked. As a New Yorker, I was violated. As an Arab American, I was humiliated." He felt he had to do something, and signed up to be a civilian interpreter for the U.S. military in the Mideast.

Two years later he wound up as Petraeus's interpreter in Iraq, used for the most crucial and sensitive meetings, not just for the general but for other senior Americans. In January 2007, he interpreted as Speaker of the House Nancy Pelosi and Representative John Murtha chewed out Prime Minister Maliki. "The meetings were very tough," Othman said, banging his fist on the table to illustrate the tone. He recalled that Pelosi told the Iraqi leader, "You have made a lot of promises, but nothing was delivered."

After Pelosi and Murtha left the room, Othman recalled, Maliki, his face pale, turned to Othman and said, "Now I understand what President Bush is going through."

He had first met Petraeus at the end of the invasion of Iraq in April 2003, as the general was coming out of a men's room at the Mosul airport. Othman, not seeing any insignia, assumed that the small, thin, smiling man in a plain brown T-shirt was like him, a civilian. Petraeus is always searching for new insights, especially from people with different perspectives. They began to talk about Iraq. Othman soon found himself assigned to be Petraeus's interpreter. He also came to admire this unusual general. One day he and Petraeus were in Mosul and encountered a man and a woman carrying a baby, with a daughter walking alongside. They looked hungry. Petraeus took out $3 in cash. The woman hesitated, and Othman urged her, "Take it—for the children." A week later the woman saw Othman again and approached him to say, "We ate meat for the first time in two years."

Petraeus and Othman stayed in touch while the general was at Leavenworth developing the counterinsurgency manual. After Petraeus was picked to be the top commander in Iraq, he asked Othman to work with him again. A member of Casey's staff called Mansoor, Petraeus's executive officer, to try to block the move. "We recommend highly you don't take him," the Casey man said. Asked about this in an interview, Othman said there had been some bad blood between him and the staffer. Mansoor, knowing how close Othman was to Petraeus, politely thanked them for their interest. In 2007–8, Othman's most important task was to be Petraeus's personal liaison with the Iraqi government. "We use Sadi a great deal," Petraeus said, "to talk to the prime minister, the minister of finance, to talk to a number of different ministers with whom he has very close personal relationships at this point." There was one major difference beween the two men: Petraeus was no schmoozer while Othman reveled in the endless hours of chatting with Iraqi officials. "When we talk to Sadi Othman and General Petraeus, we are talking to twins," said Rafi al-Assawi, a Sunni who became a deputy prime minister in 2008. "Talking to one, the message would always get to the other."

EMMA SKY

As close at Othman was to Petraeus, Emma Sky grew even closer to Odierno, becoming a kind of physical shadow to him. The birdlike British woman made a dramatic contrast to the hulking American general, both physically and intellectually. "People always thought we were funny, this huge man and this tiny British woman who went everywhere with him," she recalled.

It was a sign of how much Odierno had changed that he sensed he needed someone like Sky to second-guess him in Iraq. He had seen her in action in Iraq in 2003–4, when he was commanding the 4th Infantry Division, and she was advising the Americans on Kurdish issues in the north. Odierno asked her to come back to Iraq to be his political adviser, but she resisted. She had opposed the war, and she didn't have a lot of time for armies, especially the American one. "From my perspective, the military were the bad guys," she said one still, oven-hot summer evening, sitting on the balcony of a palace and gazing out over the darkness of one of Saddam's shallow artificial lakes. "I was about human security, not state security." A specialist in third world economics who speaks Arabic and Hebrew, she found the military approach jarring. "I come from a world where it is, first, do no harm. When you work in development, you are very conscious of that." By contrast, she said, "The military comes in like a great crashing beast." (One well-connected U.S. Army officer said he believes that Sky works for British intelligence. Upon being asked about this, she laughed.)

She surprised herself by taking the job. "Odierno, by bringing me in, has probably brought in the most opposite person he could find." She did it because she thought it was time to get the United States out of Iraq and wanted to see it happen in the least damaging way possible. "Can we exit with some dignity? Can we have relations with Iraq for a generation to come? All this is still to be decided. There is still a lot we can get from this."

Aware of the reputation Odierno carried from his time in command of the 4th Infantry Division, she agreed to join his staff on one condition, that if she ever witnessed him condoning a human rights violation, she would report him to the Hague—where the International Criminal Court prosecutes war crimes. Odierno agreed, probably a bit amused. She only learned later that the United States isn't a signatory to the statute creating the court, which it maintains doesn't have jurisdiction over U.S. soldiers or other U.S. citizens.

To her surprise, she would become one of Odierno's biggest fans. "He is the only person I would come back to Iraq for," she maintained. "I'd follow him to the end of the world. Usually when you work closely with people, you see the warts and all, and your opinion goes down. My opinion of him has gone way up."

She may have been soft on Odierno, but she retained her sharpness about the rest of the world. Asked in an interview early in 2007 about Iraqi politics, she interrupted to redefine the question. "It's not a government, it's a failing state."

She still could blow the whistle on the U.S. military, but now she did so from inside the tent. In the spring of 2007, she was in a "battle update assessment" as an officer showed gun camera footage of an attack helicopter surprising insurgents emplacing a bomb and blowing them to bits. This was red meat for officers who had spent years being attacked by anonymous roadside bombers. "They all loved it," she recalled, so much so that the officers at the briefing began talking about taking the declassification steps necessary to release the imagery to the media. "We should get this out, get it on TV," they commented.

Sky was shocked. "These are American versions of jihadi videos," she interrupted angrily, knowing they would be taken aback by the comparison to decapitation photographs and videos posted on the Internet. "Is this the image you want to present to the world? This is America killing people. Yes, it has to happen. But let's not glorify it." Furious, she stood up and strode out of the conference room.

After she left, Odierno discussed her comments with his corps sergeant major, the highest-ranking enlisted man for tens of thousands of troops. Half an hour later, the sergeant major walked into her office. "Ma'am, you're right," he said, and then hugged her.

Yet the two still had their differences. At one point in 2007, Odierno called

Sky into his office and told her she was being overly pessimistic. "I need you on this!" he said, half arguing and half imploring.

"I never liked the idea of this war anyway," Sky muttered.

At another point, she recalled, she was so tense and frustrated by one issue—she said she couldn't remember what it was—that she decided to quit. Like Odierno, but unlike Petraeus, she tended to show emotion and then get over it. She stayed.

Once, when Petraeus pointed out in a meeting to Odierno that Sky, Odierno's political adviser, made a certain argument, Odierno responded, "She's not my adviser, she's my insurgent."

To her astonishment, in the course of 2007 she would also become an admirer of the U.S. military. "I love them," she said. She added provocatively that she thinks the military is better than the country it protects. "That's the way I feel about it—America doesn't deserve its military."

The willingness of American commanders to ask for her advice consistently surprised her. "The Brits came in with more experience in this sort of operation, but over the years I think the American Army has learned a lot more. I mean, there's no way the British army would ask someone like me to come along." She also came to appreciate the meritocracy of American culture: "What I found with the Americans is they always gave me a place at the table. Once there, it was up to me to prove myself. With the British military, it's always a fight to get a seat at the table—I'm female, I'm not military, I'm a tree-hugger."

TIME WAITS FOR NO ONE

Looming over this new American team and its revamped approach was the nagging question: Was it simply too late? "The one resource that Petraeus needs, and lacks, is time," Col. Holshek, the civil affairs veteran of Iraq, said as the surge began in the spring of 2007.

Fastabend agreed. "The first thing you need," he told Petraeus, "is more time on the clock." And he would get that, Fastabend continued, only if when he went before Congress later that year he was able to show clearly understandable successes, like sharply lower violence in some parts of the country. "It can't be a 1.5 percent improvement in ministerial capacity and blah blah blah." In another Army connection, Fastabend years earlier had served as Jack Keane's executive officer.

There were many expert observers who thought the U.S. effort already was out of time. After all, this argument went, the American people had voted against the war in November 2006, and the task now was to wind it up. "It's too late to make a difference in Iraq," said Bruce Hoffman, a Georgetown University expert on terrorism who had advised the U.S. government on the war effort.

Petraeus recognized the pressing need for more time. "The Washington clock is moving more rapidly than the Baghdad clock," he said. "So we're obviously trying to speed up the Baghdad clock a bit and to produce some progress on the ground that can, perhaps . . . put a little more time on the Washington clock." But many of Petraeus's critics didn't seem to recognize what he needed that time for: not to bring the war to a close, which everyone involved thought would take years, but simply to show enough genuine progress that the American people would be willing to stick with it. That would be the real war goal for 2007.

6.

GAMBLING ON A "SHITTY HAND"

(Spring and Summer 2007)

We were dealt a really shitty hand, but we've played it to the best of our ability," Col. Peter Mansoor said as he looked back to the troubled beginning of 2007.

They had deplaned into a small civil war, and the streets of Baghdad seemed to grow bloodier by the day. On January 16, two bombs were detonated during the after-school rush at a Baghdad university, killing at least 60 people. Six days later, two more bombs devastated a street bazaar, killing at least 79 more. On January 30, 60 Shiites were killed in multiple attacks across central Iraq. "We had U.S. Air Force F-16s engaging the enemy on Haifa Street, twelve hundred meters from the embassy," recalled Kilcullen.

It is easy to forget now, after it has become conventional wisdom that the surge worked, at least tactically, how audacious a venture it was. Almost all military experts agreed with the Joint Chiefs of Staff that the U.S. troop presence was an irritant, so more troops likely would only worsen the situation. The liberal position was to withdraw as soon as possible. Hawkish centrists advocated getting smaller and staying longer. Escalation of the sort that was chosen was a radical position advocated by a small minority. At best, it was unclear what a relatively small number of additional troops might do. At worst, many thought, it simply was reinforcing failure—a cardinal sin in military operations. The consensus seemed to be that at best it probably was just delaying a horrific civil war that unfortunately seemed inevitable.

But all that pessimism had one positive side effect, because it created the conditions for strategic surprise—which as Clausewitz, the great Prussian philosopher of war, observes, is the most important and effective kind of surprise. After four years in Iraq, no one seemed to expect the Americans to develop a way to operate differently and more effectively.

The shift was all the more unexpected because it came as President Bush was politically cornered. Usually, "sustained strategic boldness . . . requires a solid foundation of popular support," Oxford historian Piers Mackesy observed in *The War for America,* his classic study of how the British managed to lose the American Revolutionary War in 1781 after appearing to have won it just a year earlier. But in agreeing to a troop escalation, Bush was operating from a position of extraordinary political weakness. Not only was he deeply unpopular, he had reversed course at a time when it seemed that stubborn persistence was his sole virtue as a leader: After years of saying he would heed the advice of his military, Bush had split with the overwhelming view of his top military leaders, from the Pentagon to Central Command to the top general in Iraq.

What probably saved Bush was his political opposition—a splintered and confused Democratic Party. The Democrats were close to paralyzed by the Iraq war, wanting to gratify their supporters by questioning it but not wanting to be responsible for the outcome. The major weapon available to them was to cut off funding for the war—but to do that would make them appear antimilitary, which would carry a political price they were not willing to pay. Put bluntly, they wanted to appear to be doing something about it without really doing anything. So, while the House of Representatives voted 246 to 182 in February 2007 to oppose the surge, it wasn't prepared to follow up that nonbinding resolution with action. This empty-handed approach would prove to be a huge political advantage to Bush, enabling him to launch and continue the counteroffensive.

PETRAEUS AMID THE PESSIMISTS

In news photographs, they are the people on the side, escorting a top official or leaning in to interpret during the photo shoot. In one such image that ran on the front page of the *New York Times,* two Petraeus aides, Col. Mike Bell and Sadi

Othman, flank the Iraqi prime minister and the American secretary of state. These were the people who studied operations, wrote critiques, and drafted papers, the plumbers and mechanics of policy. As 2007 began, few of them believed the surge would succeed. "When I first got here in January," said Emma Sky, her "sense was, the war was lost, how do we get out?" Nor, with her pacificistic tendencies, was she attracted to the new American strategy. "At the beginning of the surge, I felt violence begets violence. I felt sick. I felt horrible."

Kilcullen calculated that Petraeus would achieve his goals on security but not on politics. He went on to bet that he could summarize the situation in just ten words and did: "My bottom line: good team, right strategy, possibly too late." He even had drawn up a paper to give to Petraeus if the situation fell apart. First, he advised, you will need to recognize that you have reached a decision point. Second, act on that recognition in a timely fashion. Third, "credibly communicate" your assessment to the president and other Washington decision makers.

Nor did Capt. Liz McNally, the eager young Rhodes Scholar who was drafting Petraeus's speeches, think they were on the path to success in Iraq: "Even given the perfect amount of resources, I don't know if what we're trying to do is possible," she confessed one day in the spring.

Hearing that Petraeus might be given command in Iraq, Sadi Othman prayed that he wouldn't take it, "because the situation was very bad, and because I care about my friend Dave Petraeus." The stakes were huge, Othman believed, and the odds against success nearly overwhelming. "Let me put it this way, it is very hard to be very optimistic," he said one day in May 2007, as the casualties continued to rise. "Having said that, I strangely believe it is doable. If, God forbid, Iraq falls apart, I think it will impact the entire region in an unbelievable way. If the problems aren't solved, I believe the consequence is the whole region up in flames." It was a chilling thought. He folded his hands in his lap.

One day early in 2007, Col. Bill Rapp, Petraeus's closest adviser, was in his office watching CNN's Michael Ware, a reporter he respected, discuss the state of the war. The correspondent gloomily said to his colleague Anderson Cooper that "it just doesn't seem that there's any road forward that does not involve the spilling of so much innocent blood or the abandonment of so many of the principles that we of the West hold dear."

Col. Rapp, who was already worried, "trying to figure if we needed to get out of Dodge," was so struck by the comment that he wrote it down. Then he picked up a marker and copied it onto the big erasable white board he used with his subordinates to brainstorm. "I wrote it down as a challenge to myself and the CIG [commander's initiatives group] to help the CG [commanding general] find an alternative. Those days were fairly bleak."

Their job as the brains behind Petraeus, he instructed them, was "to prove Mick Ware wrong." Rapp's deputy, Charlie Miller, arriving in Iraq in February 2007, estimated the chances of success at 10 to 15 percent. By May he considered himself a relative optimist and raised his guess to 35 to 40 percent. It was better but still far from a safe bet.

Soon after he arrived in Iraq, Lt. Col. James Crider, commander of a cavalry squadron deploying in Baghdad, was pleasantly surprised to run into Col. Mansoor, whom he had known and admired for years.

"Hey, sir, I'm pretty optimistic, I think it's gonna work," Crider said.

"I'm not," Mansoor replied, gray-haired and expressionless behind his glasses. "I'm not sure it's gonna work. In fact, the odds are against it."

It was a sobering, even frightening exchange for Crider, who had orders to take his unit into one of Baghdad's toughest neighborhoods. He thought to himself, "This is a guy I know, and he's General Petraeus's executive officer, and he's not sure it's gonna work?"

One of the few relative optimists around Petraeus was a senior intelligence official who would be interviewed only on the condition that he not be identified by name. "I thought we had a real chance of making it work," he remembered. At the American military headquarters in Iraq, he said, "A lot of people were thinking ten percent, fifteen percent." He was at 40 percent, he said.

Despite the odds, they were going to try, especially because they didn't see a lot of good alternatives. Just because the odds were bad didn't mean there was a better choice available. There was in this period a sense of being dutiful: They had to cast a cold eye on the blunders of their predecessors while trying to be positive about their own chances. They had to risk their lives and see comrades bleed and die, all the while believing it was likely their efforts would fall short. Mixed with that ambivalence was a determination to at least try, to give it one more shot and at least salvage as much as possible.

Even the principals harbored profound doubts. "I didn't know," said Ambassador Crocker. "I thought it could work. If I had thought it absolutely would not I would be insane to come out here . . . I will not be one of those who said I saw this all along. I thought probably it was a long shot, given the levels of violence that had prevailed and the damage they had done to the political and social fabric."

Odierno also harbored doubts but was at the optimistic end of the scale. "I thought about seventy-thirty, it would work," he said, looking back. He didn't think five brigades were enough, but figured that by adding in a Marine battalion, an aviation unit, and various Special Operations units, he could get close to what he needed.

Petraeus, the apotheosis of "can-do"-ism, may have been alone in holding that the new mission was entirely plausible. "I didn't consider it a Hail Mary pass," he insisted one day that spring. He saw a series of tasks that needed to be performed, and thought they could be done with some additional troops, some reasonable improvement in the quality of Iraqi forces, and some application of the theory of counterinsurgency. At the ceremony at which he took command, he gave a short talk in which he assured his audience, "this mission is doable." But a year later he would concede that part of the role of a commander is to stay publicly optimistic.

"THE MESOPOTAMIAN STAMPEDE"

Petraeus's chosen image of his task was a Frederic Remington oil painting called *The Stampede*, a 1908 work that depicts a nineteenth-century cowboy riding for his life as a herd of cattle panics under a breaking thunderstorm. The cowboy's own pony is wild-eyed with fear, all four hooves clawing in the air. Next to the cowboy, cattle with their heads and horns down are driving as hard as they can away from the storm, which already is beginning to douse them with sheets of rain. The sky behind the cowboy and the herd is blackening. One long white streak of lightning is striking near another cowboy and cows in the misty distance, which is murky, a green and black haze of rain and storm. Everything about the painting conveys the threat of chaotic danger. If the cowboy's pony trips, or throws him to the stony ground, the unfortunate man will be ripped by the horns of the charging cows or pulped by their heavy hooves.

Petraeus included a copy of the Remington painting in a briefing on "The Mesopotamian Stampede" he would give to members of Congress and other visiting Americans. It is "a metaphor really of the need to be comfortable with slightly chaotic circumstances," Petraeus explained, seeming a bit uneasy, perhaps because of the role the image assigns Iraqis. "A stampede is not always orderly. In that particular painting the ground is rugged, the wind is howling, it's raining cats and dogs, there's lightning—and you can use the lightning as a metaphor, it could be an IED, it could be a tasker from higher headquarters, it could be some sort of political challenge in Iraq, who knows what it might be. And the concept of outriders and trail bosses—again the concept of the challenges on the trail, the idea that some issue, some cattle, some tasks, will actually get out ahead of us. They will move on their own and that's fine. We will catch up with them. But some will also fall behind and we will have to go back and round those up. That some cattle are killed along the way. There's bad guys out there, rustlers who are trying to kill us and to kill those in the cattle drive. And you can use the cattle to represent any number of different items, from the ISF—the herd is growing, they are getting stronger. There are Iraqi trail bosses out there with us, and we are gradually handing off more of the responsibility for the cattle drive to them."

He also used the painting to convey to his subordinates his notion of command. "I don't need to be hierarchical," he explained. "I want to flatten organizations. I'm comfortable with a slightly chaotic environment. I know that it's okay if some of you get out ahead of us. Some of the cattle will get out ahead and we will catch up with them. And some will fall behind and we will circle back and we won't leave them behind." He didn't show the image to Iraqis, he said. It was more useful with Americans. "We're just trying to get the cattle to Cheyenne."

Lt. Col. Nielsen, one of his aides, added that, in her view, the image is also about the limitations of high command. "A lot of it is about intent, about setting parameters, and an incredible decentralization, " she said. The message, she said, is, "I can't tell you exactly what to do," because Iraq simply was too chaotic.

Petraeus adopted a posture of much lowered expectations, and as was his wont, set the tone for his entire command. One of his most striking characteristics is his ability to discern and evaluate the reality of events. That isn't as easy as it sounds, and it is especially difficult to pick out reality through the fog of war. The first and foremost task of a commander is to understand, with a steady head, the nature of the conflict in which he is engaged. In order to achieve that understanding a commander can be neither overly optimistic nor pessimistic, and especially, not subject to McClellanesque mood swings, seeing every minor victory as a triumph and every partial setback as disaster.

Even more important, Petraeus injected a new spirit into senior commanders. At his first meeting with his division and brigade commanders and senior staff members, in February, he sought to convince them they could succeed. "I was amazed with what Petraeus did," recalled Keane, who attended the meeting.

"He took over a command with a sense of futility and hopelessness about it and almost overnight he changed the attitude and he brought them hope and a sense that we can do this, we can succeed at this."

Crocker brought a far different self-image to his partnership with Petraeus. In keeping with the morose outlook that led President Bush to dub him "Mr. Sunshine," he joked once that he saw the general and himself as resembling the lead characters in a movie about two convicts on the run from a chain gang, "shackled" together and so forced to cooperate. He seemed to be referring to *The Defiant Ones,* a 1958 film starring Tony Curtis and Sidney Poitier.

Both Crocker and Petraeus had served in Iraq before but didn't know each other until early 2007, when both arrived for their current tours. Crocker's thought after their initial meeting then was, "I had just gotten very very lucky, given his ability, his drive, his experience, and his intellect."

At the embassy, Crocker began to oversee and revive a staff that Keane found lethargic. "The whole attitude of the place changed" after Crocker arrived, Keane said. "They had passion. They were taking personal risks. They were connecting with Iraqi officials."

SMALLER GOALS . . .

One of Emma Sky's fears in returning to Iraq was that she would be subjected to endless rounds of happy talk at top American headquarters, as she had on her previous tour in Iraq, when she worked in the northeast. "They say 'Camp Victory' without any sense of irony," she noted archly.

Instead she was surprised to walk into a marathon conversation among top commanders and advisers about how to lower the goals of the mission. In the course of several weeks early in 2007, she said, "We redefined success in a much more modest way as 'sustainable stability.'" This was key: The grandiose goals of the past three years, of turning Iraq into a beacon of democracy that would transform the Middle East, or even of turning Iraq into a dependable ally of the United States, were quietly put on hold. Bush administration rhetoric didn't always reflect this shift. But on the ground in Iraq, the new goal was simply getting to a more or less peaceful Iraq that didn't explode into a regional war or implode into a civil war.

As Odierno, Sky, and others talked into the night, hours at a time, three or four nights a week, they focused on the way that parts of the Baghdad government exercised power to further sectarian agendas, undermining the legitimacy of the entire enterprise. "It is a failed state with ungoverned spaces in which the government is part of the problem," Sky summarized as their conclusion. In particular, they would target Shiite militiamen employed by the Ministry of Health, who among other things were killing Sunnis who sought medical care.

They also decided that they needed to reposition the U.S. government. In February, Odierno would tell his subordinate commanders to conduct "balanced operations targeting groups on both sides of the sectarian divide." That is, rather than act as an ally of one side, the Shiites, they would recast the American role in Iraq as an arbiter between groups.

As part of that move, Odierno ordered the abandonment of the term "AIF," for "anti-Iraqi forces," an Orwellian designation that U.S. officials had given to insurgent groups, as if Americans could decide who was a real Iraqi. They also would carefully release certain leaders of insurgent groups to see if they might begin to cooperate. The message to them would be that the U.S. government recognizes their concerns, which are legitimate, and will work with you, as long as you don't use violence against us. Finally, they decided that the key indicator of progress in security was Iraqi civilian casualties, not those inflicted on the American and Iraqi militaries.

Odierno also discussed with Keane what do to about Sadr City, the Bronx-sized slum in eastern Baghdad dominated by Moqtada al-Sadr. Keane and he concluded that "we should avoid Sadr City," and try to deal with it later politically, instead of engaging in another round of block-to-block fighting in a huge neighborhood of hostile Iraqis.

They also decided that there was a hole or a gap in the middle of Iraqi society. The people had needs, especially for security, but the Iraqi government couldn't provide it, so that opening was being filled by militias. "We need to step into that gap," Odierno ordered. The way to do that, he said to his advisers, was "to get back out into Baghdad—I want to get my people out there." In effect, they had reversed the American policy of the previous three years.

In April 2007, Maj. Gen. Fastabend, Petraeus's strategic adviser, composed a twenty-page essay, "How All This Ends"—that is, the answer to the question Petraeus had posed four years earlier—that captured the revamped approach: The United States, he wrote, needed "to settle for far less than the vision that drove it to Baghdad."

... AND BIGGER RISKS

The other shoe, Fastabend continued, was to take far bigger risks. He subtitled his essay "It's Fourth and Long, Go Deep." In the essay, which isn't classified but has been held so closely that its existence hasn't previously been disclosed, he employed the literary device of having Petraeus look back from the future—2009—to recount how he had turned around the situation in Iraq. Never one to waste a moment of his time, Petraeus kept a copy of Fastabend's essay next to the toilet in his private bathroom, taking it out occasionally to refresh his thinking.

It can end well, Fastabend explained, if the U.S. government would take more risks. But to take risks, we have to think seriously, he continued. Few antiwar critics were as scathing of the conduct of the Iraq war as are members of Petraeus's staff, such as Fastabend, his chief of strategy. "As a sole superpower, we thought we didn't have to make hard choices. We thought we could just come here, without thinking about the opportunity costs. When you just write conditions, and never have to say who does what by when—then you don't make choices and decisions. All you get is conditions: Close the border, end corruption, change the culture."

It was time, he told Petraeus, "to take some risk—not the ones you're comfortable with, but gut-wrenching, hold-your-balls risks."

He recommended six major departures:

- Get rid of extremists by working with them. We had been fighting them for four years, he said, "whacking and stacking them"—but with little to show for all that blood, sweat, and tears. Maybe, he suggested, it was time to replicate the example of Ramadi and cut some deals with tribal leaders and other insurgent organizations. Tell them they aren't militias, they are neighborhood watches. Parole insurgents to them. "Commanders will object—'catch and release.' There will be letters from mothers and fathers—'They killed Americans.' You'll have to take some heat. Make a choice!" Fastabend even called for large-scale detainee releases, which would be considered but eventually was shelved. "Petraeus was comfortable with it, but division commanders weren't," Col. Rapp explained. Petraeus agreed to drop the idea because of their concern that it would damage troop morale. But he would go on to implement the idea of local cease-fires with former insurgents.

- Another major risk Fastabend recommended taking was alienating our own allies, the Shiite-dominated central government. Push Maliki hard. And don't let him shut down the deals with former insurgents. Like Odierno, Petraeus was ready to go further there. In the following months, American commanders would sign up tens of thousands of former insurgents to become local militias, first called Concerned Local Citizens and then later, Sons of Iraq.
- Third was reaching out to Moqtada al-Sadr. Part of these negotiations were even about whether to talk to each other. "They said, we want a date for your exit," recalled Kilcullen, who was briefed on the initial exchange with Sadr's representative.

  "We can't do that," the Americans replied.

  "Well, forget it then," a Sadrist politician replied.

  But the Americans were curious. "What date did you have in mind?"

  "Well, December 2012," the Sadrist said. That brought private grins to the Americans—promising to stay in Iraq until then was a position that would have drawn protests from many in the U.S. Congress.
- Fourth was beginning to emphasize reconciliation at the local level, among Sunis and Shiites in towns and provinces, rather than a deal among national leaders, which had hit a dead end. Petraeus and Crocker would go along with this.
- Also, he argued, put the brakes on the transition to Iraq control, stopping the cycle of rushing to failure. "Casey was all about transition," said Fastabend. "Petraeus has slowed it down." One risk that surprised Fastabend was how dangerous it was to deal with the Iraqi government. While scheduling appointments, Americans had to worry about whether the government official who was being met would tip off the insurgents to set up an ambush.

Fastabend was even more bothered by how the government had reacted a few weeks earlier to the suicide bombing of the Iraqi parliament, an incident that killed eight in the worst breach of security the Green Zone had ever suffered. One Iraqi official told him, "We'll show them, we'll meet tomorrow."

"Well, I was just over there, and it needs to be cleaned up," Fastabend responded.

"Oh yeah, it will be," anotehr Iraqi promised.

He went back the Council of Representatives building the next morning just to check. It was still a bloody mess. "The motherfucker's legs were still on the floor, and parts of him were all over the walls," he recalled. He called one of the Iraqis: "You think you're going to walk the press through here in twenty minutes?"

- Finally, Fastabend was mulling something that was politically explosive back home. "I think you announce a withdrawal schedule." Moqtada al-Sadr couldn't live with a big U.S. force in Iraq, which he deemed an occupation. But maybe, Fastabend calculated, he'd want a small presence, of 5 brigades, or perhaps 35,000 troops, just to keep him safe from the Sunnis. "Some people say he wouldn't accept it. I say, 'Take a risk.'" He explained: "So we say to him, we'll give you a timetable. Maybe come down to twelve [brigade combat teams] by the end of 2008, and five by a year later."

His bottom line: "If this is the decisive struggle of our time—*be decisive.*" Fastabend didn't think he was asking too much. "Considering that the alternative is getting chased out of here, it doesn't seem that audacious to me."

There are two kinds of plans, he explained—those that fail and those that just might work. "If we fail, we are getting ready for a pretty major civil war, leading to a regional war. If things work, we are in an accommodation phase" that might lead to a preserved Iraq. So, he said, play according to the stakes.

Fastabend was correctly pointing to a major flaw in the American approach in the war from 2003 to 2006. For years, U.S. commanders had tended to seek strategic gains—that is, winning the war—without taking tactical risks. They ventured little and so gained less. By making the protection of their own troops a top priority, and by having them live mainly on big bases and only patrol neighborhoods once or twice a day or night, they had wasted precious time and ceded vital terrain to the enemy. Also, their priorities undercut any thought of making the protection of Iraqi civilians their mission. That was literally seen as someone else's job—Iraq soldiers and police.

Capt. McNally, who studied the Fastabend's essay, concluded that its core message was "It's put up or shut up time." The way forward it recommended, she explained, was, "Take risks. Otherwise, we just keep going along, and we lose six soldiers once a week when the Strykers [wheeled armored personnel carriers] get blown up."

One risk Fastabend didn't mention in his essay was the internal one Petraeus was taking on as he clashed with his immediate superior, Adm. William Fallon, who had succeeded Abizaid as chief of the Central Command, the U.S. military headquarters for Iraq and the rest of the Middle East. Petraeus was determined to speak his mind, leading to what would amount to a running feud with Fallon, his ostensible boss.

A FOUNDATION FOR STRATEGY

It is axiomatic that good tactics can't fix a bad strategy, but that a good strategy tends to fix bad tactics, because the inappropriateness of those individual actions becomes self-evident when seen against the larger scheme. For example, in a mission where the top priority explicitly is protecting the people, there would be no excuse for an incident like Haditha.

The biggest single strategic change in Iraq in 2007, the one that preceded all others and enabled them, may also have been the least noticed one: a new sobriety in the mind-set of the U.S. military. It wasn't just the Bush administration that had taken years to face reality in Iraq. The military also was slow to learn. McMaster's successful campaign in Tall Afar in late 2005, for example, seemed to be largely ignored by top commanders, or dismissed as irrelevant. Despite the attention given to Tall Afar by the media, there seemed to be no concerted effort in the Army to discern if the success there might be replicated elsewhere. By the beginning of 2007, though, the U.S. military had been fighting in Iraq longer than it fought in World War II. It had been flummoxed and humbled by its struggle in the Land Between the Rivers, trying nearly everything in its toolbox of conventional methods, and not finding much that promised a successful outcome. Finally, it was ready to try something new.

It had to come a long way. In the feel-good days after the fall of the Berlin Wall and before 9/11, and even for some time after, when the U.S. military was the armed wing of "the sole superpower," Pentagon officials liked to talk about "rapid decisive operations." That was a term for, as one 2003 study done at the Army's School of Advanced Military Studies put it, the devastating cumulative effect of "dominant maneuver, precision engagement and information operations." The technocentric notion behind it was that U.S. forces, taking advantage of advances in sensors, communications, computer technology, and long-range weaponry and precision logistics, all areas in which it excelled, would fight so quickly and adeptly that the enemy would never have a chance to catch up and understand what was happening. Blinded, confused, and overwhelmed, the enemy's will would break, U.S. forces would triumph, and everyone would live happily ever after. "We need rapidly deployable, fully integrated joint forces capable of reaching distant theaters quickly and working with our air and sea forces to strike adversaries swiftly, successfully, and with devastating effect," Defense Secretary Donald Rumsfeld said in January 2002. Thus, he continued, we would possess "the option for one massive counteroffensive to occupy an aggressor's capital and replace the regime."

One of the people in the audience that day was Gen. Tommy Franks, then the chief of the U.S. Central Command, and 14 months later the commander of U.S. forces invading Iraq. The "rapid decisive operations" approach culminated in Franks's plan for going into Iraq, in which he sought to substitute speed for control. "Speed kills" became his mantra, repeated endlessly to his subordinates. But as U.S. forces found after they raced from Kuwait into Baghdad, speed could temporarily substitute for mass in military operations but wasn't the same as control. Once the Americans got to the capital, they stopped moving. Lacking both mass and velocity, they soon lost control of the situation.

Col. McMaster would argue later that the very concept of rapid decisive operations had hamstrung American commanders as they entered the country, because it had "artificially divorced war from its political, human, and psychological dimensions. So, if flexibility hinges on a realistic estimate of the situation going into a complex situation, we were behind at the outset." It would only be after American commanders and strategists began paying attention to the most basic human elements—tribes, blood feuds, and fights over water, money, and women—that they would begin to understand the war they were in, which Clausewitz maintains is the first and most important task of the military leader.

"Our mindset was not to kill, it was to win," recalled Lt. John Burns, who led a scout platoon in Baghdad during the Petraeus counteroffensive. "We constantly evaluated our situation and made certain we were fighting the war we had and not necessarily the one we wanted."

But that sort of seasoned understanding would come only after four years of struggle that more often was counterproductive than not. As the war for Iraq began in earnest in the summer and fall of 2003, U.S. commanders, surprised by the intensity and duration of the resistance to their presence, emphasized capturing and killing their enemies. But every time they captured key leaders, more seemed to spring up. By 2007 the military had realized that this approach was not leading toward success. "I think if the last four years in Iraq show anything, it's that you can't get by on brute force alone, and our generals should understand that by now," Col. Mansoor, Petraeus's executive officer, said one day in Baghdad late in 2007.

Under Petraeus, many did indeed get it. "You can't kill your way out of this kind of war," said Lt. Gen. James Dubik, in a comment that many repeated that year.

In remaking itself in the 1970s and '80s as a blitzkrieg force, the Army may have repeated the mistakes of the German army of World War II, observed Andrew Krepinevich, the defense intellectual who wrote the seminal work on the Army's failure in Vietnam. "In World War II, the Germans were very good tactically, but they were terrible at the strategic level," he said. Thus the rebuilding of the Army during the 16 years from the fall of Saigon to the beginning of the 1991 Gulf War, rather than being new and innovative, may actually have signaled the end of an era. As retired Army Col. Bob Killebrew, a thoughtful strategic thinker, put it, "We may well look back on the '90s as the final spasm of blitzkrieg." That observation casts a new light on the two "thunder run" tank charges that the Army used to penetrate Baghdad during the invasion: They may have been not the harbinger of a new, more agile Army, but rather a last blaze of glory for the heavy conventional force, a miniature version of its glory days of 1944–45 in Europe and 1991 in Kuwait.

After four years of failure in Iraq, the U.S. military began to find effectiveness—at least tactically—as its leaders finally became resigned to the reality that the way to success was conducting slow, ambiguous operations that were built not around technology but around human interactions. "Be deliberate," Odierno would order his subordinates. Show "tactical patience," advised a brigade commander. It became common to hear American commanders counsel their frustrated soldiers to take it *"Shwia, shwia"*—Arabic for "slowly, slowly." As the new counterinsurgency manual said, they needed to be prepared to take years to succeed. The key to this mode of warfare was slowly seeking accommodation, pulling the population over to one's side, even if that sometimes meant cutting deals with people who had killed American troops. As Emma Sky said one day, "We are dealing with guys with blood on their hands."

Sky, who had advised the U.S. military for a year in 2003–4, saw the commanders as having an entirely new mind-set in 2007. "In '03, the guys were Christian crusaders seeking revenge for 9/11. Today they are advising Iraqis in a way they couldn't back then. They have completely transformed the way they work with Iraqis. It is a tremendous change. It's not just the Sunnis or the Shiites who have changed. We all have changed."

The entire approach was distinctly alien to the rapid, decisive, mechanistic, and sometimes Manichean mind-set that had been taught to a generation or two of American commanders. It had nothing to do with technology and everything to do with dealing with some of the oldest of human traits—eye-to-eye contact and heeding the values and ways of tribes and their leaders. What was going on in Iraq in 2007, as Kilcullen put it, was "a counterrevolution in military affairs, led to a certain extent by David Petraeus."

The pre-Iraq, triumphalist U.S. military also was fond of talking about "information dominance." What this tended to mean in reality was amassing data rather than understanding. For most of the time the U.S. military has been in Iraq, it actually has tended to be information poor. As Warren Buffett, the wise billionaire, once observed, if you've been playing poker for half an hour and you don't know who the patsy at the table is, then you're the patsy. Too often, U.S. troops, cut off both linguistically and physically from the Iraqi populace, operating in a harsh climate amid an alien culture, had been made patsies. This was not their fault but that of their leaders who didn't understand the task at hand of conducting a counterinsurgency campaign.

Looking back, Maj. Mark Gillespie, a military adviser in Iraq, recalled that in early 2006, he was "reaching terminal velocity and pulling my hair out and trying to figure out why people just don't get it. Well, it wasn't them who weren't getting it, it was me who wasn't getting it."

American soldiers would really only start getting the requisite amount of information after they moved out into the population in 2007. In retrospect, this seems like common sense. After all, Clausewitz, often seen incorrectly as the most conventional of war theorists, notes that the people are the greatest single source of information available. "We refer not so much to the single outstandingly significant report, but to the countless minor contacts brought about by the daily activities of our army," he explained.

The new humility of American commanders amounted to the starting point for the new strategy. After trying it their way for years, they now were going to try it the Iraqi way. So, for example, rather than try to build on their own individualistic core values of freedom and "one-man, one-vote" democracy, they began to rely on Iraq's more communitarian values, which often revolve around showing and receiving respect. "They felt disrespected, dispossessed, and disgusted," Petraeus said one day. "All they wanted was"—he began singing the letters in the old Aretha Franklin hit—"R-E-S-P-E-C-T." (Indeed, one of the new Iraqi political parties that would form called itself "Dignity.")

With humility came its twin, candor. "There's a more open environment now," Capt. McNally said. "People used to maybe think [negative] things, but they didn't say them."

This new sobriety was the intellectual context for the reduction in the goals of the war. This is a controversial point, because that shrinkage has never really been announced or even acknowledged. But it was put into practice every day as a smaller, narrower set of aims. The goal was no longer the grandiose one that somewhat murkily grew out of the 9/11 attacks and was meant to transform Iraq and the Middle East—what the old Wolfowitzian Iraq hawks had called "draining the swamp" in which terrorism grew. Instead, the quietly restated U.S. goal was to achieve a modicum of stability, to keep Iraq together, and to prevent the war from metastasizing into a regional bloodbath. That meant finding what one official called "a tolerable level of violence" and learning to live with it.

"Not rhetorically, but in practice we have" limited the goals of the U.S. effort, Mansoor said one day early in 2008. Trying out a phrase Petraeus would use publicly four months later, he said, "We are willing to accept less than a Jeffersonian democracy. . . . The rhetoric of our national leadership is still about freedom, but on the ground, there's a realization there is going to have to be Iraqis figuring this out." (In April 2008, Petraeus would tell the House Foreign Affairs Committee: "In terms of what it is that we are trying to achieve, I think simply it is a country that is at peace with itself and its neighbors. It is a country that can defend itself, that has a government that is reasonably representative and broadly responsive to its citizens, and a country that is involved in, engaged in, again, the global economy. Ambassador Crocker and I, for what it's worth, have typically seen ourselves as minimalists. We're not after the holy grail on Iraq; we're not after Jeffersonian democracy. We're after conditions that would allow our soldiers to disengage.") Petraeus began keeping an eagle eye on the president's speeches, using their weekly video teleconferences to convey caution against inflating the rhetoric. He usually succeeded but not always.

There was good reason for this quiet ratcheting down. As Steven Metz, an astute strategic analyst, put it, encouraging democracy was at odds with the larger goal of stability: "Our current strategy is based on the delusion that we can have stable, or modulated democratization," he said. "Few things are more destabilizing and prone to chaos than democratization. I think we can have either democratization or stabilization. The issue is whether we can tolerate several decades of often-violent instability while democratization takes root."

THE HARDEST STEP

The surge really began even before the first of the surge brigades arrived. That may sound paradoxical but isn't, because the surge was more about how to use troops than it was about the number of them. The first new brigade wouldn't fully arrive until February, but as the bombings increased in January, the 1st Cavalry Division, which already was in the country, escalated its efforts to protect the population, seeking new ways to protect markets, neighborhoods, main roads, and bridges, said Col. Tobin Green, the division's chief of operations, and a friend and former student of Eliot Cohen. "I believe that was a turning point," Green said, "a visible sign of commitment to protecting the Iraqi people."

Moving American soldiers from big isolated bases and into new posts of 35 men (if platoon-sized) to around 100 (if manned by a company) located in vacant schoolhouses, factories, and apartment buildings in Baghdad's neighborhoods was the hardest step. Essentially, U.S. forces were sallying out to launch a counteroffensive to retake the city.

Seeking to translate the strategy into operational and tactical sense, Odierno was looking downward, monitoring the adjustments of subordinates from division commanders to platoon leaders. "That's especially difficult with units that were already there," recalled Keane, his mentor. "He was transitioning those forces from a very defensive strategy to an offensive strategy." On top of that, having only the minimum amount of troops that he and Keane thought he needed, Odierno began to move them around in order to maximize their effectiveness. "He took risks," Keane said. "The easy thing would have been to put all the surge brigades into the city." Instead, following the "What would Saddam do?" approach, Odierno put much of his combat power outside the capital. This was the biggest difference between Odierno's plan and the one Keane and Kagan had pulled together at the American Enterprise Institute. Eventually, he would split his total available combat power evenly between the city and its surroundings, with six brigades in each.

In February, the 2nd Brigade of the 82nd Airborne Division, the first official surge brigade, was sent into eastern Baghdad. Over the next several weeks, 19 new outposts were established across Baghdad. "Get out of your Humvees, get out of your tanks, your Brads, and walk around," Army Maj. Joseph Halloran, an artillery officer, later summarized. "Stop commuting to war. . . . The concept of a super FOB [forward operating base] is more damaging to the war effort than any Abu Ghraib or Haditha incident could ever be."

The first days were surprisingly violent, with an average of almost 180 attacks a day on U.S. forces. "That was the battle of Baghdad," Petraeus said looking back 18 months later. "It was just very very difficult, very very hard." During February 2007, Baghdad suffered an average of more than one car bomb attack a day. Between late January and late February, at least eight U.S. helicopters were shot down.

In March, the second surge unit, the 4th Brigade of the 1st Infantry Division, began operations in western Baghdad. One skeptical soldier from the Big Red One told a reporter that he didn't expect the new approach to work. "It's getting worse and worse," he explained to the *Washington Post*'s Joshua Partlow. "They don't even respect us anymore. They spit at us, they throw rocks at us. It wasn't like that before." In some Shiite neighborhoods, units were greeted by stacked loudspeakers blaring the chants of the Jaysh al-Mahdi, Moqtada al-Sadr's militia. In Sunni neighborhoods that had been ethnically cleansed, patrolling soldiers often found piles of executed bodies and vacant houses with blood smeared on the walls.

This is how the operations officer for a battalion operating in southwest Baghdad recalled that time to a researcher for the official Center for Army Lessons Learned:

> When we first moved into the AO [area of operations], it was house-to-house clearing, and fighting most of the way. It took months before we could drive more than halfway north through the *mulhullas* without hitting multiple IEDs and taking fire. It got so bad that we twice had to turn over part of our battlespace to Strykers [wheeled armored vehicles]. We focused on establishing a foothold by clearing house by house and holding with a 24x7 presence. Then we began establishing our HUMINT [human intelligence] sources, pulling out

> bad guys, and building relationships with the people. We also focused on splitting the insurgency. It was composed of two main groups. First were the local mujahadin, who were truly concerned about protecting the neighborhood from the Shiite Militias, particularly Jaysh al-Mahdi (JAM). They were generally actually concerned with the people. The second element was Al-Qaeda in Iraq (AQI). The people were getting tired of all the violence in the neighborhoods, of things blowing up and getting innocents killed. Every time something happened, we'd say "AQI did this too you. Why do you allow it?" When we lost people, we'd stay restrained and not seek vengeance.

The first task was simply surviving. "Our first two weeks were tough," Lt. Jacob Carlisle, a platoon leader, later said. "We had to clear every day, and we got hit every day." Indeed, in June, he would be shot in the thigh and hit by shrapnel in the face and arm.

Not all soldiers liked the shift into the population. "My platoon sergeant came to Iraq with the idea that we were going to hide for fifteen months and all come back alive," recalled Lt. Schuyler Williamson of the 1st Cavalry Division. "When I told him that we were not going to do that, he said I was going to get my soldiers killed." The balky sergeant eventually was reassigned, Williamson added.

Lt. Col. Crider led his cavalry squadron into the Doura neighborhood in southern Baghdad and lost three soldiers in one week. "We did not know who was responsible for these attacks, and no one would tell us anything," he recalled. "Our partnered National Police unit was no help as the residents of Doura, our predominantly Sunni neighborhood, hated them." In fact, he remembered, the locals referred to the police as "the militia." Bringing them into the neighborhood was seen as a hostile act.

"Doura was a meatgrinder," recalled Command Sgt. Maj. Marvin Hill.

When Baker Company, a unit in the 2nd Infantry Division, moved into there, it was greeted with "constant enemy small-arms fire, IED, RPG, and grenade attacks, often surprisingly coordinated," recalled Lt. Tim Gross, a platoon leader. Baker began by spending three nights using shovels, screwdrivers, and tire irons to remove 18 "deep-buried" bombs in its area. The soldiers lied to the locals that they knew where all the bombs were because they had so many local sources of information. "We don't need any more information because we had hundreds of people cooperating," was the bluff, as Capt. Jim Keirsey, Baker's commander, recalled it. In fact, they began with almost no information from the people of the area, who had felt abused by Iraqi police operating in the area. Indeed, Baker later would ban the most abusive of the police, the militia-infested National Police, from entering the neighborhood.

Despite being attacked constantly, Baker Company, with roughly 125 men, began conducting patrols around the clock. It tried to be precise in the use of force. "Shooting the right guy teaches the enemy and population that evil has consequences," Keirsey wrote. "The corollary is that a poor shot—one that hits an innocent person or leads to collateral damage—is worse than not shooting at all."

Gross, the platoon leader, called this mind-set "protect the innocent, punish the deserving." He said it especially impressed the locals when one of his platoon's patrols, while amid civilians, was ambushed. After a girl was hit, his platoon sergeant picked her up and rushed her to medical care. "An informant reported the incident as a large turning point towards winning the people of our neighborhood," Gross said.

There was a new savviness to the way American forces were operating. Baker Company's most effective tactic didn't involve firepower but instead walking and talking. Its soldiers conducted a thorough census that mapped the 3,500 households in its area of operations, photographing all male inhabitants and collecting their grievances. Dubbed "Operation Close Encounters," it was done slowly and carefully, with some interviews lasting an hour. Keirsey ordered that the soldier doing the talking should sit down, take off his helmet and sunglasses, accept any drink offered, and speak respectfully. The other members of the patrol should stay in uniform and quietly focus outward on security, rather than join the conversation. In this way, they learned about suspected bomb planters and about Iraqi police abuses. As a result of ethnic cleansing, there were many empty houses. Rather than let them be used by militias, the American troops padlocked their doors and gates.

They also were told that while the area was controlled by insurgents, U.S. funds had helped finance the enemy, because the insurgents got kickbacks from contractors. "People are getting rich working with Americans in Iraq," said Keirsey. "Make sure they are the right people." It was an important lesson, but not one that many American officials had heeded in earlier years.

Visiting Iraq, Keane saw not only Petraeus and Odierno but their division and brigade commanders. He would push them. "How many of your platoons are outside the FOB and on the street twenty-four/seven?—that was always a huge dimension for me. And some of those guys would be hedging—they would have one-third of them out there. I said, 'No guys, you would have to have two-thirds, for sure. And if you could, get them all out there and be protecting yourself back in the FOB using someone else,'" such as support units or contractors.

By May 2007, the 1st Cavalry Division, which was the core unit for Baghdad, at any given point had 75 percent of combat forces off its headquarters post, said Maj. Gen. Joseph Fil Jr., the division commander. The typical cycle for a unit was five and a half days out, followed by one and a half back on post to rest, refit, check e-mail, and clean up. Having troops live where the action was added enormously to their effectiveness, not only in increased awareness but also simply in response time. "You're not driving and hour and a half to do a ninety-minute patrol," Fil said.

The 1st Cav's 1st Brigade, stationed north and northwest of Baghdad, set out to eliminate al Qaeda's safe havens and crack down on the networks sending car bombs and roadside bombs into the capital. But at first it didn't feel it had enough troops for those tasks. "I was frustrated because the only thing we were doing was terrain denial—we were so strung out securing the LOCs," or lines of communication, said Maj. Patrick Michaelis, the brigade's S-3, or chief of operations. With the troops he had, he explained, trying to keep major roads clear of ambushes and bombs was "all we could do." Dozens of soldiers were killed. The unit didn't begin to feel the effects of the surge until mid-May, after it was given an additional battalion from another division, he recalled. Thus reinforced, its operations against al Qaeda would become a model that Petraeus would cite, as the brigade pushed into the areas where al Qaeda fighters and their allies had found sanctuary. "We fought our way in," he recalled. The enemy was ready, having deeply buried bombs on the roads in the area. One had a full 1,200 feet of copper wire leading to the trigger—far further than U.S. forces were trained to look for the triggerman.

At almost every new outpost established, a series of fights and terrorist actions would ensue. Sentries found it difficult to stop truck and car bombs barreling toward them with mere rifle fire, so were issued bazooka-like anti-tank weapons. Frequently, al Qaeda would overreact to the new patrol bases, said Maj. Luke Calhoun, the brigade's intelligence officer: "They'd kidnap children, kill women, threaten tribal leaders." But that counteroffensive usually backfired, he said, because the population was driven into the arms of U.S. forces, who now were available to them 24 hours a day in the new outposts.

One of the hardest hit areas was the town of Sab al-Bor, which had a population of about 60,000. In August 2006, five months before the surge got under way, al Qaeda had begun shelling the town, located on the northwest fringe of greater Baghdad, with big 120-millimeter mortars, aiming at the primarily Shiite northwest corner of the town. But that was the only major security problem with the town, and U.S. forces were facing bigger issues elsewhere as the small civil war grew. In late September 2006, the town was turned over to Iraqi police, "so I could pull B Troop and the IA [Iraqi army] out of the town and move them to other, hotter areas," recalled Col. James Pasquarette, who commanded the U.S. Army brigade based nearby. But on October 3, soon after that move, the mortar attacks escalated. Shiites in the town retaliated by shooting up Sunni neighborhoods. Thousands fled the town, including the Iraqi police. Soon only about 5,000 inhabitants remained. The young male Shiites who were displaced became willing recruits for Shiite militias, which intensified the cycle of violence.

The turnaround for the 1st Cav brigade, commanded by Col. Paul Funk, began in 2007 after a Marine unit moved to the west side of the brigade's sector, cutting off al Qaeda's roads south to Fallujah and north to Tamariyah, Samarra, and Tikrit. Almost instantly the mortar shelling of Sab al-Bor ended. U.S. Army engineers purposely weakened a major bridge so that pedestrians could cross but not vehicles, and the car bombings stopped. By October 2007, Michaelis said, al Qaeda seemed to make a strategic decision to retreat northward to Mosul.

The improvement in security provided multiple benefits. During that period, more and more local militias came over to the American side. Turning over checkpoints and outposts to them freed up the 1st Cav units for other missions. Also, the locals began providing precise intelligence. "The info we were getting from the CLCs [Concerned Local Citizens] was phenomenal," recalled Michaelis. If they said there were six bombs in a road, and American explosives experts only detected five, the local fighters would insist that they had missed one—and would be proven right. In October, representatives of local Sunni and Shiite militias that had turned also met jointly with representatives of the Iraqi government in what the 1st Cav labeled "The Northwest Baghdad Regional Security Summit." Michaelis remembers thinking that day, "That's what 'right' looks like." Finally, elements of local governments began to surface. "We started seeing guys pop up. 'I'm the water official for the district.' 'Well, where the hell have you been for the last fifteen months?' 'There's no way I was gonna stick my head up when al Qaeda was gonna kill me.' "

By the end of the unit's tour that winter, in late 2007, Michaelis said, "We'd start seeing video shops, Internet shops, cigar shops. These are not things you buy when you are at the low end of Maslow's hierarchy of needs." And the population of Sab al-Bor was back up to 21,000. The brigade's transformative experience would be replicated in a dozen other areas in and around the capital in 2007.

THE ENEMY COUNTERATTACK

But anyone still alive to fight the Americans in Iraq in 2007 had learned a lot in the preceding years. In the spring and summer the American surge was met with a counteroffensive involving new tactics and more lethal weapons. This was arguably the toughest period of the war, as the Americans took their last and best shot only to see casualties increase without many signs of security improving. At the very least, it was the hardest part of Petraeus's time in command in Iraq. At the time he put a positive spin on it while speaking in public, calling himself a "qualified optimist." But much later he would admit, "There were days that were about the hardest that I have ever experienced." The U.S. military had committed its reserve. It was taking more risks and losing more people. As the war entered its fifth year in March 2007, there were few signs that the gamble of the surge was paying off, either tactically or strategically.

In north Baghdad, Company C of the 1st Battalion, 26th Infantry Regiment, 1st Infantry Division, spent most of its tour of duty—11 months out of 15—in the heavily contested Sunni neighborhood of Adhamiyah. On May 14, 2007, a bomb blew one of its Humvees into the air. "I never thought I was going to see my buddies running around on fire," said Staff Sgt. Octavio Nunez, one of two soldiers who would receive the Silver Star for valor that day.

The bombs grew more powerful: In June a Bradley Fighting Vehicle in the same company was hit by a huge explosion, flipping the 25-ton armored vehicle and killing 5 soldiers. The bomb had been placed not far from an Iraqi army checkpoint, a point not lost on the American soldiers. The gunner, Spec. Daniel Agami, was pinned beneath the vehicle. His comrades could hear him scream as he burned to death. Another member of the battalion, Pfc. Ross McGinnis, would posthumously receive the Medal of Honor for jumping on a grenade that lodged inside a Humvee. All told, the battalion lost 31 men during its tour, nearly half of them from Charlie Company.

Col. Galloucis, commander of the MPs in Baghdad, shook his head as he remembered the violent spring of 2007. "We started seeing the introduction of EFPs into Baghdad," he said, referring to a particularly lethal kind of roadside bomb, the "explosively formed penetrator," that can lift off the ground heavy vehicles such as the tanklike Bradley Fighting Vehicle. If the entire Iraq war was characterized by roadside bombs, as the spirit of World War I was captured by trench warfare and machine guns, then the spring of 2007 was the campaign of the EFP. These armor-piercing bombs were only the size of a coffee can, and so could be placed very quickly, unlike the big bombs that required much digging. They were used almost exclusively by Shiite militias. The bombs were manufactured in Iran, with the number radically increasing late in 2006, said U.S. officials. "They are harder to make than you think," said one American bomb expert. Designed to fire a spearlike slug of melting metal at extremely high speed, the bombs didn't work if milled imprecisely, which causes the metal to fragment prematurely and so diminish in lethality.

Galloucis's troops were also facing a sniper threat, and that "was having a real psychological impact," as well as a physical one, because some of the shooters were using armor-piercing rounds that would penetrate American body armor. He remembered moments of despair—"You had a sense that things weren't working, that whatever we'd do, they'd counter."

Crider, the cavalry squadron commander in southern Baghdad, soon realized that the time-honored tactic of simply cordoning off an area and searching it not only antagonized the very people whose support they needed but also turned up few signs of the enemy. "Insurgents have learned over five years not to hide things in their homes," he commented.

U.S. military intelligence officers began to see assaults on Americans—rather than on Iraqis—as a positive sign. "If the attacks are against us, and not against Iraqi Security Forces or the people, then we're winning," said one. It was small consolation for those being shot at.

One day Kilcullen was riding with an Iraqi battalion commander who was about to move his unit into northwestern Baghdad for a 90-day tour. They were driving behind the outgoing Iraqi commander, whose Humvee blew up in front of them, turning the old commander into a shimmering cloud of hot pink mist. Kilcullen glanced over to look at the incoming Iraqi commander. "His eyes were like dinner plates," he recalled. A few days later, a message from the insurgents arrived at the new commander's headquarters, he said: "Sorry about last week. But you know, it doesn't have to be that way. You're only here for ninety days. Can't we live and let live?" The battalion commander's reaction, Kilcullen recalled, was "Sign me up." After that, it became difficult to get that commander to do anything. For the next 90 days, his battalion was ineffective, and the sector effectively was in enemy hands.

Sadr's Jaysh al-Mahdi was extraordinarily effective in infiltrating Iraqi forces, Kilcullen said. "We did a counterintelligence assessment of an Iraqi army battalion in central Baghdad and found that every senior commander and staff were either JAM, doing criminal activity with JAM, or intimidated by JAM."

ANALYZING THE PATTERNS of Iraqi violence, Kilcullen concluded that al Qaeda attacked during the day, using car bombs to attack people around Shiite markets and mosques, while Shiite militias retaliated at night, sending death squads into neighborhoods where Sunnis slept. These different pathways of violence required different responses, he argued. The way to deter the al Qaeda attacks was to establish checkpoints at the entryways to markets, mosques, and other public places—and then to count it as a victory if a bomb exploded at a checkpoint and killed two Iraqi soldiers rather than detonating at its target and killing dozens of civilians. Likewise, the answer to Shiite revenge attacks was to protect a dozen of the remaining Sunni neighborhoods, creating "gated communities" surrounded by big cement walls. The new Joint Security Stations would emphasize helping the market checkpoints during the day and backing up the neighborhood checkpoints by night, as well as patrol through their areas.

As thousands of cement barriers were erected—the one separating Adhamiyah from a Shiite area was twelve feet high and three miles long—they were roundly criticized as an imitation of Israeli tactics. That was the most incendiary charge possible in the Middle East. Steve Niva, a Middle East specialist at the Evergreen State College in Washington, charged that they were "dividing neighbor from neighbor and choking off normal commerce and communications." What they actually were doing was dividing Iraqis from people trying to kill them and choking off the normal movements of death squads. In Adhamiyah, civilian deaths declined by about two-thirds after the wall was erected in April 2007, Kilcullen said. One sign of the value of the walls was that al Qaeda in Iraq vigorously resisted them, noted Lt. Col. Dale Kuehl, commander of a battalion in northwest Baghdad. "We were engaged in a running battle with AQI as they tried to establish holes in the barriers while we tried to keep them intact," he said.

Taking similar measures in al Anbar Province, the Marines found that the steps to limit the mobility of insurgents produced some unexpected side benefits. "The insurgency is like a shark," a Marine intelligence report stated, "it has to move to survive. Cut off its freedom of movement and its loses its effectiveness." As the fighters and death squads shifted to new locations, they were forced to communicate, and signals interception enabled the U.S. military to find them, or to eavesdrop on their reports and planning sessions. Trying to escape the new constraints, some insurgents moved out of the cities and into the desert. This in turn made it easier for the Marines to locate them and then order up air strikes. "Population control measures and the subsequent movement of the insurgency into more remote areas has a secondary positive effect on our operations," the Marine report continued. "More and more often we found ourselves engaging the enemy on terrain that maximizes kinetic effects." Also, in the emptiness of the desert, "collateral damage"—that is, killing bystanders—became far easier to avoid.

ONE OF THE SAD realizations brought by the new campaign was how disillusioned Iraqis had become with the Americans after five years. As Col. MacFarland had seen in Ramadi, the locals no longer had much faith in what American officers told them.

"The Defense of Jisr al-Doreaa," an essay written by two Army captains, Michael Burganoyne and Albert Markwardt, and based on *The Defense of Duffer's Drift,* the 1905 British military classic about small unit tactics in guerrilla war, vividly illustrates the education of Americans in Iraq—and shows why Iraqis were losing faith. One of the lessons that unfortunately appears more than once is about the failure of American officers to be able to fulfill the promises they make to local Iraqi leaders, or even to keep them alive against insurgent retaliation. "You Americans have been here for years now," the mayor of a small Iraqi riverside town says in the essay to a newly arrived lieutenant. "It's promise after promise. . . . Let us just eat so you will not have to lie to me with promises."

Later, after the fictional lieutenant patiently wins the confidence of the mayor, who tells him where the local insurgents are based, the American unit is ordered to move elsewhere. "I met with the mayor and let him know we were leaving. His face seemed like it lost its color and he almost looked through me." A few days later, the lieutenant is back on his air-conditioned Forward Operating Base, watching cable news over his breakfast of Lucky Charms cereal, only to see footage of the mayor being executed. "I saw the mayor and all the locals we have developed as informants, their hands and feet tied behind their backs, on the street in front of his house, with two masked men standing behind them. Everyone who had helped us defeat the insurgents was lined up."

Thus, after getting into the neighborhoods, the new American units of the surge were taking over an operation that was in the red. Before they could do good they had to make up for the mistakes of their predecessors. They had to restore American credibility by delivering on their promises, and demonstrating that they wouldn't make friends and then abandon them.

"We were wondering if our approach was going to work," said Lt. Jacob Carlisle. "But when we got hit, we didn't overreact." He had studied Petraeus's counterinsurgency manual and constantly sought to build bridges to local residents. For example, he said, "When we went into houses around the contact, we didn't point weapons at them and yell and swear like we used to—'You know what the fuck just happened! Tell me! You know who did this! Tell me!' Now we went in and asked first if they were okay. Were there bad people who did this around that were threatening them? Why didn't you tell us there were people digging in explosives in front of your house. . . . Call us next time."

Carlisle, from Durand, Wisconsin, also found that years of frustrated American reconstruction programs had made Iraqis skeptical. A woman complained to him about raw sewage in the street, and he replied he would fix it. "All American make promises, but nothing ever happens," she responded. Determined to show that times had changed, he made sure the problem was addressed. "Word gets out," he said. "The people say, 'This unit, they tell you something and it happens.' "

Even detainees were treated differently, the young infantry officer said. "When people are released, we bring them back to the family. We don't just dump them out the gate." During Ramadan, he gave money to widows and children, and to the family of a man he had detained. "All this stuff makes a difference."

To deepen their awareness, his soldiers were assigned shifts in their neighborhoods. His platoon patrolled during the morning, and the company's other two platoons the afternoon and evening. "We know what is normal on the streets, and see the same people in the same places every day. We know if something is out of place." As the days passed, familiarity led to more ease in communication, and even a smidgen of trust. "Now that we were in the neighborhood every day, they believed us that we would keep them safe. More and more started calling us."

There were three steps of cooperation, said Lt. Col. Stephen Michael, commander of a battalion of the 25th Infantry Division, also posted on the south side of Baghdad. "First people weren't working with us, then they would work with us covertly, and now most work with us openly."

It took time—sometimes two or three months—before the Americans and the Iraqis began to grow accustomed to each other. "When we first came over and started planting ourselves in, you wouldn't see too many people because they didn't know if we'd be here, they didn't know to trust us, and basically the extremists were still intimidating and the people were reconning us," said Col. Wayne Grigsby of the 3rd Infantry Division, commander of the third of the surge brigades, which deployed to the tough area to the southeast of Baghdad. But after about two months, in late spring, people began talking to the American soldiers. Iraqis would begin telling them things, he said, like "Hey, that guy over there has never been in this town before. He drove in with two big trucks," their cargoes covered with tarps. "I don't think it's right, and we don't want him in here if he's going to bring trouble. Can you go take care of that problem?"

Down in south Baghdad, Lt. Col. Crider found the same effect. "The days of large cordon-and-sweep operations and hoping to find something . . . were over," he said. Instead, he sent his soldiers into Iraqi homes to learn who lived in the neighborhood to converse, drink tea, take photographs and census data, and learn about local concerns. "The American soldiers was no longer a mysterious authority figure speeding by in a HMMWV behind two-inch glass who occasionally rifled through their home. . . . After repeated encounters, our soldiers began to learn who was related, which families did not get along, who provided useful insight, and many other intimate details." They found that in their neighborhood lived an international basketball referee who had worked on the side for Iraqi intelligence. They met a famous Iraqi comedian, as well as a cardiologist fluent in English and eager to help. As they began to know and see more, attacks on them and on Iraqi civilians began to taper off. "AQI could no longer threaten individuals with violence after we left, because we never did," he observed. Also, locals began to report the emplacement of roadside bombs, which forced insurgents to switch to grenades and automatic weapons, which were riskier to use.

After a detainee was released—legitimately—into the neighborhood, Crider was pleased to receive 11 tips from local citizens about his presence. U.S. soldiers were sent to visit him and talk to him "about how things had changed. . . . He never caused any problems."

In keeping with the new, more neutral stance of the U.S. military as the arbiter of events, rather than an ally of one side, Crider also reined in the National Police, which at times was indistinguishable from a Shiite militia. "Denying the National Police the ability to unilaterally operate in the neighborhoods greatly increased our credibility," he said. Commanders also learned to keep a wary eye on those allies, especially as they tried to capitalize on U.S. operations for their own ends. "Once we cleared AQI from an area, Shia extremists would try to follow and claim it as their own, essentially replacing a cleared area with a new threat," stated an after-action review conducted by Odierno's headquarters.

The fight was growing more complex. One day in May, Kilcullen noted that, in Baghdad's Hurriyah neighborhood, there were four factions of Jaysh al-Mahdi, Sadr's extremist Shiite militia, fighting each other—Noble JAM, Golden JAM, "criminal JAM," and "ordinary JAM." U.S. officials sent a message to "JAM Central" in Najaf. "We want these guys out of there." In response, he said, the JAM headquarters in Najaf sent a hit team to Baghdad to sort out the problem. "Because we treated them as the authority, they cleaned it up." There also was murky unconfirmed talk that a deal was reached under which the U.S. military would aid Golden JAM in attacking other parts of the militia deemed to have gone rogue. Petraeus stated flatly that no such agreement existed and suggested that it grew out of rumors collected from Iraqis by U.S. intelligence or deals made by local American commanders.

The trends in Shiite southern Iraq also were worrisome. "The British have basically been defeated in the south," said a senior U.S. intelligence official in Baghdad. They were abandoning their former headquarters at Basra Palace, where an official visitor from London had described them as "surrounded like cowboys and Indians" by militia fighters. An airport base outside the city, where a regional U.S. embassy office and Britain's remaining 5,500 troops were barricaded behind building-high sandbags, was being hit by rockets or mortars an average of 150 times a month. Was Basra this year a foretaste of Baghdad the next?

ON JULY 4, 2007, Lt. James Freeze, leader of a 2nd Infantry Division reconnaissance platoon based north of Baghdad, celebrated Independence Day by having a glass of sparkling cider and a cigar with his old friend Austin Wilson, another lieutenant and West Pointer who had been the best man at his wedding. They discussed what one word would best characterize the Iraq they knew. They settled on "hopeless."

By coincidence, Fred Kagan, in many ways the guiding spirit behind the surge, was in the tough south Baghdad neighborhood of Doura a few weeks earlier, visiting one of his former West Point cadets who was now a company commander. "It was a complete combat zone," he said. "There was no one in the streets. It was a ghost town." The American brigade commander declined to take him out on patrol because of the danger.

Generals tend to be optimistic by nature, said Gen. Fastabend, Petraeus's strategic adviser. "The pessimists quit as captains," he cracked.

But five months into the new strategy, even some of the optimists were feeling gloomy. The Army's new counterinsurgency strategy required soldiers to be among the people, where they would form new relationships—but it also exposed them to hellacious new levels of violence. "We had some extreme challenges, in May, June, July," recalled Brig. Gen. Anderson, Odierno's chief of staff. "We were hedging our bets that the surge would work." When Iraqi forces were sent into a cleared area to help out, he said, the chances were "fifty-fifty" they were up to the job.

"It kept getting worse," Rapp recalled. "May had very high casualties. I thought, 'Holy cow, what is going on here?'" There was good reason to fret: The possibility was growing that the situation was about to get much worse, with the Americans played out and all the ingredients of a massive civil war coming together—there was oil to fight over, plenty of weapons available, and plenty of Iraqis as well as people in neighboring states who possessed the experience and skills to intensify the fighting.

It wasn't just Baghdad, either. In May, Gen. Odierno and Emma Sky helicoptered to Baqubah, about 35 miles northwest of the capital, a city both knew from their previous tours. "I knew it wasn't right," Odierno said. "It had a black cloud." As the surge had pushed some fighters out of the capital, they had moved into Baqubah and other parts of Diyala Province.

The old guard: By mid-2006, Gen. George Casey (above, left, and below, right), Defense Secretary Donald H. Rumsfeld (above, right), and Gen. John Abizaid (below, center) were seen by many in the military as wedded to a losing strategy in the Iraq war. At the end of 2006, Robert Gates (below, left) would succeed Rumsfeld and install new commanders to implement a new strategy.

ABOVE: *Army Staff Sgt. Gary Hilliard/Defense Department* BELOW: *Cherie A. Thurlby/Defense Department*

The new approach: In 2006, Col. Sean MacFarland (above, left) and Capt. Travis Patriquin (above, right) would explore a new strategy in the war, cutting deals with sheikhs such as Sittar albu-Risha (above, center). Of the three, only MacFarland would be alive at the end of 2007. Meanwhile, the views of Australian Lt. Col. David Kilcullen (below, left, conversing with Army Lt. Col. Michael Infanti, commander of a battalion in the 10th Mountain Division) were influential in the new manual on counterinsurgency then being written under the leadership of Gen. David Petraeus.

ABOVE: *Courtesy Andrew Lubin* BELOW: *Spec. Chris McCann/U.S. Army*

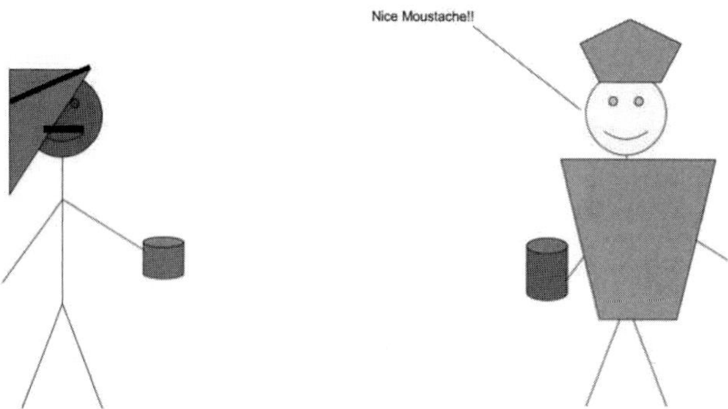

The Sheik and Joe drink Tea. Mmm good Chai.. Joe says Militias are bad, but Iraqi Police are good. Would the Sheik Let his men join the Iraqi Police? Yes, yes he will. (Iraqi Police stay in their local areas, and can effectively defeat murder and intimidation campaigns by their presence, unlike the Iraqi Army, which might send him somewhere far away..)

Patriquin created this stick-figure slide show to explain to skeptical superiors how he and MacFarland were forging alliances with Iraq tribes against al Qaeda fighters in western Iraq. His key insight was that Iraqis knew better than Americans where the extremists were—and would help the Americans if the Americans would help and protect them.

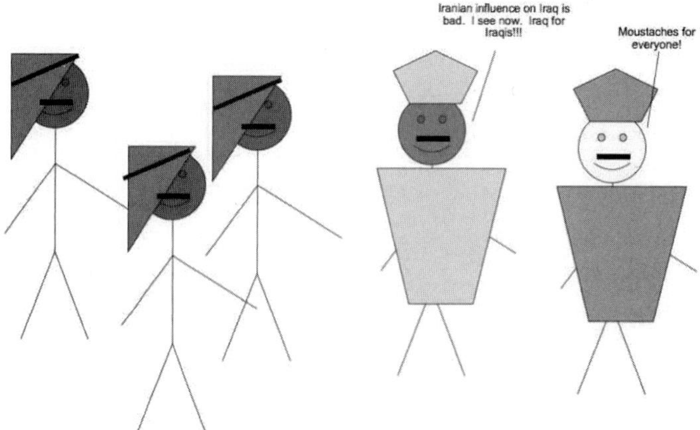

The Sheik brings more Sheiks, more sheiks bring more men. Joe realizes that if he'd done this three years ago, maybe his wife would be happier, and he'd have been home more. Mohammed gets to meet the Sheiks. They realize he's not such a bad guy, which is good for Iraq. Joe grows a moustache, because he realizes that Iraqis like people with moustaches and have a hard time trusting people without one.

Retired Gen. Jack Keane (left), seen leaving the White House after encouraging President Bush to escalate in Iraq, effectively became the chairman of the Joint Chiefs for several months in 2006, helping devise a new strategy, picking commanders to implement it, briefing Army leaders on the plan, and flying to Iraq to help the new commanders.
Brendan Smialowski/Getty Images

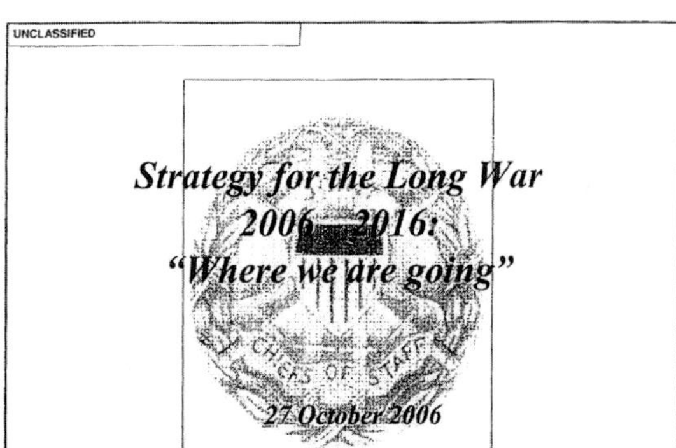

At the Pentagon, the "council of colonels" created after Keane sounded the alarm concluded in late 2006 that the war was indeed being lost and that a drastic change in strategy was urgently needed.

SECRET//NOFORN - PREDECISIONAL - CLOSE HOLD

Iraq: Impediments

- Failure to recognize the Nature of the War. We have not accepted the implications of an intensifying civil war and the strength of rejectionist sentiment in the Sunni Arab community... leads to unrealistically sanguine assessments and projections.
- Failing Strategy. "Short war" approach to a "long war" problem. Allowed political development to outpace security and other lines of operations. Aims to neutralize rather than defeat the insurgency, fails to address the civil war, and views exiting Iraq as an end unto itself.
  - *Circumscribes the will to win*
  - *Undermines Iraqi confidence*
  - *Self regulates how we define requirements (forces and resources)*
  - *Fails to generate sufficient resources and apply them to the problem (e.g. intel, inter-agency effort, troops, reconstruction)*
- We are losing because we are not winning and time is not on our side. We are not gaining the needed traction and are running out of time with US and Iraqi publics.

11 SECRET//NOFORN - PREDECISIONAL - CLOSE HOLD

But when Lt. Gen. Raymond Odierno arrived in Iraq, the orders he got from Gen. Casey were to accelerate the existing strategy of turning the security mission over to Iraqis. "Move outside all major cities" onto big bases, he was told. Within two months he would reverse almost every aspect of this order (below) and instead pursue the surge strategy of moving American troops into cities to protect the Iraqi population. *Staff Sgt. Curt Cashour/Defense Department*

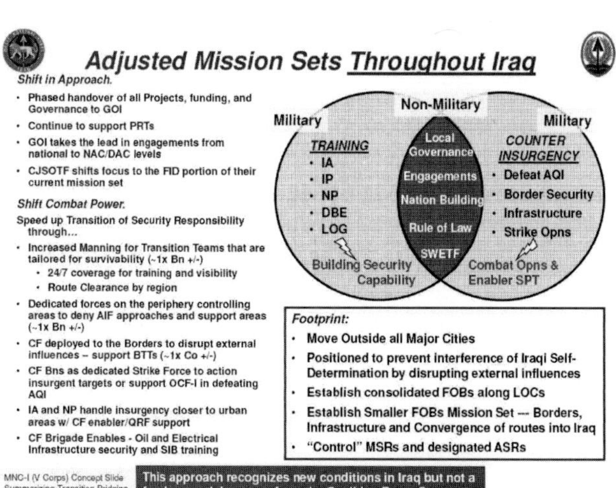

The new team: In early 2007, new leaders arrived in Iraq to revamp the American approach in the war. Gen. David Petraeus (above, left, with President Bush) took over the military effort, with Odierno (below, right) as his deputy. Ambassador Ryan Crocker (below, left) became the top American civilian.

ABOVE: *Defense Department*

BELOW: *Air Force Staff Sgt. D. Myles Cullen/Defense Department*

And new voices: Underscoring how much the American conduct of the war was changing, several foreigners became key counselors to U.S. military commanders. Emma Sky (above, right, with Petraeus), a pacifistic British expert on the Middle East, advised Odierno on politics and culture while Sadi Othman (below, between Defense Secretary Gates and Iraqi Prime Minister Nouri al Maliki), a Mennonite-educated Palestinian American, became Petraeus's ambassador to Iraqi political leaders.

ABOVE: *Army Staff Sgt. Lorie Jewell/Defense Department* BELOW: *Cherie A. Thurlby/Defense Department*

Self-images: Petraeus saw himself as a cowboy facing "the Mesopotamian stampede," and in his briefings to American visitors to Iraq used the ominous painting above, "The Stampede," by Frederic Remington. Ambassador Crocker, his civilian counterpart, could be so pessimistic that he was nicknamed "Mr. Sunshine" by President Bush. Crocker likened his partnership with Petraeus to two convicts on the lam and chained together—a plight portrayed by Sidney Poitier (below, left) and Tony Curtis (below, right) in the 1958 film *The Defiant Ones.*

ABOVE: *Gilcrease Museum, used with permission* BELOW: *Courtesy Katharine Kramer, used with permission*

The surge: The key step in the surge was not the additional troops but the decision to protect the Iraqi population. To do that, U.S. units had to establish outposts in towns and cities, a move that insurgents often challenged. Early in 2007, enemy fighters launched a complex bomb and grenade attack on the U.S. troops who had moved into the town of Tarmiyah. The photos here show the outpost before and after the battle. Of the thirty-eight soldiers there, two were killed and twenty-nine were wounded, but they won the fight. *Courtesy: 2nd Battalion, 8th Cavalry Regiment, 1st Cavalry Division, U.S. Army*

Other moves: Two other key steps in the new U.S. strategy were walling off endangered Sunni neighborhoods and Shiite markets (above), which stopped much of the ethnic cleansing, and creating the Sons of Iraq, local militias chockablock with former insurgents. Below, Staff Sgt. Michael Gonzales of the 82nd Airborne Division talks to some members of a local armed watch in Baghdad.

ABOVE: *Air Force Staff Sgt. Manuel J. Martinez/ Defense Department* BELOW: *Staff Sgt. Jason Bailey/U.S. Army*

Iraqi infighting: The first Samarra bombing, in 2006, marked the beginning of Iraq's descent into sectarian fighting. Petraeus and Crocker feared the second bombing, in 2007, would spark a new round of violence. After the second incident, Prime Minister Maliki (above, center, with his hands before him) flew to the scene to take control. Sadi Othman stands behind his left shoulder. *Iraqi Prime Minister Office via Getty Images*

American infighting: Adm. William "Fox" Fallon (left) became Petraeus's ostensible commander in 2007 and sought to revise the general's strategy. At one point the crusty Fallon sent Rear Adm. James "Sandy" Winnefeld Jr. (above) to Iraq to figure out how to get Petraeus to curtail the surge.

LEFT: *Octavio N. Ortiz/U.S. Navy*
ABOVE: *Matthew Bookwalter/U.S. Navy*

GENERAL PETRAEUS OR
GENERAL BETRAY US?
Cooking the Books for the White House
MoveOn.ORG
POLITICAL ACTION

The biggest battle: Petraeus's most important engagement in 2007 was his September confrontation with Congress (above). The atmosphere was supercharged, as evidenced by the MoveOn.org advertisement at left, which appeared in the *New York Times*. His ace in the hole was the sharp decline in violence that began just three months before his appearance (see chart below).

ABOVE: *Chip Somodevilla/Getty Images*

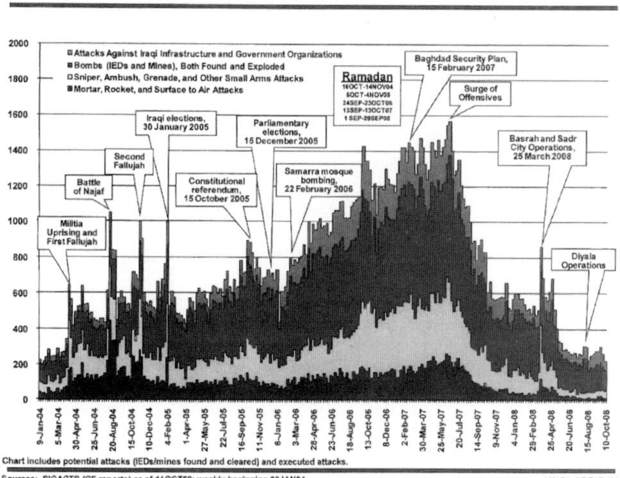

Lt. Gen. Lloyd Austin (above, center) took over from Odierno as the number two U.S. commander in Iraq in the spring of 2007. A few weeks later, Prime Minister Maliki surprised his American allies with a hastily planned assault in Basra, the biggest city in southern Iraq. Below, an Iraqi soldier patrols the retaken city with a rocket-propelled grenade.

ABOVE: *Staff Sgt. Jason R. Krawczyk/Defense Department* BELOW: *Andrea Bruce/*The Washington Post

One of the biggest risks Petraeus took was personal—moving around Baghdad and Iraq, often helmetless, as in these two photos. Above, an Iranian at an Iran-Iraq border crossing teases the general about his youthful appearance. Below, Petraeus, in a shop with Sadi Othman and two Iraqis, reacts to the Iraqi national soccer team's scoring a goal in a televised match.

ABOVE: *Army Staff Sgt. Lorie Jewell/Defense Department* BELOW: *Staff Sgt. Margaret C. Nelson/U.S. Army*

Moving up: Late in 2008, Odierno succeeded Petraeus as the top U.S. commander in Iraq while Petraeus replaced Fallon at Central Command—where he likely will work closely with the next president on Iraq, Afghanistan, Pakistan, and other issues.

ABOVE: *Cherie A. Thurlby/Defense Department* BELOW: *Army Staff Sgt. Lorie Jewell/Defense Department*

"We were gobsmacked," added Sky, using British slang for being stunned into speechlessness.

It was tough having to face the soldiers bearing the brunt of the new strategy. "There was a brief moment of *What have we got ourselves into?*" recalled Command Sgt. Maj. Hill, the veteran infantryman who had been selected by Petraeus to become the senior enlisted soldier in Iraq. Looking at the casualty reports every night that spring, he said, "would just suck the energy out of you." His days began to seem like a soul-lashing round of visiting the wounded and then attending memorial services for the dead. He learned to say a prayer under his breath before walking into the military hospitals: "God, give me strength to deal with what I'm about to see." He kept his calendar open every day from 5 to 6 P.M., on the assumption that at least one service for a dead soldier would be held.

As the casualties continued to mount, Odierno said later, "I was a little nervous." Col. J. T. Thomson, the career artilleryman who was Odierno's executive officer, would later recall those dark days as the hardest part of his tour. "May—I mean, the whole month of May," he said much later. "The wondering—is it going to get any better?"

According to unreleased statistics in the U.S. military database, there were 6,037 "significant acts" of violence in Iraq during May 2007, the highest recorded total since November 2004. "This is a period in which it gets harder before it gets easier," Petraeus said one day in May as he sipped iced tea in his office, a giant map of the city of Baghdad behind him. He was expecting a long, hard summer of violence, followed by a trek to Capitol Hill to tell Congress how much progress he was making. He was pushing all the American chips on the table, going "all-in," he said, with the surge. Whatever happened, he was going to ride this thing through to the end. "There's no combat forces left, at least, I'm aware of," he said. That is, the United States military simply didn't have replacement troops available for those he was fielding. "You can't ask for a brigade that isn't there."

Petraeus later would describe this period as "excruciating." He said he believed that the new approach would work, but "what started to develop as the question in my mind was, when will it start to show demonstrable effects?"

United States' combat deaths climbed inexorably: 70 in February, 71 in March, 96 in April, and 120 in May, which became the deadliest month for U.S. troops in two years. The additional casualties had been expected as the price to be paid in the short term for moving from big, safe bases to smaller outposts among the population. But they came even as a series of horrific killings of Iraqi civilians occurred. In February, a ton of explosives detonated in a market in a predominantly Shiite area of Baghdad, killing at least 125 and wounding 300 more. It was the single deadliest terrorist bombing ever in the capital. "They were carrying bodies like sheep," said one Iraqi witness, Abu Lubna.

The insurgents also were introducing worrisome new tactics. In February and March, they forayed into chemical warfare, detonating three trucks carrying toxic chlorine gas in Baghdad, Fallujah, and Ramadi, killing 11 people and sickening hundreds. Col. MacFarland may have found the tipping point in Ramadi the previous year, but there was plenty of fighting left in the city, as his successor unit, the 1st Brigade of the 3rd Infantry Division, led by Col. John Charlton, found in a series of battles in February and March 2007, and then again in June, when a U.S. patrol stumbled across an al Qaeda counterattack as it was forming, resulting in an all-night firefight that was called "the battle of Donkey Island." It left two Americans dead and more than 30 insurgents, and blunted what likely was a new al Qaeda offensive.

Another horrific new approach appeared in Baghdad. The driver of a car bomb managed to get through a U.S. military checkpoint and into a marketplace because he had two children in the backseat of the vehicle. Troops had been taught that cars with children were no threat. Three Iraqis were killed in the subsequent blast.

Enemy tactics were also more sophisticated, with false IEDs being strewn along with real ones, the better to slow down American troops and set them up for ambushes. "These guys are real smart," said 1st Lt. Anthony Von Plinsky. "The Iraqi insurgent as a whole has adapted well to our tactics." By this point in the war, soldiers were fond of saying, all the stupid insurgents were dead. The Americans had come and gone on tours of duty, but many of their enemies had fought nonstop for several years, and those who had survived were fit and adaptive.

The biggest threat to the success of the U.S. mission was the al Qaeda car bomb attacks against Iraqi civilians, which made it seem to many Iraqis as if the Americans couldn't provide security and that the militias was the only hope. But the biggest threat to the soldiers carrying out that mission was the roadside bombs, especially the highly lethal explosively formed penetrators, or "EFP"s. Also, an increasing number of convoys were being attacked, and American officials worried that enemy fighters were receiving Iranian training in the new tactics used in those attacks.

There seemed no limit to the forms of violence. American troops operating a new outpost in Diyala Province befriended a donkey that hung around, giving it food and water. Then "the insurgents assassinated him," said Spec. Josiah Hollopeter. "That really irritated me."

THE BATTLE OF TARMIYAH

As the new American outposts proliferated, they did appear to draw some of al Qaeda's firepower away from civilians. The more remote stations were especially enticing. For example, according to Col. David Sutherland, as sectarian killings and kidnappings declined in the late winter and spring of 2007 by about 70 percent in Diyala Province, northeast of Baghdad, attacks on U.S. and Iraqi troops increased by the same amount.

One of the most spectacular attacks was launched against 38 soldiers manning an isolated American outpost in the town of Tarmiyah, just north of Baghdad. The town of about 40,000 actually had been relatively calm until the summer of 2006, when it was destabilized by ethnic cleansing in the capital that sent thousands of Sunnis fleeing there. Al Qaeda's power in the town grew, and in December it ordered the Iraqi police there to leave—which they promptly did. The 1st Cavalry Division then established an outpost in the abandoned police station. In mid-February it was being manned by members of D Company, 2nd Battalion, 8th Cavalry Regiment, 1st Cavalry Division. It was the northernmost position in the division, poking into an area that had been a relative safe haven for Sunni insurgents.

At precisely 7 A.M. a rocket-propelled grenade detonated on the corner of the small outpost, followed by some AK-47 fire. Lt. Shawn Jokinen, who had gone to sleep two hours earlier, jolted awake in his cot. Staff Sgt. Jesus Colon, the sergeant of the guard, shouted that they were under attack. Jokinen ran to the front door of his barracks with his M-4 carbine and saw a small white "bongo" truck crash through the sliding blue front gate and roar straight toward him. He emptied the M-4's magazine into the windshield, causing the truck to swerve slightly away from the entrance, but before the driver died he detonated about 1,500 pounds of Ukrainian-made military-grade explosives, sending bits of concrete and glass sailing through the compound. "The explosion threw me against a wall and I got covered with debris," Jokinen remembered. The blast dug a crater twenty feet wide and six feet deep, shattered every window in the compound and the surrounding area, and dropped the front wall of the compound.

The battle that followed resembled the movie *Zulu*, in which a small detachment of British soldiers fends off thousands of African warriors. At first the dust was so thick that no one could see or breathe. "Everything was black, then brown," said Staff Sgt. James Copeland. He took a knee until he could get some air. Several soldiers were covered in rubble. Those not covered pulled their buddies out, then grabbed their weapons, helmets, and body armor, and ran upstairs to the roof. Some would fight for hours in their boxer shorts. Two medics began treating those with life-threatening wounds. "The rest of us wrapped up each other," Jokinen said. Copeland told the injured they were needed to shoot if they could, then grabbed a wounded soldier's M-249 light machine gun and ran to the roof, where he realized that his gear was buried and that he didn't have a helmet.

Lt. Cory Wallace, D Company's executive officer, had been walking out of the compound's command post, where he had been processing six members of an alleged al Qaeda sniper cell nabbed in an overnight raid, when the blast hurled him into a wall. The compound's 500-gallon fuel tank exploded into a fireball, knocking him out and killing Sgt. Colon. He regained consciousness and scurried back into the command post, where he saw Pfc. Pao Vang trying to stop blood squirting from a laceration on his neck. Wallace looked outside. "I noticed the front half of our barracks were destroyed. Several soldiers were staggering out of their patrol base. They were covered with dust and blood. I was still a little dazed from the blast so it took me awhile to notice that the enemy was throwing hand grenades and improvised mortar rounds over the walls." Black smoke joined the dust and grenades in the air.

Wallace shouted to Pfc. James Byington, who had picked himself up from the ground, to call the battalion headquarters for help. "Byington informed me that the radios were not working," the XO recalled. It turned out that the compound's generator had been knocked out. Wallace told Vang, who had a shard of glass protruding from the side of his head, to fix the generator. Vang tried to do it while under direct fire from a nearby building but couldn't, so said he would find batteries for the radio. They were buried under some rubble, so Vang dug with one hand to find them, the other pressed against his neck wound, which was spraying blood every time he moved.

At some point—Wallace remembers it was 90 minutes, but battalion records say far sooner—Wallace was able to transmit a situation report to his headquarters. "Once the radios were functional, I called battalion and informed them that our patrol base was under heavy attack and that our company had multiple wounded with one KIA," he said.

One of the soldiers on the roof yelled down to him, "Sir, don't let battalion pull us out, we're going to hold this motherfucker!" There was no fear of running out of ammunition, because the platoon sergeants wisely had insisted that the unit keep on hand about three times the daily requirement. On top of that, soldiers had themselves prepared "Armageddon Boxes"—extra ammunition and some water for unexpected emergencies—and kept them in their Humvees. "The only problem was our ammo holding area was located on the second floor of the barracks," Wallace said. "Soldiers kept sprinting down an exposed staircase, filling up sleeping bags with extra ammo, and running back up to their fighting position on the roof." Copeland ran from soldier to soldier on the roof, distributing ammunition and assigning sectors of fire.

The radio was in the command post, so Wallace couldn't see outside to guide the AH-64 Apache attack helicopters appearing overhead toward their targets. He had Vang assemble a portable Harris PRC-117 radio and take it to the roof, where Staff Sgt. Freddie Housey, a veteran of the capture of Baghdad in 2003, directed the air counterattack. One of the Apaches was hit and pulled away with one of its pilots wounded and his flight suit on fire. Other helicopters conducted devastating strafing runs with their 30-millimeter cannons.

Lt. Col. Scott Efflandt, the battalion commander, had been eating breakfast 12 miles away at his headquarters at Taji when he felt the concussion of the explosion and then, moments later, heard the boom. He checked with his tactical operations center, or TOC, but was told there was nothing to report, so assumed it was artillery fire involving another unit. He didn't know then that soldiers from his D Company were fighting for their lives.

Wallace reported in a few minutes later. Efflandt raced to his TOC. As he arrived, he recalled, "the streaming video from the UAV [drone reconnaissance aircraft] came online and our hearts skipped a beat." He called Wallace, found him "in charge and unflappable," and told him help was on the way.

At around 8 A.M., a unit of Stryker armored vehicles from the 2nd Infantry Division came to the rescue. One of the Strykers backed up to a hole the blast had made in the compound wall, dropped its ramp, and loaded the six most severely wounded D Company soldiers. Another unit arrived and secured a landing zone, or LZ, for medical evacuation helicopters. Wallace realized his compound wouldn't be overrun, and he would survive the day. "With our litter-urgent soldiers medevac'd and armored vehicles occupying a perimeter around the patrol base, I knew the enemy was beaten," he said.

But the battle wasn't over. "As we headed to the LZ I still heard small-arms fire, friendly and enemy," said Copeland. "The LZ was hot with the Stryker and air assets still firing as we were moved to the bird and continued as we flew away."

Efflandt, a working-class son of Rock Island, Illinois, who had gone on to teach at West Point, got to Tarmiyah later in the morning. "When we entered the town, I was stunned. It was as if we were in the wrong place, as everything looked different—battle-damaged buildings, debris everywhere downtown, no people out and about. Arriving at the patrol base I was aghast."

The outpost was destroyed. It may have been defendable but it was uninhabitable. Efflandt decided to stay and fight it out, requesting immediate delivery of a big logistics package, including thousands of tons of concrete barriers. He issued orders to take over a school building 200 meters north of the destroyed outpost and get a new patrol base up and running by sundown. "It sent a message to the insurgents that we would not be defeated and we weren't going anywhere," recalled Maj. Robert Rodriguez, the battalion's executive officer. "It was a tactical decision with strategic implications." Leading from the front, Efflandt spent the next 24 hours in the new post commanding the operation to retake the town. He had in mind Odierno's dictum that any land taken would not be given up.

When the fight was over, of the 38 soldiers who had been in the outpost, 2 were dead and 29 others had been wounded. Those who weren't hospitalized moved back to their battalion headquarters at the big base at Taji, a few miles to the southwest. The next morning Wallace woke up and went to eat. "I didn't realize what had happened until I walked out of the chow hall," he said. "For some reason, that was the best breakfast I had ever tasted in my life."

But other feelings from the fight lingered. Looking back on it now from the United States, Wallace said, "I feel guilty. I keep thinking there were a hundred things I could have done to prevent it." He is scheduled to return to Iraq in November of 2009.

When Efflandt left the battalion in 2008, his officers memorialized his command tour in Iraq with a print of Gen. Meade at Gettysburg titled *Stand and Fight It Out.* Sporadic fighting would continue in Tarmiyah through that year, at one point leading to a friendly fire shootout between American soldiers and Iraqi soldiers and police, killing 6 of the Iraqis.

BLACK THURSDAY

As the surge intensified, with the majority of the additional brigades in country, the situation actually worsened. Thursday, April 12, stands as perhaps the toughest day of this period. The previous day, news had broken in Washington that three retired generals had turned town the job of coordinating Iraq policy for the White House. It was a stunning vote of lack of confidence in the new strategy in Iraq. One of those who refused the job, retired Marine Gen. John Sheehan, explained his decision by saying, "The very fundamental issue is, they don't know where the hell they're going. So rather than go over there, develop an ulcer and eventually leave, I said, 'No, thanks.'"

On the same day, Defense Secretary Gates announced that all soldiers in Iraq, as well as those on their way, would serve 15 months there, rather than the one-year tour that had been the norm. Soldiers now had to tell their families to revise those homecoming plans, many of which involved long-planned trips to see family members or vacations at resorts. As the news spread among troops in Iraq, their reaction was expectable. "It flat out sucks, that's the only way I can think to describe it," said Pvt. Jeremy Perkins, a member of an engineering battalion in Baqubah.

On the morning of April 12 itself, a truck bomb dropped part of a key Baghdad river crossing, the Sarafiya bridge, dumping cars into the Tigris and killing 11 people. This appeared to be the first step in a campaign to prevent Shiite death squads from crossing the river into west Baghdad, or perhaps to limit the mobility of U.S. and Iraqi reinforcements. Several other bombs would hit major bridges in the following weeks. It was one more way to pull apart the carcass of a once-great city.

That afternoon, a bomber managed to get past multiple checkpoints, bomb-sniffing dogs, and body searches, and into the Green Zone building where parliament was meeting, killing a member and seven other people.

Back in Washington on the same day, Senator Joseph Biden, the Democratic chairman of the Senate Foreign Relations Committee, pronounced the surge doomed. The next day, Friday the 13th, Senate Majority Leader Harry Reid said, "I believe myself . . . that this war is lost. . . . The surge is not accomplishing anything." Even some supporters of the war were beginning to talk about what

"Plan C" might look like. Would it be, one hawk asked, a fallback to the core missions of attacking al Qaeda, protecting the embassy and providing air cover and other support to Iraqi forces?

The bad news seemed relentless. On April 14, a car bombing at the entrance to the main bus station in the Shiite holy city of Karbala killed 32. Four days later, bombings in mainly Shiite areas of Baghdad killed more than 150.

The assaults against new outposts continued. On April 24, a U.S. patrol base in an old schoolhouse in Sadah, near Baqubah, came under complex attack, with small-arms fire and rocket-propelled grenades from several directions. As the soldiers on the roof of the base returned fire, they saw two explosives-laden dump trucks coming at them. The drivers couldn't be shot because they were cocooned in steel, with only a slit to see through. The first, carrying 1,500 pounds of explosives, blew up outside the gate, leveling the obstacles leading up to it. The second one barreled through the breach just made and detonated 2,000 pounds, collapsing a building. All told, 9 U.S. soldiers were killed, all of them from the 82nd Airborne Division; 20 more were wounded. "It was the worst day of my life, to have to literally dig with your hands and carry your kids out," recalled Col. Sutherland, commander of the 1st Cavalry brigade to which the 82nd Airborne unit was attached. "That was extremely hard." The Islamic State of Iraq, a group affiliated with al Qaeda, boasted in a subsequent statement that it had sent "two knights" to attack "the Crusader American base."

One day in April, a senior non-commissioned officer in the 1st Battalion, 2nd Brigade, 1st Infantry Division allegedly led some soldiers in the execution of four Iraqi detainees. According to preliminary testimony by other soldiers, 1st Sgt. John Hatley, the top sergeant in the battalion's A Company, had four blindfolded and handcuffed Iraqis kneel by a canal. They had been captured after what *Stars & Stripes,* the official U.S. military newspaper, termed "a brief exchange of fire" and a search that turned up "heavy weapons," which in Iraq usually means mortars or rocket-propelled grenade launchers. Hatley told his men that if they passed along the Iraqis to a detention facility, they simply would be released, testified Pfc. Joshua Hartson. The Iraqis then were shot and their blindfolds and handcuffs were removed. "We then pushed the bodies into the canal and left," Sgt. Michael Leahy wrote in a statement given to Army investigators. Back at Combat Outpost Angry Dragon, Hatley gathered his troops and ordered them not to discuss the incident. He also told some soldiers to burn the blindfolds and the handcuffs, which were plastic, and to clean out the Bradley Fighting Vehicle in which the detainees had been moved. The incident only came to light in January 2008. Criminal proceedings began months later. Hatley, Leahy, and a third soldier eventually were charged with committing premeditated murder. At the time of publication of this book, they had not gone to trial, while two other soldiers pleaded guilty to lesser charges.

At 4:40 on the morning of May 12, insurgents ambushed an American unit in the "Triangle of Death" area southwest of Baghdad, first bombing it and then raking the survivors with gunfire. Five soldiers died and another three were abducted, with two of the bodies discovered finally a year later. Nine more soldiers were killed on May 23. Another 10 died on the 28th, which was Memorial Day, most of them in an incident in which an OH-58 Kiowa Warrior helicopter was shot down north of Baqubah and the mission sent to respond to the crash was hit by big two roadside bombs.

Senator Gordon Smith, the Oregon Republican who had come out against the war so vigorously the previous December, traveled to Iraq in May. He believed his emotional speech on the floor of the Senate had helped push Bush toward the surge. A White House aide, he recalled, had told him, "We recognized with your speech that not only were we losing the war, we were losing the Republicans we needed." But after touring the country and talking to Petraeus, he was no more optimistic. After he and Senator Orrin Hatch, the Utah Republican, left Petraeus's office, they were strapping into their seats in a Black Hawk helicopter for the short flight back to the Baghdad airport. "So what do you think?" Smith said to Hatch.

"We could lose this thing," Hatch glumly replied.

On June 25, a wave of bombings hit Iraqi allies of the U.S. effort. Two car bombs targeted the police station in the refinery town of Bayji, killing 30. Another attack killed 8 policemen in Hilla. But the most politically significant incident of the day was a suicide attack on a group of Anbar Awakening sheikhs meeting at the Mansour Hotel, just a short walk from the northern entrance to the Green Zone. Six of the tribal leaders were killed, as well as 6 other people.

The last of the surge brigades and their support troops finished arriving in June, elevating the U.S. troop level in Iraq to 156,000—plus another 180,000 contractors performing functions that once were done by soldiers. (Most of these were cleaners, cooks, and so on, but about 20,000 were private security guards.) By July it was beginning to look to many that the surge was failing, adding to pressure to move to a withdrawal plan. The most precious commodity Petraeus and Odierno had was time. "Everything takes time," noted Maj. Gen. Rick Lynch, who was commanding the 3rd Infantry Division in the belt south of Baghdad. "And everything takes longer than you think it's going to take."

A growing chorus of voices was saying they had run out of time. Retired Gen. Sir Michael Rose, one of the most prominent British officers of recent years, called on the Americans to "admit defeat" and bring the troops home. Senator Smith predicted that "a dozen Republican senators . . . will be with me in September." And a poll found that nearly 60 percent of Americans thought the surge would not help restore civil order to Baghdad. Tom Donnelly remained a strong supporter of the surge that he had helped design, but conceded "it's the eleventh hour and the fifty-fourth minute."

Political support for the surge, never strong, appeared to be collapsing. Senator Reid, who in April had pronounced the war lost, now attacked Petraeus personally, charging, somewhat oddly, that the general "isn't in touch with what's going on in Baghdad"—as if he could discern better from Washington, D.C. Senior Republicans weren't far behind him in heading for the exits. Senator Richard Lugar, the centrist Indiana Republican, took to the floor of the Senate on June 25 to call for an end to the surge. "I believe that the costs and risks of continuing down the current path outweigh the potential benefits that might be achieved by doing so," said Lugar, one of the most respected voices in Congress on foreign policy. "Persisting with the surge strategy will delay policy adjustments that have a better chance of protecting our interests over the long term." A week later he would be joined by Pete Domenici of New Mexico, who called for following the Iraq Study Group's recommendations and getting U.S. combat forces out of Iraq by early 2008. Senator George Voinovich of Ohio also was backing away from the president.

"The war in Iraq is approaching a kind of self-imposed climax," warned Henry Kissinger.

Al Qaeda was chortling. "Today, the wind—by grace of Allah—is blowing against Washington," Ayman al-Zawahiri, the terrorist organization's second in command, said in a video posted on a jihadist website.

DEAD MAN WITH AN IPOD

The morale of American troops seemed to be waning as they doubted if their new mission was working. "We're tired of being lost," said Sgt. 1st Class

Michael Eaglin, who was operating from a small base in Sadr City. "Have you ever been lost and at the same time getting shot at? It's miserable. . . . I want to be here for a reason, not just a show of force."

In Yusifyah, a tough little town near the southern edge of Baghdad, Spec. Yvenson Tertulien told the *Los Angeles Times* that "I don't see any progress. Just us getting killed. . . . I don't want to be here anymore."

Lt. Gregory Weber, an infantry platoon leader in the 2nd Infantry Division, recalled responding to a bombing and RPG ambush of a U.S. patrol in southern Baghdad that summer:

> We passed the top half of a HMMWV [Humvee] turret. 1st Squad was so focused on security and assaulting/clearing up to the blast site that they didn't even see [in the turret] the KIA [killed in action] Soldier, covered in soot, ACH [helmet] blown off, IBA [body armor] barely on, but an iPod headphone still in his ear. On site, there were three HMMWV destroyed. One upside down from an 8 foot deep, 15-foot-wide blast crater, 25 meters away, burning with the remains of 4 soldiers left inside. Another HMMWV was in the blast crater, partially submerged in water from a water main rupturing, and the other HMMWV 25 meters the opposite direction with its back end blown off. It was the most horrific subsurface IED detonation I saw the entire deployment.

Five soldiers were killed in the incident, but the image that haunted Weber was the first thing he saw, the dead soldier in the blasted turret, "iPod still in his ear." He still wonders, "Did his leadership know he was distracted by music; not being able to hear the battlefield?"

Indeed, there were growing signs of such demoralization and indiscipline. In the hard-hit 1st Battalion of the 26th Infantry Regiment, which had lost five soldiers in one bombing in June, life got even worse in July. The first sergeant of its Alpha Company, while on patrol, said, "I can't take it anymore," put a weapon under his chin, and shot himself in front of his men. A few days later, members of a platoon in the battalion's Charlie Company refused to go out on a mission, saying they were afraid of becoming abusive with Iraqis.

In another unusual act that verged on insubordination, seven 82nd Airborne soldiers placed an opinion piece in the *New York Times* that called the surge a failure. "We see that a vast majority of Iraqis feel increasingly insecure and view us an occupation force that has failed to produce normalcy after four years and is increasingly unlikely to do so as we continue to arm each warring side." Legally they were entitled to express their opinions, but for soldiers to write a newspaper piece on policy during a war is almost unprecedented. Three weeks later, two of the writers, Sgt. Yance Gray and Sgt. Omar Mora, would be killed after their truck veered off an elevated highway in western Baghdad and dropped about 30 feet.

The governor of Puerto Rico, Anibal Acevedo Vila, addressing the National Guard Association's annual conference, called for a new strategy in Iraq that would lead to a withdrawal. He received a standing ovation.

"I have never seen in twenty years the sort of resigned attitude I am hearing from my active-duty counterparts," reported one Army Reserve colonel. "They are conveying a 'game over' attitude where they are going to continue saluting the flag and doing what the NCA [national command authority] wants, but not without realizing it is all horseshit at this point." After the American military left Iraq, he added gloomily, the Iraqis will "turn on each other like a pack of weasels."

A SLOW TURNING

In retrospect, it appears that the pattern of the battle of Baghdad from March to June resembles, on a vastly larger scale, that of the assault earlier in the year on the Tarmiyah outpost. In both places, the new U.S. strategy was pushing into enemy strongholds and eliminating safe havens. The enemy reaction was to hit back as hard as it could. Indeed, the U.S. counteroffensive could be said to have triggered some of the bombings, as the enemy faced a "use it or lose it" prospect with its arsenal of prepared car bombs and stashed explosives. "They have previously been, you know, frankly, elusive when we actually got into an area and started to clear it, and we're seeing that in this area of east Rashid, they are standing and fighting," Maj. Gen. Joseph Fil Jr., commander of the 1st Cavalry Division, noted in June. Both sides were throwing everything they had into the fight.

Visiting Iraq at the beginning of April, Senator John McCain expressed "cautious, very cautious, optimism" about the effects of the new strategy. "We've made tremendous mistakes," he said in Baghdad on April Fool's Day, "but we're finally getting it right. And is it too little, too late? I don't know, but I don't think so."

His traveling companion, Senator Lindsey Graham, added another thought: "We're doing now what we should have done three years ago."

The two were mocked for citing a walk through a Baghdad market as evidence of improved security, but in fact they were right. There may have been soldiers protecting the market, but the market was there, with merchants and goods, because of that military presence.

As Kissinger had said, the war was approaching a climax—but not of the sort he envisioned. Quietly, in various corners of Baghdad and its environs, even as the high-profile bombings were escalating, the new strategy was beginning to show results in hundreds of ways. Every day, American troops found that more Iraqis were beginning to talk to them. Better intelligence was coming in, and was being acted on more quickly, by units that lived on the next block instead of on the outskirts of the city. A unit getting a tip on a house where enemy fighters were gathering would begin watching it, not necessarily to hit it immediately, but perhaps to see how it fit into a larger network. With that knowledge, it might then be able to cripple a gang that often had been intimidating and extorting area residents. Maj. James Allen learned this lesson in an odd way as the Iraqi troops he was advising ambushed an insurgent planting a roadside bomb. They aimed to kill the would-be bomber, but their weapons were so poorly maintained that they couldn't fire. "The dude who was emplacing the IED froze, though, so they walked over and bagged him," Allen recalled. "He rolled over on the supplier, the supplier rolled on someone else, and we essentially shut down IEDs on that stretch of road for eight weeks."

Also, having American troops in residence often dramatically improved the effectiveness of their Iraqi counterparts. Having Americans available to come to their aid—and perhaps to feed and outfit them—made Iraqi soldiers more comfortable about being out in the neighborhoods. "They feel as long as the Americans are there, they can pretty much handle anything that's going on," said Sgt. Maj. Michael Clemens, who served with the 82nd Airborne in Diyala Province from mid-2006 to mid-2007. Many of these new "partnered relationships" would begin to show results by midsummer. Of course, the locals also generally found it easier to talk to the Iraqi troops, who often would pass along the information they gleaned to the Americans with whom they shared a post.

Familiarity bred knowledge. One squad of American troops living in a Sunni area began to examine what was being sold in the markets as an indicator of the mood of the population. For example, it noticed one day that heavy portable heaters were being offered in their local market, which they interpreted—correctly—to mean that people were planning on staying there, which in turn meant that the pressure on the population to move brought by Shiite militias must be declining.

Even the language that American leaders used was changing. "There's a lot less cowboy lingo in the force—'toss the compound,' 'take 'em down,' 'roll 'em up,' 'get the bad guys,'" observed Lt. Col. Yingling, on his third tour in Iraq. Col. Grigsby, commander of the third surge brigade, still introduced himself like a traditional armor officer as "Hammer Six," but his orientation was different. "The quality of life in Jisr Diuala, one *nahiya* in the *qadha,*" was improving, he told reporters one day. He also was proud that "we worked out of eight patrol bases and four joint security sites in the middle of the population centers, [and so] we never commuted to work."

The improvements in American operations were technical as well as doctrinal, tactical, and cultural. One of the reasons that redeploying the troops into small outposts could work in 2007 better than it would have in previous years was that brigade commanders had far more aerial surveillance assets available and under their control. During 2007 the number of these drone reconnaissance aircraft operating in Iraq would increase tenfold, according to an after-action review by Odierno's headquarters. During his first tour in Iraq, in 2003–4, Odierno noted, the most that could be counted on was two drone reconnaissance aircraft available to him in all of Iraq, and they had to be shared with other divisions. In 2007 all 18 Army combat brigade commanders had their own RQ-7 Shadow UAVs, and could request more surveillance and strike aircraft as needed. This made it far easier, for example, for a commander to keep an eye on potential threats to his outposts.

In addition, in a highly classified operation, new information about al Qaeda and insurgent leaders began to get distributed much more quickly to tactical units. The officer responsible for the change was a military intelligence specialist, Lt. Col. Jen Koch Easterly, who reorganized the collection and analysis of intercepted telephone and computer communications in order to coordinate it better with other intelligence operations and with what units were doing on the ground. She also focused more on going after the networks that were assembling, delivering, and detonating roadside bombs, which has been the single greatest killer of U.S. troops during the war. According to one senior officer, her military intelligence unit's successes became the undisclosed key to the success of the surge. Her work still remains largely unknown because so much of what was done remains highly classified. But as one operations report by the 1st Cavalry Division put it, "synchronization of ISR/HUMINT/SIGINT [intelligence, surveillance, and reconnaissance/human intelligence/signals intelligence] has significantly reduced IED cells and threat." Asked about that, Maj. Patrick Michaelis said, "It was a major factor. . . . Cryptological support from Colonel Easterly was critical." She declined to be interviewed, citing classification issues.

In midsummer, intel people picked up some interesting indications that the insurgency was running out of steam. One smart U.S. Army intelligence officer in Baghdad said that he just didn't see the signs of a vibrant counterattack forming. "There's nothing that shows any kind of [enemy] surge in the making," he said. On intercepts of telephone conversations between insurgent leaders, he noted, "There's a lot of bitching and moaning, 'What have you done today?'" The response, he said, was often along the lines of, "I haven't done anything, there are too many around, I can't move."

One of the emerging lessons was that the increase in regular U.S. troops on the streets of the city improved the effectiveness of the Special Operators who were targeting al Qaeda. It also helped that Odierno was an old friend of Lt. Gen. Stanley McChrystal, the head of Special Operations in Iraq, whom he had known since their days together at West Point. Until that point, "We didn't see how essential conventional forces are in the counterterror fight," remembered Rapp. American commanders, he said, were surprised to see that having their troops moving around effectively sponged up the sea in which al Qaeda swam. As insurgents found it more difficult to move, they began to communicate more electronically, in part because as senior leaders were caught, they tended to be replaced by younger, less experienced men, which in turn made them more vulnerable to Lt. Col. Easterly's signals interception operation. "When you stay in the neighborhood, they have no place to stay, they have to talk more, because they're mobile, so we can catch them, " Rapp said.

Even as U.S. troop deaths increased, Iraqi civilian deaths appeared to be declining, decreasing steadily from January on. Essentially, by moving out into the population, the military had interposed itself between the attackers and the people. And some of the attacks on them that succeeded were not as bad as previous ones. For example, in March and April, the bombs that detonated were hitting more checkpoints and fewer of the markets and mosques those checkpoints were intended to protect. Roadside bombs also were becoming less effective, for two reasons. Partly, emplacers had less time to dig holes, and some bomb cells were resorting to the hasty method of simply lowering small pressure-detonated bombs through a hole in the floor of a car and then driving off. Soldiers comfortably dismissed those relatively ineffective devices as "drop 'n' pops." Even some of the bigger devices used low-grade homemade explosives, indicating that the bombmakers were running low on more lethal material.

COUNTERINSURGENCY INSIDE THE PRISON CAMPS

Two other institutional initiatives also were beginning to have an effect. These were how the Americans handled prisoners and how they raised Iraqi forces. Neither one held the excitement of combat operations, but improving them was essential if the American effort was to become more effective.

For years handling detainees had been the Achilles' heel of the American operation. Holding and treating prisoners decently didn't seem the hardest of tasks, but their abuse and torture at the Abu Ghraib facility had been one of the biggest embarrassments, and strategic setbacks, of the war. "We have learned an enormous amount, the very hard way," Petraeus said later. One hard lesson he listed was that "you cannot safeguard our values by violating them in another country in an endeavor like this."

Despite that, his counterinsurgency manual didn't offer much new on the way to deal with detainees. It advised that they should not be abused, but didn't really have much to say about what to do with them besides that.

Not long after Petraeus took command, he picked Maj. Gen. Douglas Stone, a Marine reservist who had worked for Hewlett-Packard and IBM, to take over the detention operation. At first, there was some question about Stone, with a few officers recommending against him. Petraeus called Gen. James Mattis, a Marine who has had a kind of parallel career to his—first when they were both assistants to a top Pentagon official, then when they both commanded divisions during 2003 in Iraq, and finally overseeing their services' educational and training establishments. Most important, they are two of the most highly educated generals in today's military. "Jim, what's the deal?" Petraeus asked. "Some people advised not to take him."

"He is the kind of guy you need," Mattis reassured him. "There will be some degree of care and feeding required, but knowing you, Petraeus, and knowing him, you will be a great team."

Stone would rewrite the book on effective detention operations. His beginning insight was that there was an insurgency inside the prison camps, and that simply warehousing the prisoners only intensified the opposition there, creating more insurgents out of civilians and more dedicated ones out of existing insurgents. As Stone later put it, "by not emphasizing population protection and the exemplary treatment of detainees, our facilities became breeding grounds for extremist recruitment." In an official review, he termed U.S. detainment policies for the first several years of the war "an abject failure, a strategic risk to the MNF-I mission and a failure from a counterinsurgency perspective." In April 2007 alone, the month he took command, there were 10,178 acts of detainee violence inside U.S. prison camps in Iraq.

What was needed, Stone thought, was a campaign that paralleled the larger counterinsurgency effort overseen by Petraeus. He dubbed it "COIN inside the wire." Stone told his guards to secure the prison population, and especially isolate the roughly 1,000 extremists who had been intimidating the 20,000 other inmates, to the point of holding "trials" of inmates who refused to join them. The first step in separating out the hard core was to learn more about the prisoners, who until that point had been separated by sect but not by ideology. (The sectarian split was about 80 percent Sunni, 20 percent Shiite.) Despite Western perceptions, only a tiny percentage were foreigners. Who were they? What motivated them? The answers they gave in surveys surprised their captors. They were tribally oriented, with 78 percent reporting that they would use their tribal leaders to solve problems. They were not strikingly religious—only 28 percent reported attending services at their mosque on most Fridays. More than 10 percent had been police, soldiers, or security guards at the time of arrest. Most important, only about 4 percent were deemed to be hard-core cases. The vast majority, it seemed, were motivated not by ideology or a sense of grievance, but by minor economic necessity. They planted bombs not to feed their families, but for the cash al Qaeda would pay them, so they could buy small luxuries such as air conditioners or DVD players.

The second move was to begin providing services to the prison population. Basic literacy courses were offered. A civics course was made mandatory. Some 160 Muslim clerics were hired to begin teaching moderate Islam, in courses offered on a voluntary basis. Other courses were given in Arabic, English, history, science, geography, and math. "There is a danger that the insurgency is becoming a vocation," warned a briefing prepared by Stone's headquarters, so vocational training was begun in carpentry, textiles, and masonry. The notion was to provide a pathway back to a life in the civilian world where they would not seek to benefit from violence. Stone even proposed giving released detainees a stipend of $200 a month for six months, just to get them on their feet and keep them away from temptation, but that idea died for lack of sufficient support. Instead, he opened a brick factory inside one prison, Camp Bucca, and paid the prisoners for their work, enabling them to build small nest eggs. Typically, the flamboyant Stone had each brick stamped in Arabic, "Rebuilding the nation brick by brick." After concluding that prisoners who saw their families were less likely to become violent, he set out to enable family visits, running regular bus trips from the cities to the camps.

Stone also urged his subordinates to recognize their own cultural limitations. "Our own individual view of the world tends to limit our perceptions," he wrote in an overview document, "creating risk when we make the mistake of judging a detainee's actions in the context of our own culture rather than his own. This is one of the most significant challenges we face in detainee operations." One of the best ways to defuse a confrontation with guards, they found, was to turn on the large-screen television and play a video of a recent soccer match. And, in another move to reduce tensions and also improve understanding, a pamphlet in Arabic was created to explain the detention process to new arrivals, with a comic book version created for those who were illiterate.

American commanders also seemed to be getting the word. Preparing to lead a brigade of the 10th Mountain Division into Iraq, Col. David Paschal made a point during a training exercise by wearing a *dishdasha*—the Arab robe that most Iraqi men wear—and playing the role of "an uncooperative detainee." He threw food and insults at his guards until he finally was tackled and handcuffed. "By participating in the training I was able to experience the level of professionalism and proficiency of my soldiers while at the same time see how they are maintaining our detainees' safety as well as dignity," he explained.

Such training continued to be important, because there continued to be a hard core of such uncooperative Iraqis. Even after all of Stone's improvements were implemented, incidents still occurred. One day many months later, six Navy personnel working as prison camp guards grew tired of having inmates' feces hurled at them and locked the offenders in a room, then set off pepper spray and turned off the ventilation.

But the strategic view of how to handle detainees had changed, probably irretrievably, as had the atmosphere in most parts of the camps. In April 2008, there were 178 acts of violence recorded in the prison camps, about one-tenth the figure a year earlier. At his farewell ceremony in June, Gen. Stone commented: "History has shown us that leaders often rise from the most difficult of times and circumstances, and we should not be surprised if Iraq's future leaders are today being held in coalition force custody." The way they were treated today might shape the country's policies in the future, he warned.

SURGING THE IRAQIS

An old military aphorism holds that amateurs talk tactics, but professionals talk logistics. In fact, real military insiders often focus on larger personnel issues—raising, training, and equipping the force—because that is the key to long-term, sustainable success.

The U.S. effort to create a new Iraqi military had never gone particularly well. Part of that grew out of the political obstacles facing Iraq: A member of the Mahdi Army, for example, might not be well equipped or trained, but he knew what he was fighting for. By contrast, a member of the Iraqi army, despite having reliable American gear, didn't know if the government for which he fought would even exist a year later. Even under Petraeus in 2004–5, the training effort had a slow, haphazard feel to it. This was one reason he seemed to shy away from discussing that tour of duty. He maintains that he succeeded then. "It was a massive task and what we inherited was a pretty modest effort," he said. But still that tour carries about it a whiff of something inconsistent with the rest of his stellar military career.

Years later there was still plenty of room for improvement. In April 2007 a platoon of American soldiers was pinned down outside a mosque in western Baghdad's Kadhimiyah neighborhood and looked around for some help from Iraqi soldiers. "Of the twenty-seven hundred Iraqi security forces that are in Kadhimiyah, no Iraqi unit would respond," said Lt. Col. Steven Miska, deputy commander of a U.S. brigade.

Early in 2007, Petraeus asked for Lt. Gen. James Dubik to come out and take over the program to train, equip, and advise Iraqi army and police units. Dubik is an unusual figure, lower key than Petraeus, but like him a light-infantry intellectual. He had spent about half his military career in infantry and paratroop units, and the other half studying and teaching at military schools such as West

Point and Fort Leavenworth School of Advanced Military Studies, and civilian universities, including Harvard, Johns Hopkins, and the Massachusetts Institute of Technology. Before joining the Army he had intended to become a priest and had spent a year at seminary.

In an echo of Petraeus's "Mesopotamian Stampede," Dubik called his training effort "Meanwhile, Back at the Ranch." That is, he explained, "We all feel we're the part of the movie where the spotlight isn't. The posse is going after the rustlers, rescuing the stagecoach, and running the bad guys out of town." Meanwhile, Dubik was trying to create a more effective Iraqi security force. In some ways, this was a key counterinsurgency move, because it is axiomatic that it is indigenous forces that finally put down insurgencies, not foreign militaries. Dubik wasn't particularly taking a page out of the new counterinsurgency manual, but he was consistent with the new strategy in another, larger way: He increased the risk taking in his part of the effort.

First, he deemphasized the transition to Iraqi control. "It's the indirect approach," Dubik said. "It's right out of Aristotle: If you want a happy life, don't aim for happiness, aim for virtue." In other words, create an effective Iraqi force, and the transition will follow naturally, without being forced. In Maoist terms, Iraqi forces would not be given power, they would take it.

Second, rather than downplay the infiltration of Iraqi forces by Shiite militias, especially in the National Police, Dubik confronted it, purging its ranks. This wasn't just a matter of personalities and personal connections, but also of the politics of the country. As Stephen Biddle, who advised Petraeus on the issue, put it, "The problem is, in a country at war, the same pressures will exist against the next commander. The guys in the black baklavas will visit him at midnight." So the issue was not how to go after individual commanders but how to reduce sectarian influence—again, an instance of the indirect approach. The key, Biddle said, was to initiate a "virtuous cycle" where militias were weakened, so their pressures were less, so Iraqi commanders acted in less sectarian ways, and so the Iraqi population's opinion of Iraqi forces improved, making those forces stronger.

But there also plainly were some commanders who had to go. "We have gradually cleaned them up," Petraeus later said. In the National Police, he said, "They replaced the overall commander, both division commanders, all of the brigade commanders, and about seventy to eighty percent of the battalion commanders—and in some cases did it twice." In the course of those removals,

Dubik noted, some 15 internal affairs investigators at the Ministry of Interior, which oversees the police, were killed, and another 14 were wounded.

Third, and probably most important, Dubik accelerated the growth of Iraqi forces, knowing that they might not be as effective at the outset. His goal was "sufficient quantity of sufficiently capable." He halved the time dedicated to basic training. This was essentially a step away from the professional U.S. military approach of the last 20 years and toward the World War II approach of churning out troops and letting quality show itself and rise up. Under Dubik, the size of the Iraqi security forces increased from 400,000 in June 2007 to 560,000 a year later—actually becoming larger than the active-duty United States Army.

FINISHED BUSINESS

There was also one more American commander who had to go. In June, just as the surge was about to take full effect, Defense Secretary Gates effectively fired the chairman of the Joint Chiefs of Staff, Gen. Pace, who was the last member of the old Rumsfeld team still in place, having been vice chairman of the Joint Chiefs starting in October 2001 and then chairman since October 2005. Gates blamed the removal on Congress, saying he decided not to renominate Pace for the customary second term because "the focus of his confirmation process would have been on the past, rather than the future, and further, there was the very real prospect that the process would be quite contentious." That may be so, but Gates was also effective at ridding himself of unneeded trouble. Pace became the first chairman in more than 40 years to serve such a short term. With him went the vice chairman of the Joint Chiefs, Adm. Edmund Giambiastiani, who had been seen as even closer to Rumsfeld than Pace.

7.

SIGNS OF LIFE IN BAGHDAD

(Summer 2007)

Like a summer thunderstorm tapering off, American losses began to drop sharply in July. From a distance it all still looked like a solid wall of thunder and lightning, but those underneath it began to see patches of blue. In some neighborhoods, the streets were growing more crowded. More shops were open. Parents were allowing their children to play outside. The biggest change was the general absence of the clatter of gunfire and the roar of bomb blasts, which a year earlier had been common in Baghdad. There were five major reasons for this change. First, and most obvious, was the new force posture of putting troops out among the people and giving them the mission of protecting those people. Eventually there were some 75 outposts established across the city, and their presence was beginning to produce benefits. Much of the city was beginning to feel safer.

Second was that by the time they got there, the ethnic cleansing of Baghdad had been largely completed, with some neighborhoods that once were heavily Sunni becoming overwhelming Shia. Shiite militias patrolled their streets and sometimes rented out the houses from which Sunnis had been driven. "Now that the Sunnis are all gone, murders have dropped off," said Capt. Jay Wink, the intelligence officer for a 1st Infantry Division battalion that was operating in one newly Shiite neighborhood in southwest Baghdad. "One way to put it is they ran out of people to kill."

Third, and later in the year, came the declaration of a cease-fire with the Americans by Moqtada al-Sadr, the anti-American Shiite cleric.

There was also a less noticed fourth reason: For the first time since the invasion, U.S. forces were all pursuing the same goal in the same way. Putting out an official document is one thing; getting commanders and their troops to actually implement it is another. For example, when Gen. Kinnard surveyed his peers who had served in Vietnam for *The War Managers,* one senior general, asked about how a newly issued campaign plan had affected his operations, responded, "I never read them, it would only confuse me."

Odierno's great accomplishment may have been making sure that all his forces were dancing to the same tune and at the same time. Rather than permit each of his subordinate units—divisions or brigades—to carry out their own operations independently, he coordinated and even synchronized them, especially after the last surge brigade arrived as summer began, so that insurgents and terrorists couldn't just shift to quieter areas where there was less pressure. "In July, Odierno had all his forces, and he was able to put down the hammer, keep the squeeze on, everywhere," said Keane. "He just kept hammering and hammering and hammering."

Unity of effort radically increases the effectiveness of military operations. The new counterinsurgency manual was officially issued only in December 2006, but within months it was being implemented on the streets of Baghdad. That was a sharp contrast to the first years of the war, when every unit pursued its own fight, often in very different ways, said Col. James Rainey, who had been a major in Iraq during the 2003 invasion, then commanded a battalion of the 1st Cavalry Division in Iraq in 2004–5, and then returned in 2008 as the G-3, or director of operations, for the 4th Infantry Division. "The biggest difference is, we have doctrine now," he said, "Everyone's doing it now, protecting the population." That was also a much more concrete mission than "stop the insurgency," an order that only raised a series of additional definitional questions, such as what the insurgency was and what tactics were appropriate in countering it.

Listening to Rainey, Maj. Gen. Jeffrey Hammond, the division commander, added, "Petraeus's view of counterinsurgency changed the way we all look at it." That was an overstatement, as Petraeus was not alone in developing the new manual on counterinsurgency. Yet Hammond's basic point was correct: It is rare for a single person to have as dramatic effect as Petraeus did on how a large institution operates, and especially in how the U.S. Army wages war.

Illustrating how the new view permeated the force, Craig Coppock, who led an infantry platoon in Iraq in 2006–7, compiled a "Counterinsurgency Cliff Notes" for his peers. In this seven-page essay, lessons from the Vietnam War, from the French campaign in Algeria in the 1950s, and, most of all, from earlier in the Iraq war are woven together. The innovations of past years that had been considered only by dissidents now were becoming common sense. Once Army commanders had thought shows of force were the way to impress the locals and so prevail. Now Coppock admonished, "Use minimum force. Basically, try not to break stuff or kill anyone you don't have to." While top American officials had let the lynching of four U.S. contractors provoke them into ordering an attack on Fallujah in the spring of 2004, the young officer warned, "Avoid emotional responses to an operational event. . . . Knee-jerk reactions waste energy, effort, and are in most cases counterproductive to COIN strategy." And while the Army had spent years improving the anti-bomb properties of Humvees, Coppock instructed soldiers instead to get out of their rolling cocoons: "You should be out on foot in your AO [area of operations] every time you roll out of the wire." (Coppock also spoke with the tone of hard-won wisdom: "Never leave your AO the same way you went in.")

A SEPARATE PEACE

The fifth—and by far the most controversial—reason for the decline in violence was the turning of parts of the Sunni insurgency. This may have been the biggest gamble Petraeus took as the commander of the war in Iraq. He was going behind the back of the Baghdad government to put its enemies on the American payroll. Strikingly, he didn't seem to think he needed to get clearance from the American government, either. When asked about how he had gotten the president to agree to the program, he indicated that he hadn't asked Bush about it. "I don't think it was something that we needed to ask permission for. We had the authority to conduct what are called security contracts, and that was how we saw these." But, he added, "to be truthful we didn't see it growing to 103,000"—its peak in 2008, and a huge addition to the firepower the U.S. military could bring to bear in and around Baghdad. At its height, the monthly payroll was $30 million, which sounds like a lot but amounts to a few hours of what the war costs the American taxpayer twenty-four hours a day, every day of the year.

Some experts, such as retired Gen. Abizaid and Stephen Biddle, a sometime adviser to Petraeus, argue that the change in the loyalties of Sunni fighters was the single most important cause of the improvement in security in 2007. It had begun before the surge, in the fall of '06, with the deals Col. MacFarland was cutting in al Anbar Province.

"It reached critical mass in Ramadi, and set off a chain reaction up the Euphrates River Valley," Petraeus said. The turning accelerated during the winter and spring of 2007. The membership rolls of these new neighborhood militias exploded later in the year, going from a few thousand to more than 60,000 by the winter, and then to 103,000, the majority of them Sunni and many of them former insurgents. They were not supporters of the Baghdad government, but they were allies of the American effort—at least, most of the time.

In simple manpower terms, this was a huge bonus to the Americans. As Gen. Keane put it, tens of thousands of fighters who had been trying to kill Americans now "were not shooting at you. That helps a lot when you only have thirty thousand of your own additional troops to address the problem."

It was effectively a second marriage for both sides, which had become estranged from their original partners. The Americans weren't quite divorced from their allies in the Shiite-dominated government in Baghdad, which wasn't interested in a program of centrally driven reconciliation, but there was a new distance between the two. The Sunnis had split from al Qaeda in Iraq, rejecting its program of violent religious extremism. "The possibility of forming a de facto alliance with the tribes emerged only once the Sunnis had themselves become disenchanted with AQI, and once the United States had also grown equally disillusioned with the prospects of achieving a 'top down' process of reconciliation through the auspices of the al-Maliki government," commented Australian political scientist Andrew Phillips.

The turned insurgents at first tended to refer to themselves as "the Sunni Awakening." Tellingly, Petraeus and other American officials used a variety of euphemisms, as if not to face head-on the sensitive reality that they were negotiating cease-fires with the enemy. Some units initially used terms such as "security contractors," "neighborhood watches," and "provisional security forces." Then the official name became "Concerned Local Citizens," until that Orwellian term was dropped for something marginally more realistic, "Sons of Iraq." There was a small irony in this last term, because until Petraeus and Odierno took command, American officials often had labeled insurgents "Anti-Iraqi Forces," even using the acronym "AIF" in briefings. Now those fighters had gone from being deemed to be against Iraq to being its progeny.

The cease-fires didn't quite amount to an amnesty, because there was no explicit forgiveness. But there was an implied one. Nor were they surrenders, because the fighters remained armed, and in some cases were given new and better weapons. They also went on the American payroll at about $10 a day per man, hardly a punitive step. The CIA paid bonuses to favored sheikhs. In reality these were paid truces of an uncertain duration and with a limited writ. The insurgents hadn't come over to the American side or even necessarily endorsed American goals. Maj. Mark Brady, a reconciliation specialist with the 1st Cavalry Division, noted that one Sunni leader said to him, "As soon as we finish with al Qaeda, we start with the Shiite extremists."

But the turning proved the answer to the sticky problem seen in Baghdad in 2006 of U.S. forces being able to clear but Iraqi forces being unable to hold. That was especially true in Sunni areas, where Iraqi forces tended to be seen as tools of the Shiite-dominated government in Baghdad. The answer: Have the Sunnis do it themselves.

At first, this new policy of paying off a former enemy was largely being done without informing the Baghdad government about it. "In the initial months, we weren't even telling them [Iraqi government officials], we were just doing it," said Emma Sky. Upon learning of the talks, she added, officials in the Baghdad government "accused us of creating a Sunni army that could lead to warlordism and possibly to a civil war." These were concerns that would remain alive for years.

During the spring many Iraqi commanders resisted meeting with the former insurgents who were volunteering to turn sides, said Col. Green, chief of operations for the 1st Cavalry Division. "They hadn't received any orders from the Iraqi government," he said. But soon, he said, many Iraqi battalion and brigade commanders began to work with the groups, even without direction from Baghdad. "They were finding ways to accommodate it, to share information, to deconflict the battlespace, even though they hadn't had orders," he said.

Nor were the front-line troops being asked to work with their former enemies told much about the changeover. Cpl. David Goldich, a smart young Marine in al Anbar Province, recalled simply seeing local guys showing up with weapons and setting up a rudimentary checkpoint on a main road. To a Marine eye, they didn't look impressive—"unshaven men wearing civilian clothes carrying rusty AK-47s milling about," he wrote. But he soon concluded that "they are worth their weight in gold. . . . an amazing force multiplier that denied the enemy freedom of movement in a manner we could not." They spoke the language, they knew the area, and they knew who wasn't from it. Higher-ups wouldn't approve giving supplies to the new guards, so Goldich's unit decided to help them out and scrounged weapons and food for the men and bullet-proof glass and concertina wire for their checkpoints. "What we gave them we stole from base, and probably would have been punished if caught," he recalled. (Goldich, who graduated from the University of Virginia before enlisting, also showed a far greater understanding of counterinsurgency than the Marine chain of command had after the Haditha incident. He took more risks, such as sometimes approaching Iraqis without carrying a weapon, because he thought it would help his unit achieve its mission. "My job is to defeat the enemy, not protect myself," he reasoned.)

Later in the spring, the process became more formalized. Odierno established a "reconciliation cell" in his headquarters to track the turnings and to advise commanders on how to do it. This was partly because commanders were asking for guidance about who they were allowed to talk to, whether they should treat with insurgent leaders, and how to respond to those leaders' requests for money, weapons, and official support. Odierno laid down some informal guidelines: Don't talk to war criminals. Don't give them ammunition. And if they ask you to stop doing raids in their area, tell them you can't promise that. Powell, the planner, recalled that "General Odierno's guidance was, 'We are going to be striking deals with people who have killed American soldiers. That may turn your stomach, but that's the way forward.' "

Once brigade and battalion commanders grew comfortable with the process, "it really started to catch on," said Brig. Gen. Mark McDonald, who was overseeing the new cell. The new opening with the Americans offered the Sunnis a way out from their unhappy alliance with al Qaeda. It is probably no coincidence that in April, as the top American commanders threw their weight behind the turning, the Islamic Army, a group of Sunni insurgent militias, posted on jihad websites a nine-page letter denouncing al Qaeda. It complained that al Qaeda had killed more than 30 of its fighters that spring. Abu Mohammed al-Salmani, a member of the group, said that the terrorist organization was killing far more Sunnis than the Americans were. "People are tired of this torture," he told a reporter. "We cannot keep silent anymore."

But as the turning edged closer to Baghdad, the central government grew more vocal about the deals being made. Maliki began sending alarmed messages asking exactly what the Americans thought they were doing. "They are trusting terrorists," charged Ali al-Adeeb, a prominent Shiite politician. "They are trusting people who have previously attacked American forces and innocent people. They are trusting people who are loyal to the regime of Saddam Hussein."

"It's like raising a crocodile," Saad Yousef al-Muttalibi, a member of the Maliki cabinet, told the *Washington Times.* "It is fine when it is a baby, but when it is big, you can't keep it in the house." The Baghdad government feared that the American government was going to feed baby crocodiles for its own purposes and then leave Iraq—just as the reptiles were beginning to snap at Baghdad. Later in the year, Maliki's Shiite bloc, the United Iraqi Alliance, would issue a statement condemning the American embrace of "those terrorist elements which committed the most hideous crimes against our people" and demanding "that the American administration stop this adventure." Other Shiites charged that after the Americans left, there would be two armies in central Iraq—one loyal to Baghdad, and one not.

There also was some suspicion that that was precisely the American plan—that is, create a balancing force of Sunnis to deter the Shiites from wholesale suppression of the Sunnis once the Americans were out of the way. Petraeus flatly denied that the new groups were a helpful counterweight to the Baghdad government, but planners below him were perhaps more candid. "As their growth grows, the national government will be in jeopardy," said Lt. Col. Jeff McDougall, one of Odierno's senior planners. "So it's a forcing mechanism," he said, posing a useful "or else" to the Shiite political leaders in Baghdad.

Even neutral observers had some qualms. Patrick Porter, an Australian military historian, later would call the new American allies in Iraq "a coalition of gangsters, tribal leaders and opportunists."

Not all American military officials were comfortable with the approach, worrying that the short-term security gain obtained would create long-term political problems. "What we're doing is creating a secessionist state out west," said a senior U.S. military intelligence official. "The Anbar tribes will be capable of keeping order, and also of keeping a Shiite-dominated army out of Anbar." In other words, argued retired Army Col. Andrew Bacevich, the Americans were avoiding military defeat by embracing political failure.

Some American troops were antsy about working alongside men who had fought them, and probably killed some of their comrades. "If Jack Bauer doesn't negotiate with terrorists, why does the American army?" asked Spec. Alex Horton, a young Texan who served in Baghdad and Baqubah in late 2006 and early 2007.

Horton reported a cold exchange between a member of his platoon and a turned insurgent. "Do you want to kill me?" the American soldier asked.

"Yes," replied the Iraqi, who had been a member of the 1920 Brigade, an insurgent group that broke with al Qaeda in 2007. "But not today."

But most American commanders liked what they were seeing. Some, in fact, soon seemed to grow more comfortable with the former insurgents than they did with the Iraqi police.

One day in late May in the western Baghdad neighborhood of Amiriyah, some local militiamen painted a sign on a wall, "Down with al Qaeda, long live the honest resistance." It was a classic ploy: Members of al Qaeda angrily arrived to paint over the disrespectful graffiti, only to be greeted by an explosion that killed three of them. Al Qaeda sent in reinforcements, who were caught in a firefight that lasted several hours, killing another nine al Qaeda members.

A few days later, on May 29, Lt. Col. Dale Kuehl, commander of the American battalion operating in the neighborhood, got a call from a local religious leader. "We're going after al Qaeda," he said. "What we want you to do is stay out of the way." It was in effect a replication of what MacFarland had experienced in Ramadi nine months earlier.

The next day at noon, loudspeakers in mosques broadcast a call to attack local members of al Qaeda. Black-clad militiamen began moving through the streets. Kuehl was inclined to stand back and watch the situation unfold. But after al Qaeda counterattacked the next day and surrounded the militia members, he had second thoughts, and dispatched Stryker armored vehicles to rescue the militiamen. It was a confusing fight for his troops, because both sides were wearing similar outfits and wielding AK-47s and other weaponry. (Soldiers frequently identify the enemy not by sight but by the sound of their guns.) The Americans were impressed with the tactical skills of the militiamen. "These guys looked like a military unit, the way they moved," Capt. Andy Wilbraham told the *Washington*

Post's Joshua Partlow. "Hand and arm signals. Stop. Take a knee. Weapons up." The leader of the militia was a former Iraqi army captain who called himself Haji Abu Abed.

GETTING TO KNOW YOU

Upon meeting your insurgent enemy, Kilcullen had told American officers, you will be surprised: "Your worst opponent is not the psychopathic terrorist of Hollywood, it is the charismatic follow-me warrior who would make your best platoon leader."

He was right. In July 2007, for example, Col. Martin Stanton, chief of reconciliation at Odierno's headquarters, met with some newly former insurgents outside the ragged little town of Mahmudiyah, one corner of the area south of Baghdad that American troops had dubbed the "Triangle of Death." They were in farmlands, he said, "but these guys didn't look like farmers. They were lean, tough, in their twenties. Their answers were crisp. Their weapons were clean and well oiled. . . . These are serious men, disciplined. They were very polite. They weren't effusive." That impressed him: They were acutely aware of how strong they were, and they weren't kowtowing. They clearly didn't feel they had lost the fight. His analysis was that "here was an enemy that, for reasons of their own, have come forward. . . . We had not defeated the Iraqi insurgents. What I took from that meeting was that they were still a going concern, but they were willing to take a chance with the Americans."

Biddle, the sometime adviser to Petraeus, was even more impressed by the former insurgents he met a few months later in Arab Jabour, south of Baghdad. "They were by far the most professional military organization I'd seen in Iraq, aside from the Americans and the British," he recalled. "They had a military bearing. They stood up straight. Their shirts were tucked in. I was simultaneously impressed, and glad that it was daylight."

The Americans also were willing to be forgiving on motives, in part perhaps because it made it easier to work their with former enemies. Lt. Col. Mark Fetter, another officer working on reconciliation issues, said that in his experience, insurgents were young men who "have got to eat. There are so many we've detained and interrogated, they did what they did for money."

Maj. Gen. Rick Lynch, commander of the U.S. division just south of Baghdad, summarized, "They're honorable men and they want to take care of their families."

The Americans learned a lot from their new friends. The police chief of Fallujah, Col. Faisal Ismail al-Zobaie, wanted to deter the manufacture of car bombs, so he ordered his force to monitor car mechanics' shops, where the bombs were assembled, and also to count the oxygen tanks at the hospital, because the canisters were used as bombs. He knew to take those steps because he was a former insurgent. The downside was that along with his knowledge, he had brought his Saddam-era attitudes. While he insisted he didn't torture prisoners, he did concede that he sometimes had them beaten. "Iraq obeys only force," he explained to the *Washington Post*'s Sudarsan Raghavan. He also said he had come to a better understanding of the U.S. presence: "I have realized that Americans love the strong guy." His view of his country's political future was equally blunt: "No democracy in Iraq. Ever." Two months later, he would be given new reason for his harsh view of life in Iraq: Insurgents executed his uncle, a school principal, apparently in the hope that Zobaie would attend the funeral. The police chief cautiously stayed away, but a boy walked into it wearing a suicide vest, and many of his relatives were among the 23 dead.

If there was a question about motives, it was asked more of the Americans by critics of the process, who worried that the Americans were just paying the insurgents to stop fighting without any plans to ensure that the payments would continue as long as needed. One critic of the surge, Col. Gian Gentile, a thoughtful officer who commanded a battalion in Iraq in 2006, called the deals with militias "cash for cooperation." He skeptically asked, "Have they really sided with us? Or, are they siding with their own side and using us and our money to prepare for a bigger fight down the road they know is coming?"

One officer involved in reconciliation issues, Maj. Brady, agreed that at least some insurgents were doing just that. "They watch TV," and so are aware of the American political debate over leaving Iraq, he said. His guess was that they had decided "to get themselves into a position to defend themselves, if there is going to be a civil war. They are coalescing their forces."

But others involved in the policy said such criticisms didn't grasp what was happening. Foremost, said Mansoor and others, was the ability of Americans to help protect people, which turned groups and especially the sheikhs leading them. These men were angry with al Qaeda, and had asked the Americans to shield or help them. "You don't get public rejection of al Qaeda if the people don't feel secure, if they are going to get their heads lopped off," said Rapp. "Our having troops in the population gives them confidence to do that, and that helps the Awakening spread." Thus the surge reinforced and spread the turning of insurgent groups.

Months later, U.S. troops on a raid in southern Salahuddin Province found the revealing diary of a regional leader of al Qaeda in Iraq. The repeated theme of his entries in the fall of 2007 was how the flipping of the insurgency was eroding his group. "There were almost 600 fighters in our sector before the tribes changed course," he wrote. "Many of our fighters quit and some of them joined the deserters." Now, he said, he had "20 or less" fighters deemed reliable—and he wasn't even sure about a few of those who seemed to be avoiding him. One former member kept possession of some 2,000 C-5 rockets and a sophisticated RPG-9 grenade launcher, he complained. "We have to keep trying with him to get our weapons and ammunition back," he noted.

He had plans for revenge on those who had abandoned him. "We were mistreated, cheated and betrayed by some of our brothers who used to be part of the jihadi movement. Therefore we must not have mercy on those traitors until they come back to the right side or get eliminated completely."

THE INSURGENT WHO LOVED *TITANIC*

Capt. Samuel Cook, who was commanding the 3rd Armored Cavalry Regiment's C troop in the northern Tigris Valley in Salahuddin Province, a bit north of where that diary was discovered, had been pursuing the local leader of al Qaeda in Iraq, whom he considered a "very passionate, eloquent speaker, well educated." The terrorist leader offered to talk, and Cook took him up on it. "He was tired of being on the run, and he no longer believed in what he had once been preaching," Cook said. He provided information on the whereabouts of a higher al Qaeda leader for the province, who was killed in a firefight two weeks later.

He also told them that al Qaeda in Iraq had three major sources of funding: crime, the Kurds, and the Iranians. Cook would use this information adroitly, asking local Sunni insurgents why they thought al Qaeda was their friend, if it was on the payroll of the dreaded Persian power. The insurgents, who had affiliated with al Qaeda as the surge began to hit them, also were growing tired, Cook recalled.

Cook had a light touch. In December 2007, he sent a letter to the community wishing them a happy Eid al-Fitr, a festival that marks the end of the Muslim holy month of Ramadan, and one of the most significant Muslim holidays. At the beginning of the Eid feast, he met with the al Qaeda man, telling him that he had enough evidence to detain him. The man responded that Cook was wading into a fight between tribes, implying that he didn't understand the situation. Cook countered, "We have far too many reports from people in your own tribe to make this a tribal affair." Cook then told the man and some sheikhs who had waited outside that the reconciliation process is not easy and that the al Qaeda man and he disagreed on his guilt, but that out of respect for the Eid holiday, he wouldn't detain him at this time. As Cook hoped, those three actions—the letter, the meeting, and the show of respect— persuaded other insurgents to come see the thoughtful American.

One man who came in to talk was Sarhan Hassan Wisme, a local legend, described by Cook as "the Robin Hood figure at the height of the insurgency in 2006." Sarhan boasted of having planted more than 200 bombs for attacks on U.S. troops, a claim he later happily repeated to Cook. His other specialty was killing locals who cooperated with the Americans. "The thing that intrigued me about him is that he was not afraid to tell us exactly what he had done to U.S. forces—proud of it almost." The Americans had raided his house six times but never caught him.

Cook, an inquisitive man who grew up partly in Belfast, Northern Ireland, where his father was a professor of religion, had several extensive conservations with Sarhan, beginning on the first day of 2008. These meetings weren't deemed official interrogations because Sarhan wasn't in custody and was told he was free to leave at any time. Cook didn't want to capture one man; he wanted to turn his entire organization, or destroy it, if that became necessary. To ensure his knowledge was accurate, Cook had a soldier sit quietly in the room and take verbatim notes.

"Captain, you just make me out to be a very bad man, saying I have murdered, raped, and stolen," Sarhan protested, according to those notes. "I fight only the Americans, and all of Sharqat is my witness."

"What about car bombs?" Cook asked.

"If you have witnesses that I was part of a car bombing, then you can kill me right now," the insurgent responded indignantly.

"You are part of a group and ideology that is destroying Iraq," Cook said, not willing to cede any moral ground. "We have enough evidence to shoot you on sight. . . . When you leave, unless this meeting goes very well, I will still try to kill you."

During several more meetings in January, Sarhan told Cook his life story. He worked at a fertilizer factory in nearby Bayji, home of a major oil refinery, and obtained some of his bomb-making materials there. He had started attacking the Americans in the spring of 2004, motivated by news of the American abuse of prisoners at the Abu Ghraib prison west of Baghdad. He insisted that he attacked only Americans, not the Iraqi army or police. That wasn't just a matter of ideology. His organization, the Islamic Army, had thoroughly infiltrated the police, who actually became quite helpful, warning him by cell phone when there was an American patrol coming to the town, one reason he was never found at home. Indeed, he said, one police major had donated his sniper rifle to the insurgents. He explained that the local police colonel had an agreement: "As long as JAI [the Islamic Army] does not attack Iraqi police or the Iraqi army, they are free to attack coalition forces." Also, he said, the city council chief had an understanding under which contracts given by the Iraqi government and the U.S. military for local projects were steered to members of the insurgency, or at the very least made sure it employed them.

In January 2007, he had affiliated with al Qaeda after hearing its local mufti speak about the need to unify because the Americans were retreating from Iraq, and the insurgency had to stand as one to oppose the inevitable Persian attempt at domination. Here he hesitated. "There are things I don't want to talk about because if we do talk about them, you may kill me," Sarhan said.

"You are here as a guest and I will honor that," Cook reassured him.

As the two men got to know each other better in subsequent meetings, their discussions would meander, as Cook sought to understand his onetime and perhaps future adversary. Hedging his bets, he used his company sniper team as his bodyguards during some meetings so they would get a good look at Sarhan in case they needed to shoot him in the future. The two men talked about Sarhan's children, who were playing "Mujahadeen and Americans," instead of the traditional "Cowboys and Indians." Cook knew that Iraqis of all stripes loved American movies, particularly the 1997 epic *Titanic.* Sarhan told him that he didn't watch any American movies, that they were products of the devil. Cook jokingly asked him if he liked *Titanic,* knowing it was enormously popular in Iraq. Why, yes, the insurgent confessed. He recounted watching it seven times and crying every time at the ending, as Kate Winslet lets the dead Leonardo DiCaprio slip into the freezing North Atlantic.

When Cook asked about another local insurgent cell, and whether they were responsible for the kidnapping and murder of five Iraqi soldiers four months earlier, Sarhan was contemptuous. "No, they couldn't kill a chicken," he sneered.

The exchange that struck Cook most was one in which he didn't speak, but instead listened to a conversation between two Iraqis. In mid-January he brought Col. Ismael, a local Iraqi police commander he respected enormously, to sit down with Sarhan. Both were Sunnis, and in fact from related tribes, but had never met. "They are tribal cousins, and both chose very different paths to deal with the crushing loss they felt after the invasion," Cook said. Their dialogue, which Cook recorded, does indeed read like a David Mamet version of recent Sunni history, as they jab and parry about the dilemma of feeling squeezed between two enemies, the United States and Iran.

"You know that your jihad is all bullshit," Ismael asserted. "You cooperate with Iran"—a cardinal sin for a Sunni. "You know Iran is our number one enemy."

Sarhan hit back: How could you call yourself an Iraqi yet cooperate with the American occupiers? "You are sworn to defend your country, is that right?"

"Yes, I defend my country," said Ismael, who had been a colonel in the Iraqi army under Saddam Hussein and was wounded in Iraq's war with Iran. "But you know the result of that. It is Saddam Hussein." He pushed Sarhan to consider the consequences of an American departure. "You know if U.S. forces withdraw from Iraq, Iran will come. Their occupation will be intolerable."

Sarhan was ready to take them on. "Then we will fight Iran and force them to withdraw from Iraq as well."

"You are not thinking!" chided Ismael. "They will destroy this country!"

Ismael repeatedly attacked Sarhan on the issues of dignity and respect, the core values of Iraqi culture. "A lot of people are talking shit about you." People in town were saying things behind his back, he said. "They say to you, 'Hi, you are doing a good job of fighting the Americans,' but when you leave, they say, 'Let him go to Hell.' . . . They make fun of you and talk about how you fucked up Iraq."

Ismael knew his man. "Sarhan is a cold-blooded man, but I could see his eyes tearing up while Ismael lectured him," Cook wrote in a patrol report. His interpreter told him after the meeting that as he had listened, he had "relived all the pain of the last five years."

But Sarhan still wasn't quite persuaded to give up. The Iraqi policeman who had arranged the first meeting with Sarhan informed Cook that the situation in the town was growing more dangerous. In late January, Iraqi police found a propane tank that had been rigged to explode and was being taken to Cook's outpost. Also, a former coworker of Sarhan's from the fertilizer factory was caught looking for a photograph of Cook, apparently to help in planning a sniper attack on the meddlesome American commander. More reports came to Cook that the insurgency might be preparing a new round of attacks—this time under Sarhan's leadership. Cook had Sarhan brought in and tried to persuade him to give up. The insurgent agreed, but as a matter of pride, insisted that he be arrested not by the Americans but by the Iraqi police. On February 4, after a few more meetings, Sarhan finally turned himself in.

The effect of the turning of the insurgent groups was extraordinary, "the game changer," Cook concluded. "The mufti for al Qaeda who had been so potent in his rhetoric against us gave the opening remarks at the reconciliation conference in mid-February in front of over a thousand people. He was now telling most of his erstwhile colleagues in the insurgency why it was time to lay down their weapons." In the following days, 184 people came in to "reconcile" and be given parole. "It was a mass surrender in effect," and it later spread to the rest of Salahuddin Province, Cook said. In order to be deemed "reconciled," insurgents were required to:

- state publicly their commitment to lay down their arms,
- turn in all weapons,
- promise to help provide security,
- come in with a guarantor, who becomes subject to arrest if the insurgent can't be found, and
- be ready to come in any time they are summoned.

They had seven days to consider those terms, after which they would be targeted. Most obeyed these rather strict rules of parole, Cook noted, and those who didn't were arrested.

The rounds of conversations that followed "flipped the light switch on and allowed us to see the insurgency, the leaders, the structure, their tactics, everything," said an amazed Cook. American tactics and practices immediately improved in myriad ways. For example, the new commander of the turned insurgents, now working with the Americans, strongly recommended that Iraqi police not be permitted to keep cell phones at checkpoints. He also named the Iraqi police officer who was responsible for keeping top insurgent leaders informed about the whereabouts of planned American raids. One such leader would tell Cook later about being warned and so hiding in a prepared hole next to his sister's house, where a cow conveniently sat while the Americans looked for him.

Cook's bottom line was that many low-level fighters had joined the insurgency for the money. By taking them away from al Qaeda and putting them on the American payroll, he said, the huge economic advantage of the United States was finally brought to bear in Iraq. "They could not compete with the sheer volume of cash we were able to put in people's hands," he said. Payments of $300 a month each to 1,500 local security guards amounted to nearly a half million dollars a month, he noted. "Instead of devoting twenty-five to fifty percent of my combat power to route security—patrols, sniper outposts, et cetera, I have been able to spend my time hunting—intelligence gathering, raids, overwatching enemy houses with snipers."

Having former insurgents as guides also meant there was suddenly much more information on which to act, both because the insurgents were talking but also because they were no longer violently preventing civilians from doing so. Indeed, there were so many new informants that it made it difficult for the remaining insurgents to pinpoint the origins of the new American intelligence. They "knew where the [arms] caches were, they knew all the names of the al Qaeda leaders," said Capt. Zane Galvach, a platoon leader in the 2nd Infantry Division's 3rd Stryker Brigade.

All told, the Americans arrived at local cease-fires with 779 local militias, some as small as 10 men in a neighborhood, some as large as 800 armed fighters, said Army Lt. Col. Jeffrey Kulmayer, who oversaw the U.S. military's relationship with the groups in 2008. Permitting the Sunnis to field militias, commented Carter Malkasian, the counterinsurgency adviser to the Marines, was probably "one more step toward the fragmentation of Iraq." Despite that concern, he endorsed the idea. It was time to select "least bad" choices. "Optimal is no longer a luxury the United States can afford," he wrote. "Right now, we must focus on avoiding the worst possible outcome."

A little noticed aspect of this embrace of former enemies was that it was a second major instance of the leaders of the U.S. effort quietly imitating Saddam Hussein. The first was Gen. Odierno's decision that in order to secure Baghdad he had to focus on the surrounding Baghdad belts. After being weakened by his partial defeat in the 1991 war, Saddam also had reached out to Sunni tribal leaders. Just as Petraeus would allow former insurgents to keep their arms and patrol their neighborhoods, after the 1991 Gulf War, Saddam had "embraced auxiliary tribalism by allowing sheikhs to create their own private armies equipped with small arms, rocket-propelled grenades, mortars, and allegedly even howitzers," noted Austin Long, a RAND Corporation expert on counterinsurgency.

But, Long noted, the U.S. policy faced an additional difficulty: It was opposed by the Baghdad government, while Saddam's earlier move had been implemented by Baghdad.

Making peace with some of one's foes made sense when one's allies were sometimes secret enemies. In January 2007, for example, insurgents assaulted a police station in Karbala where U.S. advisers were based. One of the Americans was killed, three were wounded, and four were kidnapped, only to be shot and killed later. A subsequent investigation found strong evidence that some of the Iraqi police colluded with the attackers. Some left the compound before the assault began, and a back gate had been left unlocked. Also, the attackers somehow had obtained the uniforms worn by U.S. bodyguards. Later that year, the head of police intelligence in Karbala Province was detained after roadside bombs and other weapons were found in his house. In Baghdad, U.S. troops detained an Iraqi police lieutenant suspected of being a Shiite militia leader, only to have other policemen open fire on them from a checkpoint and from nearby rooftops. Six of the police were killed.

A study done at the U.S. embassy later in the year concluded that corruption was "the norm" in many of the ministries in the Iraqi government but that its extent couldn't be determined, in part because "several ministries are so controlled by criminal gangs or militias so to be impossible to operate without a tactical force protecting the investigator." The report singled out two ministries in particular as problematic. Unfortunately, they were two of the three most important: the oil ministry, loaded with revenue, and the interior ministry, which controls the police and other law enforcement organizations, such as the border patrol. Leakage at the oil agency was said to be "massive," with much of the money going to the insurgency, the report alleged. It likened the interior department to a Racketeer Influenced and Corrupt Organization: "MOI is a 'legal enterprise' which has been co-opted by organized criminals who act through the 'legal enterprise' to commit crimes such as kidnapping, extortion, bribery, etc."

ARMY 2006 VS. ARMY 2007

A sharp but illuminating squabble would break out later among some Army officers who had commanded in Iraq about whether the U.S. approach in 2007 really was that different from earlier years. Some contended that the manner in which the surge troops were being used wasn't, in fact, a real departure. Nor did some of those earlier commanders think they had been on a losing trajectory. One such credible expert is Col. Gentile, the savvy officer who commanded a battalion in the southern part of Baghdad in 2006. "We did not fail" that year, he later argued. "In my opinion, we succeeded."

In fact, he wrote, "there is little difference between what American combat soldiers did in 2006 and what they are now doing as part of the 'surge.'" In his view, they were out doing what needed to be done, conducting some 3,500 patrols. "We cleaned up the garbage, started to establish neighborhood security forces, rebuilt schools and killed or captured hostile insurgents, both Shiite and Sunni." Most important, Gentile contended that "our fundamental mission was to protect the people"—just as it was a year later under Petraeus and Odierno.

Strikingly, Gentile argued that the decline in violence in 2007 was primarily the result of the cease-fires with the Sunni insurgents and the Sadrist militias rather than from anything the surge did. "The dramatic lowering of violence in summer '07 had more to do with the decision to ally with our former enemies to fight al Qaeda and the reciprocating effect of them not attacking us anymore combined with Sadr's decision to stand down attacks explains the lowering of violence," he wrote.

But there were some fundamental flaws in Gentile's argument. Pete Mansoor, before working with Petraeus on counterinsurgency theory and then becoming his executive officer, had commanded a brigade in Baghdad in the 1st Armored Division. As intellectual antagonists, he and Gentile were well matched: Both had commanded large units in combat around Baghdad, and both had earned doctorates in military history at elite institutions. Mansoor responded emphatically to Gentile in a posting on the website of the *Small Wars Journal:*

> The troops did not fail in 2006, but the strategy did. Gian Gentile is wrong when he writes about 2006, "Our fundamental mission was to protect the people." In fact, the fundamental mission in 2006 was to transition the mission to Iraqi forces. And there were not just "fewer Combat Outposts" in Iraqi neighbor-

> hoods in 2006; in fact, there were almost none. Gentile's troops were forced to try to protect the Iraqi people by commuting from Camp Victory and other large bases on the periphery of the city.

Gentile flatly rejected that challenge. "My mission was to protect the people, period!" he responded on the website.

No, countered Mansoor, quoting the overarching document that guided the 2006 campaign plan, which stated that "completing this transition [to Iraqi self-reliance] . . . is the focus of the Campaign Plan." Not *a* focus, Mansoor noted, but *the* focus.

Others in Baghdad greeted Gentile's arguments with a mix of bewilderment and anger. "Gentile had a different stance," said Maj. Gen. Hammond, commander of the 4th Infantry Division, which replaced the 1st Cavalry Division in Baghdad early in 2008. "It was night and day. He was FOB-centric. We are JSS-centric"—that is, with operations built around the "Joint Security Stations" out in the city.

Indeed, Gentile's account omits certain key differences between how the Army operated in Iraq on his watch and then a year later. Most important, almost all his troops lived on a big base, Forward Operating Base Falcon, and interacted with the Iraqi population only while on patrol outside it. No matter how many patrols they conducted, they didn't live among the population. Early in 2006, I was embedded with his unit, the 8th Squadron of the 10th Cavalry Regiment, 4th Infantry Division. One night at the base I was sleeping in a small building that was separated from the world of Iraq outside only by a series of tall cement barriers. As I dozed off in my sleeping bag, there was a small firefight going on just on the other side of the wall, but it was between Iraqi forces and someone else, and seemed very distant. I inquired the next morning, but no one on Gentile's staff seemed to care much about what had happened on the other side of the wall. So I disagree with his argument that "the accuracy of reports that tout differences between counterinsurgency methods in 2006 and 2007 are mostly off the mark." By contrast, I remember being astonished in January and February 2006 at how invisible the American military presence had become on the streets of Baghdad. If troops are not present, they almost certainly aren't protecting anyone who is.

Most conclusive was a comment made by the operations officer for an Army battalion operating in Gentile's old area during the surge. Interviewed by an officer from the Army's Center for Lessons Learned, he reported that locals who had once been insurgents told them that until the surge increased the U.S. presence in the area, they had largely ignored the occasional American patrol. Their practice, the former insurgents reported, was, "Just let them drive through, we won't see them again for weeks."

THE GENERAL WHO LOVED GERTRUDE BELL

But Gentile was correct in noting that American officials were indeed cutting deals with all sorts of characters they previously had shunned, and that these agreements were significantly reducing violence. In some ways, the story of the Iraq war in 2007 was the Iraqification of the American effort. Not only had Americans stopped trying to Americanize Iraq, they were themselves willing to become more Iraqified. After an American soldier got into a lethal fight with an Iraqi policeman in Ramadi in the spring of 2008, his commanders acted as if they were Iraqis. Rather than go directly to the family or tribe of the dead policeman, they followed local custom and approached a sheikh of another tribe and asked him to act as a mediator. He quizzed them about the incident and then escorted them to the family, which followed the expected routine and acted emotionally, with hundreds of related tribesman shouting "Death to America" and "The occupiers must leave." After a series of meetings, Col. Charlton, commander of the brigade that replaced MacFarland's, agreed to step up a reconstruction project that the tribe wanted—effectively paying blood money. This lengthy process averted "a potential disaster" in which the tribe could have turned hostile, concluded Capt. Elliott Press, an intelligence officer under Charlton.

The embrace of the tribes and their ways could have happened earlier, but was discouraged by senior U.S. officials for ideological reasons, said an Army officer who had served as a strategist in Iraq. "In '03, the commanders were working with the tribes and they got hammered for it," he recalled. "I was in a meeting with [Deputy Secretary of Defense Paul] Wolfowitz and we said, 'These tribes are a powerful part of the social structure.' Wolfowitz said, 'This disturbs me greatly. Iraq is a cosmopolitan society.' "

In 2007 the American effort, overall, stopped fighting Iraq's tribal structure and instead started to cooperate with it. "Tribal society makes up the tectonic plates in Iraq on which everything rests," concluded Brig. Gen. John Allen, the deputy commander of the Marines in Iraq that year. Acting on that insight, Allen effectively became the Marine ambassador to the sheikhs of al Anbar Province, flying frequently to Amman, Jordan, to meet with them there in private homes and at the Sheraton Hotel, whose three-tiered lobby of rich marble and divans nestled in lush vines has an almost Babylonian feel of hanging gardens.

The Marine Corps has a greater tolerance for outliers and even flat-out eccentrics than the Army does. Allen is no oddball, but he is unusual. He has three master's degrees in international relations and related subjects, had taught political science at the Naval Academy in Annapolis, Maryland, and was a member of the Council on Foreign Relations, where it is more common to see diplomats, academic, and investment bankers than Marine officers. Like Petraeus, Allen also thrived in command. For example, as a company commander, he won the Leftwich Trophy, awarded in the Marines every year to one captain who has demonstrated outstanding leadership skills.

Allen's task was to expand the accomplishment of Sean MacFarland's brigade and its attached Marine units in Ramadi. MacFarland had run into a lot of skepticism in the Marines about what he was trying to do in Ramadi, but not from Allen. "I felt like he got it immediately," MacFarland said. "He was finishing my sentences for me. He was Mozart to my Salieri."

Allen was ready to take the reconciliation talks to a new, regional level. "It became clear to us that this Anbar fight was being fought over the region, in hotel lobbies and rooms around the Gulf," Allen said. "You'd have a meeting with a sheikh in Amman or an Iraqi businessman in Dubai, a phone call would be made, and something beneficial would happen" back in Iraq, such as hundreds of tribesmen showing up at a police recruiting office.

In a June 2007 meeting in Amman, for example, he expressed a desire to see Sheikh Mishan al-Jumayli, who was living in Damascus. One of the sheikh's sons had been killed by mistake at an American checkpoint in 2003. A second one was murdered by al Qaeda in 2005. After that, his wife died of a broken heart, the sheikh said. An Iraqi businessman at the meeting whipped out a cell phone, hit one button, and got Sheikh Mishan on the line. The next morning they met first on neutral ground in Amman and then in Allen's room at the Sheraton. Allen asked the wary sheikh to return to Iraq, telling him that his presence in his tribal lands in al Anbar could turn the tide against al Qaeda. Mishan demurred: "It's not time. I will return when Allah wills it." Well, proposed Allen, if you should change your mind, I will fortify your compound and train your bodyguards. One of the lessons he had learned was that working with the tribes requires "tactical patience," a military virtue the American armed forces tend to neglect or even disparage.

Several weeks later Allen was contacted by an intermediary in Amman. Sheikh Mishan's third son had been killed by an IED near Fallujah, and he wanted to know if the offer was still good. The next day Allen and a team of Marines from al Anbar were on a Marine C-130 cargo plane to Amman. The sheikh, his sole surviving son, and his spiritual adviser flew back with them, with the sheikh sitting in the cockpit and emotionally looking out over the western desert of Iraq. As they landed at a Marine base, helicopters were waiting to fly the sheikh to Fallujah, where he was met by local sheikhs. "They took him home, and that began the turning of Karmah," which had been a persistently tough town for the Marines. Each of these "turnings" would have concrete results as tribal members manned the police and brought their militias into alliance with the Americans.

Not that the job was done. "Al Qaeda counterattacked right away," Allen remembered. "They put about ten members of his family in a house and dynamited it." Then one of the sheikh's subordinate leaders was shot by a sniper, and Allen stayed with him through his surgery. Then his brother's house was mortared, wounding several family members.

The attacks diminished but never really ended. In June 2008, a suicide bomber hit a meeting in Karmah and killed 13 other sheikhs, the town's mayor, and the commander of a Marine battalion and also the CO of one of his rifle companies.

Another problem was the relatively low stature of the main American ally among the tribal leaders, Sittar albu-Risha. Farther up the Euphrates River Valley, Allen recalled, "They'd talk about Sittar the criminal, the smuggler, the second-tier sheikh of a third-tier tribe. At this point many of the sheikhs from the older, larger tribes were unwilling to subordinate their prestige or tribal equities to Sittar, even though he'd apparently been able create a strong relationship with the U.S. Army brigade in Ramadi." Also, Sittar was pushing for greater political representation, arguing that he and his followers had liberated Ramadi, the provincial capital and so should receive half the seats on the provincial council. He didn't get that, but he got a voice. And by August 2007, when Sittar sponsored a meeting at his compound, nearly all the sheikhs in the province showed up, "voluntarily," said Allen. When President Bush visited al Anbar Province the following month, Sittar was seated next to the president, at the recommendation of the governor. Always smooth-tongued, Sittar told Bush that as soon as the fighting was done in Iraq, "We're ready to go to Afghanistan to help you."

Only 10 days later, just after Petraeus testified to Congress and just before the first anniversary of the crucial meeting in Ramadi, Sittar was blown up in his backyard by a buried bomb.

Allen is an unusual Marine. "I probably would have been an archaeologist had I not wound up where I am," he said. He was particularly influenced by the writings of Gertrude Bell, the British expert on the Middle East who was a colleague of T. E. Lawrence's and spoke far better Arabic than him but lacked his skill at self-promotion. She worked extensively in Iraq advising the British government, especially on tribal affairs. An heiress, the author of many books, translator of Arabic and Persian poetry, and a mountain climber, she also founded what became the Baghdad Archaeological Museum before committing suicide in Baghdad in July 1926, likely because she knew she was suffering from cancer. "She had the life I perhaps would have liked to have had," Gen. Allen said. He read her books, letters, and diaries, especially after he found some of them posted on a British university website. He studied her writings on the Iraqi tribes. "When the tribes are at their best they live in a condition of splendid equilibrium," he said, quoting from her diaries. Lifting a book from his desk, he read aloud her comment about the British campaign in Iraq during World War I: " 'Before the smoke of conflict has lifted, within the hearing of the guns, the work of reconstruction has been initiated.' "

Bell had a gimlet eye for the politics of Iraq. In commenting on the rebellion against the British occupation after World War I, she wrote, "The tribes witnessed the withdrawal of British administration and were convinced that their efforts would, as they had been assured, drive the British out of Mesopotamia. This conviction spurred on those who had already risen and won over the half-hearted, who could not risk being left on the losing side."

Allen saw Iraq through the lens provided by Bell. "If you are not a member of a tribe in Anbar, you have no status," he said. "You're probably a dead man." He was fascinated to see former al Qaeda fighters petition for reentry into their old tribes. In the fall of 2007, Allen recalled, Sheikh Khamis of the Albu Issa tribe issued an edict: "You have to put your name on a public statement that you will fight al Qaeda. And then you must have the blood of al Qaeda on your hands."

Tribal justice was far from unsophisticated, Allen advised other Marines. "It's about mediation, conflict resolution," he would say. "Remember, there's a thousand years in this operating system." As al Qaeda's leaders fled the province, leaving behind their foot soldiers, he began to see many more such statements, he said. An entire IED cell came in one day and simply surrendered out of the blue. "They were simply exhausted by the relentless pursuit of Coalition and Iraqi security forces and had lost hope in their cause."

A BALANCED STRATEGY

Petraeus hadn't said so publicly, but he had brought the means and ends of U.S. strategy more into balance. Not only had he and Odierno increased the resources devoted to the war, primarily with the addition of 30,000 troops, his new, more realpoliitik approach had reduced the size of the opposition, even if that mean negotiating with people who had killed American troops. Finally, after years of driving its enemies together, the U.S. effort was splitting them apart, thus obeying Andrew Krepinevich's law of the conservation of enemies: Never make more than you need to have at any one time.

With the new approach, it was possible to make better distinctions. "The insurgency had three levels," Capt. Keirsey, the Baker Company commander in southern Baghdad, said he realized. "Top was the true AQI hard-core leaders. Next were those who were truly trying to protect their neighborhoods. Others were simply the criminals and such that try to exploit the situation for their own benefit or make a living." The second group could be enticed simply by allowing them to maintain checkpoints and patrols if they cooperated and coordinated with U.S. and Iraqi forces. They and the third group could be bought off for surprisingly little—usually $10 a day, plus some reconstruction contracts for the sheikhs who brought them in. That was a small price to pay to keep alive American soldiers.

Keirsey gave the Iraqi security volunteers tough love. The volunteer group in his area was at first called "Heroes of Mulhalla Organization," but the acronym HOMO made them decide to change it. Each member was vetted with a local member of the community. The Americans kept track of each endorsement. If the volunteer went bad, the endorser could be fined or even jailed. Those accepted were then issued a numbered badge. Every day an assignment sheet indicated by badge number which volunteers were on duty, and if a patrol found that the volunteer wasn't there, they would report him so his pay could be docked. "We were extremely harsh on discipline," Keirsey said. "Late for work, lose twenty percent of your pay for the month. Shirt not tucked in, lose twenty percent of your pay."

In turn, he found the volunteers far more effective than the Iraqi police or army. After he asked for a list of the area's poorest families, they developed one with 55 names, plus phone numbers and addresses. His patrols checked it out and found "the information was one hundred percent accurate." Just to be careful, the company also developed "target packets" in case any of the volunteer leaders turned against them again. "Fortunately, that was never an issue," Lt. Gross, the platoon leader, said.

With the passage of time they were able to build trust. "We picked up a lot of credibility in one incident," Keirsey recalled. Local Iraqi volunteers came under attack without American troops nearby. After they called Keirsey's unit on a cell phone, desperate for help, he was able to get U.S. attack helicopters to fly to their defense. Later that day, the Iraqi militiamen wanted to come visit him to express their gratitude but were detained at a checkpoint. "We got them out."

One nagging question is whether Petraeus and Odierno had tried only to harmonize policy and strategy—or actually had overstepped their bounds by setting policy. There is evidence that they did overstep to a degree, but in a forgivable way, because there was a strategy vacuum at the White House. As part of this, they quietly downsized American goals in Iraq, lowering their sights to trying to achieve sustainable security, but not necessarily aiming for an Iraq that is democratic, respects human rights, and is an ally of the United States. Thus they brought means and ends more into balance—despite Bush's continuing presidential rhetoric about victory and liberty. The two big American bases just west of downtown Baghdad were called Camp Victory and Camp Liberty. But if they were labeled truthfully, they would have been renamed Camp Accommodation and Camp Stability, as those were the new goals of the American effort.

The danger of making policy on the fly and not vetting it through scrutiny and debate is that it may win short-term advances without recognizing long-term costs. As Long, the counterinsurgency expert at the RAND Corporation put it, "The tribal strategy is a means to achieve one strategic end, fighting al Qaeda in Mesopotamia, but it is antithetical to another, the creation of a stable, unified, and democratic Iraq."

It was no coincidence, added Marc Lynch, a Middle Eastern expert at George Washington University, that after the United States began cutting deals with local militias, both the Sunni and Shiite communities began "fragmenting at a remarkable rate." There was still a scramble for power in the future Iraq; the Americans had just made sure there would be some Sunni entries in the race.

BAGHDAD SATURDAY NIGHTS

One reason Petraeus was able to bring Bush along into these hazy areas of half deals with enemies and threats to friends was that he is skilled at managing upward, especially at the strategic level. Part of the job, as Petraeus saw it, was to "make sure your bosses understand the mission." For him, much of that educational task came during his weekly video-teleconferences with President Bush.

Preparation for those sessions began with Lt. Col. Charlie Miller, who had known Petraeus for well over a decade, having been a second lieutenant in Petraeus's battalion in the early 1990s. Indeed, Miller had been across the street at a different firing range when a sergeant told him the battalion commander had just been shot. Miller didn't believe it at first, thinking that the NCO was pulling a green lieutenant's leg.

Now, 16 years later, the two were in Baghdad. Every Saturday night Miller would sit down and write one of the world's most exclusive memos, about what he thought the president needed to know and understand about this week of the war. Miller—smart, boyish, and sincere—would take notes all week, as would his boss, Col. Rapp, the head of Petraeus's internal think tank, who traveled around Iraq with the general. Miller also would review the week's operations. In particular, he would look for a theme, something that pulled together the events and data of the week.

At around 7:30 on Saturday evenings, Miller would walk across the bridge from the palace at Camp Victory, over the shallow artificial lake, to the path winding to the mess hall, where he would get a take-out meal. He would bring it back to his desk in a cubbyhole just outside the office Petraeus kept there. Then he would begin writing, sipping big cups of coffee as he did. His first paragraph summarized the security situation. His second was about politics and economics. By midnight he would have about 2,500 words on his computer screen.

On Sunday morning he would send it to Col. Rapp, who would edit it. "We try to use it to push Petraeus, see if we can get some edge into it," Rapp said. On Sunday night, Petraeus and his writing aide, Liz McNally, would go over it. "He handwrites all over it," Rapp said.

On Monday morning, Rapp would take back the memo, by now edited down to four or five pages long, and e-mail it to just a handful of people—the defense secretary, the chairman of the Joint Chiefs of Staff, and the chief of the Central Command. Not even the other service chiefs, or the White House, were copied in—President Bush would get the message directly from Petraeus during their electronic meeting that afternoon. "When they are declassified, these weekly reports will be a big part of the history of the war," Rapp said. "He doesn't pull any punches."

In late October 2007, for example, Petraeus began to worry that the president would again begin talking about how everything was going well in Iraq, in part because of assertions by some Special Operations officers that al Qaeda in Iraq had been defeated, so one memo then focused on avoiding presidential triumphalism. "I just wrote for him, 'Mr. President, you need to be measured, you need to say, "We are putting the hurt on al Qaeda, but they are not finished," ' " Rapp said.

On Monday afternoon, at 3:35 Baghdad time, which during much of the year was 8:35 in the morning back in Washington, Petraeus would talk by videoteleconference with the president. Ambassador Crocker usually would also participate. These sessions usually would go on for about an hour, with Petraeus and Crocker on camera, and Mansoor and Rapp sitting to the side. Rapp said Bush was far more imposing in the sessions than his public persona would lead one to expect. "I think America's view of the president, whether they like or dislike him, is what they see of him reading a statement at the podium, which isn't impressive, in my opinion," Rapp said. "In these meetings, he is masterful—good political insights, good handle on the subject."

Miller agreed that the private Bush was strikingly different. "I wish he would come across a little more in public like that."

If Bush and Petraeus disagreed, Rapp said, Bush would make his view clear but still give the general a green light. "He'll say, 'I've got some concerns about that, but if you think that's the way to go, Okay, let's try it,'" he said. Overall, the tone of these meetings was remarkably more collegial than they had been when Rumsfeld was defense secretary, said one Army officer. "The VTCs I sat in on, I was just fucking amazed at how that guy treated people," he recalled. "He was just exceedingly combative in an unhelpful way." Now, with Gates's becoming a quiet force at the Pentagon and Petraeus's bonding with the president across the oceans in a way the American people never saw, the American conduct of the war moved forward, perhaps less grandly, but with a coherence and unity of effort it had lacked since the invasion long ago in 2003.

8.

THE DOMESTIC OPPOSITION COLLAPSES

(Summer and Fall 2007)

At 9 A.M. on June 13, 2007, insurgents dynamited the two minarets remaining at the shell of the Golden Dome Mosque in Samarra, which had been bombed 16 months earlier. The renewed attack on one of the holiest sites for Shiites clearly was meant to spark sectarian fighting. Petraeus's heart sank as an aide told him about the attack. "You know, you have moments where you can feel the blood coursing through your body as news comes in." He had previously endured only two such moments during his three tours in Iraq, he said. The first time was when his 101st Airborne Division took casualties during the invasion of Iraq, and the second was later in 2003 when two Black Hawks collided over Mosul, killing 17 of his soldiers.

Petraeus's Green Zone office is only a few steps from Crocker's. He immediately walked over to see the ambassador, who listened and then said, "Oh, shit!" They were both thinking that this could be like the first bombing of Samarra that had preceded the small civil war of 2006.

The two immediately decided to go see Maliki. As they were driving across the Green Zone, with Sadi Othman, Petraeus's interpreter and counsel on Iraqi affairs, also in the car, Crocker recalled, "Dave and I just looked at each other, didn't say anything—didn't need to say anything—because we both knew that this was where the whole thing could spin out of control." Upon their arrival at the prime minister's office, Maliki told them the same thing. Everyone was terrified that this would kick off another round of sectarian fighting.

"It was a hard meeting," recalled Othman. Maliki was furious. The prime minister complained that his commanders in Samarra had said they had control of the city and promised to him that the remains of the mosque would be protected. He worried that Shiites in the capital would soon be in the streets hunting Sunnis, burning their shops, homes, and mosques. That in turn might confirm to the Sunni Arab world what it had suspected all along about Maliki, that he was simply the head of the biggest Shiite gang in Iraq, not a real national leader who deserved diplomatic recognition.

Petraeus suggested sending in one Iraqi unit he knew that was trained and competent. But, as he knew, it was also 40 percent Sunni. Maliki resisted. Later that day, Maliki's office would dispatch another more Shiite unit, the 4th Brigade of the 4th Division, that the Americans regarded as unready. "There was a big tug of war over that," Petraeus said. Asked if he threatened to pull U.S. support for the operation, as some U.S. officers have claimed, Petraeus said, "I don't know if I went that far, but I certainly raised it as a very serious concern. I am pretty sparing about ever saying that we are not going to support an operation of the importance of that one, [but] it was very clear that . . . we had very serious reservations about moving forward with a predominantly Shia, largely untrained, new unit that had a very low number of the leaders that it needed as well."

The first two Iraqi units sent in weren't ready to fight, Petraeus said. Some of them melted away rather than go into Samarra, a majority Sunni city. "It was unbelievably painful," Petraeus said.

They also discussed whether to impose a nationwide curfew. Maliki said, "No, it's going to be Baghdad, obviously up in Salahuddin, in Mosul," but not anywhere else. The reason, he told the Americans, was "I don't want to send the signal that we are panicking."

That afternoon Maliki, Odierno, and Othman flew to Samarra. Upon arrival at the ruins of the mosque, Maliki fired some Iraqi commanders, Othman said.

Lt. Gen. Dubik, who had only been in the country a few weeks as the new overseer for training and advising Iraqi forces, also hurried to Samarra, where he was shocked. Months later, sitting in his Green Zone office late at night, he folded his arms and gazed up at the ceiling. "It was a harrowing day for me," he recalled. "The first time I went up there it wasn't chaos, but it was near. I thought, you got to be kidding me." But he was impressed to see the minister of defense step in and personally reorganize the operation. "It improved over the following weeks." Still mulling the memory, he folded his arms and again looked up. Overall, the battle was a huge learning experience for him, because his initial assessment was that the Iraqi military likely would fail—but it improved in a way he said he didn't expect. "That was a big couple of weeks for me."

Fourteen Sunni mosques were attacked in the days following the Samarra bombing, but after that, violence was no worse than usual. A full week later, Crocker began to relax a bit. "We just kind of took it day to day. I think it was probably day six or seven that I unclenched a little bit." He had the sense that the Iraqis had looked into the abyss and turned away.

At Odierno's headquarters, Maj. Kent Strader had a similar reaction. "You're waiting for something bad to start happening"—he paused—"and then, nothing's happening!" Intelligence officials began to speculate that the political atmosphere in Iraq was changing.

AN ADMIRAL IN THE HALLWAY

The battle of Samarra that never happened was one of three significant engagements Petraeus would face during the summer of 2007, events that would shape the next phase of the war. None of them came close to approximating a normal military campaign. Most important would be Petraeus's confrontation with the U.S. Congress in September.

But well before that, he found himself engaged in a sharp and significant quarrel inside the U.S. military about how quickly to reduce the numbers of American troops in Iraq and also when to make those cuts. It began in March, when Adm. William Fallon took over at Central Command, headquartered in Tampa, Florida, but with a forward base in Qatar. He was new to the region and unfamiliar with ground warfare, but he was one of the most senior officers in the U.S. military—and indeed one of the few veterans of the Vietnam War still on active duty. Petraeus, by contrast, was one of the first members of the post-Vietnam generation, taking his first duty assignment as a platoon leader in May 1975, days after the last Marine helicopter lifted off the roof of the U.S. embassy in Saigon and North Vietnamese troops crashed a tank through the gates of the Presidential Palace there. In 2007 Fallon had been an admiral for 13 years, having received his first star in October 1994, when David Petraeus was still a lieutenant colonel.

The Iraq war was the first extended campaign fought under the 1986 Goldwater Nichols Act, which reorganized the command structure for U.S. military operations, made the chairman of the Joint Chiefs the principal military adviser to the president and the defense secretary, and also cut the service chiefs out of combat operations. The law also made the "combatant commanders"—the chiefs of Centcom, European Command, Southern Command (for Central and South America), Pacific Command, and two specialized headquarters, Special Operations Command and Strategic Command (for nuclear weapons)—the powerful princes of the American military. Until Petraeus and Fallon, the top pair of U.S. commanders in the Iraq conflict—Franks, Abizaid, Sanchez, and Casey—had all been Army generals, operating as much under its culture as under the formal structure of the U.S. military. But with Fallon's move to Centcom, for the first time, the regional commander, or "CinC," was from a different service than the war commander, the officer actually in the country leading the effort. Formally speaking, Petraeus answered to Fallon. But in practice he reported to President Bush. Indeed, Petraeus probably had a more direct relationship with his president than any field commander in an American war had enjoyed since the Civil War, when Lincoln could summon a general to Washington or board the *River Queen* to steam down the Potomac and up the James and meet with Grant and Sherman at City Point, Virginia. Defense Secretary Gates, like Edwin Stanton, Lincoln's secretary of war, was welcome to listen.

But Fallon prided himself on being a strategic thinker, a sense he may have developed because there was little competition in that arena in the Navy, which in recent years had tended to be weak intellectually, aside from its elite counterterror force in Special Operations, which is practically a separate service. It is difficult, for example, to think of a senior Navy officer who has played a prominent role in shaping American strategy since 9/11, or of an active-duty Navy officer who has written a book or essay as influential as those produced by the Army's Col. H. R. McMaster, Lt. Col. Paul Yingling, and Lt. Col. John Nagl. There was some forewarning in his confirmation hearing that Fallon wouldn't step aside simply because Petraeus was an Army general who talked weekly to the president while Fallon was a novice both in the region and in this type of war, and was arriving just after a new strategy had been hammered out. "I'm not going to hesitate to dive down and ask the tough questions if I don't think we're getting results," he told the Senate Armed Services Committee at that January session. "And that's the key thing that's missing in this entire program of late." Just in case the senators didn't get the message, he added later that day, "I am not a particularly patient man."

Petraeus went out of his way to be respectful of Fallon, who had been shaped by the Navy, the most tradition-conscious of the armed services. "In e-mails and conversations he always ensures that he calls Admiral Fallon 'boss' or 'sir,'" observed one Centcom official who watched the two interact. "This is a big point with Admiral Fallon as he has the Navy mentality of formality."

In April, just weeks after taking command at Centcom, Fallon called into his office Gen. Barbero, who was preparing to replace Fastabend as Petraeus's strategic adviser in Iraq. For about half an hour, the admiral held forth on what was wrong with the way the Iraq war was being conducted. The theme of Fallon's lecture, Barbero recalled, was, "I think we have too many troops there, we have to relook this." Barbero, who had been thinking about the Middle East since 1989, when he wrote his master's thesis on the Iran-Iraq war, thought the admiral didn't have his eye on the ball. What Petraeus needed, he thought, was help with regional influences on the Iraq war, such as intervention by Iran's Quds Force. "What we didn't need is someone to tell us what to do in Iraq, which is where we were" at that point, he said.

Fallon began by holding up troop requests that until then had been considered routine, such as for a company of engineers or some specialists in traumatic wounds to the brain. "We were putting in requests and getting fucked continuously," recalled Fastabend. "Fallon's default position was No. You had to prove why he was wrong." After a lot of back and forth, the admiral would accede to the request, having made his point. To smooth the way, senior Centcom staffers began to send back channel notes to Baghdad, telling Petraeus's subordinates what not to ask for, because they wouldn't get it.

Fallon's next step, in June, was to quietly send an emissary, Rear Adm. James "Sandy" Winnefeld Jr., to Iraq to review Petraeus's strategy. It was a surprisingly inept move for Fallon to make. The strategy had been in place for just a few months, and was at the make or break point. If it didn't work, it would be time not to revise it but probably to pull the plug on the war and begin planning a strategy to contain post-American Iraq. Also, Winnefeld was a career naval officer, out of step with the Iraq environment. "Why don't we put a general in charge of a carrier strike group?" laughed Charlie Miller, who referred to the admiral as "the spy." There were plenty of Army and Marine officers at Central Command whom Fallon might have sent to Baghdad. Winnefeld might bring a fresh view, but it was an ignorant one, painfully unaware of many of the bruising lessons learned by the Army and Marine Corps—let alone Iraqi civilians—over the previous four years. Nor was he steeped in counterinsurgency theory, as were all major U.S. commanders in Iraq by the summer of 2007. Fallon, inexplicably, thought he knew more about counterinsurgency than did Petraeus, telling Bob Woodward that the new manual was okay as far as it went but was outdated. Most unforgivably, Fallon, for all his emphasis on formality, didn't seem to give people a heads-up, a violation of military courtesy that unnecessarily antagonized commanders in Baghdad. "What surprised me is I didn't know he [Winnefeld] was here wandering around, for the longest time," said Odierno. "When you have a two-star here for three weeks—that's strange."

Officers in Baghdad didn't see Winnefeld, who had served as Fallon's executive officer, as stupid. "You don't get to be where he is by being a dumbass," Rapp observed. But they didn't find him intellectually honest in his mission. "He came here with a conclusion and was looking for evidence to fit above that final paragraph of recommendation in his report."

Winnefeld's proposed solution echoed Fallon's inclination to withdraw the U.S. military from the fighting, and move completely into training of Iraqi forces. "Great idea, sir," Rapp commented sarcastically. "Who's gonna do it? And who's gonna fight while those people train?" Fallon's hope was to make the main mission of the remaining U.S. forces sealing the border to stop the flow of foreign influences into Iraq. Meanwhile, Special Operations troops would continue to go after al Qaeda in Iraq, and U.S. forces would draw down to 10 brigades during 2007—that is, halve the U.S. combat power in Iraq, not only going back to the pre-surge level of combat power almost as soon as the five brigades had all arrived, but then taking away another five brigades.

To officers in Baghdad, Winnefeld's views amounted to a recommendation to dump everything that was beginning to work—the troop increase, the use of counterinsurgency tactics, and making the mission the protection of the population—and instead return to the failed policies of 2003–6, which in their view had brought the United States perilously close to the edge of defeat in Iraq. His conclusions, said one senior officer, shaking his head, were "so simplistic." This in turn deepened their unease with Fallon: This was his idea of helping out?

Fallon apparently liked what Winnefeld had to say. In midsummer, he sent word to Petraeus, recalled Barbero: Get ready for a change of mission this fall. Security was going to be downgraded as a goal, and the top task would be transition—that is, exactly what it had been until Odierno and Petraeus arrived. And as part of the change, a drawdown in forces would begin in the fall of 2007.

Petraeus sent word that he disagreed. He wanted to continue the mission. He offered some thoughts about the points at which future decisions could be made about the size of the U.S. troop presence.

"This wasn't just a disagreement between flags, but a military command structure that was, in effect, fighting the president's direction by nibbling away at the general he'd picked to carry out his mission," retired Army Col. Bob Killebrew commented in reviewing this bureaucratic infighting. "By bucking Petraeus, he [Fallon] was bucking the commander in chief." Fallon's disruptive role was beginning to be talked about back in Washington. Eliot Cohen, who had joined the administration earlier in the year as counselor at the State Department, noticed this during his assessment trips in Iraq. "Fallon was just a disaster," he concluded. "He left people seething. The Marines were saying, "We were trying to tell him what is happening in Ramadi, and he starts telling us.'" Petraeus had the same experience, with Fallon flying to Baghdad to tell him what was going on in Iraq.

Petraeus generally was open during a series of interviews done for this book in 2007 and 2008, but the subject of his relationship with Fallon was one area where he not only grew close-mouthed but testy. "Look, this isn't a soap opera," he snapped in January 2008, showing more anger than is his wont. "This is a deadly serious endeavor and we talked about things in a deadly serious way, but not some kind of great emotion." He dismissed a rumor circulating at the time that Fallon had called him "chickenshit." Among other things, he noted, he wouldn't stand for it. "It's bullshit," he said, "If some fucking guy told me that, I would walk out of the office. I'd say, 'Here, you got it, take over.' "

Fallon declined to be interviewed for this book. But in a previous interview with me, in December 2007, he conceded that he might occasionally have stepped on subordinates' toes. "If you're trying to lead," he explained, "you're never going to have everyone wanting to do the same thing." Fallon never seemed to grasp that even though Petraeus was technically his subordinate, the general held all the cards. As long as Petraeus, Odierno, and Crocker held a united position, and Keane was in the background conveying their views to Cheney, they outweighed not just Fallon but the entire Joint Chiefs of Staff as well. As one of Petraeus's aides put it, "If there is a beauty contest between the chiefs, Fallon, Casey, and I don't know who else—well, Petraeus wins."

As the friction between Fallon and Petraeus went on for months, some officers in Baghdad wondered whether they were getting the support they deserved and indeed needed at a very difficult phase of the war. This would especially hit them when they went home for leave or consultations. "You go to the Pentagon, and there's no sense of a war going on, there's no sense of everybody surging," said Charlie Miller. "People ride the bus to work, ride the bus home, and go on. There's been no inclination to accept institutional risk—like shutting the War College for a year, and sending the colonels out here as advisers."

Nor did Fallon seem to grasp that with the ascendancy of Petraeus and Odierno during the winter of 2006–7, a generational shift had taken place in the war. Petraeus was the first officer to serve as top commander in Iraq who had fought in the war on a previous tour. So had Odierno. And many of the officers around them had commanded brigades or battalions on their own previous tours. They had been bloodied. They had been targeted for death by insurgents and militias. They had looked men in the eye and sent them to their deaths. For the first time in the war, younger officers could feel that they were being led by men who had some sense of what life was like for soldiers out in the streets, palm groves, and deserts of Iraq. "These are people who have moved forward through a very, very tough crucible," said Abizaid, who had known them for years. They were far less inclined than their predecessors to tolerate peacetime protocol or bureaucratic chickenshit. And that was what they thought they were getting from Fallon in the spring and summer of 2007.

There also was a growing suspicion that while Fallon was meddling in Petraeus's arena, he was neglecting his own responsibilities, with the result that Petraeus had to take on some of those tasks. Maj. Rayburn, who had worked for Central Command, for McMaster, and for Petraeus, and also had helped devise the American Enterprise Institute plan for a surge, offered as one example working with the Gulf States to lay the groundwork for their support of political compromise in Iraq. It was something that Fallon should have been doing, but it was being left to Petraeus. "It seems to me he's had to do the job of the Centcom commander," he concluded. "There's a vacuum up there."

Dubik, one of the most senior generals in Iraq in 2007, argued that the friction between Petraeus and Fallon wasn't entirely a bad thing. "There's a healthy tension that comes from an alternative path being considered. It adds to the intellectual energy. I think both sides grew, and I think it helped Petraeus and Crocker prepare for the congressional hearings in September. It sharpened their thinking."

That was not the dominant view. One senior intelligence officer in Iraq called Fallon's attempt in the summer of 2007 to rewrite the strategy a "disaster." Mansoor, Petraeus's executive officer, just shook his head: "Boy, that was weird."

But it carried serious implications for the future conduct of the war. As the summer went on, it appeared that the Joint Chiefs might be closing ranks with Fallon against Petraeus. They were growing impatient, pushing for a swifter end to the surge and more emphasis on transitioning to Iraqi security forces. They also tried to shut down Petraeus's back channel through Keane to the White House. In August, Gen. Casey, the chief of the Army, told Petraeus to back away from Keane. "You need to understand that Jack is perceived by the Chiefs as going around them," Casey told Petraeus.

Petraeus wasn't buying it. "The president should be able to get advice from anyone he wants," he said, according to a senior officer who heard him express his strong views on the subject.

Petraeus's direct line to the president made it difficult to slap him down. But his support could be nibbled away. That summer, Keane, who had worked to bolster support for Petraeus among White House aides, ran into Gen. Casey at the Walter Reed Army Medical Center in northwest Washington, D.C. Casey was seething. "We feel—the Chiefs feel—you are way too out in front in advocating a policy for which you are not accountable," Casey said to Keane, in a conversation first reported by Bob Woodward in his 2008 book, *The War Within.* "We're accountable. You're not accountable. And that's a problem." It was a particularly fatuous argument for Casey to mount, because there had been extremely little accountability for military officers—or others—in the Iraq war. Gen. Tommy Franks had designed an inept war plan and then retired as the insurgency erupted in the summer of 2003, only to be awarded the Presidential Medal of Freedom, along with two other officials who had made grave mistakes, former CIA chief George Tenet and former occupation chief L. Paul Bremer. Other Army generals had taken actions that had enflamed the insurgency, only to receive promotions at the ends of their tours. Indeed, Eliot Cohen, among others, pointed to the lack of accountability for generals as a major flaw in the conduct of the war. There seemed to be no relationship between battlefield performance by officers and subsequent promotions and assignments. By helping White House officials ask tough questions about the conduct of the war, Keane was injecting accountability into the system—and that was making the generals uncomfortable. "I always felt as a professional military officer that if he felt he had something to offer to the mission, he ought to have called me or contacted me in some way," Casey said. "He never did."

SUCCESS ON THE BATTLEFIELD

The summer of 2007 gave Petraeus the trump card he needed to prevail over Fallon. By late June and early July there was a new feeling emerging in parts of the American military across central Iraq. Despite the hard hits taken during their counterattack, there was a sense of having regained the initiative. That is an extraordinary accomplishment—typically, once one loses the strategic initiative in war, it is difficult, if not impossible, to regain it.

The effects first starting appearing at the bottom and began filtering upward. Capt. Keirsey, the commander of Baker Company, operating in southern Baghdad, began in the spring to notice "a shift in the mentality of the Iraqi populace." In the beginning of the year, his men were attacked repeatedly every day. During the last quarter of 2007, they would not be attacked once. "The populace went from being entirely complicit with the insurgency to being supporters of our efforts," he said later.

Overall, no clear improvement could be discerned. In fact, violence was increasing in many areas in reaction to the new presence of U.S. troops. But even as that happened, soldiers like Keirsey were noticing, here and there, that the mood of the people, the vibe in the air, was different—there is no more precise way to put it. One day in early spring a senior intelligence officer argued in a Baghdad meeting that despite the rise in U.S. causalities, the situation was improving radically. "When everyone was saying it was worse, I said, 'Hey, this is working,' " recalled this officer, who until then had been known for his dour assessment of the situation. "I said, 'We've turned the corner.' " He was greeted with disbelief. No, he persisted. "We are seeing it in interrogations." Sunni fighters were reporting fatigue and disappointment. Their anger against the Americans seemed to have dissipated.

"Let's be careful," Petraeus admonished him. Everyone at the table knew that the American effort in Iraq had been plagued for years by assessments that overly accentuated the positive, to the detriment of understanding what actually was happening.

In past years this intelligence official had been sent to the White House to deliver his dark, contrary views of the Iraq war. Now, still contrary, he was ready to stand by his more hopeful evaluation—and once again he would find it unwelcome. "No," he responded, "the enemy can no longer achieve his objectives."

Another veteran intelligence official who was familiar with his longtime pessimism about the war and had heard about his conversation ran into him in Iraq that fall and asked, seriously, "Have you gotten Baghdad-itis? Are you just a cheerleader or do you really believe things are better?" The answer, of course, was the latter.

In April, Ambassador Crocker went to Doura, the same south Baghdad neighborhood whose devastation had so shocked Petraeus two months earlier. There he saw theory turned into practice: that is, that having an American soldier on the street corner would have a different political effect than having several Iraqi soldiers in the same spot. In response to the new presence of U.S. troops in the neighborhood, about three dozen shops had reopened. When he spoke to the shopkeepers, he recalled, "They said, 'You're back.' I said, 'We're back because you're here.'" They also told him that they didn't trust the Iraqi National Police, which had acquired the reputation of being a Shiite militia in uniform, and still weren't confident of the Iraqi army, but felt that the U.S. troops treated them decently. "Damn, this might work," Crocker thought. By midsummer, he would be confident that it was, at least in improving security.

May proved to be an odd month, with contradictory signals: U.S. military deaths peaked at 126 lost, with more than another 600 wounded, yet there were also some signs of improvement. "There was a real clash of the data," said Lt. Col. Douglas Ollivant, a planner for the 1st Cavalry Division who had been a prominent advocate of moving troops out into the population. "The casualty statistics were godawful. But it began to feel like it was working. We could sense the progress before it was measurable—we could feel it." For the first time, he was getting upbeat messages from officers out in the streets, he said, with company commanders calling to say, "This is different, people are finally coming to us, and telling us what we need to know."

In June, Barbero went on a foot patrol in Baqubah. "I was talking to company commanders, second-tour guys"—that is, officers seasoned enough to judge events on the ground—"and they were saying, 'We're beginning to see something different. The Sunnis are rejecting al Qaeda"' He came away thinking, "Hey, this has got a chance."

By midsummer, as the full surge took effect, with a total of about 155,000 U.S. troops in the country, the signs were becoming measurable. "It began cascading," said Ollivant.

Sadi Othman began to think things were changing when he was in a market one midsummer day in Yusifiyah, one of the hard little towns just southwest of Baghdad, along the fault line between Shia and Sunni, an area, he noted, where a few months earlier "you couldn't go in a tank." He strayed away from the official party and its bodyguards to buy some figs. An aide to Petraeus took a photograph of him alone in the market and e-mailed it to him. Looking at the photo that night, he gulped: This was the street where just a few months before, "they used to dump bodies and decapitate people."

Galloucis, the hawk-nosed, bald MP commander who had been so gloomy earlier in the year, began to see improvements in the quality of Iraqi forces immediately after a Baghdad Operational Command was established in March to coordinate their efforts, which had a "surge" effect of its own. "By July, you started seeing Iraqi forces out on the street—Iraqi army, local police, National Police. There was people all over the friggin' place. Over time, the attacks, the deaths, the found bodies, all started going down. You started to feel better."

On Baghdad's northwest fringe, Maj. Michaelis, the operations officer of the 1st Brigade of the 1st Cavalry, began to notice in July a change in the "atmospherics" around the outposts the unit had established, in "the engagement we were getting from people who had been ignoring us, or had been hostile."

For some Iraqis, the sign of improving security was a decline in the price of cooking gas, from $22 a tank, the price charged by some Shiite militias, to $2, the normal cost. Suddenly, with the Americans nearby and saying they would stay there, it no longer seemed like a bargain to pay high prices in exchange for militia protection against Sunni death squads.

Returning in midsummer from ten days of leave in London, Emma Sky was struck by the security improvement described in the military's morning briefing. But, "as a matter of principle," she had a policy of not believing anything she heard in official briefings. "I don't believe statistics," she explained. "Also, I don't believe violence can stop violence. I didn't have confidence in these population security measures, like these big concrete barriers." She wanted to hear it from Iraqis. In late July, she said, to her surprise, Iraqis began telling her that American troops were protecting their communities. "Around Baghdad, we started seeing whole neighborhoods start to revive. We see neighborhoods start to sign agreements, and the government starting to bring in services. You started seeing ink spots—and ink spots spreading."

Spec. Mark Heinl, a soldier posted in Doura, told an officer from the Center for Army Lessons Learned that the new posture of living among the people was working. "I've built real relationships and care about these people. And they care about me. . . . I've taught myself Arabic and can converse pretty well. Many people call on my private cell to let me know of a problem or something bad happening. At first, most of the ISVs [Iraqi Security Volunteers] were bad folks. But they realized AQI lied to them. Now they are willing to work with us as long as they see progress." His conclusion: "This could work."

Lt. Jacob Carlisle, his platoon leader, said that Petraeus's new manual on counterinsurgency had changed his thinking. "We had read the COIN manual while at the IZ [International Zone, or Green Zone], and now it really began to come to life in our minds. We started to treat the people differently." He added, "You must get to know the people. It's only been recently that people started waving to us and treating us like people. It took us treating them like that first."

For years, one of the major killers of U.S. troops had been attacks on supply convoys, both with bombs and with small arms such as rocket-propelled grenades. In response, U.S. commanders had outfitted trucks with armor and machine guns, but enemy tactics also improved, with the result that the number of attacks actually increased fairly steadily in 2005 and 2006. They peaked early in 2007. In January and February of that year, the chances of a civilian supply convoy being attacked was 1 in 5. By December, it would drop to 1 in 33. (And by April of 2008, it would be 1 in 100.) Also, the attacks were becoming less effective. "By the end of 2007, less sophisticated forms of IEDs—such as command wire- and pressure-plate detonated devices—had become the most common, possibly indicating a degradation in the supply networks or ability to coordinate and operate of the adversary," the Congressional Research Service reported.

Reflecting such trends, in the second half of 2007, U.S. combat deaths declined steadily. After peaking in May at 126, there were 93 KIAs in June, when the surge troops all were in country, then 66 in July, 55 in August, and—eventually—just 14 in December.

Also, the Army's annual survey of the mental health of troops in Iraq found that morale had rebounded sharply in 2007. Despite the hard fighting of the first half of the year—one-third said they had been exposed to sniper fire during their current tour of duty—the researchers found fewer reporting being depressed, anxious, or acutely stressed. "The surge hammered us at first but over the past couple of months it seems to be working," one soldier told the mental health researchers. "Things are calmer now." Soldiers also reported being more satisfied with the units' leadership, cohesion, and military readiness. "If we were a football team, we are just now having a winning record," another soldier stated.

One especially strong feeling was that of relief in not having to constantly keep "retaking" cities such as Samarra and Fallujah, which had become almost annual events. As a third soldier said, "I understand the surge and I believe the surge. I went into Fallujah three times and I could never understand why we kept having to retake things."

There also was an intense debate going on inside the U.S. military about whether al Qaeda in Iraq had been defeated as an entity. The cascade effect that Capt. Cook had seen in one town was being replicated across central Iraq. In every city but Mosul, to which al Qaeda fighters were retreating, the terrorist organization was far weaker than it had been a year earlier.

Still, it was a near-run thing. In early August, just weeks before he would have to return to Congress to deliver his assessment of the state of the war, Petraeus began to think the surge was working. He later would insist that he always had thought it would, but conceded that actually doing it was a far tougher proposition. That is, he had believed that getting troops out with the mission of protecting the population would have a strong positive effect. "We were seeing the facts validate the academic proposition. The COIN manual has it—but it's one thing to write it, another thing to operationalize it." He began to write another letter to his troops that would say, "my sense is that we have achieved tactical momentum and wrested the initiative from our enemies in a number of areas of Iraq." Coming from the careful Petraeus, that was a strong statement of optimism.

The sign that persuaded Campbell, the assistant commander of the 1st Cavalry, that the war was turning was that the locals "were turning in people." They wouldn't do that if they thought those they turned in would be on top again one day.

There were still plenty of problems—a huge bombing of the Yezidi people, an obscure sect in the north; the assassination of two Shiite governors in the south; the deterioration of Basra, the biggest city in the south and a vital center of commerce, into gangland warfare over control of oil exports and other sources of revenue. A study by the International Crisis Group found that city plagued by "the systematic misuse of official institutions, political assassinations, tribal vendettas, neighborhood vigilantism and enforcement of social mores, together with the rise of criminal mafias that increasingly intermingle with political actors." A new phenomenon occurred there as religious extremists began killing women who appeared without the head scarf called the *hijab.*

But even some of the violence helped American aims. In August a day of Shiite-on-Shiite violence in the holy city of Karbala killed 49 people. Moqtada al-Sadr apparently was embarrassed by the incident, which had pitted his Mahdi Army against fighters from the the Badr Corps, the other major Shiite militia. He announced that he was putting a "freeze" on his militia's operations for six months, a period he later expanded. Sadr was taking a gamble of his own, that he could survive as a political power without having a fielded force to protect his turf and generate revenue from various forms of racketeering, extortion, and property seizures.

On the hot, dusty day of August 10, 2007, Petraeus and Rapp were flying from the U.S. base at Taji back to the capital. Rapp, who accompanied Petraeus to most of the general's meetings, often used the time in flight to talk through new ideas. As they wheeled over the Abu Ghraib area, west of the city, Rapp turned to Petraeus and offered what he thought the next step in the war might be. "The violent way is the short way, and the peaceful way is the long way," he said over the Black Hawk's intercom. "Sir, if we want this competition in Iraq for resources to be resolved peacefully, then we have to prepare people for a long, drawn-out process."

Petraeus liked the idea coming through the headphones. "You know, that's really good," he replied. He asked Rapp to write a memo on this thought. Over the following four weeks, it would become the core idea of his congressional testimony.

The bottom line, as Charlie Miller, who also worked on the testimony, thought of it, was: "This is going to be a long-term effort, it isn't going to be easy, but if we keep plugging away, it just might work."

That notion also would lead to more conflict with Adm. Fallon, because it argued that looking for a quick exit likely would lead to a replay of the violence of 2006. The long view "wasn't exactly what Admiral Fallon wanted to hear,"

Rapp said. "He had a shorter timeline than the CG's"—that is, the commanding general's.

As Petraeus came to think of it, the point he would make to Congress was that in late 2006, there was an average of more than 50 murders a day in Baghdad. "If you didn't like where Iraq was then, you'd hate it if we just let it go," he thought.

But he was still running into strong internal opposition from above in his chain of command. On a Saturday in late August, Col. Rapp recalled, Fallon flew to Baghdad to try to talk Petraeus out of the recommendations he was planning to deliver to Congress the following month. Petraeus planned to say, recalled Rapp, that "we have the right strategy, the surge is showing initial results, and we need to stay the course. And if you're looking for a drawdown, it isn't going to happen." By contrast, Rapp said, at the meeting at Camp Victory, Fallon pushed for an accelerated transition to Iraqi forces, with faster training of them. "What Fallon wanted was a change of mission." (In an interview, Petraeus said he didn't recollect that meeting, saying only, "There were constant conversations during that period." But Rapp's memory of the day is so precise that it suggests Petraeus was just being discreet.)

A few days later, President Bush approved Petraeus's mission statement, which called for security while transitioning—that is, continue the mission to protect the people, and keep the troops necessary to carry that out.

Fallon's emphasis not only added to the friction with Petraeus, but also made officers in Iraq chary of talking about progress, for fear that it would be used against them. "Centcom is seizing any good news from Iraq to call for a quicker drawdown," Miller said "I still think he [Adm. Fallon] sees it as his role to draw down in Iraq as quickly as possible. He seems to be operating out of the old playbook."

Miller thought Fallon was a hypocrite. "He'll be in public applauding the efforts in Iraq, but behind the scenes, it's 'cut, cut, cut.'"

PETRAEUS VS. THE CONGRESS

The third and most significant battle Gen. David Petraeus fought in 2007 took place more than 6,000 miles from Iraq. His two days of hearings on Capitol Hill in September of that year altered the course of the war, both in domestic political terms and in how it was viewed on the ground in Iraq. His approach to the hearings was adversarial, and it worked.

For months, Democrats had expected the September hearings to be decisive, even a conclusive point in the war. For example, Representative James P. Moran Jr., a Northern Virginia Democrat, had said in May, "If we don't see a light at the end of the tunnel, September is going to be a very bleak month for this administration." Some Republican allies of the president agreed that the Iraq strategy was doomed. Senate GOP leader Mitch McConnell of Kentucky said the same month that "the handwriting is on the wall that we are going in a different direction in the fall, and I expect the president to lead it." His counterpart in the House, John Boehner of Ohio, said, "By the time we get to September, October, members are going to want to know how well this is working, and if it isn't, what's Plan B."

Listening to such comments, Iraqis began calculating not only that the surge would end soon, but that Americans would be heading to the exits in six months or so. "You saw them hardening their positions, because they thought we were going to leave," Odierno observed.

Col. Steve Boylan, Petraeus's communications adviser, calculated that the key to the hearings was understanding that it was not Petraeus but congressional Democrats who were in a bind. "My feeling was that Congress wouldn't be able to put together enough votes to override a presidential veto, because then they'd own it," he said. Here he put his finger on a basic dilemma the Democrats hadn't been able to resolve: how to end the war without being blamed for how it ended.

Fastabend, Petraeus's strategic adviser at this time, offered similar counsel: If you can put together enough small victories, you can demonstrate that defeat is not inevitable—and so he wrote to Petraeus "that the 'bring 'em home' crowd risked snatching defeat from the jaws of victory." What's more, he noted, "they risked incurring the blame."

It would indeed turn out to be the anti-war Democrats who ended September feeling forlorn. Before the hearings, the dominant political question had been how to get out of Iraq with the least damage. After them, the question would become how to find the least damaging way to stay in Iraq.

Petraeus and Crocker knew that after four years of consistently overoptimistic reports, the credibility of American officials remained low with the American people and especially with congressional Democrats. They were determined to deliver a sober, evenhanded assessment that wouldn't leave them open to the same charge.

Petraeus laid the groundwork for that approach in the letter he issued to the troops as he left Iraq. While the initiative had been retaken, he expressed disappointment about the political state of Iraq. "Many of us had hoped this summer would be a time of tangible political progress at the national level," he wrote. "One of the justifications for the surge, after all, was that it would help create the space for Iraqi leaders to tackle the tough questions and agree on key pieces of 'national reconciliation' legislation. It has not worked out as we had hoped." It would be hard to charge that he was being rosy about Iraq.

As they ran together on Sunday mornings during the summer of 2007, Petraeus and Crocker had talked about how they would handle Congress in September. Petraeus's calculation was that the debate back in the United States was stalemated, especially in considering the consequences of a pullout. "My job is not to make it easy on people back in Washington," he said in his office over a cup of coffee in a 101ST AIRBORNE coffee mug. "Some of the debate has lacked a full discussion of the implications of various courses of action."

On the Friday before the hearings, Petraeus gave Capt. Liz McNally, his staff writer, a printout of the statement he planned to deliver at the outset. She and Col. Mansoor cut it by about one quarter.

At the Pentagon, Boylan set up a "murder board" to rehearse Petraeus over the weekend. "The questions asked in our rehearsal were tougher than anyone asked" at the hearings later that week, Boylan said.

"Is it worth it, given the strains on the military and the divisions in the United States?" asked Charlie Miller. His suggested response was that only time would tell, but that it "definitely won't be worth it if we fail due to a precipitous withdrawal." As for divisions in the U.S., he advised, that was for the political system to sort out, not a general.

Boylan's most pointed question in the Sunday rehearsal was, "Sir, explain to me why we have to lose one more American life in Iraq."

Petraeus responded, "Okay, what's your answer?" Boylan didn't have one, but he wanted Petraeus to think about it.

On the day the hearings began, MoveOn.org, an anti-war group influential in the Democratic Party, ran a full-page advertisement in the *New York Times* that mocked Petraeus as "General Betray Us." Petraeus, it charged, was "at war with the facts." And the facts, as MoveOn saw them, were that "the surge strategy has failed." In addition, it said, "General Petraeus will not admit what everyone knows: Iraq is mired in an unwinnable religious civil war."

In a narrow sense, the advertisement was understandable. For 15 years, beginning with the endorsement of candidate Bill Clinton in 1992 by former Joint Chiefs Chairman Adm. William Crowe, senior retired military officers, some of them fresh from active duty, had been acting in a more politicized manner. Powell, the most political of active-duty generals, had written an op-ed on the eve of that election. In subsequent campaigns, candidates scrambled to line up slates of retired generals and admirals as endorsers. At the 2004 and 2008 Democratic conventions, old flag officers would parade on the stage in scenes oddly evocative of a beauty pageant. In the MoveOn advertisement, Petraeus was reaping what all those politicized generals and admirals had sowed: If generals wanted to influence politics, then they would be treated as part of the political arena.

Yet with regard to Petraeus, the attack was deeply unfair, as there was no evidence that he had been part of that trend toward politicization. True, he had been a Republican—registered in rural New Hampshire, where he owned some land west of the tiny town of New London—but he had kept that quiet, and thought he had been careful to avoid intruding on politics. He felt he had been a professional soldier doing his duty. "I've been deployed three of the last five years," he said later that week. "My family has given a lot." He was puzzled by the attack. (The *Times*' ombudsman later would criticize the newspaper for giving MoveOn a discount, and also for violating its policy of not allowing personal attacks in advertisements.)

On the morning the advertisement ran, Rapp rode with Petraeus in a car from Fort Belvoir, Virginia, near George Washington's home at Mount Vernon, to the Capitol. "Petraeus did a good job of not showing it, but I know it stung," he said. "He was just a little quieter than usual."

Nor did he mention it later. "But I think he was personally affected" by it, said Charlie Miller, who noted that Petraeus grew up in Cornwall, New York, reading the *New York Times*, and continued to take it at West Point. Likewise, Capt. McNally, who had always read the newspaper, talked to her parents that night about the advertisement. Her father told her it was just "free speech," but she was angry. "There was this institution I've always admired, so it was really disappointing."

Crocker, the lifelong diplomat, took a less emotional approach. Upon first seeing the advertisement, he thought he was reading it incorrectly. "I couldn't believe it, I thought I didn't see this, that it can't be what I thought it was." He read it again and shook his head. As he read it through, his disbelief gave way to outrage, and then a grim smile. "They've screwed themselves." His calculation was that he knew what Petraeus planned to say, and that it would amount to a "word-by-word rebuttal of that allegation."

Senator Joseph Biden, chairman of the Foreign Relations Committee, began his panel's session. The president had said that the purpose of the surge was to buy time for a political breakthrough, he noted, and that hadn't happened. "It's time to turn the corner, in my view, gentlemen," he said, "We should stop the surge and start bringing our troops home. We should end a political strategy in Iraq that cannot succeed and begin one that can."

Petraeus was conscious that one of the senators facing him that day—Barack Obama, McCain, Clinton, and Biden—likely would become his commander in chief in just over a year. "The cameras on these people were astonishing," he recalled later. "When Biden went and sat down next to Obama, there was an explosion of clicks."

While Petraeus and Crocker testified for almost two full days, on September 10 and 11, crouched in small chairs, being both berated and slimed with praise, their lower backs began to ache. "Those witness tables are diabolically designed to get you at just the wrong angle, and you sit at one for eleven hours or whatever it was, it's a physical endurance test," Crocker said.

In Petraeus's case, it was especially painful because the effects of a recreational skydiving accident make it difficult for him to sit in chairs that don't offer strong back support. One day in the autumn of 2000, he was above the Raeford Drop Zone, near Fort Bragg, North Carolina, descending well and making his final approach, when his parachute failed and he plummeted to the ground. "Basically, the nose collapsed about eighty feet off the ground going through what's called dirty air," he recalled. Even as he worked the chute to get back some lift, "I could tell I was going in for a hard landing." The accident smashed his pelvis, which is now held together by seven screws and one large flat metal plate. He also emerged from the hospital a quarter inch shorter on his left side than on his right. What pained him almost as much was that to ease the strain on his mending pelvis, he had to sell his old manual-shifting Volkswagen Golf and buy a car with an automatic transmission—as it happened, a BMW. During breaks from the hearing, Petraeus gobbled Motrin pain-relief pills, taking 1,600 milligrams on the second day.

Crocker said later that he understood why the hearings had to occur. "It was important that that happened, and I can understand all the reasons for it, but if you are the one that's sitting there over eighteen hours for two days, it's less than fun, particularly the tone of some of the questions, which gets repeated and repeated and repeated. You can tell yourself look this is a part of politics and that's the American system—but if you are the guys who are out there doing everything you can to make this work under pretty tough circumstances, when you get that kind of personal edge to it, that gets kind of tiresome." He would find it growing a bit heavy. "There is some kind of mental deadening process sets in."

Petraeus offered very little in his opening statement. He began by establishing his independence. "I wrote this myself and did not clear it with anyone in the Pentagon, the White House or Congress," he said. The military aspects of the surge were going fairly well, he asserted. "The security situation in Iraq is improving, and Iraqi elements are slowly taking on more of the responsibility for protecting their citizens." If both those trends continued, he thought that by mid-2008, he could reduce his combat forces to the pre-surge level. That was it. He made no promises whatsoever—keeping a vow he had made to himself. He and Ambassador Crocker essentially said that they thought it was possible that there might be a light at the end of the tunnel, but they couldn't say how long the tunnel was, or how much time it would take to get through it, or actually where it led us.

"This is a sober assessment, but it should not be a disheartening one," Crocker said in his own opening statement.

John McCain used his own time to break another set of Democratic arrows. While a strong supporter of the war, he took the lead in criticizing how it had been handled for the first four years. "The American people are saddened, frustrated, and angry over our past failures in Iraq," he said. "I, too, have been made sick at heart by the terrible price we've paid for nearly four years of mismanaged war. Some of us from the beginning have warned against the Rumsfeld strategy of too few troops, insufficient resources, and a plan predicated on hope rather than on the difficult business of stabilization and counterinsurgency." Now, he asserted, we were finally "getting it right, because we finally have in place a strategy that can succeed."

That left Democrats little running room, but Russell Feingold of Wisconsin tried to find an opening. How could Petraeus claim progress when the first six months of 2007 had brought higher numbers of deaths than the first half of the previous year? "So, to suggest that there was some decline in the number in June and July, versus other months, does not address the fact that the number of troops' deaths has greatly increased." What Feingold couldn't know was what troops on the streets of Baghdad had been sensing in various ways in recent months, that there was indeed a major change in the feeling of the place. Between June and December, the number of bomb, rifle, mortar, and grenade attacks in Iraq would decrease by some 60 percent, from an all-time high of 1,600 a week in June to below 600 a week by year's end. Some 44 car bombs were detonated in Baghdad in February, killing 253 and wounding another 654, while there would be only 5 in December, killing 12 and wounding 40.

Well, yeah, Petraeus responded, I was leading a counterattack. "When you go on the offensive, you have tough fighting."

The Democrats were beginning to sense that the sessions were going to have a far different result than they had expected. "General Petraeus, you indicate that hopefully within ten months, we will be able to get our troop levels down to one hundred thirty thousand, which is where we started, which is no troop reduction," said Benjamin Cardin of Maryland. "We're back to where we were before the surge, which doesn't seem to be the goal we set out last January." Petraeus wasn't given time to answer, but there was almost no need. The fact of the matter was dawning on the Democrats—yes, that was indeed all that he was offering. As one officer at Centcom gleefully summarized it, "It was like doing a fifty percent markup, and then offering a half-off sale."

Two exchanges that day lingered in Petraeus's mind. The first came with Senator Obama, who took seven minutes—the entire period allotted him for questions and answers—to cast doubt on the strategy and pose a series of questions. "How do we clean up the mess and make the best out of a situation in where there are no good options, there are bad options and worse options?" he asked. If Petraeus and Crocker had been given time to answer, they likely would have said a polite version of, Well, duh—welcome to our lives. "How long will this take? And at what point do we say enough?" Obama continued. "[Y]ou said . . . the Iraqi people understand that the patience of the American people is not limitless. But that appears to be exactly what you're asking for in this testimony." Obama had put his finger on the Democrats' dilemma. But he didn't appear to have a way out of it. By the time he finishing posing his questions, time was up, and Petraeus didn't get a chance to respond to any of it. The Illinois Democrat was not at his best that day.

Obama said nothing that day about the scurrilous MoveOn advertisement, but his political skills should never be underestimated. Nine months later, as he was preparing to visit Iraq as the Democratic presidential nominee, he would use a speech on patriotism to revisit the issue. "All too often our politics still seems trapped in these old, threadbare arguments," he said, "a fact most evident during our recent debates about the war in Iraq, when those who opposed administration policy were tagged by some as unpatriotic, and a general providing his best counsel on how to move forward in Iraq was accused of betrayal." It was a smart fence-mending move to make before going to visit Petraeus in Baghdad.

The comment that would irk Petraeus most that day came from Hillary Clinton. He was surprised when, late in the proceedings, she came at him swinging. "You have been made the de facto spokesman for what many of us believe to be a failed policy," she chided. "I think the reports that you provide us really require the willing suspension of disbelief."

Those last four words were powerful. As one friend of Petraeus's later commented, "You're either calling him dishonest or stupid."

Gen. Keane felt a personal sense of duplicity. He had encouraged Petraeus to spend hours with her, explaining the war and his approach to it. Now she was attacking him personally, following the MoveOn course. "I knew she would ask tough questions, but"—here he paused—"well, I talked to Dave about it at his house [the next day], and he was disappointed by her comment and in general with the entire hearing. He was emotionally and psychologically wounded. He knew he was sitting in a chair where his predecessors had lost credibility. The fact that he was in uniform and got attacked in terms of his character was something he wasn't prepared for."

Many generals possess a strong sense of honor and a long memory, and Petraeus probably does more than most. He also has the ability to veil his emotions well. He responded in a neutral but essentially unhelpful manner. "As you know, this policy is a national policy that results from policies put forward at one end of Pennsylvania Avenue, with the advice and consent and resources provided at the other," he said, offering the senator, and former first lady and law professor, an introduction to the Constitution. He didn't show it publicly, but he was furious, friends said. Not only did Petraeus feel that his integrity had been questioned, he also felt a sense of betrayal, because he had given Clinton a lot of his time. Also, he respected her intelligence.

There was one other notable exchange that day. John Warner of Virginia asked if Petraeus's campaign in Iraq made Americans any safer.

The murder board hadn't prepped Petraeus for that one. "Sir, I don't know, actually," he said. This was probably as close as he came during the hearings to breaking with the Bush administration. Nothing was said at the time, but seven months later, the president would state in a speech delivered, notably, at the Pentagon that "because we acted, the world is better and the United States of America is safer."

Petraeus also may have gotten out ahead of the administration on the issue of how long American forces might have to fight in Iraq. David Kilcullen, his sometime adviser on counterinsurgency, went over to the White House a few days after the hearings and came away thinking that "there's still a fundamental reluctance to 'fess up to the American people what the costs are, and what the duration is."

Capt. McNally watched it all a little wide eyed. It was the first congressional hearing she had ever attended, and she was surprised to see that the senators—"these are important people"—each had only seven minutes in which to pose their questions. "I'm one of those dorks who enjoys watching C-SPAN. I was thinking, this is democracy at work."

Crocker and Petraeus were less pleased. The general's conclusion was that he had underestimated the depth of anti-war feeling in the United States, which he termed "industrial strength." But he also seemed to understand that he had prevailed.

The ambassador looked back on it as "one of the least pleasant experiences of my professional life"—this from a man who was blown against a wall at the U.S. embassy in Beirut when it was bombed in April 1983, killing 64 of his friends and colleagues. On September 12, as the two left the public television studio where they had appeared on *The NewsHour with Jim Lehrer,* Crocker turned to Petraeus and muttered, "I am not doing this again."

"HEY, WE WON!"

Petraeus and Odierno had opponents in places besides Iraq and Capitol Hill. Their boss at Central Command, Adm. Fallon, and some others inside the national security establishment, still wanted to see the number of troops in Iraq come down quickly.

To wrap up the impact of the hearings, the president was giving a nationally televised speech on the evening of September 13. Late that day, the White House sent a late draft of the speech to Rapp. Scanning it, he saw immediately that "the mission wording had been changed to what Fallon wanted," Rapp recalled. He was told that the Iraq staffers at the White House had made the change. He showed the draft to Petraeus, who then made a telephone call to get the wording changed back, Rapp recalled. (Petraeus remembers this moment differently, saying the wording change was just the work of White House speechwriters "who weren't sensitive to the balance between security and transition," and that the fix was made by e-mail, not by phone.)

That night the president told the nation that the mission in Iraq would change eventually, but not now. "Over time, our troops will shift from leading operations, to partnering with Iraqi forces, and eventually to overwatching those forces," he said. "As this transition in our mission takes place, our troops will focus on a more limited set of tasks, including counterterrorism operations and training, equipping, and supporting Iraqi forces."

Fallon's influence was waning. A few weeks after the hearings, Adm. Michael Mullen succeeded Gen. Pace as chairman of the Joint Chiefs. Mullen would prove to be a more effective chairman than the Marine general. Perhaps more important for Petraeus, the admiral was a longtime friend of Fallon's, and was able to reduce friction between Petraeus and Fallon. Indeed, word in Iraq was that Defense Secretary Gates had told the new chairman to get Fallon off Petraeus's back. "He has played a calming role," Lt. Col. Miller said appreciatively a few months later.

But Mullen also seemed determined to reduce the traffic between Petraeus and the White House, a pattern that under Pace had effectively cut the chairman of the Joint Chiefs out of the decision loop. The chairman officially is the president's principal adviser on military affairs, but even if he participated in Petraeus's meetings with the president, he still couldn't know what Keane was quietly cooking up with Cheney's staff. As Bob Woodward first reported, the new chairman told colleagues that he felt Keane, by stepping into policy making, had diminished the office of chairman of the Joint Chiefs. This was an inaccurate assessment by Mullen, because it was Pace and his predecessor, Air Force Gen. Richard Myers, who had reduced the office and created the vacuum into which Keane had stepped. It also was a politically naive step for the new chairman to take. Keane, a career Army officer, had more credibility on ground warfare than did Mullen, a career Navy officer. More significant, Keane had been encouraged in his role by the White House, even to the point of Cheney's asking Keane to take command in Iraq.

"You really don't want me to help Petraeus?" Keane asked Mullen.

"No," the chairman said, "I don't want to take the chance." Once more, the leaders of the American military establishment had shown a tendency to avoid risks, and to prefer following established ways of doing business rather than take difficult but necessary steps to become more effective. Keane went back to the White House and got the chairman's roadblock removed.

Two Mondays after the hearing, in a video teleconference, President Bush brought up the MoveOn advertisement with Petraeus. "On behalf of all Americans, I want to apologize to you for that," Bush said, according to people who were present at the meeting. "No public servant should have to endure that." He also told Petraeus that his performance before Congress had altered the domestic political debate on the war.

Crocker had the same sense that something fundamental had shifted in the politics of the war at home. "We kind of saw the air go out of the whole thing," he said. "I still kind of wonder if maybe it really wasn't so much what we said but simply that we said it. . . . [T]his thing had been hyped as the event of the decade, and then, 'Well they came, they testified, they left, so now what?'"

The congressional Democrats were stumped. As Senator Webb later put it, "There are a couple of problems with the Democrats and Iraq. One is that there is a wide divergence of opinion inside the party, and the other is that the Democrats are a very fragile majority, and in fact aren't a majority in the Senate because Lieberman always votes with the Republicans."

That said, something had changed in the way Democrats talked about the war. On September 26, two days after the president's apology to Petraeus, the Democratic presidential candidates debated in Hanover, New Hampshire. None of the top candidates would promise to have the U.S. military out of Iraq by January 2013, more than five years later. "I think it would be irresponsible" to state that, said Senator Obama.

"It is very difficult to know what we're going to be inheriting," added Senator Clinton.

Seeing those comments, Boylan exclaimed to himself, "Hey, we won!" He had been right. The hearings were supposed to have been climactic. They were, but instead of seizing control of policy, the Democrats essentially had yielded.

They hadn't quite endorsed Bush's position, but they had conceded much in agreeing to go along with Petraeus's approach. They were resigned.

From Kilcullen's point of view, the September hearings were a kind of a parallel to the battle that didn't happen in Samarra in midsummer. Just as Iraqis had looked at the possibility of a full-blown civil war and turned away, he said, so too the U.S. public had considered a leap into the unknown—and declined to take it. "America," he said, "has taken a deep breath, looked into the abyss of pulling out, and decided, 'Let's not do it yet.'"

AMERICA TUNES OUT THE WAR

The American public had heard all it needed to hear. The people might not have liked what Petraeus was offering, but it was better than anyone else was proposing. They understood that the United States was stuck in Iraq. But that didn't mean they had to like it. So they would let him continue—but they also would tune it out.

The best evidence for that new hands-off attitude was the sharp decline in news coverage of the war in the weeks and months after the September hearings. In the first half of 2007, the Iraq war was the top running story almost every week on television networks' evening news broadcasts. After the September hearings, its ranking declined rapidly, from taking up 25 percent of coverage at the time of the hearings to just 3 percent in mid-2008. Starting a month after the hearings, the network broadcasts began consistently to devote more time to presidential campaign politics and the state of the economy. The broadcast networks' evening news shows are the most sensitive to demand, because they have only about 22 minutes to use every night, roughly equivalent to the number of words a broadsheet newspaper typically carries on its front page. In the spring of 2008, networks would begin to cut back on their staffs covering the war. CBS no longer kept a correspondent in Baghdad, and it was widely expected that other organizations would follow suit after the U.S. presidential election later that year.

Meanwhile, newspaper coverage of the war declined by about half between early 2007 and early 2008. "It seems like a bad dream, and the public's not interested in revisiting it unless there is a major development," Hunter George, the executive editor of the *Birmingham* (Ala.) *News*, told the *American Journalism Review* in early 2008. "If I'm outside the newsroom and Iraq comes up, I hear groans."

A series of anti-war movies bombed, despite having high-power actors and directors: *In the Valley of Elah,* directed by Paul Haggis and starring Tommy Lee Jones and Charlize Theron; *Lions for Lambs,* with Robert Redford, Tom Cruise, and Meryl Streep; Brian De Palma's *Redacted;* and *Grace Is Gone,* featuring John Cusack. Hollywood wasn't telling moviegoers anything they didn't know already. The best movies to come out of Iraq were documentaries, such as *Baghdad Diary* and Deborah Scranton's innovative *The War Tapes,* which was filmed by giving video cameras to deploying National Guardsmen.

When the fifth anniversary of the war arrived in March 2008, the anti-war demonstrations were tiny. In Washington, D.C., where anti-war marches during the Vietnam era brought out at least 250,000 or more, there appeared fewer than 1,000 souls. In San Francisco, where an estimated 150,000 people had turned out against the war in 2003, just 500 protestors showed up in 2008.

"I think the debate has moved on," Secretary Gates said. He was right. Iraq was just part of the national wallpaper, always kind of there, but not particularly noticed.

Hadi al-Amari, the head of the Badr Corps, the militia of the Islamic Supreme Council of Iraq, the largest Shiite party, told Gen. Barbero that Petraeus returned to Iraq with much more *wasta.* "He went there, he went into the teeth of the opposition, and he came out with his plan intact," the militia commander explained.

Sadi Othman noticed a similar effect in the rest of the Middle East. "That was huge," Othman he said. "The hearings in the States [changed] the debate on Iraq in the Middle East and around the world."

But it is axiomatic in military affairs that every strength carries its own weakness. Petraeus now "owned" the war—that is, he has made it his. He had implemented the changes he wanted to make, and had some tactical success to show for it. But the surge hadn't led to national political reconciliation. That left Petraeus in the position of just keeping his fingers crossed, hoping against hope for a political breakthrough in Iraq. His predicament left him in the same position as Rodney King, who famously pleaded for an end to the 1992 riots in Los Angeles: "Can we all get along?" The answer from many Iraqi factional leaders was negative.

Part Three

WAR WITHOUT END

9.

THE TWILIGHT ZONE

(Winter 2007–8)

At the turn of the year, Lt. Freeze, the reconnaissance platoon leader in Diyala who on Independence Day had despaired for Iraq, revised his characterization of the country. The one word to summarize it now, he thought, would be "progress."

That was a distinctly relative term. Baghdad was more secure, but still far from safe. Violence had decreased to the level of 2005, which at the time had seemed nightmarish, but now, coming after the horror of 2006, felt like a welcome relief. Civilian deaths were plummeting. The bloodshed that did occur now seemed to resonate less, especially because there was a new air of desperate improvisation in al Qaeda's attacks. "None of 'em add up to anything particular," Brig. Gen. Anderson, Odierno's chief of staff, said of that winter's car bombings. Baghdad had moved from the seventh circle of Hell, which Dante reserved for the violent, to the fifth, the destination of those overcome with anger and sullenness, or as the poet put it in Canto VII, "those who swallow mud." It was a notable improvement, and it was in the right direction—but it was still a version of Hell. Al Qaeda's usual methods of bomb delivery—cars or young men—were deterred by a proliferation of checkpoints, so it began using bicycles, women, and preteen boys to bomb Iraqis. Eventually it would perversely turn to mentally handicapped or disabled girls. In a sign of how much checkpoints run by the turned militias were impeding its operations, al Qaeda fighters also began launching sophisticated ambushes against them, in one instance wearing Iraqi police uniforms so they could get near. U.S. military operations continued, with large offensives in Diyala and Nineveh Provinces, but they had a desultory feeling of mopping up.

Iraq still was far from a functioning state. "We had a much better government in Vietnam than we do in Iraq right now," one colonel warned ominously.

One day I was traveling from Camp Victory, near the airport, to downtown when my driver and I came to a National Police checkpoint manned by perhaps eight men. We, and our bodyguards in a chase car, waited about half an hour, and then were waved through. Fifty yards later we came to an Iraqi army checkpoint, manned by another eight men. The two checkpoints apparently were stationed closely so the police and army could keep an eye on each other. After another half-hour wait, we were through. About 200 yards later, we arrived at a bridge over the Tigris, only to find one side of it closed for repairs, pushing all the cars to the other side. There, where a police officer really could have helped, there was no one directing traffic, nor were there even lanes demarked for the two opposing directions. The river crossing felt like a civilian demolition derby, with Iraqis driving head on at each other at high speeds, flashing their lights as warnings to swerve out of the way. That was how Iraq worked in 2007.

"It's ironic that the Iraqis, who we built up into such a threat, now seem so entirely helpless," observed Lt. Col. Miller.

As Iraqi's rainy, surprisingly chilly winter set in, Petraeus was pondering whether the war might change. "It's going to continue to morph," he said. "We think we are going to be quick enough to adjust."

It was a time of assessment. What had we gained with tactical success? Where has the new strategy taken us? How much further do we need to go? Who are our friends, and who the foes, in reaching our goals? Was the Baghdad government part of the problem or part of the solution? Asking these questions led to reexaminations not only of the strategy but of the major players it was intended to affect: the Iraqi government, the former Sunni insurgents, and the Shiite militias. The new American strategy also had the unintended side effect of casting a new light on the tens of thousands of mercenaries—also known as "private security contractors"—that the Americans had brought to Iraq.

REVISITING A STRATEGIC ASSUMPTION

"The surge is doing what it was designed to do," President Bush asserted in the spring of 2008. But it hadn't done what he had *hoped* it would—that is, lead to political reconciliation. As Defense Secretary Gates had phrased it, "The purpose of the surge was to create enough space that the process of reconciliation could go forward in Iraq."

On the ground in Iraq it was clear that anything resembling genuine reconciliation wasn't occurring, and probably wouldn't anytime soon. "We had a faulty logic, February '07, that the surge protects the people, then government will reconcile," Col. Bill Rapp said one day later that year. "We still haven't seen that knitting together at the top."

Col. Mike Bell, Rapp's successor as consigliere to Petraeus, found pretty much the same situation obtained in mid-2008. It took him back to Petraeus's persistent need for more time. "I think what we haven't thought through as a government is how much time you need from improved security to a political change," Bell said.

Despite a reputation for stubbornness, President Bush had become quite flexible as he searched for a way out of the labyrinth of Iraq. In a speech at the National War College he offered a fallback assumption. Political movement at the local level ultimately would lead to change at the national level, he argued. The goal of this new approach, he said, was "to help Iraqis make progress toward reconciliation," which in turn would lead to freedom, human rights, democracy, and so on.

But here again, there had been little evidence of that happening. As Maj. James Powell, one of Odierno's planners, was preparing to leave Baghdad early in 2008, he said that bottom-up moves "buy us time." But, he added, "As I've heard one Iraqi say, it takes two hands to clap. At some point it has to be met by movement at the top."

Rapp at first was an advocate of the localized alternative. But by the winter of 2007–8, he also had given up on that idea. "In retrospect, it was a dumbass thing to say." There was something happening at the local level, he said, but "it wasn't reconciliation, it was bottom-up accommodation, or calmness. They weren't reconciling with anything."

Some top Iraqi leaders dismissed the entire notion the Americans were peddling. "I don't think there is something called reconciliation," said Barham Salih, the deputy prime minister. "To me, it is a very inaccurate term. This is a struggle about power." Maliki, meanwhile, began to argue almost the opposite, that the necessary reconciliation already had occurred, so there was no need to talk about it anymore.

The lack of political movement raised the unhappy question of just what it was that U.S. forces were fighting for. In the Army's survey of the mental health and morale of soldiers in Iraq, one sergeant commented, "They are at the watering trough but choose not to drink. . . . I don't think we're doing anything at all—they're not changing." It is not too much to say that American troops were dying to give Iraqi politicians the chance to find a way forward—but that it wasn't clear if Iraqi politicians wanted that chance.

So what were the Americans waiting for? "This is the dilemma we're in right now," said a senior U.S. military intelligence officer with long experience in the Middle East. "We've bought some time, but for what? We're still waiting for someone to pull the rabbit out of the hat. But so far there is no indication that anything is going to stave off the breakup of the country. So right now we are in a kind of twilight zone of neither peace nor victory. But I think we are drifting toward a breakup."

To some, that meant it was time to pull the plug. "To date the Iraqi political process has not demonstrated the capacity to deal successfully with any of these issues," said Senator Jack Reed, a Rhode Island Democrat who was growing increasingly influential on defense issues. "And if they're not dealt with, then you've got a failing state that is not helping itself."

But to others, the failure of Iraqi politics raised the question of whether the next step was to revise the American mission—and in some ways return to the grandiose vision that the Bush administration held when it sent American forces into Iraq, that of making it a democratic beacon that would change the politics of the Middle East. "We've built a state, and now we have to build a nation," Col. Allen Batschelet, chief of staff of the 4th Infantry Division, said early in 2008. "At the tactical level, we've been buying time for that to happen."

TIME FOR MALIKI TO GO?

The impasse led to a new and grimmer understanding of the limitations of the people at the top of the Iraq government. There was a growing feeling that perhaps they just weren't capable of doing what the Americans thought they needed to do. "We thought that once they weren't being shot at, they could start being statesmanlike," Col. Rapp said. "It turns out we have a bunch of guys who survived the Saddam years by being secretive and exclusive, instead of being open and inclusive."

Some of those around Petraeus were coming to see the intransigence of the Maliki government as the key threat in Iraq, rather than terrorists, insurgents, or militias. "I think the reason that we're in the twilight zone is the Maliki government is very dysfunctional, and unwilling to reach out to his enemies," Mansoor said. "He has a conspiratorial mind-set, and is fearful of a coup."

The Americans were especially antagonized by what they saw as Maliki's footdragging on bringing in the former insurgents who had turned onto the Iraqi government payroll. An Army officer in Baghdad reported that after his unit sent in applications for local Sunnis to join the police, they were returned because they had been filled out with a nonprescribed color of ink. "The longer the Iraqi government stalls, . . . the greater the danger that tens of thousands of tough, armed Iraqis will stray," said Wayne White, a retired State Department specialist on the Middle East.

There was an undercurrent of distrust in dealing with Iraqi officials. Top officials not only didn't do the right thing, they didn't seem to want to do it. "The ministers, they don't get it," said Campbell, the assistant commander of the 1st Cavalry Division. "They don't know what the hell is going on on the ground." By contrast, he said, the Sunnis, waiting to be given a place at the table by the Baghdad government, had in his view shown great patience. "You don't want the Sunnis that are working with you to go back to the dark side."

After years of insurgent attacks and criminal kidnappings, anyone in the Iraqi government who was still alive was viewed with some suspicion. Had he cut unsavory deals, or worse, did he have a foot in both camps? One battalion commander in Baghdad, talking about a neighborhood official, called him "a good guy," but then wondered aloud about how he alone on the local political council had survived: "Why is he the original member who wasn't touched?"

Americans worried that the Baghdad government would fritter away the opportunity won for it by their bloody counteroffensive of the spring and summer of 2007. "The tipping point that I've been looking for as an intel officer, we are there," said a senior U.S. military intelligence officer. "We are at the critical juncture. The GOI [government of Iraq] and ISF [Iraqi Security Forces] are at the point where they can make or break it." He was especially worried that if the top

Iraqi officials didn't make more of an effort to reach out to the Sunnis that the country would slide back into civil war. "If the Sunni insurgents are disenfranchised by the GOI, guess what? It's game on—they're back to attacking again."

Americans quietly debated whether to look for an alternative to Maliki. "As I arrived, Maliki had kind of a questionable future," recalled Col. Bell, who got to Baghdad in February 2008. "It wasn't clear that he had the political support or the personal leadership to remain there [in office] very long."

Arguing against Maliki was his track record. There were concerns that he might prove to be a leader who needed to have a war, who thrived on its divisiveness and feared peace for two reasons. First, any fair election would diminish his power, because greater Sunni participation in the vote would cut the Shiite hold on government. Also, an absence of violence would push to the fore the divisive questions to which he had no answers: How to divide oil revenue among the peoples of Iraq? How to decide the future of the disputed city of Kirkuk, claimed by the Kurds as their capital, but sitting on top of much of Iraq's oil? And who really led Iraq's Shiites, still learning how to exercise the power of the majority?

Maliki's advocates responded that it wasn't clear that anyone else could do better. As Kilcullen had observed, we shouldn't blame the Iraqi officer who cuts deals with insurgents to keep his family alive, we should fix a system that can't protect his family and so forces him into such arrangements. Maliki may be in the same position on a national scale. Also, there was fear that pushing out Maliki could return the country to the situation in early 2006, when it took five months to form a government, during which Baghdad drifted into a municipal civil war.

THE SUNNI SIDE OF THE STREET

Many American officials considered the turning of the Sunni insurgency to be more significant than either the surge or the new tactics associated with the surge. But no one knew how long the loyalty of these new allies could be retained, especially if they believed they weren't getting a fair deal from the Baghdad government. In 2008 there were 103,000 of these armed men—a ceiling the Iraqi government had asked the U.S. military to stop at—and there were plans to absorb only 20,000 of them into the police and army. It wasn't clear ultimately what would happen to the rest, especially if the Sunni community continued to feel estranged from the Baghdad government.

But the central government in Baghdad had never warmed to them, seeing them as little more than warlords for hire. "They are like mercenaries," one aide to Maliki told the Associated Press. "Today they are paid by the Americans. Tomorrow they can be paid by al Qaeda." Other Iraqi officials scorned the groups as "American militias."

The American view was rather different. "Clearly the coalition and the government of Iraq and I think the Iraqi people realize that these are very brave, courageous people that stood up in a time of need of their country," said Brig. Gen. David Perkins.

Maj. Gen. John Kelly, commander of the Marines in western Iraq, reported that more than two-thirds of the Sons of Iraq, most of them turned Sunni insurgents, in his area wanted to join the Iraqi army or police. How would the thousands left hanging react? "Despite the repeated assurances of the Maliki government, there is no evidence to date that the governing coalition has resolved its sectarian concerns" about the groups, "or begun to formulate a comprehensive plan for integration of their members," noted Michael Hanna, an expert on Iraq law and politics.

In the short term, such a reliance on local militias didn't appear to be such a bad bet. But what would happen to them in the long run? As Col. Jon Lehr, commander of one of the surge brigades, prepared to leave Iraq, he explained the role that the Sons of Iraq had played in improving security in Diyala Province, north of Baghdad. "From Baqubah, emanating out from Baqubah, we have conducted a strategy of clear, hold, and tactical build in a series of concentric rings," he said. "And clearing is one thing, but holding the ground is another. And that's where the CLC/Sons of Iraq part of the strategy is very important. You can clear an area, but if you can't hold it, it's all for naught." In other words, Lehr appeared to have succeeded by turning over control of cleared areas to a force that may or may not respond to orders from Baghdad. That raised the question of whether basic problems of security weren't being solved as much as deferred. If so, when push came to shove, there almost certainly would be far less U.S. combat power available to back up Baghdad than was available during the surge of 2007–8.

Likewise, in Tarmiyah, the rough little town where a U.S. outpost had been besieged for four hours in February 2007, the U.S. military finally cut a deal with the local Sunni sheikh and made his son the chief of the local contingent of the Sons of Iraq. But the Americans and the Iraqis seemed to have different notions of the long-term purpose of this force. The father, Sheikh Sa'd Jassim, had been accused of providing funds for al Qaeda operations in the area, but the U.S. military now chose to interpret that as simply a case of blackmail in which the victim shouldn't be blamed. The son, Sheikh Imad, oversaw a force of 500 armed men, each paid $300 a month. "He does not seem to regard the U.S.-paid Sons of Iraq as a short-term transition, but as a long-term means to protect Sunni areas against Shiite persecution," reporter Nathan Webster wrote in the blog "The Long War Journal."

U.S. troops tended to praise these local allies, but some were indeed genuine thugs, despite American assurances to the contrary. The British newspaper the *Guardian* published a hair-raising profile of Haji Abu Abed, the former insurgent who a few months earlier had arrived at an alliance of convenience with the U.S. military in Baghdad's Amiriyah neighborhood. The Americans dubbed his group "the Baghdad Patriots," but it preferred to be known as "the Amiriyah Knights." The *Guardian* portrayed him screaming at Iraqi bystanders while waving a pistol and shouting, "Oh people of Iraq, I had come to you with two swords, one is for mercy, which I have left back in the desert, and this one"—the gun—"is the sword of oppression, which I kept in my hand." His men piled into cars and drove around his territory, waving weapons out the windows. On a raid looking for an alleged cache of sniper rifles, he told a boy he would cut off his head "and put it on your chest if you don't tell us where the guns are by tomorrow." He then tried to put his shotgun in the boy's mouth, the newspaper said.

Nine months later, Abu Abed had fled to Amman, Jordan, after being ousted by a subordinate. His former U.S. military adviser still supported him. "Many times he had the opportunity to do the wrong thing and never did," former Army Capt. Eric Cosper told the *Los Angeles Times.* "I have absolute faith in him."

Spec. Horton, the Stryker brigade soldier who had qualms about working with former insurgents in Baqubah, later wrote that under American tutelage, "they've grown into a much more organized, lethal force. They use this organization to steal cars and intimidate the local population, or anyone else they accuse of being linked to Al Qaeda. The Gestapo of the 21st century, sanctioned by the United States Army."

Maj. Gen. Rick Lynch, commander of the forces just south of Baghdad, said early in 2008 that he understood how tenuous the situation was. "I mean, a good portion of our concerned citizens were probably insurgents yesterday, and they could be insurgents tomorrow, and what we're doing right now is working hard to keep them on the right side of the fence."

The Iraqi government was less interested in that approach, and in the summer of 2008, began to talk about setting a deadline sometime in the winter for the groups to unilaterally disarm—or suffer the consequences.

THE ONCE AND FUTURE SADR

"There's something going on above us," an Army intelligence officer said one day in 2007. He knew there were some sort of contacts between U.S. officials and representatives of Moqtada al-Sadr, but he didn't know the details.

This was a form of reconciliation by the United States government, which was reaching out to an anti-American leader whose followers had killed American troops in two rounds of fighting in 2004, and who continued to be a threat. U.S. policy toward Sadr resembled that of President Johnson toward FBI director J. Edgar Hoover, of whom he said he would rather have him inside the tent pissing out than outside it pissing in. "Sadr isn't going to go away," said a senior U.S. military intelligence officer. "So how do you deal with him in a way that facilitates the continued growth of the GoI?"—that is, the government of Iraq.

"We are now meeting with them, for the first time," Odierno said in January 2008. Of Sadr, he said, "He's clearly moving more toward a humanitarian approach, and less of a militia." In public comments, American commanders began to refer to Sadr as "the honorable." Petraeus took it a step further a month later, calling him "al-Sayyid Moqtada al-Sadr," using the honorific for descendants of the prophet Muhammad.

It wasn't clear where the talks were going, especially because the Americans had almost no sense of what was happening in Basra, the largest city in the Shiite south. One of the few reporters to venture there at this time was Solomon Moore of the *New York Times*, who in February 2008 found a "deeply troubled" city where doctors, teachers, politicians, and sheikhs were being kidnapped and murdered. "Most of the killings are done by gunmen in police cars," Sheikh Khadem al-Ribat told him. A senior Iraqi police officer reported that Shiite militias had taken 250 police cars and 5,000 pistols.

"I think all hell is going to break loose down there," said an American military intelligence officer.

THE AMERICAN MILITIA: FRIENDS OR FOES?

The last nongovernmental armed group in Iraq that was being reevaluated that winter was the genuine American militia, the 20,000 to 30,000 private security contractors who, loosely controlled and operating under a hazy legal regime, guarded American diplomats and other contractors. One of the side effects of the new U.S. strategy, founded on protecting the people, was to cast a harsh new light on the security contractors, and especially their willingness to open fire on civilian vehicles.

The heavy use of these contractors long had been an anomaly in the Iraq war. When historians look back on the conflict, one aspect on which some are likely to focus is how American forces relied heavily on contractors to truck supplies, cook food, and provide technical support. But they probably will look most closely at the armed civilians hired to provide security to State Department personnel and other American officials, as well as to many of their fellow contractors engaged in reconstruction projects. This group of mercenaries by far constituted the second largest group in the "coalition," after U.S. forces. (Indeed, the so-called coalition continued to crumble, with the shrinking British contingent of 4,100 based at the Basra airport doing almost nothing, and the next largest troop contributor, the former Soviet state of Georgia, being forced in the summer of 2008 to precipitously withdraw its 2,000 soldiers from Iraq, where they had been operating checkpoints along the Iranian border, so they could help fight the Russians back home. Oddly, of the 24 nations in the group, some of which contributed just a handful of soldiers, 17 were former Communist states.) In the post-9/11 world, one security company, Blackwater, was paid around $1 billion by the U.S. government, much of it for work in Iraq.

Many of the private security contractors carried noticeable chips on their shoulders, the likely effect of really being responsible to no one for their behavior. One day in 2007, for example, a knot of about seven white American males stood in the airport in Amman, Jordan, waiting for one of the two daily Royal Jordanian Airlines flights to Baghdad. They were dressed in "mercenary casual"—short-sleeved shirts, multipocketed khaki cargo pants, and wraparound sunglasses on their heads. Some sported tattoos on their biceps. Two carried daypacks that had B+ and A+ stitched on them, denoting their blood types. They conversed in the distinctive acronym-heavy jargon of the U.S. military. One Kiplingesque story of desert intrigue began, "There was this TCN in the secondary QRF," referring to a Third Country National, who ranks low in hierarchy of status in the world of mercenaries, on a Quick Reaction Force, a group that is supposed to stand ready to aid elements in trouble.

A bedraggled Jordanian baggage handler in baggy blue overalls pushed his cart up to the point where the group of Americans blocked his way. "Ex-coo," he said deferentially, and too quietly. "Ex-coo."

The men gazed at him as he tried to ease his cart through them. They hadn't heard his soft voice, and they didn't move. "Be polite!" ordered one of the Americans. "Say, 'Excuse me'!"

The small Jordanian man looked up at the American and repeated, "Ex-coo."

"Okay, then," the mercenary said, and stepped aside.

"What's up?" asked one of his colleagues.

"I'm just telling this motherfucker to be polite," he explained. This occurred not in Iraq, but in Jordan, where the group had no legal standing or protection.

Once in Iraq, security contractors behaved even more brusquely, leading Iraqis to loathe them. The bodyguards were notorious for moving around Baghdad without regard for other cars or even pedestrians, driving on the wrong side of the road and even on the sidewalks. Ann Exline Starr, a former adviser to the American occupation authority, recalled being told by her protectors, "Our mission is to protect the principal at all costs. If that means pissing off the Iraqis, too bad." (The *Washington Post*'s chief of security in Baghdad once asked me to change my shirt before going out because, he pointed out, the outfit of black polo shirt and light khakis that I was wearing resembled too much the typical dress of many security contractors.)

For some, angering Iraqis was a sport as well as a business. One widely watched video showed some contractors firing from the back of their vehicle on an Iraqi highway, hitting cars behind them, apparently for fun. "The Iraqis despised them, because they were untouchable," Matthew Degn, an adviser at the Iraqi Interior Ministry, told the *Washington Post*'s Steve Fainaru about the contractors. "They were above the law." He said that Blackwater's Little Bird helicopters, bristling with armed men, often buzzed the ministry, "almost like they were saying, 'Look, we can fly anywhere we want.'" (Fainaru, who would go on to win a Pulitzer Prize for his coverage of the use of mercenaries in the Iraq war, also reported in his book *Big Boy Rules* that a Peruvian told him that among the Peruvian security guards in Iraq were former members of the Shining Path, the Maoist guerrilla organization that, Fainaru noted, in Peru "had massacred thousands of peasants during the eighties and early nineties.")

On Christmas Eve in 2006, a Blackwater man while drunk shot and killed a bodyguard for Adel Abdul Mahdi, one of Iraq's two vice presidents. Two months later, a Blackwater sniper shot and killed three guards at the Iraqi Media Network, a state-funded television station. In May, a company team shot and killed a civilian at the gates of the Interior Ministry, provoking an armed confrontation with Iraqi police.

Few American commanders ever liked having armed men in their area who were ostensible allies yet who were not subject to American rules and laws. But in the first several years of the war, when commanders put "force protection" above all else, there wasn't much daylight between the approach taken by the U.S. military and the private trigger pullers. Then, in early 2007, as the top priority in the U.S. mission became protecting the people, there suddenly was a huge difference between how the two types of armed Americans were acting in Iraq.

Matters came to a head on a Tuesday afternoon in September 2007, when employees of Blackwater who were guarding a convoy just outside the Green Zone shot and killed at least 17 Iraqis. The Blackwater men said they were responding to an ambush, and the company would back them up, saying they acted in self-defense. But several Iraqi eyewitnesses disputed that, and parallel investigations by the U.S. military and the Iraqi government would conclude that no one fired except the contractors. Iraqi police said the shootings occurred just outside the headquarters building of the Iraqi National Police, an area heavily protected by checkpoints in every direction, making it difficult for anyone to set up an ambush. Maliki would call the incident a cold-blooded crime. A U.S. military report, based upon interviews with soldiers who arrived on the scene and with Iraqi eyewitnesses reported that there was "no enemy activity involved," and that many of the Iraqi civilians were wounded as they tried to drive away from the American convoy. "It had every indication of an excessive shooting," said Lt. Col. Mike Tarsa, a battalion commander in the 1st Cavalry Division. Capt. Don Cherry concluded that "this was uncalled for." Five of the Blackwater guards involved in the incident were indicted in December 2008 by a federal grand jury on charges of manslaughter and assault.

FROM BERLIN TO BAGHDAD

It was striking that the most thoughtful of those around Petraeus, the advisers who knew most about the region and took the longest view, also tended to be the most skeptical about political progress. Pundits back home began declaring victory in Iraq, but the closer one was to the country, the more one saw the potential problems. "There is a chance of this breaking down at a whole range of points," Crocker said in January 2008.

Emma Sky was optimistic about security but pessimistic about politics. She flew to Washington, D.C., to deliver the keynote speech to a CIA conference on Iraq. "The psychological impact of the surge has been huge," she said in that talk. "We have shown to ourselves and our critics that we are not defeated, and we have shown Iraqis that we are trying to help them. So there is a whole new psychological dynamic." But, she continued, "we also have created a whole new load of risks. We have created this huge bottom-up momentum on the Shia and Sunni street."

The purpose of the surge, she said, was to buy time and space for the government of Iraq to reach accommodation. But she had concluded that wasn't going to happen. "What I came away thinking was, you could buy time and space for the government of Iraq, and it wouldn't reach accommodation, because the system isn't capable of it." That is, the political structure of Iraq as it existed in early 2008 simply couldn't do what the Americans were asking it to do. The best thing the Americans might be able to get from it was time while waiting for a new generation of political leaders to emerge.

Likewise, Joel Rayburn, the savvy strategist on Petraeus's staff who had helped shape Fred Kagan's thinking about a surge and then came out to Baghdad to work on Iraqi affairs in the context of the region, said he saw little chance of political progress. "My own view, and it is at odds with the institutional view, is I don't see us moving forward politically." He gave the surge "an incomplete." The test, he said, would be provincial elections, if and when they came—not only whether they would be held, but whether they would be fair enough to achieve balanced representation.

Retired Army Col. Joel Armstrong, who also had been involved in the planning that Gen. Keane took to the White House, agreed that the theory of the surge hadn't played out. "It hasn't worked as well as I hoped," he said in 2008.

"There are lots of people in Iraq who want to put together a better life, but there are lots of people in power who don't seem to want that."

One way to understand Iraq in 2008 was through the prism of the Cold War. It took decades to be resolved, and during that time, Germany was divided, millions were deprived of their basic human rights for decades, and uprisings in Hungary, Czechoslovakia, and Poland were suppressed along the way. But full-scale war never erupted, and eventually Germany was reunited and the walls dividing people came down. The surge, said one White House aide involved in Iraqi affairs, pointed toward a similar minimal way forward. "It has shown Baghdad how a bare minimum modus vivendi can be had," he said. "They can have their own neighborhoods and live in peace, even if it's in Sunni ghettos." At some point, he said, they would start blending together again—perhaps, he ventured, three years in the future or perhaps in thirty.

The Americans first had been seen as liberators by Iraqis, Barbero said, and then as occupiers. But by the end of 2007, he continued, they were more trusted by the major factions than those groups trusted each other, and were beginning to be seen as protectors and intermediaries. "I think our presence is one of the moderating forces," agreed a senior U.S. Special Operations officer in Baghdad. "It provides a venue for discussion, dialogue." No longer the sand in the gears, they had become the glue in the situation, perhaps the only thing holding Iraq together. As in Europe after World War II, that amounted to a recipe for keeping U.S. forces in Iraq for a very long time.

Stephen Biddle, an astute defense expert and sometime adviser to Petraeus, argued that by cutting deals with dozens of local Sunni insurgent groups and Shiite militias, the U.S. military indeed had put itself on the hook for staying in Iraq for decades. "A continued presence by a substantial outside force would be essential for many years to keep a patchwork quilt of wary former enemies from turning on one another," he concluded.

In retrospect, the winter of 2007–8 appears to be a time of missed opportunity, when Iraqi leaders should have made great strides politically but didn't. It was at this point that the surge began to fracture: It was succeeding militarily but failing politically.

10.

BIG *WASTA*

(Spring 2008)

"You know, we all feel much older than we did in 2003," Petraeus said one day early in 2008 after being asked about the impending fifth anniversary of the war. "And not just five years older, but vastly older. It seems like light-years ago, frankly." As he spoke he sat stiffly erect in a straight-backed chair, the better to ease the strain on his damaged pelvis. Despite being in phenomenal physical condition, the fatigue was evident on his face. He long had looked about a decade younger than his age, but now was beginning to look like what he was, a man in his midfifties carrying a heavy load.

"His patience level is much lower," noted Brig. Gen. Joe Anderson, who had commanded a brigade in the 101st Airborne under Petraeus. "His sense of humor is diminished. He's a bit disconnected, distant."

One day U.S. forces lost five troops in two different bombing attacks. Petraeus, like Col. MacFarland in Ramadi two years earlier, reminded his staff of Gen. Grant's prediction after being beaten on the first day of the Shiloh battle: "He is sitting there with a soggy cigar at the end of this terrible day, confused as all get out, and says, 'Yup, lick 'em tomorrow,'" Petraeus recalled. For him, Grant's terse comment symbolized the need for willpower: "I think it takes that kind of indomitable attitude and sheer force of will at times in these kinds of endeavors." Gesturing at an aide, he said, "These guys have heard me say it a couple of times."

Petraeus's *wasta* was growing. He couldn't know it then, but the following months would bring resolution in several areas that had been nagging him.

FALLON OUT, PETRAEUS PEOPLE UP

In March, Adm. Fallon finally went too far. The offended party wasn't Petraeus but, significantly, the White House, as the admiral shot his mouth off in a feature article in *Esquire* magazine that made him look like the only thing standing between President Bush and an American war with Iran. The profile, written by Thomas P. M. Barnett, a former professor at the Naval War College, portrayed Fallon as "brazenly challenging" President Bush on whether to attack Iran, pushing back "against what he saw as an ill-advised action." Barnett was clearly an admirer, praising the new Centcom chief as "a man of strategic brilliance" whose understanding of the tumultuous situation in Pakistan "is far more complex than anyone else's"—a questionable assertion, given that Fallon was new to the region, while some American officials, such as Ryan Crocker, had been dealing with it for decades. Fallon clearly had cooperated with Barnett, with the author accompanying him on trips to Egypt and Afghanistan over the previous year. The article quoted Fallon as saying one day in Cairo that "I'm in hot water again" with the White House, apparently for telling Egyptian president Hosni Mubarak that the United States would not attack Iran.

But Barnett hadn't done Fallon any favors in return. Asked about the article by e-mail, the admiral confusingly called it "poison pen stuff" that is "really disrespectful and ugly." He did not cite specific objections. Nor did he seem to understand during the first few days after the article appeared how much trouble he was in. Some at the Pentagon saw the quotes simply as Fox Fallon being Fox Fallon. But the article was raising eyebrows elsewhere in the government, including the White House. He might have kept his job under Rumsfeld, who barked more than he bit, and under Pace, the chairman of the Joint Chiefs, who just wanted everyone to get along. But Gates and his new chairman of the Joint Chiefs, Adm. Mullen, were a different team. Gates spoke softly but acted quickly. A few days later, Fallon began to understand it was time to go "when the SecDef stopped taking his calls," said a White House aide.

"Admiral Fallon reached this difficult decision entirely on his own," Gates said in an unscheduled news conference announcing the departure. "I believe it was the right thing to do, even though I do not believe there are, in fact, significant differences between his views and administration policy."

Not only would Fallon be pushed out of Central Command after barely a year in the job, he would be replaced by his erstwhile nemesis, Petraeus. Surprisingly, Petraeus wasn't happy about any of this. After Iraq he had wanted to go to European Command, not Centcom. And he felt that after months of wrangling, he and Fallon had worked out a way of living with each other. Indeed, when Petraeus had briefed Fallon on his plans for Iraq after the end of the surge, Fallon had been so agreeable that after the briefing, Pete Mansoor had turned to Petraeus and said, "You know, he couldn't be more supportive."

By the time Fallon was on the way out, Petraeus said, "Actually we had a very good relationship." He began the next morning's briefing by saying to his staff, "We're sorry to see this happen to Admiral Fallon. We want to thank him for his help to MNF-I."

Fallon, who had arrived in Baghdad a few hours earlier and was participating in the briefing, then added, "I made a decision that it was an unnecessary distraction in a time of war, so it is time for me to move on."

Petraeus had hoped that at European Command his wife could join him as he rebuilt NATO to deal with Afghanistan and the future. Instead he was made Fallon's successor at Central Command, condemning him to several more years of wrestling with Iraq and the Middle East. His aides said that Petraeus actually had recommended several other officers to Gates for the Centcom post. Among the names floated, they said, were Marine Gen. James Mattis and Army Lt. Gen. Pete Chiarelli. But Petraeus insisted that he didn't bring up names with Gates, but simply had said, "You know, I think that there are certainly others who could do the job."

Interestingly, the officer chosen to be Petraeus's deputy at Central Command was John Allen, the Marine general who reached out to the sheikhs of Anbar, following in the footsteps of his beloved Gertrude Bell.

Odierno had gone home in February to become vice chief of the army. He left Iraq with his reputation redeemed. "General Odierno has experienced an awakening," said retired Army Col. Stuart Herrington, who in 2003 had written the intelligence report critical of Odierno. "I've now completely revised my impression of him." Two months later, when Fallon's departure created an opening, Odierno was told instead to succeed Petraeus as the top U.S. commander in Iraq.

The advice Odierno prepared for his subordinates underscored just how much he had changed. His "key message" at an April 2008 conference, according to an internal Army document, was that "planners must understand the environment and develop plans from an environmental perspective vice an enemy situation perspective." This was classic counterinsurgency thinking—that is, focus on the overall situation, and seek to make the enemy irrelevant to it. This was what David Kilcullen, the Australian counterinsurgent, had been advocating for some time, but it was almost the opposite of the approach that Odierno and most of the rest of the U.S. Army had taken in Iraq in 2003–4, when they emphasized a "kill and capture" approach.

Emma Sky, Odierno's political adviser, had planned to put Iraq behind her as a chapter in her life. She left in February and went hiking in New Zealand to mull her future. She was thinking about settling back in London and becoming a consultant. But a few months later, after Odierno was tapped to replace Petraeus, he called her. "What possessed you to take the job?" she asked.

"You know that flag you make fun of?" he responded, referring to the American colors he and all other Army soldiers wear just below the right shoulder. He also told her with amazement that he had been at a birthday party in Texas for a ten-year-old, and the entertainment had been target practice with rifles. She thought that meant he was looking at his own country differently. "He wouldn't have noticed that before," she thought.

He asked her to come back for a third tour in Iraq, advising him in his new position. "I will never again do anything like this without having someone like that," he has said of Sky. "I have a lot of respect for MI [military intelligence], but you have to have someone with a different view. It is very helpful." She agreed to return to Baghdad, joking that if she was going to serve the U.S. military so much, someone should grant her American citizenship.

A major personnel move led by Petraeus a few months earlier also began to leak out about this time. In November he had left Iraq to come back to the Pentagon to run a promotion board to select the Army's new brigadier generals. It was unprecedented for a commander to leave the war zone to do that, but it showed how influential he had become. Among the 40 new generals his board tapped were H. R. McMaster, Sean MacFarland, and Steve Townsend, who had commanded a highly mobile Stryker brigade that Odierno had employed as a quick reaction force in 2007. The board also was notably heavy in veterans of

Special Operations, including Kenneth Tovo, who had lead a task force in Iraq; Austin Miller, a former commander of the secretive Delta Force; and Kevin Magnum, a former commander of the 160th Special Operations Aviation Regiment. One of the signs of an effective military is rewarding battlefield success, and Petraeus's board, which was widely watched inside the military, did just that. For more than a decade, the Army had been led by post-Cold War officers—the group that did the Gulf War, the invasion of Panama, and the peacekeeping missions in Somalia, Haiti, Bosnia, and Kosovo. Now, a new generation of generals was emerging, the leaders of the post-9/11 Army.

"MARCH MADNESS"

At almost the same time that Fallon was defenestrated, Prime Minister Maliki surprised the Americans with an unexpected move that would alter the relationship between the U.S. and Iraqi governments. He had been watching and learning many things from the Americans. One of those things was how to roll the dice and take risks. He was ready to gamble.

The occupation of Basra, the biggest city in southern Iraq, had been a miserable experience for the British, the only major European government to stand with the Bush administration through five years of war in Iraq. At the outset, the British military had felt rather superior to the clumsy Americans. Not only did they have more experience in the Middle East, they also seemed to have a better feel for how to conduct a counterinsurgency campaign, reaching back to operations in Malaya, Kenya, and Cyprus.

But as one crusty defense expert, Anthony Cordesman, put it, "By late 2007, the British position in Basra had eroded to the point of hiding in the airport." Daniel Marston, an American who taught counterinsurgency at Sandhurst, the British military academy, noted that it had been a humiliating experience for British officers, especially as they watched Petraeus and Odierno regain the initiative in Baghdad. "I'm not going to go into details, but the frustration . . . when I've been with commanders, to see how bad they were doing things, and that the Americans turned it around, was incredible," Marston said. "There was a lot of upset, and honor was a problem in the army." (Underscoring that unhappiness, British military commentary, so vocal at the beginning of the war in grading the American performance, fell almost silent in 2007.) Islamic extremists and thugs were running Basra, siphoning off oil revenue and inventing new ways to impose their religious rules, not just banning the sale of alcohol but also shutting down a plastic surgeon's practice on the reasoning that he was altering what God had made.

On the evening of Friday, March 21, 2008, as the sixth year of the war began, and just before the U.S. military death toll hit 4,000, Petraeus was being briefed on a very deliberate plan to take Basra. Developed by Iraqi Lt. Gen. Mohan al-Furaiji, the Iraqi commander there, it would take months to carry out and called for the United States to provide money, machine guns, tanks, and concrete barriers. It probably would begin in September or maybe October. It certainly was seen as something that would happen in the distant future and last for months.

But Maliki had a different idea. Mowaffak al-Rubaie, the national security adviser to the prime minister, interrupted the briefing with an urgent message: The prime minister wanted to see Petraeus the next morning at eleven, he said. "It's about doing Basra," Rubaie explained.

"*Mosul,* you mean," responded Maj. Gen. Barbero, Petraeus's chief strategist, thinking the aide had intended to refer to the largest city in the north. American intelligence had reported that some Iraqi brigades were being moved by Maliki, but the word was that they were heading north.

"No," Rubaie said, "He means *Basra.* He is tired of the lawlessness there."

So began a major turning point in the war, and even more in the course of relations between the Iraqi government and the U.S. occupation force.

The next morning Maliki told Petraeus, "I'm going to go in there forcefully, now. We've got to clean these people out." He had been briefed that criminals and militias were running and looting the city, killing anyone who stood in their way and raping many women they encountered. He presented the general his plan, frequently employing the term "lines of operations," which he had heard incessantly in briefings by American officers. "He laid out, there is going to be a tribal engagement line of operations, a political engagement line of operations, an economic/humanitarian assistance line and a security line of course," Petraeus said. "And he talked about how he was going to go down personally with a number of the ministers—Interior, Defense, Justice—the commander of the National Police, commander of the Iraqi ground forces, and a number of others, and they were going to work these different lines of operations."

His question for Petraeus: "Will you support me?"

In Petraeus's mind, there was no question about that. Of course he would.

The general had worked, he recalled later, "very hard to build what I think now is a relationship of mutual trust, respect, and confidence, informed by an awareness of the demands of our different positions and the context in which we perform our different responsibilities." He sometimes had spoken bluntly to Maliki, but, he thought, never disrespectfully. "Occasionally guys think I just went in there and had it out with him a couple of times—you don't do that with a prime minister of a sovereign country." Nor would it fit Petraeus's style. Even when his relationship with Fallon was on the rocks, for example, it always remained correct.

Maliki's decision to move precipitously was especially a shock because Petraeus and his staff had just gone through interminable briefings on Mohan's cautious plan for Basra. Also, the Americans had understood that consideration of retaking Basra would commence only after Mosul was quiet. "I was planning to defeat al Qaeda in the north, hold the center, and not pick a fight in the south," recalled Lt. Gen. Lloyd Austin, who had replaced Odierno as the corps commander, in charge of day-to-day operations in Iraq.

Instead, Maliki said, the operation would begin on Monday, March 24—that is, two days later. "He thought it would be quick and easy," said Sadi Othman, who attended the Saturday meeting. "That's what his commanders told him." Petraeus was a bit uneasy, but didn't try to talk him out of it. Instead he gave him advice about how to operate, how to set conditions for the assault.

On Easter Sunday, the day before the hasty offensive was to commence, powerful rockets began to rain down on the Green Zone. From that day through mid-May, more than 1,000 rockets would be fired at the Zone, mainly from the Sadr City area, making a mockery of the truce Sadr supposedly was following. By the U.S. military's count, the attacks killed or wounded 269 people. Looking back, some officials came to believe that word had leaked inside the Iraqi government of Maliki's intent to crack down on his erstwhile allies in the Sadrist movement. Others, such as Maj. Rayburn, a regional strategist for Petraeus, argued that such a barrage takes many days to prepare and coordinate, with stockpiling and planning, and that both Maliki's decision and the rocket attacks from Sadr's turf simply reflected the growing tension between the two. Rayburn's analysis was that the Sadrists were moving to oust Maliki, not really caring who replaced him, so long as they were able to show themselves to be the kingmakers who could remove a sitting prime minister. If they succeeded, he said, "They would have looked like they have veto power, like Hezbollah in Lebanon."

It was an unsettling moment. "I called it 'March madness,'" Barbero said a few months later in his Green Zone office, which faces east, toward the Sadr City rocket launching sites. "Basra was going on. We had rockets coming in here. The worst case was that all of southern Iraq would go up in flames with the Mahdi Army." The U.S. military had seen what that might look like back in 2004, when as the first battle of Fallujah got under way, Sadr's followers began attacking U.S. and allied forces in central and southern Iraq. For several weeks the American fought a two-front war, and grew seriously concerned that the Shiite militias would cut their major supply line that stretched across the south to Kuwait. For a short period, Baghdad was entirely isolated, with every road leading into it deemed too dangerous for travel.

Assaulting Basra piled gamble upon gamble. Maliki was betting that his security forces could do it. Other political parties calculated, after some hesitation, that they should back Maliki. It was clear that the Iranians were active in Basra, which is not only the biggest city in the south but the key to Iraq's only seaport, and so the lucrative home of much of its export trade. The Americans crossed their fingers, hoped for the best, and prepared to bail out Maliki if necessary.

The attack didn't begin well. Iraqi troops moved surprisingly quickly, but upon arrival simply were thrown into the city, often without supplies and with the barest of orders, such as, Go take that area. Some commanders were handed bags of cash and told to buy food after they settled into the city, Petraeus said. "It was difficult to understand for a wee while whether it was a work of genius or folly," said Lt. Gen. John Cooper, a British deputy to Petraeus who was on his second Iraq tour. "For the first few days, we were badly concerned about it—to that extent, had the prime minister bitten off more than he could chew?"

Or, as Col. Bell put it, American-style, "It was a huge mess."

There were very few Americans in Basra, and almost none with the Iraqi units, so the American headquarters in Baghdad was almost blind. What it did hear didn't sound good. Some 883 soldiers in the Iraqi army's 52nd Brigade, which numbered only about 2,500, refused to fight, along with about 500 members of the Basra police. Sadr's Mahdi Army launched counterattacks in Baghdad and in towns across southern Iraq, but not a full-scale assault that would mean the truce was entirely dead. "There were some very tenuous moments during the first forty-eight to seventy-two hours," recalled Lt. Col. Nielsen. She began to worry that it ultimately would be a tactical victory but a strategic setback—that is, so expensive a win that it would undercut Maliki and make the United States look inept as well.

The early conclusion was that Maliki had gambled and lost. "It was ill advised and ill timed," said Mahmoud Othman, a Kurdish politician. "I think Maliki had a setback and America had a setback because Iran and Moqtada al-Sadr were victorious."

On Thursday, March 27, Gen. Austin, Odierno's successor as the commander of day-to-day operations in Iraq, flew south to take a look. "The smell of fear [in Iraqi officials there] was palpable," said a senior Army intelligence officer who accompanied him. That night Austin ordered one of his deputies, Marine Maj. Gen. George Flynn, to go to Basra to help the Iraqi army, especially with planning and coordinating support, such as supplies, aerial reconnaissance, and air strikes. Flynn flew down the following morning and soon was joined by a group of planners. As he arrived, he recalled, "the situation on the ground was tense and uncertain." The British were at the airport, outside of town. Maliki was downtown in a government complex that was being shelled steadily by mortars. The chief of his personal security force was killed at about this time by mortar shrapnel. Soldiers inside the compound, including Americans, hesitated even to go outside to another office because of the incessant fire, which made it difficult to communicate inside the headquarters.

The first step, Flynn decided, was to get armed Predator drones in the air to begin finding and destroying the mortar emplacements and killing the mortar teams, to get the shelling off the back of headquarters so they could begin to operate normally. The second was to get U.S. liaison troops embedded with Iraqi units, so they could report back and call on U.S. resources to help out.

By the fourth day, the hastiness of the operation began to impede Iraqi units, as nearly every unit in the fight ran low on fuel, food, water, ammunition, and money, recalled Marine Sgt. Alexander Lemons, who was deployed to Basra. The Iraqi troops to whom he was attached fed themselves by dropping hand grenades into a canal and collecting and cooking the fish that floated to the surface.

On March 30, the sixth day of the battle, Sadr ordered his followers to stand down, apparently after receiving reassurances from Maliki that the attacks on his loyalists would cease. Many of his fighters did lay down their arms. But the statement he issued was hardly conciliatory, calling the Americans and their Iraqi allies the "armies of darkness." Word seeped out that the cease-fire had been brokered by the Iranian government, which apparently was alarmed to see the Shiite-led Baghdad government crack down on the Shiite militias that dominated Basra. "JAM [Jayash al-Mahdi, Sadr's Mahdi Army] wasn't really broken so much as they were chased underground," Lemons concluded. But they were clearly on the wrong foot: Sadr's organization began to threaten to hold a "million-man march" to protest the offensive, a tactical retreat for an outfit that a few days earlier had been willing to fight Maliki and the Americans for control of a major city. A few days later, Sadr took another step back from confrontation and cancelled the march—only to issue a blustery statement later in the month threatening "open war until liberation."

The militias in Basra that had continued to fight began to show signs of weakness. A series of raids by Iraqi special operations troops killed or captured about two dozen of their commanders, as well as some top criminal gang leaders. Other militia captains began to flee the city, leaving behind a headless force. Then the air strikes began to kick in, shutting down most of the remaining mortar sites. Supplies began to flow into the city. Sadi Othman received anguished telephone calls from his Sadrist contacts, saying, he said, "This is crazy, we need to talk to Maliki, this is unnecessary bloodshed." But, he said, the prime minister wasn't in the mood to negotiate. Still in Basra, Maliki received calls from some erstwhile political opponents saying, "We are with you."

"As those factors accumulated you could sense the shift," Petraeus said. "The targeted operations started to really bear fruit, the Iraqi SOF [Special Operations Forces] really got some traction. You also have the negotiations ongoing, Iran realizing that they don't want to bring the government down, so they are starting to pull on the reins. And frankly the leaders of these organizations typically do not stay and fight, and so they were starting to exfiltrate to Iran and so you have them, the Iranians and presumably Sadr, realizing that their forces are getting beaten up pretty badly, realizing that the people are frustrated with them."

By mid-April, the crisis had passed. "We were beginning to feel pretty good," said Flynn, the Marine general, who was still in Basra, coordinating American support. In a symbolic move, an Iraqi army battalion occupied the building that had housed Sadr's headquarters in the city. Maliki felt so vindicated that he fired Gen. Mohan, who had developed the more deliberate plan that would have taken months. On April 19, Iraqi forces went into the "flats" on Basra's southern side that were considered to be the Sadr City of the south, deemed hostile and nearly impregnable. They were unopposed. The battle was over, and Maliki had won it, more or less.

"Basra was a colossal failure in execution, but the decision to attack was a key step forward for the government of Iraq," concluded Brig. Gen. Dan Allyn, Gen. Austin's chief of staff at the American military headquarters for day-to-day operations in Iraq. "They chose to take on Shia militias for the first time. That was a courageous decision not properly prepared for."

MALIKI: FROM OVERWHELMED TO OVERCONFIDENT?

One of the harsh lessons of the Iraq war, as well as earlier ones such as Vietnam, has been that a military victory doesn't necessarily translate into a political gain—which is one reason that military operations can't be judged just in tactical terms. The reverse can also be true, that a military stalemate can be a victory for one side. That is what happened to Maliki in Basra. In military terms, the outcome was ambiguous. "It was totally unclear who won or lost on the ground," said Lemons, the Marine sergeant. But in political terms, Basra was a clear victory for Maliki and his army, he and others said. "Every Iraqi I have spoken to since then about how the prime minister did claims Maliki proved he is a strong leader willing to crack JAM."

Cooper, the British deputy to Petraeus, was more optimistic. "It was nip and tuck up" to the cease-fire, he said, but after that, "we got the sense that JAM had taken a pounding, and had their own logistical problems."

The operation's political effects were clearer. "Iraqi politics were just muddling along," said Maj. Rayburn. "Then there was this watershed: They were forced to make a choice between the prime minister and the Sadrists. After some quick deliberation, they all decided against the Sadrists." Also, the quality of life improved for more than a million Iraqis who lived in Basra, which effectively rejoined Iraq.

American officials came to see the operation as a psychological tipping point for both Maliki and his army. "He went into Basra an uncertain political leader with an uncertain future," said Bell, the head of Petraeus's think tank. "I think he emerged very different."

"It wasn't tactically pretty but it was a decisive and strategic move," concluded Col. Richard Daum, a top military planner in Iraq in 2008. Sitting in his blue cubbyhole amid an ocean of cubbyholes in the headquarters complex at

Camp Victory, he said, "I think Basra will be looked at as an enormous turning point. It signaled that the government isn't going after only Sunni insurgents, but also Shias. It also signaled to the Iranians that they needed to stop meddling. And it sent a signal to the moderate Arab states. The prime minister emerged with a lot more *wasta.*" In the wake of Basra, several Arab nations announced they would open embassies in Baghdad, after years of resisting American pressure to take that step. A few months later, King Abdullah of Jordan would become the first head of a Sunni Arab state to visit Iraq since the American invasion. Of course, what he was looking for was the kind of breaks on oil prices that Saddam Hussein had given Jordan. But that would be a small price for Maliki to be recognized as a peer by the Sunni Arab world. In September, Syria sent an ambassador to Iraq. In October, the Egyptian foreign minister visited, along with his country's oil minister.

"Six months ago, people were saying about Maliki, 'He is a Shiite prime minister, he is an Iranian guy,'" said Othman, who spent hours a day talking to Iraqi politicians. "Now, after Basra and Mosul, he is looked upon much more as an Iraqi." The Americans were also pleased that upon his return to Baghdad, Maliki established a new government committee to gather intelligence on Iranian influence in Iraq.

The Iraqi army had surprised the Americans and gained new respect, even deference. "The lesson of Basra is that the Iraqi army has come a long way," said Flynn, who spent a total of six weeks in Basra assisting the operation. "I don't think they could have done this a year ago. But they also have a long way to go."

Hammond, the commander of the 4th Infantry Division, described the battle of Basra as a transformative event for Iraqi troops. "Until then, they were a checkpoint-based security force, and that was kind of hit and miss," he said. "It's kind of like they found a whole new level of confidence. Even the checkpoints are different than they were a month ago—higher level of professionalism, greater pride, greater sense of purpose. I think they've tasted success, and they like it."

On the American side, this led to a new readiness to defer to Iraqi officers. "I do think there is more of a willingness to engage Iraqi counterparts in a serious way, a greater willingness to see problems through Iraqi eyes, to take their advice even if it doesn't seem to make sense," said Lt. Col. Paul Yingling, who in 2008 was on his third tour in Iraq.

When Emma Sky, Odierno's erstwhile politcal adviser, got back to Iraq to prepare for the change of command from Petraeus to Odierno, she headed down to Basra, where she went on patrol with Iraqi troops. "They had a terrific esprit de corps—'This is where we fought this battle.' It was like a glimpse into the future. It's not the way we'd do it, but it is an Iraqi way." She also was impressed by the new confidence she saw in the way Maliki talked and moved. "I've not seen him for four months, and he's a different man. He's growing into power."

Other American advisers agreed that Basra fight illuminated the pathway for Iraqi forces and their American allies. Iraqi forces would lead the way, and their generals would make the big decisions—but the Americans would stand ready to provide support in key areas, such as close air support, medical evacuation, intelligence and surveillance, and communications. That was a recipe, the Americans believed, for big U.S. troop drawdowns in 2009—but also for a smaller, long-term presence built around those advisory and enabling missions. "To me, the big lesson learned is, that's the way forward," said Barbero.

Later in the spring, the fighting in Sadr City in eastern Baghdad was resolved in a similar way to Basra. Iraqi officials did it their way, and despite American apprehensions, it worked. At first U.S. forces were intensely involved as they bit off an arc of southern Sadr City, targeting the portion that had been the launching point for most of the rockets and mortar shells that were raining down on the Green Zone. In several weeks of combat, at least 200 Mahdi Army fighters were killed, many of them members of the launching teams. But in mid-May, Maliki's government cut another deal with Sadr. Rather than conduct a joint U.S.-Iraq assault on the heart of Sadr City, the Iraqi forces negotiated their entry, and went in alone, slowly and with permission. It was a sharp contrast to 2006, when Maliki had ordered the Americans to stop raiding into Sadr City or even to put up checkpoints at its entryways. Apparently under orders from Sadr, residents greeted them with flowers and Korans—an ironic echo of the Bush administration's view that American troops would be met with bouquets in 2003. Hammond, the division commander, said he wasn't entirely comfortable with the negotiated entry, but said, "They're doing it their way. They're not looking for my approval." He said he wasn't issuing orders to Iraqi commanders, but instead advising them—and often seeing his advice rejected. "More often, I have to fight for my point of view," he said. His forces played an overwatch role, establishing Joint Security Stations on all four sides of the city. Two aerostat balloons were lofted alongside the city to provide 24-hour surveillance. In addition, said Hammond, at any given time, five Predator and Shadow drone aircraft and four Apache attack helicopters were orbiting above the city, ready to fire missiles at any rocket or mortar teams that emerged.

By June a new Sons of Iraq program began in the huge slum. But Sadr's men continued to fight in quiet ways. In June Brig. Gen. Jabar Musaid, who had been head of Basra's military intelligence operations during the crackdown there, was shot to death in east Baghdad.

In June 2008, Austin, the new corps commander, noted that, "For the first time, the government has positive control of the three strategic nodes—Basra, Mosul, and Baghdad." It was indeed an accomplishment, even if it came during the sixth year of the war. At Umm Qasr, Iraq's only port, just south of Basra, the amount of cargo arriving daily tripled from the spring to the summer.

By the summer of 2008, the American military actually was ahead of its schedule. "Where we are now is where we thought we'd be in January of next year," said Col. Bell. That is, the security situation was about what they had hoped to be able to turn over to the next American president. Petraeus winced when he heard such open talk of timetables, but others confirmed that they were indeed ahead of their secret plan at that point.

By June a new worry began to grow about Maliki: that he was overconfident and didn't fathom just how much essential support he was getting from the Americans, especially from the nightly Special Operations raids that were keeping al Qaeda in Iraq from reforming and being able to launch a new wave of attacks in Baghdad. During June and July 2008, the terrorist organization, still on its heels, suffered a new round of losses from a series of raids along the Tigris River Valley. In one operation near Tikrit, U.S. forces not only captured several people but also found suicide vests and a readied car bomb. In nearby Bayji they captured the man who housed incoming foreign fighters. In Mosul, they killed a leading figure and captured more than $100,000 and more suicide vests.

Maliki, feeling his oats, began to distance himself from the Americans, and especially from the Bush administration. In midsummer he appeared to endorse Senator Obama's plan to get American combat forces out of Iraq within a year or two.

"It's been a good thing and a bad thing," Gen. Odierno said later in 2008 of Maliki's victory in Basra. The benefit, of course, was that the side allied with the Americans won. "The bad point is, it's a bit of an overestimation by Maliki of how it happened." Odierno eventually put together a briefing for the prime minister to teach him just how much the United States had helped win the battle of Basra and continued to support Maliki in hundreds of ways every day.

ROUND II WITH CONGRESS: NO WAY OUT

"Nothing succeeds with the American public like success," Petraeus had written in his 1987 doctoral dissertation at Princeton, about the influence of the Vietnam War on the thinking of the U.S. military leaders about how to use force.

But in his second round of congressional testimony, in April 2008, he would find that limited success doesn't sell as well. In September 2007, he had been able to testify that the war was being turned around, and so had stymied Democrats advocating a swift pullout. Seven months later, as far as Washington was concerned, the tactical gains of the surge were old news. Now it would be the turn of congressional Republicans to feel frustrated. They had given him time, and now they wanted to hear more about how that success was going to get the United States out of Iraq. He had little for them in that regard. Instead, he was looking to freeze the U.S. military presence near the level of 130,000, where it had been in 2006, before the surge began. On top of that, he was telling Republicans that the light at the end of the tunnel wouldn't be the bright beacon of democracy that the Bush administration originally envisioned as the payoff for invading Iraq. Reflecting the lowered goals of the U.S. effort in Iraq, Petraeus pointedly called himself a "minimalist."

Unlike the previous September, this time members of Congress knew from the outset what they would be getting. Even before the hearings began, Senator Norm Coleman, a Minnesota Republican, posed the basic question: "How do we get out of this mess?" The answer, of course, was: We don't. This was not something they wanted to hear.

Lawmakers must have sensed Petraeus wasn't going to be of much help in assuring them that the American commitment to Iraq wasn't open-ended, because they gnawed at the issue throughout the hearings. "I still have a hard time seeing the big picture and what constitutes success," fretted Republican Representative Jeff Flake of Arizona. "That's not just one side of the aisle with those kind of concerns. Many on this side of the aisle have that as well."

"The people of the United States have paid an awful price," noted Republican Representative Dana Rohrabacher of California. "It's time for the Iraqis to pay that price for their own protection."

Senate Republicans were no happier. Bob Corker of Tennessee said, "I think people want a sense of what the end is going to look like."

"Where do we go from here?" asked Senator Chuck Hagel, a Republican but a longtime skeptic of the war.

Senator George Voinovich of Ohio said, "The American people have had it up to here."

"We're a generous people," said Senator John Barrasso of Wyoming, another new Republican, "but our patience is not unlimited."

Welcome to the club, Senator Carl Levin, chairman of the Armed Services Committee, seemed to say. Petraeus's plans to draw down U.S. troops to pre-surge levels, he asserted, were "just the next page in a war plan with no exit strategy." He was more or less correct: While there was an exit strategy, the exit was years away, in fact so far in the future that it was hard to discern.

As for presidential candidates, McCain seemed most detached from reality, essentially not listening to Petraeus and instead laying out a concept for an ending that seemed unreachable. The day before the hearings began, he described Iraq in terms that were eerily similar to how the Bush administration had described it on the eve of the invasion, as a country that the Americans would transform and turn into an engine of change for the entire region. "The fact is, we now have a great opportunity, not only to bring stability and freedom to Iraq but to make Iraq a pillar of our future strategy for the entire region of the Greater Middle East," he had told the national convention of the Veterans of Foreign Wars. "If we seize the opportunity before us, we stand to gain a strong, stable, democratic ally against terrorism and a strong ally against an aggressive and radical Iran."

At the hearing, McCain summarized his view: "We can now look ahead to the genuine prospect of success. Success, the establishment of a peaceful, stable, prosperous, democratic state that poses no threats to its neighbors and contributes to the defeat of terrorists, this success is within reach."

McCain's grand vision was not only at odds with the more restrained goals in Petraeus's campaign plan—simply of "sustainable security"—but verged on fantasy. It resembled President Bush's 2003 rhetoric, but flew in the face of five additional years of painful evidence about the imprudence of that grandiose approach. It was unlikely that Iraq would wind up a strong or genuinely democratic nation, with not only elections but also rule of law and respect for the rights of its minorities. There was even less chance that Iraq would be an ally against Iran, given that the Shiite politicians that the United States had helped to power had taken refuge in Iran during Saddam's time, and had maintained close ties even during the U.S. occupation. Rather, the best case scenario was that in the long run, Iraq would calm down, be mildly authoritarian, and probably become an ally of Iran, but, with luck, not one that threatened the rest of the Arab world.

Senator Clinton asked sharp questions that underscored the vagueness of Petraeus's answers. You keep on saying that your decisions will be based not on time but on conditions, she said, so please describe those conditions. Petraeus didn't, instead describing how he would measure the situation. His response is worth quoting at length for its masterful evasiveness:

> With respect to the conditions, Senator, what we have is a number of factors that we will consider by area as we look at where we can make recommendations for further reductions beyond the reduction of the surge forces that will be complete in July. These factors are fairly clear. There's obviously an enemy situation factor. There's a friendly situation factor with respect to Iraqi forces, local governance, even economic and political dynamics, all of which are considered as the factors in making recommendations on further reductions. Having said that, I have to say that again it's not a mathematical exercise. There is not an equation in which you have coefficients in front of each of these factors. It's not as mechanical as that. At the end of the day, it really involves commanders sitting down, also with their Iraqi counterparts and leaders in a particular area, and assessing where it is that you can reduce your forces so that you can again make a recommendation to make further reductions. And that's the process. Again, there is this issue, in a sense, this term of battlefield geometry. And as I mentioned, together with Ambassador Crocker and Iraqi political leaders, there's even sort of a political-military calculus that you have to consider, again, in establishing where the conditions are met to make further reductions.

It was as if, after being ambushed by Clinton in the September hearings, Petraeus had crossed her off his list. He wasn't prepared to engage with her except at an unhelpful, arm's-length distance. Mess me around, he seemed to be saying, and all you'll get from me is empty but correct answers. (Meanwhile, Senator Roger Wicker, a new Republican from Mississippi, managed to get in a subtle dig at Clinton, throwing back at her that loaded phrase from last September. "There is no question that the situation is better now," he lectured. "It's better than when the surge began and it's better than in September. It would take a major *suspension of disbelief* to conclude otherwise, to conclude that things are not much improved.")

Senator Obama was much more focused in his questions than in the September hearing, when he had rambled. Obama this time seemed to be thinking like someone who might have to make real decisions in a year's time. He wanted to know two things: If we are never going to totally eliminate support for al Qaeda in Iraq and we are never going to totally eliminate Iranian influence, then what are we really trying to do with those two issues? Or, he asked, are we going to try to stay there for two or three decades, until everything is really solved? "I'm trying to get to an end point," Obama said. "That's what all of us are trying to get to."

Obama's bottom line wasn't really much different from that of Petraeus and Crocker. If we wanted to entirely eliminate al Qaeda and have a solid Iraqi state, we'd be there for decades. "If on the other hand," he said, "our criteria is a messy, sloppy status quo, but there's not, you know, huge outbreaks of violence; there's still corruption, but the country's struggling along but it's not a threat to its neighbors and it's not an al Qaeda base; that seems, to me, an achievable goal within a measurable time frame." That was what the campaign plan called "sustainable security."

Crocker's message was even starker. He used the hearings to raise concern about what he termed the "Lebanonization" of Iraq—this is, the weakening of the government, the division of the people into sectarian groups, and the rise of militias that rival the government in reliable firepower. Also, in both Lebanon and Iraq, Iran played an active role, supplying and training certain armed groups. "Iran is pursuing a Lebanonization strategy," Crocker said. And if the U.S. left Iraq quickly, he added, "Iran would just push that much harder."

The evocation of Lebanonization raised the haunting possibility of the American war in the Middle East continuing for decades. A generation of Arab fighters had taken on the United States presence in Iraq, and some had survived to go back home, reported the *Washington Post*'s Anthony Shadid. "Iraq is a badge of honor for every Arab and Muslim to fight the American vampire," he was told by Abu Haritha, the nom de guerre of a man who was wounded while fighting in Fallujah and then returned home to his home in Tripoli, Lebanon's second-largest city. Crocker's warning was effectively dismissed by the members of Congress quizzing him and Petraeus, despite the ambassador's persistence and his familiarity with both Lebanon and Iraq. It was as if no one even wanted to hear it.

After the hearings, I asked Petraeus over a lunch why he hadn't taken more risks and simply laid it out plainly, saying something like this: *Look, the best case scenario is we're going to be there a minimum of another three or four years, though I think with about half the troops we have there now, and with fairly steadily declining casualties. This isn't a lead-pipe cinch, but I think it is plausible, and it sure beats any alternative I can see.* He responded that he thought he had said that, more or less.

I didn't think he had made that clear. But some military professionals disagreed, saying that they had heard that message. This didn't necessarily make them hopeful. Retired Marine Col. Robert Work, an insightful former adviser to the secretary of the Navy, observed that Petraeus subtly had shifted from a conditions-based strategy to a time-based one:

> We have given up on having a shining beacon of democracy in Iraq. We want a nation that is relatively stable, not a threat to its neighbors, and can protect its borders. We have also largely given up on sectarian reconciliation; we now simply hope for some type of sectarian accommodation that will reduce the likelihood of widespread sectarian conflict when we leave. Crocker and Petraeus cannot describe the conditions for this except that it will take time. Every gain is potentially reversible, for far into the future. Our condition for leaving is now simply: We'll wait and hope that through the passage of time for bottom up accommodation and the formation of a functioning state. We've planted the seeds and will know the time to leave when the flower blooms. Unfortunately, we cannot tell the American people how long this particular flower takes to bloom. In the meantime, as part of our time-based strategy, we will expend the majority of our time, money, blood, sweat, and tears building up Iraqi security forces, not the government or the society. We leave that for natural development; it is funded and resourced in a relatively paltry fashion. This seems to me to be a highly risky strategy. It is arming all three of the major sectarian groups to the teeth.

Retired Maj. Gen. Robert Scales Jr., a former commandant of the Army War College, thought the strategy was even riskier than Work did. Petraeus was caught in a fundamental contradiction, he thought: Petraeus had the correct strategy, but was on thin ice because time was running out on it. "The counterinsurgency strategy implemented by Petraeus is the right one and cannot be substantially altered," Scales said. But, he continued, "The crucible of patience among the American people is emptying at a prodigious rate and very little short of a complete shift in conditions on the ground is likely to refill it." On top of that, by early 2008 the Iraq war had cost roughly $650 billion, at minimum. That price tag would grow even more significant as the U.S. economy slipped into a recession and a burgeoning financial crisis.

It appeared that Obama might be the person who would have to address the contradiction. After securing the Democratic nomination in early June, he used part of his victory speech to talk about Iraq, beginning with a comment that echoed Kilcullen's crack that just because you invade a country stupidly doesn't mean you should leave it that way. "We must be as careful getting out of Iraq as we were careless getting in," Obama said. " But start leaving, we must. It's time for Iraqis to take responsibility for their future."

Bush certainly understood the point Petraeus had been making. The two had breakfast after the April hearings, along with Crocker. "I've told him he'll have all the time he needs," the president said afterward.

DRAWDOWN

Before he moved to his new post at Central Command, Petraeus had to continue to plan in Iraq. In June 2008, his strategic planners began working on the following year. He told them to begin thinking about a transition from a mission of "securing the population" to one of "sustainable security." They already could see four hurdles ahead. The Muslim holy month of Ramadan would start this year in September, and in every year of the war it had brought a spike in violence. Second, the better security was in Baghdad, the more refugees would return home from Jordan and Syria, where many of them were running out of money. Their homecomings promised to provoke sectarian fighting and test Iraqi forces as Sunnis returned to neighborhoods that had been cleansed by Shiite militias that had taken possession of Sunni houses. Provincial elections almost certainly would increase violence. The planners also knew, finally, that the American election would be closely watched in Iraq, and that there might be violence intended to influence American voters. That election could go a long way toward determining the future U.S. mission in Iraq: Under Obama it would be to reduce the presence, while under McCain it would be to prevail and help confront Iran.

For years, the U.S. military had fretted about "mission creep." Beginning with the Somalia operation in 1992–93, top commanders worried that once U.S. forces were committed to a situation, the tasks assigned them would continually expand, from security to providing a variety of services to standing up a government, until they were mired in what was derogated as "nation building." Many in the military had listened with relief with George W. Bush had denounced this tendency during the 2000 presidential election campaign, saying it was not a proper use of the armed forces. "I don't think our troops ought to be used for what's called nation building," he said during a debate with Al Gore, the Democratic candidate. "I think our troops ought to be used to fight and win war." Then, of course, he went on to invade Iraq and inadvertently launch perhaps the most ambitious and expensive nation-building effort in the history of the United States.

In Iraq in 2008, the U.S. military would face a new variant of the mission creep problem. As the 5 brigades sent for the surge began to go home, commanders were facing "force shrinkage." That is, the mission would remain the same—ensuring that Iraq was developing sustainable security—but there would be fewer and fewer U.S. troops available to carry that out. The key would be to "hold" (under "clear, hold, and build") with less combat power. But to make that happen, Iraqi forces would have to shoulder more of the burden. Always wanting to take it slowly, Petraeus recommended holding the troop level in Iraq to about 15 combat brigades until it was clear how provincial elections were going to play out. Pushed by the Joint Chiefs, he ultimately agreed to a compromise under which one brigade would leave in January 2009 without being replaced, but another one would be on tap to replace it if needed.

11.

AFTER THE SURGE

(Summer 2008)

As the surge ended in mid-2008, with the last of the five additional combat brigades heading home, Baghdad felt distinctly better. Kebab stands and coffee shops had reopened across the city, and many ordinary Iraqis felt safe enough to venture out of their homes at night, in part because stores were remaining open to evening shoppers. Some women discarded the head scarves that Islamic extremists had insisted they wear, with violators being attacked. Even as Iraq's factions remained murderously divided, violence was at its lowest level of the entire war, with only a dozen American soldiers dying in July 2008. Contrary to expectation, the holy month of Ramadan didn't bring a major spike in violence, as it had in the previous five years. Some 39,000 displaced families safely returned to Baghdad.

Some optimists, such as Fred Kagan, pronounced that Iraqi politics were moving forward smartly and that the war was all but over. But that assessment confused starting to win with having won. There was no question that under Petraeus, the U.S. military had regained the strategic initiative, an extraordinary achievement. "He has pulled off something that is unparalleled, really, and without much support from Washington or Centcom, and with active hampering from the Joint Chiefs," said David Kilcullen. Yet most of the basic questions about the long-term direction of Iraq remained unanswered. It is striking that of the predictions General Fastabend made in his 2007 essay written for Petraeus about "How All This Ends," many of the military ones came true while the political ones didn't. As Fastabend had urged, the U.S. government was indeed able to arrive at cease-fires with tribes, to turn former insurgents and put them on the payroll, and even to chip away at the power of Sadr's militia. But on the political side, Fastabend had predicted that Maliki would be ousted from power by January 2008 and then disappear a few months later while traveling in Iran. He saw provincial elections rolling across Iraq in 2008, another event that didn't happen. (He did make one good call on the political side: foreseeing that the Republicans would lose the White House in the November 2008 elections.)

Iraqi politics felt stuck, and American officials were beginning to fear that an entire generation of embittered, distrustful former exiles would have to pass from the scene before genuine and lasting progress could occur. This struck me especially one day late in 2008, when Maj. Gen. Guy Swan, Odierno's director of strategic operations, told me in his Green Zone office that "with the security gains, there is a window of opportunity. . . . Only they can do it. We have set the conditions for them. They have an opportunity to pursue their own destiny." Almost exactly a year earlier, Gen. Odierno had said almost exactly the same thing to me. A window of opportunity had opened for the government to reach out to its former foes, he had explained then, but said "it's unclear how long that window is going to be open."

Analyzing the lack of progress in Iraqi politics one day late in 2008, Emma Sky recalled Petraeus's image of "the Mesopotamian Stampede." "We've stopped the stallion from running off the cliff, but then it runs off in another direction," she said. "Right now it is frantically running around in circles." By that she meant that the existential questions that faced the country before the surge—and indeed since the day the Americans invaded—were still hanging out there.

What, then, had the surge accomplished?

THE SURGE FALLS SHORT

The surge was the right step to take, or more precisely, the least wrong move in a misconceived war. Petraeus's final letter to his troops, dated September 15, 2008, stated that "your great work, sacrifice, courage and skill have helped reverse a downward spiral toward civil war and wrest the initiative from the enemies of the new Iraq." That assessment captured what the surge and associated moves did, but not what they didn't do.

The surge campaign was effective in many ways, but the best grade it can be given is a solid incomplete. It succeeded tactically but fell short strategically. There is no question that the surge was an important contributor to the reduction in violence in Iraq and perhaps the main cause of that improvement. But its larger purpose had been to create a breathing space that would then enable Iraqi politicians to find a way forward and that hadn't happened. As 2008 proceeded, not only were some top Iraqi officials not seizing the opportunity, some were regressing, Odierno worried one day as he sat in the Green Zone office he recently had inherited from Petraeus. Iraqi politicians had found that they didn't necessarily have to move forward, he said. "What we're finding is that as Iraq has become more secure, they've . . . moved backwards, in some cases, to their hard-line positions, whether it be a Kurdish position, an Arab position, a Sunni position, a Shi'a position, a Da'wa position, an ISCI position"—these last two being the two major Shiia parties.

Odierno argued that progress was being made politically. But the analysis he then offered of Iraqi politics seemed instead to support the argument that the breathing space given Iraqi leaders had enabled them to retreat from reconciliation and dodge tough problems. "Security is good enough where I worry about them going back," he explained. "They're not going back to solve the old problems which we've pushed. They've continued to delay the tough ones, like the problem with land up in the north with the Kurds, the problems with the Peshmerga, oil, Kirkuk." Nor had international actors, most notably Iran, agreed to back off and let Iraq solve its problems by itself. Indeed, a senior U.S. intelligence officer in Iraq told a reporter that there were four locations in Iran at which Iraqi Shiites were being trained to assassinate Iraqi judges and other officials.

Marine Col. Tom Greenwood, who had been a member of the critical "council of colonels" that in the fall of 2006 had pushed the Pentagon toward recognizing some hard truths about Iraq, said the surge essentially had papered over the problems of Iraq without solving them. "I still think that the Maliki government is riddled with sectarianism and is dysfunctional," he said in mid-2008, and "that we have de facto partition between the Kurds, Shia and Sunni, that Iraq is little more than an Iranian proxy, that we have destabilized the region worse than Saddam Hussein ever did, that the downward trend in U.S. casualties will be short-lived."

What's more, some of the country's political tensions were worsening, most notably between Arabs and Kurds over oil and the status of Kirkuk. "As Nouri al-Maliki has become more capable and more confident, he's actually become less inclined to reach out to those he most needs to reconcile with," said Colin Kahl of the Center for a New American Security, a Washington think tank. Masoud Barzani, the president of the Kurdish region, charged the Baghdad government with forgetting its commitments and acting like "a totalitarian regime."

Violence had declined much less in Kirkuk than in Baghdad, added Michael Knights, an expert on Middle East defense issues, who dubbed the disputed city "the land the surge forgot."

One White House official worried aloud that there were signs that the axis of the Iraq war was shifting from Sunnis versus Shiites to Arabs versus Kurds. After visiting Iraq in late 2008, Gen. Barry McCaffrey agreed, saying that "the war waiting in the wings is the war of the Kurds and the Arabs." The Kurds also were causing friction in Mosul, where much of the Iraqi army is Kurdish but the majority of the population is Arabic. Significantly, that city, the largest in the north, was the last redoubt of al Qaeda in Iraq, which was able to play on anti-Kurdish feeling with the locals.

Judging by the frustrated mood of officials in Baghdad, it wouldn't be surprising in an Arab-Kurd showdown to see an American "tilt" in favor of the Arabs. "The Kurds have gotten away with everything for the last five years, taking more than they should," Emma Sky, Odierno's political adviser, said that same month. "I think the Kurds overplayed their hand, and we helped them do it."

In August, Maliki seemed to redirect an offensive in Diyala Province, making it less against Sunni insurgents and more against the Kurds. Iraqi troops pushed Kurdish military units northward, provoking the Kurds' Barzani to issue an ultimatum that the Kurds would never give up Kirkuk. "The Iraqi army's campaign in Diyala, ostensibly directed against al Qaeda in Iraq, has turned against Maliki's ruling coalition partner, the Kurds," reported one veteran observer, Joost Hilterman of the International Crisis Group. Baghdad's forces also raided government offices in Diyala, arresting a provincial council member and a university president, a Shiite who was led away in a hood and handcuffs.

The lack of a breakthrough meant that after the last of the surge troops went home, the U.S. military faced essentially the same set of missions, but had fewer troops to carry them out. Some analysts worried that the first task to be curtailed would be the most important one: protecting the population, which also required the greatest use of troops. "I can't see them having all the same missions with less people," said Joel Armstrong, the retired Army officer who helped plan the surge. "All the training and security missions are still there." So, he worried, Iraq would backslide into "a downward spiral." American officials insisted that Iraqi forces could step into the void. That assertion will be tested in 2009, as American troop numbers begin to fall below pre-surge levels.

The surge, while making short-term security gains, also may have carried hidden long-term costs that will only become fully apparent when Obama is president. "The surge may have bought transitory successes . . . but it has done so by stoking the three forces that have traditionally threatened the stability of Middle Eastern states: tribalism, warlordism, and sectarianism," argued Steven Simon, a Council of Foreign Relations expert on the Middle East. If continued, he predicted, the U.S. support for tribes, local militias, and other centrifugal forces will undermine central authority and lead to a divided, dysfunctional sate "that suffers from the same instability and violence as Yemen and Pakistan."

OBAMA IN IRAQ

He arrived in late July, escorted by two senators who are Army veterans, Democrat Jack Reed of Rhode Island and Republican Chuck Hagel of Nebraska. He flew from Kuwait to Basra, where he met with British and American generals. Then it was on to Baghdad.

When Obama walked into the U.S. embassy, Petraeus and Crocker had him where they wanted him: on their turf. This was their chance to answer all the questions he had posed so well during the hearings and not given them a chance to answer. They assembled a huge, extremely detailed briefing and walked the candidate through the Iraq they knew, one where some progress had been made but where it could all fall apart. The meeting went nearly two hours, half an hour longer than scheduled.

"We noted that we didn't have the opportunity to answer [his question] . . . in the dialogue that we had in the hearings," Petraeus said later. The issue for Obama, he said, was "We sought to . . . provide an answer to that question.

And to do that we basically had an executive overview of the joint campaign plan, laid out the lines of operations, supporting activities."

The senators were a bit surprised to be given such a formal briefing, rather than a candid informal conversation. "This was a rare opportunity to have a discussion, not a step-by-step presentation that you would give to a committee or large audience," said one participant who termed the meeting "serious but civil."

It was an oddly contentious encounter, in part because the two men are essentially similar—more cerebral and reserved than their peers, but also lean, focused, ambitious, and extraordinarily successful in their chosen fields. One is a paratrooper who went to graduate school at Princeton, the other a community activist who went to law school at Harvard. Most important, their vision of what America can and should do in Iraq is fundamentally fairly close, with both inclined toward what Petraeus has called a "minimalist" position, a polite way of rejecting the grandiose Bush vision and instead acknowledging that Iraq isn't going to be a stable, quiet, peace-loving democracy anytime soon.

Yet in this meeting, according to two participants, they tended to concentrate on their differences—at least when Obama was permitted to interrupt the lecture. Petraeus made it clear that he strongly opposed Obama's notion of getting all the combat troops out by mid-2010, especially because security conditions in Iraq are always changing. Obama made it clear that his job as president would be to look at the larger picture—an assertion that likely insulted Petraeus, who justly prides himself on his ability to do just that. This is far from over, Petraeus said. Obama responded that it's on the mend, and it's time to divert resources elsewhere.

"We are coming down, but I need the flexibility of not having a timetable," Petraeus responded. The three senators observed that the Iraqis wanted a timetable—and so did they. At that point, Petraeus just looked at them. Some officers around Petraeus found Obama to be so self-confident that they privately referred to him as the "presumptuous nominee."

Obama left the meeting unswayed. Later that day, he said that he understood that Petraeus had "deep concerns," especially about a timetable, but that "my job is to think about the national security interests as a whole and to weigh and balance risks in Afghanistan and Iraq. Their job is to get the job done here."

He also said he wouldn't be "boxed" into either "rubber-stamping" the advice of generals or rigidly following a time line. At a press conference the next day, Obama elaborated on that apparent flexibility, saying that even after combat forces were pulled out, he expected a substantial military presence to remain.

The senators spent the night in VIP trailers behind the embassy. The next day they boarded a Marine V-22 Osprey, which takes off like a helicopter but then tilts its rotors to fly like an airplane, and headed west to Ramadi, where they met with Marine officers and then with the brother of Sheikh Sittar, the tribal chief who had worked so effectively with Col. Sean MacFarland in Ramadi in 2006. Also attending were about 30 other sheikhs, clad in white robes with gold and black trim, as well as some Iraqi officials. "He came to us," Mamoun Sami Rasheed, the governor of al Anbar Province, later said. This was about as big as *wasta* gets—having the future president of the United States haul out to the bank of the Euphrates to explain his views. "He asked many questions," Rasheed continued. "We asked him not to pull out of Iraq." Obama told him that he wanted to get the American combat forces out of Iraq in about 16 months. Rasheed replied that the U.S. military would need to stay at least three more years, because the Iraqi military isn't ready to take over the mission. To that, he said, Obama promised, "The United States will not abandon Iraq."

That last promise may prove decisive in shaping the future of the U.S. effort in Iraq. If Obama keeps it, he almost certainly will have to break his vow to get all U.S. combat units out of Iraq by mid-2010. On the other hand, there is less to that promise than meets the eye. The phrase "combat units" is really meaningless in the context of the Iraq war, where there is no front and where all troops, front line or not, are vulnerable. What the American people care about is whether U.S. troops of any sort are getting killed. Most deaths in the war have been caused by roadside bombs, which don't distinguish between front-line infantry and support units. Indeed, a transport soldier whose mission is to conduct convoys is more likely to get bombed than an infantryman who mainly operates on foot.

Gen. Austin, the number two commander in Iraq, said that his impression was that Obama "really took to heart some of the things we told him." Obama left people in Iraq with the sense he would be flexible and consider conditions on the ground and would be able to adjust his 16-month timetable if he saw the need. In sum, Obama, Bush, Maliki, and Petraeus all seemed to be saying more or less the same thing: We all want the U.S. military out of Iraq eventually, but want to do it in a way that doesn't push the country over a cliff. The long war view appeared to have won.

PETRAEUS OUT OF IRAQ

It has happened to hundreds of thousands of soldiers. Leaving Iraq is a moment of ambivalence. One is pleased to be going home and anticipating a reunion with one's family, but is also conflicted by the nagging sense of leaving in the middle of the fight, with much unfinished business. There is a sense of lightness, of a weight being lifted, followed by a recognition of how much a mental and physical strain it has been to fight in Iraq. When Petraeus got on the airplane to leave Iraq in mid-September 2008, he experienced all these mixed emotions. He and others felt "a quiet pride," he said, "that we helped Iraq step back from the brink of civil war and to essentially go . . . from the brink to the mend." But in his case, the sense of relief didn't last long. "I think there might have been a lifting of the weight for five minutes and then someone started talking about Centcom."

At his new assignment at Central Command, Petraeus would face a new round of troubles, and also would be dealing with a new president who had made it clear that he has strong strategic views of his own. Looming largest before Petraeus was the war in Afghanistan, which is really a war in both that country and Pakistan, with Pakistan the more important part of it, because Pakistan possesses nuclear weapons and remains a hotbed of Islamic extremism. On top of that, the world financial crisis was already beginning to hit Pakistan and threatened to put a new crimp in the U.S. military as America was forced to tighten its belt. In addition, the American face-off with Iran over that country's nuclear ambitions continued to threaten to escalate into a crisis that could change the region. Nor was Iraq going to be resolved anytime soon.

Even before yielding command in Iraq, Petraeus flew to Lebanon. The trip suggested that if no one else had heeded Crocker's concerns about the possible "Lebanonization" of Iraq, he had. He entered Beirut just after a new government was created that gave Hezbollah—an armed militia independent of government control—and its allies 11 of 30 seats in the new cabinet. The visit came as American intelligence analysts in Baghdad were suggesting that the Sadr organization's future course would be to try to become the Hezbollah of Iraq, an armed force outside the government that provides services and also holds great influence over the actions of the government. A major difference between Sadr and Hezbollah is that thus far, Iran has not provided Sadr's militia with Kornet anti-tank laser-guided missiles and the other sophisticated weaponry it is said to have shipped to Hezbollah in Lebanon. Hezbollah used that matériel to great effect in its 2006 war with Israel, fighting the Israeli military to a standstill and gaining *wasta* across the Arab world. If Iran provided such weaponry to its allies in Iraq, it would be escalating the war there significantly, and likely would require the U.S. government to reevaluate its approach to the war and even consider actions inside Iran.

It was a high-profile trip for Petraeus to take as his first move as the incoming chief of Centcom. He insisted it wasn't the harbinger of a more aggressive stance. "This is not a provocative-type initiative," he said, but rather "to get a sense of the situation in a country where Iran has been asserting substantial influence."

The biggest change Petraeus is apt to bring to Centcom is in the handling of Afghanistan, where he likely will reach out to "reconcilable" enemies while trying to isolate and kill those deemed "irreconcilable." The best indication of this isn't anything he has said, but his pick for his deputy at Centcom: John Allen, the Marine general who loved Gertrude Bell, and also had become the de facto American ambassador to Anbar's sheikhs, playing a major role in the turning of the Sunni insurgency in that province.

I'd be surprised if Petraeus remains at Centcom for more than two years. I wouldn't be surprised to see him at some point in the Obama administration, picked to be national security adviser or for another senior national security position. Petraeus wouldn't have to leave the military to move to the White House. For example, Colin Powell did it as an active-duty officer late in the Reagan administration. He said he wasn't interested in writing a memoir. "I am not interested in a sort of rehashing." He cited Gen. George Marshall's refusal after World War II to write an autobiography, even when doing so would have made him a wealthy man. "It would cause some discomfort and I don't have any desire to do that," Petraeus said. Crocker had a similarly clear response: "absolutely not." If they stick to that, one of many oddities of the Iraq war will be that the officials who failed—L. Paul Bremer, Lt. Gen. Ricardo Sanchez, even Lt. Col. Nate Sassaman—will leave behind memoirs while those who were more successful remain officially silent.

SURPRISES AT HOME

When Petraeus got home, he was moved to be invited to the State Department by Condoleezza Rice, who surprised him with an award for distinguished service. He was pleased especially because his time in Iraq had followed a spell in which the State Department and the Pentagon often viewed each other as enemies. He had brought about reconciliation. Always looking for opportunities to teach, he used the occasion to underscore "the importance, the imperative, of unity of effort in endeavors such as the one in Iraq." Crocker also was recognized, but had to accept his medal remotely, because he was still in Baghdad. He had plans to retire in February 2009 and retreat to a hideaway in the high desert of eastern Washington.

After being home for a few weeks, Petraeus grew dismayed that people didn't seem to understand quite how difficult the previous 18 months had been in Iraq, especially for the troops who had implemented the new approach on the streets and in the palm groves of Iraq. In his view, it was a "horrific nightmare" that simply was being forgotten. During the surge, some 1,124 American soldiers had been killed and 7,710 wounded. About another 24,000 Iraqi soldiers, police officers, and civilians were killed, according to an accounting based on news reports.

At about the same time, Odierno was surprised when Bob Woodward's book, published just as he took command from Petraeus in Iraq, credited White House aides and others in Washington with cooking up the surge. From Odierno's perspective—and that of many other senior officers in Iraq—it had been more or less conceived and executed by Odierno in Baghdad, with some crucial coaching from Gen. Keane. "We thought we needed it [the new strategy] and we asked for it and we got it," he said, puzzled that President Bush's aides would present such a different account to Woodward. "You know General Petraeus and I think . . . [that] I did it here, [and] he picked it up. That's how we see it. And so it's very interesting when people back there see it very differently." Of course, he said, ultimately the president had to make the policy decision to do it, and some White House aides encouraged that step. But, he continued, "I mean, they had nothing to do with developing" the actual way it was done, he said. "Where to go, what they [the soldiers] would do. I mean, I *know* I made all those decisions."

Different people have different views. Even so, without question, Odierno hasn't gotten the public recognition he deserves, not only for his role in developing and implementing the surge, but also for his overall adaptation to the Iraq war. If the ability to adjust effectively in wartime is the measure of generalship, then Odierno has come further than any other American general in the war and is as successful as any of them, including Petraeus.

A FRAYED MILITARY

One of the themes of this book is that the U.S. military adjusted as a whole in 2007 making radical, far-reaching, and unexpected changes in its approach to the Iraq war. "I think in the last two years, the Army feels different," observed Lt. Col. Suzanne Nielsen, an aide to Petraeus and a professor at West Point. "It really began to think about outcomes. Before that, it judged itself a lot by processes and inputs." That is, it had been judging its performance by effort expended rather than by results achieved—a metric that tends to waste resources and be counterproductive, often encouraging mindless activity more than insight or patience.

The improvement has come at a cost we can only guess at. This worry surfaces publicly on occasion, but is a major subject of discussion among military leaders. In the short term, there is worry about readiness and about bad actors around the globe thinking that Uncle Sam might be too preoccupied with Iraq, Afghanistan, and a global financial crisis to respond to other challenges. But the deeper and more abiding worry is about the military of ten or fifteen years from now. How long will it take to recover from Iraq? It required years to rebuild the Army and Marine Corps after the Vietnam War, and especially to recruit and train a new cadre of professional non-commissioned officers, the backbone of the American ground forces.

The last few years have seen soldiers burning out after repeated tours of duty in the war, with high rates of posttraumatic stress disorder among combat veterans. Rates of suicide and divorce have been increasing. Officers and sergeants are leaving in greater numbers. Some 50,000 soldiers now have prescriptions for narcotic pain relievers. In one unit, the 509th Engineer Company, based at Fort Leonard Wood, Missouri, about a third of the soldiers were found to be abusing drugs. In another worrisome sign, in the fall of 2008, five soldiers at Fort Carson, Colorado, were suspected in a series of killings after their return from Iraq.

The quality of recruits also has been dropping, with only 70 to 80 percent of new Army enlistees having high school degrees, well below the salad days of the 1990s, when the figure regularly was above 90 percent. (Repeated studies have found that recruits who finish secondary school are much more likely to succeed in the armed forces than are dropouts.) The military also has been admitting more recruits with criminal records, with 511 convicted felons entering the Army in fiscal year 2007. In that year, more than 27,000 "conduct waivers" were issued to troubled recruits by the Army and Marines.

Lower quality recruits also affect how other soldiers perceive their service. In the mid- and late 1970s, the surge in recalcitrant, poorly educated, and ill-disciplined new soldiers deepened the downward cycle of the Army, making some sergeants decide to get out. No one can tell at this point whether that unhappy pattern will again plague the Army.

In recent years many seasoned but still young officers have left the Army, despite the lure of big bonuses to stay in. Lt. Col. Charlie Miller taught at West Point from 1999 to 2002 and knows many of the young officers who are at the point of deciding whether to leave, having served their obligatory five years. "They are just flying out," he said.

What types of captains are getting out? "Almost all of them," said Capt. Liz McNally, another Petraeus aide. That includes her, and most of her friends from West Point, she said. A big part of this decision is the desire to have a normal life, and raise a family, after seeing two or three tours of duty overseas since 2001. Heavy deployments are inflicting "incredible stress" on soldiers and their families and posing "a significant risk" to the military, Gen. Richard Cody, then the Army's vice chief of staff, said early in 2008. "I've never seen our lack of strategic depth be where it is today."

But the nature of the war in Iraq also is causing some to leave the military. As Lt. Col. Ollivant, a key planner in the surge, had noted, during the first several years of the war it was deeply frustrating for younger officers to report to men who had never done what they were doing, and often didn't understand the situation. Until recently, many senior officers did not recognize how ill prepared they had been. The Army could be quite unforgiving of the missteps of younger soldiers, but enormously understanding when it came to much larger mistakes by generals. Captains were subjected to rigorous after-action reviews, but generals, inexplicably, were treated with kid gloves. As Lt. Col. Paul Yingling put it in a widely noticed essay, "a private who loses a rifle suffers far greater consequences than a general who loses a war."

12.
OBAMA'S WAR

(Fall 2008)

When he delivered his victory speech on the night that he was elected president, Barack Obama alluded to the war twice. Both references were telling and, though his powerful speaking style smoothed it over, somewhat contradictory. The first mention underscored his ambivalence about the war. It came in his list of the problems his administration would face, including "two wars"—and then, in a pattern he has shown in the past, he immediately raised a competing domestic need, in this case the difficulty Americans face in paying their bills for health care, mortgages, and college tuitions. The second allusion, less noted, came when the new president-elect was sending explicit messages to the world. "To those who would tear the world down," he vowed, "we will defeat you."

Looming before him that night was the knowledge that upon taking office, he would face an almost immediate dilemma, torn between what his supporters expect and what his generals advise. Newly confident Democrats want him to follow through on ending the war. This was brought home when Gordon Smith, the emotional Oregon Republican who had broken so dramatically with President Bush over the Iraq war, was narrowly defeated in his bid for a third Senate term. Smith was downed by Jeff Merkley, who in his own victory speech gave a hint of the troubles Obama may face in reconciling his goals for getting out of Iraq while defeating terrorism. Merkley was far clearer than Obama was about where he stood on Iraq. "That bold agenda for change involves ending this war in Iraq and bringing our sons and daughters, our husbands and wives, home," he told his followers unambiguously.

Public sentiment is likely to flow in the same direction. "A democratic republic fighting an unpopular war, with limited war aims, for an unlimited time period is a bad combination," commented retired Navy Capt. Rosemary Mariner, an expert on national strategy.

But like Congress, the military has also gone through some major changes recently. Chastened by the performance of its leaders in the first part of the war, the Army is no longer chasing the chimera of "rapid, decisive operations." As Col. Karlton Johnson, an official in the Iraqi training and equipping program, put it one day in the summer of 2008, "We're not looking at doing things fast. We're looking at doing things right." The new president's front-line military advisers, most notably Petraeus and Odierno, are likely to tell him that doing the right thing, including defeating "those who would tear the world down," is going to take much longer than he likes, and with more fighting than he wants.

By the time Obama made that vow in Chicago, the sun already had dawned on a pleasant, sunny, California-like day in Baghdad. There were more soldiers smiling and more black soldiers watching television news than is usual, but it felt much like any other day in the war. Soldiers stood guard duty in watch towers, conducted foot patrols, trained Iraqi counterparts, and piloted Black Hawk helicopters over the city. Some staff officers reviewed details of how to ensure that the Iraqi government paid the Sons of Iraq on those groups' first payday on the Baghdad payroll. (Discussing that exercise, Gen. Jeffrey Hammond, commander of American troops in Baghdad, invoked the film *Jerry Maguire:* "I keep on telling my guys, like that Tom Cruise movie about sports agents, 'Show me the money!'") Long-term planners were looking at the run-up to Iraqi provincial elections at the end of January. It all felt like the previous day—yet the war had changed overnight. It now was effectively Obama's war. It may change him more than he changes it.

Obama indicated during the campaign that he doesn't view Iraq through the lens of Vietnam. "The Vietnam War had drawn to a close when I was fairly young," he said. "And so that wasn't formative for me in the way it was, I think, for an earlier generation." Rather, the Iraq war seems to have taught Obama several lessons, among them to be wary of the unilateral use of force. For all his idealistic rhetoric about hope, he also seems to be essentially a realist about Iraq, willing to limit the American commitment by stating during the campaign that "Iraq is not going to be a perfect place." Yet he also said that as long as the Iraqis made some political progress, he would plan to keep troops there to pursue al Qaeda, protect the embassy and other American personnel, and train and support Iraqi security forces. "I have never talked about leaving the field entirely," he explained. "Nobody's talking about abandoning the field." Rather, he said in a December 2008 press conference, he expects "to maintain a residual force" in Iraq.

Depending on the amount of support provided to the Iraqi forces, the mission as described by Obama could be surprisingly large, requiring anywhere from 25,000 to 50,000 troops.

Military planners have been mulling the shape and size of the "post-occupation" force ever since it became clear in mid-2007 that the surge was working tactically. Such a long-term presence would have four major components. The centerpiece would be a reinforced mechanized infantry division of 15,000 to 20,000 soldiers assigned to guarantee the security of the Iraqi government and to assist Iraqi forces or their U.S. advisers if they get into fights they can't handle. Second, a training and advisory force of close to 10,000 troops would work with Iraqi military and police units. In addition, there would be a small but significant Special Operations unit focused on fighting the Sunni insurgent group al Qaeda in Iraq. "I think you'll retain a very robust counterterror capability in this country for a long, long time," an American official in Iraq said in 2007. Finally, the headquarters and logistical elements to command and supply such a force would total more than 10,000 troops, plus some civilian contractors. Again, this would amount to a long-term commitment in the area of 35,000 troops.

Interestingly, that is about the figure that Gen. Odierno cited in my last interview with him for this book in November 2008. Asked what the U.S. military presence would look like around 2014 or 2015—that is, well after President Obama's first term—Odierno said, "I would like to see a . . . force probably around 30,000 or so, 35,000," with many training Iraqi forces and others conducting combat operations against al Qaeda in Iraq and its allies. To justify such a force, Odierno or Petraeus could read back to Obama the statement the candidate made in July 2008, not long before that trip to Iraq: "My 16-month time line, if you examine everything I've said, was always premised on making sure our troops were safe," Obama had told reporters in North Dakota. "And my guiding approach continues to be that we've got to make sure that our troops are safe and that Iraq is stable." Indeed, they could argue that that last word is overambitious, because it will be a long time before anyone can confidently call Iraq stable.

Obama is likely to find Odierno and other generals arguing passionately that to come close to meeting Obama's conditions of keeping the troops safe, keeping Iraq edging toward stability, and keeping up the pressure on al Qaeda and other extremists, he will need a relatively large force for many years. In addition, they will argue that adhering to any timetable will risk giving up the security gains already made. "Now is not the time to take your foot off the gas," said Gen. Swan. "If you assume the war is won, that would be a faulty assumption. We've got the bad guys down. Don't let them get back up."

Clearly Odierno has been mulling what he will say when he sits down with Obama. Just before the election, Odierno said in my interview with him that one of the points he would make to the new president would be "the importance of us leaving with honor and justice. . . . For the military it's extremely important because of all the sacrifice and time and, in fact, how we've all adjusted and adapted."

For Obama to reject such an argument, made by soldiers such as Odierno who have seen their own children fight and bleed, would risk a confrontation with the military early in his administration perhaps akin to but more contentious than President Clinton's battle early in his first term over gays in the military. Like Clinton, Obama also would face the prospect of a de facto alliance between the military and congressional Republicans to stop him from making any major changes. My bet is that Obama and his generals eventually will settle on what one Obama adviser calls "a sustainable presence"—and that that smaller force will be in Iraq for many years.

A NEW CAMPAIGN

As Obama prepared to take office, Iraq faced its own electoral upheaval, and in its own rough fashion. Elections feel different in Iraq than they do in the United States, where they tend to mark the end of contention. Few outsiders know the politics of Iraq as well as Ambassador Crocker. Asked in November 2008 what one word best describes Iraq, he didn't hesitate: "fear." Among other things, that shapes campaigns and their aftermaths.

In late 2008, a new form of terrorism was becoming popular in Baghdad, using small magnetic "sticky bombs" that were attached to the bottoms of automobiles. The goal of the bomber wasn't mass murder, but rather targeted assassination of individuals. Perversely, this new form of killing was a sign of political ferment. Another round of electoral politics was getting under way, with provincial elections likely in early 2009, and the bombings were effectively a form of Iraqi primary system.

If events go according to the revised schedule devised by the Iraqi parliament—and in Iraq that is a major condition—then 2009 will be the year of elections in Iraq. The first round is supposed to be provincial elections, which have been postponed repeatedly but are supposed to come early in the year. Next comes a round of district voting. Finally, the end of the year may bring national elections.

Americans tend to view elections in Iraq as goals to be reached. In Iraq, they are better seen as tests to be passed. That is, the important thing is not just doing them, but doing them well. The next round of elections, noted Nazar Janabi, an analyst at the Washington Institute for Near East Policy, "marks the beginning of a vital transition that could lead either to a unified democratic country or to a fractured sectarian one that is prone to foreign influence."

Holding fair elections is only the first step. The next question will be whether they are perceived as legitimate, especially if the new parties emerging for the election suspect, rightly or wrongly, that they've been cheated in the counting of votes. Following that will be the issue of whether and how those ousted by the vote give up power. Finally, those elected will have to learn the ropes and begin governing.

Odierno said his major concern is not so much the period leading up to the elections but rather the 60 to 90 days after them. "I still think the major parties will be the people who are successful in the elections. And so what I worry about is those who feel they've had these new movements, how much effect will they gain from these elections? I think it's going to be less than they expect." Significantly, some of those newcomers are leaders of the Sons of Iraq, who not only have local support, but also are a paramilitary force.

A suspicious election could be especially damaging in Anbar, where the turning of the insurgency began. "One particularly ominous aspect of Anbari politics is the continuing influence of high-ranking former regime officials," observed Navy Reserve Lt. Cdr. Jon Lindsay, who served in Anbar Province in 2007–8 and who in civilian life is a political scientist at MIT. If they feel spurned by the electoral process, they have not only alternatives but, Lindsay noted, the means to pursue them. "Considerable Baath resources remain available to support an attempt to regain what they see as their right to govern Iraq."

The rank and file of the Sons of Iraq presents its own problems. Current plans call for only 20 percent of its membership, which peaked at 103,000, to move into the security forces, with the remainder who didn't go into the private sector getting government jobs of some sort. But as Emma Sky noted in late 2008, "These jobs don't exist." This raises the prospect of tens of thousands of armed men, many of them former insurgents, feeling rejected twice by the Baghdad government—first politically and then economically. Sky's hope was that some of the leaders of the militias would be elected and then "be in a position to offer their guys jobs, contracts and bribes." American generals also said that if Baghdad didn't pay the militiamen, they would. But it isn't clear how long they can fulfill that promise, which costs more than $20 million a month.

"These guys will keep their AKs under the bed," Lt. Gen. John Cooper, a British deputy to Petraeus, observed early in 2008. "They haven't come to a moral conclusion that violence is wrong."

Finally, a major destabilizing factor in Iraq in 2009 will be the smaller size of the American military presence. Counterintuitively, the effects of drawing down troops will become more pronounced with the passage of time. When the surge ended in mid-2008, the first areas left relatively uncovered by a U.S. military presence were the safest, most dependable parts of Baghdad. As more soldiers are withdrawn and the U.S. presence falls below pre-surge levels, the pullouts will become riskier. "We've taken on the easy places," Odierno said. "The next ones get tougher because they become the mixed regions and the areas where it is more difficult. So I would say we've kind of taken the low-hanging fruit here in terms of where we've withdrawn our forces. Every decision now gets a bit more difficult." Every decision also may underscore the differences in the views of Obama, on the one hand, and of Petraeus and Odierno on the other.

Current U.S. long-range plans envision radically reducing the U.S. presence in Baghdad beginning in the summer of 2009 and accelerating in the fall and winter. At the same time, a series of volatile elections will be held. By the end of the year, said Odierno, we could enter a time of particular danger. "We'll probably see it a little bit in the summer of 2009 and then, really, at the end of 2009 and 2010 will be the real test probably."

For all these reasons, 2009 could prove to be a particularly difficult year in the war. "In many ways the entire war was a huge gamble, risking America's future power and prestige on a war that, at best, is likely to be inconclusive," commented Shawn Brimley, a former Canadian infantry officer who became a defense analyst at the Center for a New American Security. He predicted that Bush's gamble will force Obama into a series of his own gambles and trade-offs—between the war and domestic needs, between Iraq and Afghanistan, between his political base and his military.

In sum, the first year of Obama's war promises to be tougher for America's leaders and military than was the last year of Bush's war.

EPILOGUE

THE LONG WAR

In 2007, on my way home from my first reporting trip in Iraq for this book, I stopped in Rome and spent a day in its Forum. For all the faults of its governments, Italy feels to me like the most civilized land in the world, and that spirit was something I craved after being in Baghdad. I was looking to get away from thinking about wars in Iraq and the Middle East, which have dominated my life since September 11, 2001. But I found instead that the Forum took me back to those wars. There, at one of the two or three most important sites in the history of Western governance, I was struck that the two triumphal arches that bracket and dominate the Forum commemorate Roman wars not in Transalpine Gaul or Germany but in the Middle East. On the south end, the Arch of Titus, completed in A.D. 81, honors victories in Egypt and Jerusalem. On the north, the Arch of Septimius Severus, built 122 years later, celebrates a triumphant campaign in Mesopotamia. As I walked the foot-polished stones of the Via Sacra, I was reminded of the argument that getting the U.S. military out of the Middle East is simply unrealistic. In this analysis, it has been the fate of the West's great powers for thousands of years to become involved in the power politics of the region, and since the Suez Crisis of 1956, when British and French influence in the region suffered a major reduction, it has been the turn of America to take the lead in the Middle East—though until 2003, the United States managed to avoid becoming enmeshed in sustained ground combat there.

In October 2008, as I was finishing this book, I again was in Rome. I sat on a stone wall on the south side of Rome's Capitoline Hill, after which our own Capitol Hill is named, and again studied the two arches of the Forum. It was a week when U.S. forces had engaged in combat in Syria, Iraq, Afghanistan, and Pakistan—that is, with the exception of Iran, we were fighting in a string of countries stretching from the Mediterranean Sea to the Indian Ocean, following in the footsteps of Alexander the Great, the Romans, and the British. The more we talk about getting out of the Middle East, the deeper we seem to be engaged.

I don't come to this conclusion about being stuck with any satisfaction. Even as security improved in Iraq in 2008, I found myself consistently saddened by the war, not just by its obvious costs to Iraqis and Americans, but also by the incompetence and profligacy with which the Bush administration conducted much of it. Yet I also came to believe that we can't leave.

By the end of 2008, Iraq stood a good chance of becoming America's longest war, passing the American Revolution and even the Vietnam War. As long as U.S. troops are in Iraq, it is likely that some will be dying violently—the all-important difference between Iraq and the many decades of postwar U.S. military presence in Germany, Japan, and Korea. A continuing U.S. mission in Iraq also would continue to drain the U.S. Treasury, strain the military, polarize American politics, and provoke tension with other nations, especially in the Middle East.

Many Americans seem to think that the Iraq war is close to wrapped up, or at least our part in it. When I hear that, I worry. A phrase associated with this war that particularly haunts me is one that Paul Wolfowitz, then the deputy secretary of Defense, used often in the winter before the invasion. "Hard to imagine," he would say. It was hard to imagine, he would tell members of Congress, the media, and other skeptics, that the war would last as long as they feared, or that it could cost as much as all that, or might require so many troops. Wolfowitz's failure of imagination—his flaw of thinking that if he couldn't conceive of something happening, then it didn't merit discussion—did great damage to this country, and even more to Iraq. I worry that now again we are failing to imagine sufficiently what we have gotten ourselves into and how much more we have to pay in blood, treasure, prestige, and credibility. The research of cognitive psychologist Gary Klein has shown that one of the causes of catastrophic failures such as aircraft disasters sometimes is a lack of imagination in assessing a situation. I don't think the Iraq war is over, and I worry that there is more to come than any of us suspect. This is a concern I heard expressed much more often by American officials in Baghdad than in Washington, D.C.

To imagine where Iraq is going, we need to pay attention to where it is and also to what history can tell us. As I was walking in the Forum, Anthony Cordesman, the CSIS defense analyst, was also thinking about those lessons of the past. "History provides countless warnings that states as divided and weak as Iraq is today rarely become stable—much less stable, liberal democracies—without a long series of power struggles," he warned.

What outsiders don't see but many insiders do in examining post-surge Iraq is that a smaller but long-term U.S. military presence is probably the best case scenario. The thought of having small numbers of U.S. troops dying for years more in the deserts and palm groves of Iraq isn't appealing, but it appears to be better than the most likely alternatives, of either being ejected or pulling out—and in either case letting the genocidal chips fall where they may. There also is the alarming possibility that, years after such a pullout, the U.S. military eventually would have to return to fight another war or impose peace on chaos.

Almost every American official I interviewed in Iraq over the last three years agreed that the key ingredient was time. "This is not a campaign that can be won in one or two years," said Col. Pete Mansoor, who was Petraeus's executive officer during much of the general's tour in Iraq. "The United States has got to be willing to underwrite this effort for many, many years to come. I can't put it in any brighter colors than that."

Likewise, at the strategic level, said Maj. James Powell, Odierno's most articulate planner, "the American military is trying to persuade the American people that this is going to take a long time, and we have to be very clear and deliberate in our goals."

The foreign advisers to the American military effort were adamant in their sense that the United States would need to stay in Iraq for a good number of years. "We have to buy time in the U.S. to complete the mission," said Emma Sky. "We have to re-frame the issue for the American people."

One of the lessons of the twentieth century, noted David Kilcullen, the counterinsurgency expert, was that "there has never been a successful counterinsurgency that took less than 10 years." (But, he emphasized, he wasn't thinking about U.S. forces being in combat for 10 years.)

When I asked, few were willing to venture a guess as to just how long the American military might need to stay. One who would was Stephen Biddle, an occasional adviser to Petraeus, who argued that the way forward in Iraq was through hundreds of local cease-fires that eventually might become national, but then would require monitoring and enforcement by U.S. peacekeeping troops. "This mission will be long—perhaps 20 years long," he wrote. But, he continued, it was the best chance the United States had—as long as it didn't try to creep away, and instead resigned itself to keeping more than 50,000 troops there for many years to come.

Sgt. Alexander Lemons, the Marine reservist who fought in Basra, thought an even longer time line would be required. "The surge has done incredible things in Iraq but it is not enough," he wrote after returning home in the summer of 2008. "Change of the sort envisioned by most Americans . . . requires a long-term commitment, for as long as five decades, with enough American forces to assist the unprepared and sometimes lawless security forces while protecting the country's open borders."

AT THE END OF THE RAINBOW?

Nor, at the end of many more years of struggle, is the outcome likely to be something Americans recognize as victory. Instead these additional years of sacrifice promise to be made for markedly limited objectives. A senior intelligence officer in Iraq described the long-term American goal as "a stable Iraq that is unified, at peace with its neighbors, and is able to police its internal affairs, so it isn't a sanctuary for al Qaeda. Preferably a friend to us, but it doesn't have to be." He paused, then pointedly noted that his list doesn't include democracy or the observation of human rights.

That is a surprisingly common view among officials in Iraq, even if it hasn't yet sunk in with many Americans. Few foreigners are as steeped in Iraqi issues as Emma Sky, who is now on her third tour in the country. "The idea that you bring democracy to Iraq and they all become secular, liberal supporters of Israel—well, there are a lot of scenarios I can imagine before that one," she said. "It's not going to end that way."

Another British official in the midst of the American effort was Lt. Gen. Cooper, the top British adviser to Petraeus. In the future, he said, "Iraq is not going to look like the United States. It is not going to look like Western Europe.

The country is violent. It would not surprise me if there were significant bits of violence around the country."

Yet even another 10 or 15 years of struggle might not produce that minimal result. "There's a fifty percent chance of it succeeding in a middling way, and a fifty percent chance of the flaws in Iraqis preventing what needs to be done from getting done," estimated Marin Strmecki, a conservative national security thinker who sometimes advises the Pentagon.

Col. Gian Gentile, who commanded a battalion in Iraq in 2006 and later became a critic of the surge, came to a similar conclusion, arguing that "only a decades-long American occupation can prevent the country from coming apart at the seams."

Even more, many insiders worried that as American influence waned, the Iraqi tendency toward violent solutions would increase. This inclination would be made worse by the American efforts during the surge phase to arm and train the Iraqi army and police while also creating a cohesive, better-trained cadre of Sunni militias. "It's a risk—there is no doubt it's a risk," conceded Lt. Gen. James Dubik, who ran the training and equipping effort in 2007.

John McCreary, a veteran analyst for the Defense Intelligence Agency, predicted in September 2008 that the arrangement imposed by the U.S. government on Iraqi factions would unravel, likely with a Shiite attack on the U.S. presence. The Americans have imposed power sharing on Iraq's factions, he said, and that should worry us for several reasons. First, it produces what looks like peace but isn't. Second, in such situations eventually one of the factions seeks to break out of the arrangement. "Thus," McCreary wrote, "power sharing is always a prelude to violence," usually after the force imposing it withdraws.

That analysis points toward an outcome akin to the battered state of Lebanon. In fact, many of those closest to the situation in Iraq expect a full-blown civil war in the coming years. One colonel who served in Iraq saw that renewed bloodshed as inevitable. "I don't think the Iraqi civil war has been fought yet," he said. "I suspect Sadr is recruiting and amassing weapons and resources for that day we pull down our troop levels to the point where he can make a grab for the seat of power in Baghdad. I'm sure his boys are infiltrating all levels of the Iraqi army and police, and he is smart enough to wait until he realizes we are drawn down to a point where we can't effectively stop him without a massive rebuild of troops, . . . a point where the American public will not stomach another buildup."

Sky, for all her relative optimism in mid-2008, shared that concern. "This country has much more fighting that's potentially there," she calculated one day in Baghdad. "If you look at countries that have been in civil wars, I think it is more than fifty percent fall back into civil war. And that's especially true of countries with great resources—like Iraq."

There also were doubts about the sustainability of changes the Americans had made. Soldiers on the ground tended to be pessimists. "If the Americans leave, the sectarian violence will flare up," Staff Sgt. Jose Benavides told a reporter from the *Christian Science Monitor* after a year of serving in one Baghdad neighborhood.

Skeptics noted especially that the Americans had altered the surface of the country but not its fundamentals. "The emerging U.S. reconstruction project in Iraq increasingly comes across as a colossus with feet of clay," concluded Reidar Visser, an Oxford-educated expert on Iraqi Shiites. "Only Kurdistan is being represented in government by politicians who enjoy widespread popular backing; substantial segments of the Arab population are either being bombed into submission (the Sadrists) or bribed and armed (the Sunnis) instead of becoming genuinely integrated in national politics." So, he argued in an essay that was passed around Petraeus's headquarters, even if the American goal of a democratic Iraq were momentarily realized, it would be unlikely to last. The Iraq that is being built, he said, "is based on an appetite for power and extreme opportunism alone, [so] it cannot survive except through the application of brute force and the use of material power." He predicted a long-term trend toward "increased authoritarianism."

Some insiders agreed, worrying that Iraq was drifting toward a military seizure of power. Kilcullen, who had moved on to advise Eliot Cohen at the State Department, worried that the classic conditions for a military coup were developing—a venal political elite divorced from the population, isolated inside the Green Zone, while the Iraqi military outside the zone's walls grew more capable and also became closer to the people, working with them, finding their local leaders, and trying to address their concerns.

The less the Iraqi generals need American support, the more they might be inclined to take control of the government, so one reason to keep a substantial number of troops there, said Biddle, was to deter them from launching a coup. One nightmare scenario, he noted, leads eventually to a Shiite general who takes over explicitly as a Shiite out to suppress the Sunnis—and who has at his disposal a military and an economy more effective and efficient than Saddam Hussein's ever were. "Imagine an Iraq-Iran axis with their oil wealth, a modern equipped army, in cahoots with each other," he said.

WHAT HAVE WE DONE?

The embrace of former insurgents had created many new local power centers in Iraq, and the faces of those so empowered remained obscure in many places. "We've made a lot of deals with shady guys," said Col. Mike Galloucis, the MP commander in Baghdad in 2007, at the end of his tour. "It's working. But the key is, is it sustainable?"

One of the least understood of those "shady guys" was also one of the most prominent—Moqtada al-Sadr. The U.S. government consistently has underestimated him, first in going into Iraq and then in 2004, when he violently confronted the American superpower. He not only survived those encounters, but also emerged more powerful and was brought into the American-created Iraqi government. If he can stay alive, more power is likely to flow to him, as his two main rivals for Shiite allegiance, Hakim and Ayatollah Sistani, are both old and ill.

Some American officials believe that the United States can live with Sadr, despite his support for Hezbollah, arguing that he is the least pro-Iranian of the likely leaders of Iraq. "Sadr and his group put me in the hospital for sixteen months, so I have a bias," said one American officer who was wounded in an attack by Sadr's militia. "But after talking to his people, I think Sadr is as close as we come to a Shiite nationalist." He said he can live with that outcome.

For reasons of nationalism, if Sadr can be drawn into the political arena, he may effectively become an ally of convenience to the Americans, albeit one who remains closer to Hezbollah. "It should not be forgotten that the Sadrists are Tehran's historical main enemy among the Shiites of Iraq," noted Visser, the specialist in Iraqi Shiism.

Indeed, given that Sadr is more of an Iraqi nationalist than many of the people the U.S. government has supported in Iraq, it isn't clear why the U.S. government holds that diminishing him will restrain Iranian influence in Iraq. "That's the million-dollar question," said Capt. Jeanne Hull, a military intelligence veteran who during 2008 was on her third tour in Iraq, all of them working for Petraeus. She also was almost certainly the only soldier serving in Iraq who was simultaneously doing research for a doctoral dissertation for Princeton

University. She had been assigned to work on Sadrist issues on this most recent tour. "I don't think we've looked at it deeply enough to know if backing the GOI [government of Iraq] is the same as backing Iranian interests."

Others contend that Sadr, working on a longer time scale than the Americans, is just lying low until the United States draws down its troops and declares its combat role concluded in Iraq. Then, this analysis continues, Sadr can launch the civil war he wants. "The reason I am distrustful of Sadr is that we know that in private conversations, he has said, 'There are two million who must die,'" said an Army officer who served in a key position in Iraq. This wasn't hearsay, he said, indicating that it came from an intercept of communications. Another official who also declined to be named said he too had heard of this.

TEHRAN ON TOP?

Americans still don't fathom how the Iraq war is likely to end, Emma Sky said after addressing the CIA conference on Iraq early in 2008. "I expect Iraq is going to ask us to leave," she said. That is, Iraqi leaders no longer would see any utility in keeping U.S. forces on hand, which would permit Iraq's deep-seated xenophobia to roar back in full strength. Once they felt they had amassed sufficient power to survive without American protection, they would kick them out. That expulsion would probably only come when and if the government of Iraq felt secure, both internally and with its neighbors. But it also could develop if the Baghdad government came sufficiently under the sway of Tehran to become a subsidiary of Iranian power—-a situation that would promise long-term instability, both internally and regionally.

The role of Iran remains problematic. At this point it appears to be the biggest winner in the Iraq war, and perhaps in the region—both in the short term and long term. As former Iranian president Muhammed Khatami boasted to the scholar Vali Nasr, "regardless of where the United States changes regimes, it is our friends who will come to power." In other words, all Iran really has to do is stand back and collect its winnings as Iraqi Shiites take power and realize they have few allies in the region aside from Iran.

"Iran's influence will remain and probably grow stronger," said Jeffrey White, a former Defense Intelligence Agency specialist in Middle Eastern security affairs. "As Sunnis become politically and militarily more powerful, Shia political elements will look for allies. The Iranians have many contacts and agents of influence in Iraq, their border with Iraq is a strategic factor of permanent consequence, and their role in the Iraqi economy is growing. Iran does not have an unconstrained opportunity in Iraq, but the situation is strategically strongly in its favor."

What's more, noted Toby Dodge, a British defense expert who was an occasional adviser to Petraeus, "the current Iraqi government is full of Iranian clients. You'll almost certainly end up with a rough and ready dictatorship of three groups that will be in hock to Iran." But, he added philosophically, "that's better than where we were in 2006." To this, Capt. Hull, a more frequent adviser to Petraeus, replied that Gen. de Gaulle took refuge in London during World War II but hardly became a toady to the British and Americans after that war. Indeed, both de Gaulle and Maliki were said to nurse deep resentment over the way their hosts treated them in exile.

A senior U.S. military intelligence officer also was thinking about that sour postwar Parisian point of view. "The best you can hope for is an Iraq strong enough to defend itself but not attack others or be repressive," he said. "And they'll vote against us eighty percent of the time in the UN. They'll make the French look grateful."

One view that attributes a particularly cynical strategy to Iran holds that it wants the U.S. military to stay in Iraq for as long as possible, in part because of the steady drain on American resources, but mainly because as long as American troops are in Iraq, it has a quick and easy way to retaliate against any U.S. action against Iran. That is, the Iranian government may believe that as long as the Americans are in Iraq, they are constrained from striking Iran. Thus the American presence grants near impunity to the Iranian pursuit of nuclear weapons. "I think there's probably a real belief that they have weathered the storm," the same U.S. intelligence officer in Baghdad said one day in 2008. Every indication was that Tehran would wind up with a Shiite-dominated government in Baghdad that it sees as a friend, he noted. "They are very comfortable with the way it's going. They want us out, but gradually."

Cooper, the British general who had watched the Iranians in the south as commander of a multinational division there, agreed with that analysis. "First, they wish to see a Finlandized Iraq in their orbit," he said. "Second, they want us out, but not too quickly, because that could collapse the first aim."

But Rayburn, the regional strategist for Petraeus, warned against simply blaming the Iranians for future setbacks in Iraq. Rather, he said, the Shias of

Iraq, after decades of dispossession, were still bloodily sorting out who among them would wield power and how. The Iranians, he said, "made it worse, more violent—but they didn't cause it."

The wild card in all this is Israel. U.S. commanders worried that if it chose to attack Iran's nuclear installations, the U.S. effort in Iraq would be knocked badly off course, with the possibility again of the nightmare of 2004—twin Sunni and Shiite uprisings against the U.S. presence.

WAITING FOR SADDAM?

For all the worry about Iran, the view of many American soldiers who have served in Iraq is that the biggest threat to American aspirations won't be the Iranians but the Iraqis themselves.

The Iraqi military is getting better, especially in 2008, after its surprising victory in Basra. "Each operation after Basra, we saw incremental improvements," said Brig. Gen. Daniel Allyn, chief of staff for Gen. Austin.

Yet it still is a deeply flawed institution, even with tens of thousands of American soldiers keeping an eye on it. "The Iraqi army is a predominantly Shia institution," said Sgt. Maj. Michael Clemens. "They tend to react to things as Shia first and as soldiers second. . . . We had to remind them that they're an apolitical organization and they couldn't drive around in their Humvees with pictures of Moqtada al-Sadr plastered on the back and their green Shia flags. They couldn't march in support of the Shia tribes during holidays." (Indeed, in mid-2008, as Iraq's political parties began to gear up for possible elections, there were reports of troops tearing down posters publicizing the registration effort in Sunni areas.) Clemens also mentioned, without offering specifics, the case of a commander's bodyguard who also was "in a Shia death squad that runs around at night hacking the heads off Sunnis."

The Americans who should be heeded most on the attitudes of Iraqi commanders are those who saw them up close during tours of duty as advisers to Iraqi units. Some of their accounts should give pause to anyone who sees Iraqi forces as the key to an American exit. Those doubts should extend even to the Iraqi army, which has a far better reputation than the Iraqi national police. Maj. David Voorhies said that he was given "unsubstantiated" statements that Lt. Col. Sabah, the Iraqi commander he advised, had subordinate officers who disagreed with him killed. Voorhies didn't seem to think it unlikely. "You'd probably get a good idea of what it's like to work with him by watching *The Sopranos* or watching *The Godfather* trilogy. He's very persuasive and he leads through fear."

Some American advisers reported that their Iraqi counterparts would candidly say they were just waiting for the Americans to depart so they could revert to their old methods of population suppression. Older officers "would sit and tell us they wanted to go back to the old way underneath Saddam and were just waiting for the U.S. to leave," reported Maj. William Arnold, who in 2007 advised a battalion of the Iraqi 9th Division (Mechanized), a particularly significant unit because it was part of the only armored brigade in the Iraqi army and so would be key to launching a military coup d'état. "We felt that those guys would listen to us just because they were using us as a checkbook."

Maj. Matt Whitney, who spent 2006 advising Iraqi generals, predicted that once U.S. forces were out of the way, Iraqi commanders would relapse to the brutal ways of earlier days:

> Saddam Hussein taught them how to do that [suppress urban populations] and we've just reinforced that lesson for four years. Sad, huh? . . . . These guys think they're the shit and they can do it. They're ready to kill people—a lot of people—in order to get stability in Iraq. They just don't have enough weapons as far as they're concerned. . . . If you think you can leave them in charge and not wind up with a real kinetic solution that would kill a lot of people, you're wrong.

Another adviser, Maj. Stephen Burr, who worked with a major Iraqi military intelligence headquarters in 2006, was even more emphatic. "They're going to be ruthless about it," he warned. "They're not going to be concerned about body counts, they're not going to be concerned about media, and they're not going to be concerned about collateral damage. If it requires leveling the city of Najaf, they will do that. That's what they did after the Gulf War. They have no problem with that. They feel that these things are acceptable losses."

Gen. Odierno said in my last interview with him in November 2008 that he thinks Iraqi commanders have improved and that they no longer will automatically revert to Saddam-era viciousness. "I think two years ago that was true. I think maybe even a year and a half ago it was true. I think a year ago it was a little less true. I think today it's less true." He added that there clearly are still problems and cited that as one reason why the American military presence will be required for some time.

But that hopeful assessment conflicts with the frequent statements of Iraqi commanders themselves. As one Iraqi police chief boasted to an American officer, "one week in his [police] custody was worse than twenty years in prison."

Maj. Chad Quayle, who advised an Iraqi battalion in south Baghdad during the surge, said that he "got consistent answers" from Iraqi officers about the political future of their country. "When you got to know them and they'd be honest with you, every single one of them thought that the whole notion of democracy and representative government in Iraq was absolutely ludicrous."

Or as the police chief in Fallujah had phrased his bottom line after leaving the insurgency to come over to the American side: "No democracy in Iraq. Ever."

If these forebodings are borne out, then unlike in the Saddam era, the United States will bear some of the blame for creating a brutal Iraq run by younger, tougher versions of that dictator, who by the time of the invasion was an aging, almost toothless tiger. What's more, American forces probably would still be in the country, advising and supporting this new Iraqi military and police, but with fewer troops and so less ability to know what is happening on the ground. Capt. Justin Gorkowski, who advised an Iraqi brigade in 2006–7, told the story of a Turkmen Shia police chief who used his pull with an Iraqi general to call an air strike on a Sunni village, as part of his ethnic cleansing work. As it happened, Gorkoswki said, the American gunships, seeing no hostile actions or threats in the village, declined to fire into it. In future such situations, American forces, thinner on the ground and so lacking awareness, might not be able to be so discerning.

HOW DOES THIS END?

So to address the perceptive question David Petraeus posed many years ago during the invasion: How does this end?

Petraeus himself wasn't keen to take on the question. Asked if the gloomy formula once proposed for Vietnam of "eight divisions for eight years" applies in Iraq, he said that it clearly wasn't going to take that many troops. As for duration, he said, "I don't know how long, you can only see so far." But such operations, he said, seeking refuge in vagueness, take "a long time."

I posed the question to several other American commanders and officers in Iraq. Probably the best answer came from Charlie Miller, the member of the Petraeus think tank who did the first draft of policy development and presidential reporting for the general. "I don't think it does end," he replied one day in 2008. "We are going to be in this centrally located Arab state for a long time. There will be some U.S. presence, and some relationship with the Iraqis, for decades." In many ways, this was the best case scenario for Petraeus and those around him, because they saw the alternative as a chaos that could eventually drag the United States into another Middle Eastern war sooner or later. "We're thinking in terms of Reconstruction after the Civil War," Miller added. That may be a historically insightful way to think about the duration of the American presence in Iraq, but it probably is not a good sign politically, given that Reconstruction was a failure, giving rise to the Ku Klux Klan, a terrorist organization that for the next century violently intimidated American blacks and any whites who might seek to help them exercise their civil rights. Nor have Americans signed up for a century-long mission in Iraq.

The American public is unlikely to put up with such a long-term effort, which in turn raises the danger that, as Dodge, the British analyst put it, "America will have bequeathed a highly unstable state to the Middle East and a great deal of suffering to the Iraqi people, for nothing."

No matter how the U.S. war in Iraq ends, it appears that today we may be only halfway through it. That is, the quiet consensus emerging among many people who have served in Iraq is that we likely will have American soldiers engaged in combat in Iraq until at least 2015—which would put us now at about the midpoint of the conflict. "The story of the new Iraq is going to be a very, very long time in unfolding," Ambassador Crocker said one day in 2008.

The heart of the Iraq matter still lies before us, Crocker maintained in both my interviews with him in Baghdad in 2008, and he likely is correct. "What the world ultimately thinks about us and what we think about ourselves," he said, "I think is going to be determined much more by what happens from now on than what's happened up to now."

In other words, the events for which the Iraq war will be remembered probably have not yet happened.

AFTERWORD

THE UNRAVELING

"We are going to bring this war to an end," President Obama, barely a month in office, said in February 2009. Despite what he and many other Americans seemed to think, the war in Iraq wasn't over as that year came to a close. Bombings and deaths declined but hardly stopped, with smaller blasts routinely killing Americans and Iraqis in Mosul, Tall Afar, Ramadi, Fallujah, and Kirkuk, in addition to some spectacular explosions in central Baghdad. In late 2009, there were still 117,000 U.S. troops in Iraq, close to the average American commitment under the Bush administration from 2003 to 2006. The president plans to halve that number during the first six months of 2010, but my sense is that that remains more an aspiration than a certainty.

In July, Col. Timothy Reese, an Army officer based in Baghdad, wrote a memorandum that amounted to a pretty good summary of the state of the politics of Iraq:

> The ineffectiveness and corruption of GOI [government of Iraq] Ministries is the stuff of legend. The anti-corruption drive is little more than a campaign tool for Maliki. The GOI is failing to take rational steps to improve its electrical infrastructure and to improve their oil exploration, production and exports. There is no progress towards resolving the Kirkuk situation. Sunni Reconciliation is at best at a standstill and probably going backwards. Sons of Iraq (SOI)

> or Sahwa transition to ISF [Iraqi security forces] and GOI civil service is not happening, and SOI monthly paydays continue to fall further behind. The Kurdish situation continues to fester. Political violence and intimidation is rampant in the civilian community as well as military and legal institutions. The Vice President received a rather cool reception this past weekend and was publicly told that the internal affairs of Iraq are none of the U.S.'s business.

Caring about the internal affairs of Iraq certainly has become less an American preoccupation, by any measure. To a surprising degree, since the departure of Gen. David Petraeus in September 2008 and his replacement by Gen. Raymond Odierno, the Mesopotamian conflict became a war hiding in plain sight. It was increasingly difficult to track what was happening, because the international media was less engaged, having trimmed its Baghdad presence for two major reasons—first, events there were deemed less newsworthy, and second, because the journalism business was in collapse, under financial pressure even before the Great Recession of 2008 began. A third and lesser reason for the lack of coverage was that even though security had improved somewhat, reporters didn't feel able to move about freely. The violence in Iraq, oddly enough, as a running story had migrated from the front pages to the local sections of newspapers, where it was covered as something that occasionally killed soldiers from a given area.

The result was that large parts of the country seemed to go off the radar screen. It was hard to know what was happening just west of Baghdad in al Anbar Province. There were numerous bombings and attacks on police there, but who was doing them and why was hard to know. In the south, Basra had always been a bit of a mystery during the war but in 2009 became even more veiled. This especially struck me because I suspect that the government of Iran covets Basra more than it does Baghdad. Influence in the capital may be prestigious, but it also promises to be a continual headache as Iraqi factions shift and split. Basra, the biggest city in the south, sitting atop the Persian Gulf, is a more straightforward proposition: Control it and one has a hold over much of Iraq's foreign revenue. And because that money derives from the export of oil, one may also be able to regulate the size of the outward flow of that commodity, which would help Iran's position in the world oil markets.

The U.S. military presence didn't shrink as much as the media's, but its operational presence was sharply curtailed. With the pullback from smaller outposts into big bases, the U.S. Army's feel for the situation seemed to grow less sure. I noticed this not only in official statements but also in e-mails I got from soldiers in the field. One infantry officer wrote to me that during his time in Baghdad in 2009, he was struck by the comment that Ambassador Ryan Crocker made at the end of the hardcover edition of this book, that the events for which the Iraq war would be remembered have not yet happened. "This is quite true," the officer told me, "and the troubling fact is that these events are going on right now and we don't even know what to do about them." In addition, there seemed to be new friction between the U.S. military headquarters and the U.S. embassy, with the soldiers wanting to intervene as they had in the past, but the diplomats arguing that it was time to take American hands off and let Iraq find its own course.

WHITHER SECURITY

So what course is Iraq on? It is possible to be overly pessimistic about Iraq. I made that error in the early spring of 2009, because I thought that the deals that General Petraeus and Ambassador Crocker had cut with Iraqi politicians and insurgents during the surge era were beginning to unravel quickly. My worries peaked in March, when fighting broke out in the streets of Baghdad between "former Sunni insurgents" and Iraqi government forces. During the surge, the Sunni fighters had entered into a cease-fire, not a surrender, keeping their weapons and organizations and even in some cases their areas of operation. After the surge, as the Americans tried to turn over security functions to Iraqi forces, some of these people went back into violent opposition. American units were dispatched to support the Iraqi forces fighting these erstwhile enemies turned allies turned enemies again. This is how the *Washington Post* described one of those springtime confrontations:

> As Apache helicopter gunships cruised above Baghdad's Fadhil neighborhood, former Sunni insurgents fought from rooftops and street corners against American and Iraqi forces, according to witnesses, the Iraqi military and police. At least 15 people were wounded in the gunfights, which lasted several hours. By nightfall, the street fighters had taken five Iraqi soldiers hostage.

Despite such incidents, security didn't deteriorate as quickly as I thought it would, and instead the confrontations between the Sons of Iraq and Iraqi forces tailed off. Then, in late June, when American troops closed outposts in the cities and moved back to big bases, there was a spate of bombings and other violence, with a series of blasts against Christian churches. But again the violence seemed to decline somewhat. Sunni and Shiite militias didn't start re-emerging, as many Iraqis feared—and as I did, having seen Iraq in 2006—when there was a small civil war in and around Baghdad.

Yet much worry remains just under the surface, especially among Iraqis in sensitive positions. As the Americans pulled back, people who had allied with them at the local level expressed alarm. "I never expected we'd come to this point," Hassan Shama, the head of a "district council" in Baghdad's Sadr City, told a reporter. "The U.S. Army and the U.S. Embassy have abandoned us. After six years of very hard work, we're worthless. They call us agents, spies for the Americans." Such fear is noteworthy especially because it is expressed while the American military still maintains a large presence in the country. The apprehension is likely to grow in 2010 if the Obama administration is able to draw down as planned, with more than ten thousand troops leaving every month from spring through late summer.

The best answers of the future of the security situation have been offered in two forward-looking analyses, one by an American, the other by an Iraqi. The first, by Adam Silverman, who in 2008 served as a political adviser to a brigade of the 1st Armored Division on the outskirts of Baghdad, found several indicators that the central government was not taking the steps necessary to bind it to the people. Shiite sheikhs as well as Sunni ones perceived the central government as a subsidiary of the Iranian government. "Even by Shia . . . the members of it are viewed as either Iranian agents or Iranians," he wrote.

Also, Silverman wrote, the central government wasn't providing services, and so was disconnected from the tribes. "The lack of tethering . . . of governmental structures to the most powerful socio-cultural dynamic in Iraq, the tribal system, is worrying." This lack threatened to undo the political gains of the surge era, he warned. "The concern is that unless the population layer, which is tribally oriented, is fully activated and brought into the mix, the hard work, grounded in the COIN [counterinsurgency] reality of empowering the lowest levels . . . will fail." Silverman also concluded that the two groups enjoying broad indigenous support were the former insurgents known as the Sons of Iraq and the Sadrists. These groups—one Sunni, the other Shiite—are bitter foes. Their commonalities are their inclination to use violence and their anti-Americanism. This certainly wasn't where the U.S. government had placed its bets.

The second discussion was by Najim Abed al-Jabouri, the former mayor of Tall Afar, the northwestern Iraqi town that saw the first major successful sustained counterinsurgency campaign in the war. In a different place than Silverman and with a very different perspective, he came to a remarkably similar set of conclusions. In contrast to American views of the Iraqi security forces, or ISF, he wrote, "Iraqi assessments suggest that without separating the ISF from the incumbent ethno-sectarian parties, the ISF will be a tool for creating instability in the country. Iraqis realize that the reasons and justifications for a civil war are still at play in Iraq." In other words, the Iraqi military and police were not a force for stability any more than the politicians were.

A major reason that the army and police were likely to fracture the country, al-Jabouri continued, was that political meddling had created a divisive situation within those forces. "The majority of [Iraqi army] divisions are under the patronage of a political party," he asserted. Unusually, he then listed the political affiliations of various units: the 8th Iraqi Army division in Kut and Diwaniya was heavily influenced by the Dawa party, the 4th Division in Salahudeen was under the sway of Iraqi President Jalal Talabani's Patriotic Union of Kurdistan, the 7th Division was responsive to the Iraqi Awakening Party, and the 5th division in Diyala heeded the Islamic Supreme Council of Iraq. It was as if the U.S. Army's 82nd Airborne cleared its movements with Nancy Pelosi, the 101st Airborne vetted its orders with John McCain, and the 4th Infantry Division was hard-over libertarian or dominated by Texas separatists. Similarly, al-Jabouri added, many of the forces of the Ministry of Interior actually operated beyond the control of that ministry and instead reported to political parties. Officers who blow the whistle on the influence wielded by political parties over Iraqi army units risk losing their personal security guards as well as their jobs, he noted.

Listening to this veteran of the Iraqi military and politics, I think the security situation is worse than it appears from a distance, and the slow unraveling of 2009 is likely to accelerate in 2010 as American's sway wanes and Iraqis vie for post-American power.

IRAN WINS

By contrast, I think Iranian influence, already powerful, will grow. Iran is the big winner in this war, as I said at the end of the hardcover edition of this book. "They have run circles around us since the beginning and now they are really in charge," agreed Alexander Lemons, the Marine sergeant who was unusually involved in Basra and other parts of the south.

It is striking to me how uneasy American officials are about discussing the Iranian role in Iraq. This is not because they know so much that is classified, but rather, I think, because the facts of the matter make them uncomfortable: Iran has been empowered by the American invasion of Iraq and the capture and hanging of Saddam Hussein, who led Iraq in eight years of war with Iran, from 1980 to 1988. The Americans transferred much power in Iraq from the Sunnis to the Shiites, who are not universally allies of the government in Tehran but are certainly closer to it than was the Baath Party.

A veteran Iraqi intelligence official interviewed by *Washington Post* columnist David Ignatius in mid-2009 predicted that in five years, "Iraq will be a colony of Iran."

A few weeks after his first e-mail, that infantry officer who had written to me on his return from a year of fighting in western Baghdad sent me a note that came to the same conclusion. "When I was in Iraq," he wrote,

> I read a bunch of books to include Robert Baer's *The Devil We Know*, which is about Iran's growing influence in the Mideast. Baer's first two sentences in Chapter 2, 'How Iran Beat America,' are: 'Iraq is lost. Iran won it.' Given what we've seen in classified reports and in the revolving door of Iraqi army commanders in select Baghdad neighborhoods, his thesis is spot on. Plus, Shia militiamen have melted into the army and police over the past few years making it much easier for them to create Shia havens throughout the city. It'll be interesting to see where Baghdad is in about 5 years.

Anyone who still talks of an American "victory" in Iraq should be asked to address this question: For many years to come, the government in Baghdad is not likely to be stable or very democratic, but almost certainly it will be closer to Tehran than to Washington. What part of that constitutes success for the U.S. government?

2010: HOW THIS DOESN'T END

The national elections scheduled for early in 2010 will tell us a lot about Iraq's direction, especially in the two to three months after the actual voting. One of the most acute observers of the Iraq war, British defense analyst Toby Dodge, notes that it is clear in retrospect that the national elections of 2005 "actually hastened Iraq's descent into civil war." An additional complication will come if, as is widely expected, Defense Secretary Robert Gates steps down in late spring 2010, depriving the Obama administration of its only top official who has dealt closely for several years with the intricacies of the situation.

In stable countries, elections tend to be the end of contention and the beginning of compromise. That isn't the case in Iraq, where there tends to be a "winner take all" mentality. This is how *New York Times* reporter Alissa Rubin put it recently as she left Iraq after years of living in Baghdad:

> . . . Army checkpoints—legal ones—are the only ones that stop you, but huge posters of Imam Ali punctuate the streets, a signal that this is now Shiite-land. Imam Ali is revered as a founder of the Shiite branch of Islam, but a poster of him is also a silent rebuke to Sunnis, a way of marking territory, of reminding them that the Shiites run things now. It is a sign of victory as much as peace.
>
> And victory in Iraq almost always begets revenge.
>
> In my five years in Iraq, all that I wanted to believe in was gunned down. Sunnis and Shiites each committed horrific crimes, and the Kurds, whose modern-looking cities and Western ways seemed at first so familiar, turned out to be capable of their own brutality.

I thought about this observation when a small firefight broke out in Baqubah between Iraqi soldiers and police officers in November 2009. It was a minor, murky affair, and I couldn't determine what provoked it. But I wondered if it was a portent of the Iraq of 2010. A few weeks later, when thirteen people affiliated with an Iraqi political leader in eastern Anbar province were murdered, the vice president of Iraq charged that the slaughter had been carried out by Iraqi soldiers.

President Obama's troop withdrawal plan will be hostage to the behavior of Iraqis during the aftermath of the election. It is possible that things will go quietly—after all, they went better in the spring and summer of 2009 than I thought they would. If Iraq indeed is quiet in 2010, then the American pullout likely will be able to proceed as planned, with a swift drawdown in the first half of the year. But if Iraq reverts to form and the security situation appears to be unraveling quickly, then it will be difficult to maintain pace of the planned pullout. That would be doubly difficult for American policymakers because it likely would mean that there aren't enough troops available for the parallel and intensifying effort in Afghanistan.

It would be even tougher for Iraqis. As one longtime observer, Joost Hiltermann of International Crisis Group, put it,

> . . . just as Odierno will be pulling out his first combat brigades, starting in March, Iraq will be entering into a period of fractious wrangling over the formation of a new government. If Iraqi national forces fail to impose their control, an absence of political leadership could thus coincide with a collapse in security; if politicians and their allied militias resort to violence, the state, including its intelligence apparatus so critical for maintaining internal stability, could fracture along political, ethnic, and sectarian lines.

For those reasons, I suspect 2010 may come to rival as a turning point two earlier times in this war—2003, when the invasion occurred and gave rise to an insurgency, and 2007, when the American military finally became effective in its operations in Iraq.

The basic problem facing Iraq is that all the problems that have divided Iraqis for many years are still hanging fire, unresolved and threatening to lead to renewed fighting. Pessimists argue that Iraqi politicians have learned how to use this turbulence to further their own goals. "Perhaps the biggest challenge," warned security analyst Michael Eisenstadt,

> is that key political parties have successfully exploited ethnosectarian grievances as a means of mobilizing support. These parties have a vested interest in perpetuating the political status quo and would stand to lose a great deal if a post-sectarian style of politics in Iraq were to emerge as a result of a successful reconciliation process.

In other words, they now have a stake in perpetuating violence and tradition. Peace and stability threaten their positions of power and influence. So the real question, I think, is not whether there will be violence in Iraq for many years to come, but how severe the violence will be, and how disruptive to neighboring countries.

So, to once more evoke General Petraeus's famous question during the invasion of Iraq about eight years ago, *How does this end?* I think the question was best answered over the last year by his successor as the top American commander in Iraq, Gen. Odierno, who said one day in Baghdad that

> it's not going to end, okay? There'll always be some sort of a low-level insurgency in Iraq for the next five, 10, 15 years. The issue is, what is the level of that insurgency? And can the Iraqis handle it with their own forces and with their government? That's the issue.

That indeed is the issue, and is the reason that we are likely to see tens of thousands of American soldiers in Iraq for many years to come. The U.S. government may say they are not combat troops, and we may not pay attention to them. But they will be there.

APPENDIXES

These four documents capture key points in the American approach to the Iraq war during late 2006 and early 2007.

The first is the conclusion in August 2006 of Col. Pete Devlin, the senior Marine intelligence officer in Iraq at the time, that al Anbar Province had been lost.

The second is the mission statement Lt. Gen. Odierno received from Gen. Casey upon becoming the number two officer in Iraq in December 2006.

The third is a briefing Odierno gave to Gen. Petraeus two months later and represents almost a complete reversal of what Casey had told Odierno to do.

The last is Petraeus's summary of how to fight in Iraq. It is dated June 2008 but captures the changes in the tactics and disposition of U.S. forces that began 18 months earlier.

A. COL. DEVLIN'S INTELLIGENCE ASSESSMENT

State of the Insurgency in al-Anbar
I MEF G-2
SECRET//REL MCFI//20310816

17 Aug 06

General Situation: As of mid August, 2006, the daily average number of attacks exceeds 50 per day in al-Anbar Province. This activity reflects a 57% increase in overall attack numbers since I MEF assumed control of the province in February. Intensifying violence is reflected in the preponderantly negative outlook of the Sunni population, in the continuing inability to develop adequate Iraqi security forces, and in the near complete failure of reconstruction and development projects across western Iraq. *The social and political situation has deteriorated to a point that MNF and ISF are no longer capable of militarily defeating the insurgency in al-Anbar.*

Social Collapse: Underlying this decline in stability is the near complete collapse of social order in al-Anbar. The tribal system has wholly failed in AO Raleigh and Topeka, and has only limited efficacy in AO Denver. Prominent leaders have exiled themselves to neighboring Jordan and Syria, including some leading imams. Despite the success of the December elections, nearly all government institutions from the village to provincial level have disintegrated or have been thoroughly corrupted and infiltrated by al-Qaida in Iraq (AQI) or criminal/insurgent gangs. *Violence and criminality are now the principle driving factors behind daily life for most Anbar Sunni;* they commit violence or crime, avoid violence or crime through corruption and acquiescence, or become victims.

Isolation from Baghdad: Already embroiled in a daily fight for survival, al-Anbar Sunni have little hope for national reconciliation or re-integration into the national polity. From the Sunni perspective, their greatest fears have been realized: Iran controls Baghdad and Anbaris have been marginalized. True or not, this paranoia directly undermines Sunni willingness to envision a unified Iraq under the current structure. These fears also are reinforced by actions of the Shi'a-dominated government, including the failure to pay ISF in al-Anbar, attacks by official Shi'a paramilitary groups against Sunni civilian targets in Baghdad, the unwillingness to confront the Jaysh al-Mandi, bureaucratic attacks on popular Sunni political and military leaders, and minimal support for local government institutions and initiatives from Ramadi to al-Qa'im. This sense of isolation directly undermines Sunni willingness to work within IG and MNF defined social and political boundaries.

Lack of Resources: Although recent reports appear to confirm the presence of natural gas and some oil reserves along the western Euphrates river valley, there is no prospect for exploitation or development of these resources in the foreseeable future. In the absence of security, even the most aggressive investors are unwilling to risk an al-Anbar venture. Wealthy expatriate Ba'athists talk a strong game of support from Amman and Damascus, but have been unwilling to reinvigorate the al-Anbar economy from their accounts. The only resource that matters - oil - is in the hands of the Shi'a government. From the Sunni perspective, oil is the source of real power in Iraq. With oil money comes government largesse, structured public investment, personal position, and cronyism. Because they lack faith in the political system, many Sunni see the only way to regain control of Iraqi oil is through violence. This sentiment directly feeds the insurgency and is used to justify violent criminal behavior. Anbaris have begun overtly to blame the province's inadequate resource allocation, from the national power grid, for example, to sectarian motivations in Baghdad ministries.

Al-Qaida in Iraq: AQI is the dominant organization of influence in al-Anbar, surpassing nationalist insurgents, the Iraqi Government, and MNF in its ability to control the day-to-day life of the average Sunni. Transitioning to a primarily Iraqi organization in late 2004, *AQI has become an integral part of the social fabric of western Iraq.* With this "I Iraqification" came devolution to low-level, semi-autonomous, and criminally financed cells of varying loyalty to the larger AQI organization. While this diffusion has weakened the original Salafi zeal of AQI writ large, it has eliminated the opportunity for a decapitating strike that would cripple the organization - this is why the death of Zarqawi had so little impact on the structure and capabilities of AQI, especially in al-Anbar.

AQI effectively has eliminated, subsumed, marginalized or co-opted all nationalist insurgent groups in al-Anbar. This very deliberate AQI campaign against rival insurgent groups began shortly after national elections in December 2005, when nationalist insurgent groups cooperated to prevent AQI from disrupting polling throughout al-Anbar. Faced with this blatant challenge to their hegemony, AQI destroyed the Anbar People's Council of Mohammed Mahmoud Latif through a highly efficient and comprehensive assassination campaign, thereby eliminating the sole rival nexus of insurgent leadership in al-Anbar. Following this calculated purge, AQI cunningly employed their greater financial resources, superior organization, proven leadership, and brutal tactics to consolidate their hold on most other nationalist insurgent cells in al-Anbar. Parallel to this effort, AQI enacted a tactical alliance with the small Ansar al-Sunna cells operating in some parts of al-Anbar, particularly in the Haditha Triad.

Al-Anbar Sunni now see an entrenched, Iraqi AQI that in some cases has taken on the mantle of nationalism, or more recently, "defender of the faithful" against the Iranian-backed Shi'a. Although most al-Anbar Sunni dislike, resent, and distrust AQI, many increasingly see it as an inevitable part of daily life and, in some cases, their only hope for protection against a possible ethnic cleansing campaign by the central government.

The remaining core of AQI Salafists retain the capability to guide the organization in broad terms; they can shift resources, fund specific groups, and mass combat power for short "campaigns" by pulling in disparate cells from across western Iraq. The zeal of the vanguard remains relatively intact - there can be no realistic expectation that AQI will negotiate with the IG or MNF short of accepting absolute surrender and ascension to power. The perceived indecisiveness and moral weakness of both the IG and MNF directly feed the resolve of AQI, as well as the grudging acceptance of AQI by the populace. As long as the status quo between the central government and the al-Anbar Sunni remains, AQI is an intractable problem.

Sunni Outlook: From the al-Anbar Sunni perspective, there is little hope that the status quo will lead to a better future. The economy in western Iraq provides bare sustenance to the average citizen while enriching criminals, insurgents, and corrupt officials. The potential for economic revival appears to be nonexistent. Violence and fear are the dominant factors in daily life, reinforcing a predilection for survival behavior nourished under the sanctions period. This behavior in turn feeds criminality and corruption and undermines faith in government institutions.

Increasingly, there appears to be little chance for national reconciliation with the Shi'a. Deep-seated fears of Iranian domination have been realized and embodied in the central government. Although more trust has been placed in MNF to protect and support the average citizen, there is little hope that American troops will remain long enough to provide true stability. Faced with the prospects of an increasingly brutish future, there is every reason to support the insurgency.

Tactical and Operational Considerations: The Sunni outlook underlies the dramatic increase in attacks since February. However, several tactical and operational considerations have contributed to the rise in violence. Despite some success in isolated areas of the province, the insurgency has strengthened in the past six months. Insurgent groups are better organized, increasingly achieve effective operational security, have improved their capabilities to cache and distribute weapons, and have refined and adapted their tactics. Control of criminal enterprise means the majority of insurgents are now financially self-sustaining at the lowest levels. Broad control of the illicit oil trade from Bayji provides millions of dollars per year to AQI, while official profits appear to feed Shi'a cronyism in Baghdad.

With the slight increase in MNF and ISF units operating across al-Anbar, there is more presence in insurgent-dominated terrain; increased presence provides an increase in targets and opportunity. Continuation of the mass prisoner release program feeds the cycle of recidivism across western Iraq, repopulating insurgent groups at regular intervals and preventing tactical progress against their force structure. Although it is likely that attack levels have peaked, *the steady rise in attacks from mid-2003 to 2006 indicates a clear failure to defeat the insurgency in al-Anbar Province.*

Way Ahead: Barring the deployment of an additional MNF division and the injection of billions of dollars of reconstruction and investment money into the Province, there is nothing MNF can do to influence the motivations of al-Anbar Sunni to wage an insurgency. Federalism provides a possible solution:

–Federalism is legally possible under the current constitution. Creating a successful federated Sunni state in al-Anbar would require considerable political and legal wrangling by a unified political block.

–A federated state might provide the Sunni of western Iraq with the general sense of "buy-in" lacking under the centralized, Shi'a-dominated government. This in turn may tempt expatriate Anbari elites, exemplified by the Central Council of al-Anbar, to return to the province or at least increase their support and involvement in al-Anbar economic development.

– Successful federation, providing al-Anbar with a specified and locally controlled budget, could lead to a broad revival in Ramadi. This would in turn necessitate the formation of effective local governments to appeal to the Governor for resources.

– Although a centralized budget carries considerable temptation and risk in such a corrupt and criminal environment, ownership of the budget might encourage an increase in local responsibility and accountability in Ramadi.

– In Iraq, all politics are local, and local politics and government in al-Anbar is anemic or dysfunctional due to insurgent intimidation - Fallujah being a notable exception. That many local officials remain in office despite threats from insurgents and little support from Baghdad is a testament to their resilience and forbearance. This natural impetus to create effective government at the local level will help address a wide range of social and economic problems that feed the insurgency. Unlike a MNFsponsored government, a self-generated government with a real and accountable budget holds promise for long-term success.

– Al-Anbar potentially could control a sizeable and legally approved paramilitary force, offsetting the fears of Iranian domination or Shi'a pogroms. This force would have a better chance of encouraging local recruitment than a national, Shi'a-dominated military force likely to station Sunni recruits far from their homes.

– Despite a vicious insurgent intimidation campaign, the Iraqi Police in al-Anbar have proven remarkably resilient in most areas, especially when they can rally around an effective leader. When fully formed and properly supported, the Iraqi Police can pose a credible challenge to AQI in al-Anbar.

However:

– Currently, there is no unified Sunni political block interested in establishing a federal state in al-Anbar. The majority of Sunni politicians vocally oppose federalism, primarily based on the fear of economic/budgetary isolation.

– Federalism brings with it a host of potential social problems, including forced migration, sectarian cleansing, and the very real chance of national isolation.

– Iraqi federation could spark a wider conflict between Iran and Sunni Arab countries and interests within the MEF Area of Interest.

– Despite recent friction, there is very little long-term, grass roots friction between Iraqi Sunni and Shi'a. Most al-Anbar Sunni see Iran, not the Iraqi Shi'a, as their most pressing threat. At a visceral level, many Anbaris may not support federalism based on sectarian considerations.

– Federalism will not eliminate AQI or immediately address most of the underlying social issues that feed the insurgency.

Final Consideration: The insurgency in al-Anbar and the suffering of al-Anbar citizens undoubtedly would be far worse now if it was not for the very effective efforts of MNF operations. That we cannot end the insurgency in al-Anbar within the present political conditions is not an indication that our efforts have not had a very real suppressive effect on the insurgency.

B. THE ORDERS LT. GEN. ODIERNO RECEIVED IN DECEMBER 2006

Transition Bridging Strategy

Concept and Background Slides (Dec 06)

1

Adjusted Mission Sets Throughout Iraq

Shift in Approach.

- **Phased handover of all Projects, funding, and Governance to GOI**
- **Continue to support PRTs**
- **GOI takes the lead in engagements from national to NAC/DAC levels**
- **CJSOTF shifts focus to the FID portion of their current mission set**

Shift Combat Power.

Speed up Transition of Security Responsibility through…

- **Increased Manning for Transition Teams that are tailored for survivability (~1x Bn +/-)**
  - **24/7 coverage for training and visibility**
  - **Route Clearance by region**
- **Dedicated forces on the periphery controlling areas to deny AIF approaches and support areas (~1x Bn +/-)**
- **CF deployed to the Borders to disrupt external influences -- support BTTs (~1x Co +/-)**
- **CF Bns as dedicated Strike Force to action insurgent targets or support OCF-I in defeating AQI**
- **IA and NP handle insurgency closer to urban areas w/ CF enabler/QRF support**
- **CF Brigade Enables - Oil and Electrical Infrastructure security and SIB training**

Military | **Non-Military** | **Military**

TRAINING
- IA
- IP
- NP
- DBE
- LOG

Building Security Capability

Local Governance
Engagements
Nation Building
Rule of Law
SWETF

COUNTER INSURGENCY
- Defeat AQI
- Border Security
- Infrastructure
- Strike Opns

Combat Opns & Enabler SPT

Footprint:

- **Move Outside all Major Cities**
- **Positioned to prevent interference of Iraqi Self-Determination by disrupting external influences**
- **Establish consolidated FOBs along LOCs**
- **Establish Smaller FOBs Mission Set --- Borders, Infrastructure and Convergence of routes into Iraq**
- **"Control" MSRs and designated ASRs**

MNC-I (V Corps) Concept Slide Summarizing Transition Bridging Strategy (briefed 4 Dec 06)

2

Background

Rationale for Accelerating the Transition of Iraqi Security

- Sectarian violence in Iraq is impeding reconciliation
- Iraqi security challenges require an Iraqi solution
- ISF improving but not yet able to neutralize the sources of sectarian violence
- PM has expressed a desire to expedite the transfer of security responsibilities
- Acceleration of ISF assumption of control will enable transition to self-reliance and is in the best interest of both the Iraqis and the Coalition
- Without tangible progress toward reconciliation, stabilization, and transition, achieving the MNF-I endstate is at risk

MNC-I Slide Summarizing MNF-I Strategic Directive
(Accelerating Transition of Iraqi Security, 5 Dec 06 [draft])

3

MNF-I Mission and Intent

- **MNF-I Mission** (no change from 2006 JCAP, 9 Jun 06)
  – US Mission and Coalition Forces will, in partnership with the GOI, contribute to an environment where Iraqis can develop representative and effective institutions capable of meeting the needs of the Iraqi people, creating the conditions for the Rule of Law, defeating the terrorists and irreconcilable insurgents, bringing other insurgents into the political process, reducing sectarian tensions and denying Iraq as a safe haven for terror
- **Intent**
  – Purpose: To enable the accelerated transition of Iraqi security
  – Approach: "Bridge" the ISF capability gap between what currently exists and what is needed to transition security responsibility to the GOI
    - MNF-I will prepare the ISF to assume the lead more rapidly by enhancing transition teams, providing capable enabling functions, and building capacity in the national security ministries
    - Improvements in ISF execution to standard should come at a more rapid pace under closer and more detailed coaching, teaching, and mentoring by MNF-I; the same approach applies at ministerial level
    - This shift in operational approach acknowledges that there is a finite amount of time available
  – Endstate: Legitimate ISF are the dominant security forces in Iraq; CF are positioned to interdict irreconcilable groups that threaten Iraqi self-reliance; ISF have control in Baghdad and the nine key cities; the GOI is in control of national security, supported by CF

MNC-I Slide Summarizing MNF-I Strategic Directive
(Accelerating Transition of Iraqi Security, 5 Dec 06 [draft])

4

Concept of Operations

- MNF-I shifts its main effort to supporting the ISF and Border Forces
- Baghdad the primary focus
- IOC – 1 Jan 07; FOC – 31 Mar 07
- Key tasks include:
  - Repositioning to the periphery of urban areas, following a deliberate process of handing over battlespace to the IA
  - Continuing to provide required enabling logistical support and QRF capability to the ISF (with eventual transition to GOI)
  - Methodically handing over responsibility to the ISF for the apprehension of criminals, SWETF projects, guard forces for gov't buildings and facilities, and the development of gov't capacity at provincial and city levels
  - Gaining GOI concurrence on:
    - The bridging endstate
    - MNC-I's bridging operational concept
    - The transition from the Baghdad Security Plan, Phase II to the ISF
    - The division of responsibility for security between MNF-I and the GOI
    - The transfer of infrastructure development and security to the GOI
  - Supporting the GOI in the implementation of a reconciliation plan
  - Controlling MSRs and ASRs
  - Contributing to an interagency effort that more rapidly addresses ROL issues
  - Defeating AQI by summer 2007

MNC-I Slide Summarizing MNF-I Strategic Directive
(Accelerating Transition of Iraqi Security, 5 Dec 06 [draft])

5

C. HOW ODIERNO CHANGED THE MISSION

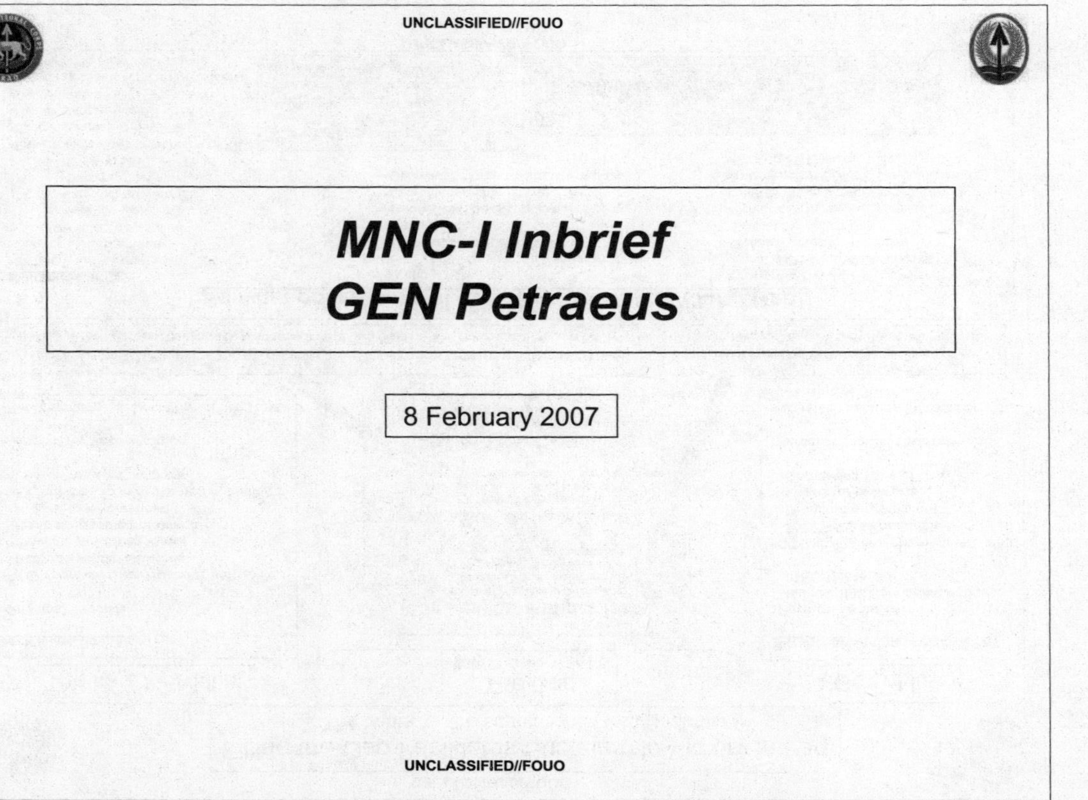

UNCLASSIFIED//FOUO

Filling the Gap Facilitates Sustainable Victory in Iraq

The battle for the population of Iraq/Baghdad

The Iraqi Individual

Needs and Desires:

- **Physical Security**
- **QOL improvements-Hope for better life**
  - **Basic Essential Services**
  - **Sewage and Clean Water**
  - **Honorable job-employment**
  - **Rule of Law--balanced**
  - **Expectation to improve home, family, neighborhood, society**
- **Respect for Tribe/Religion**
- **Representation in Local/Provincial Govt.**

The Gap

Who is going to fill it?

Shia militia and parties?
Power and historical revenge
Sectarian EJKs/Cleansing
EFPs Against MNC-I forces
Internal power stuggles (BADR/JAM)

Iraqi Sunni Resistance?
Return to Power
Protection from Shia Revenge
Co-location/Support with AQI, but tiring of tactics

AQI and the Caliphate?
First step in safe-haven for Regional Caliphate
Foreign Fighters and Terrorists
High Profile attacks (SVIED, VBIED)

Gov of Iraq

Slowly developing capability for:

- **Physical Security**
  - **Issues of ISF actions/inaction**
  - **ISF Loyal to GoI**
- **QOL improvements minimal, need**
  - **SWET-F advancement**
  - **Dignified employment**
  - **Loans for enterprise**
  - **Consistent Rule of Law**
- **Perceived as Shia biased**
- **No representation in Local or Provincial Govt**

External Influences

Syria--Safe Haven/Source of support for Sunni Insurgents

Iran--Influence in Iraqi (Shia) affairs, keep US engaged

This is the historical fault line betwenn the Arab Sunni majority and the Persian Shia minority--Arab Sunnis are nervous, and Persian Shias are optimistic.

So what do we have to do? Get the GoI to fill the Gap!!

Military/Security
- Iraqi led, CF support--Joint Plan
- Control COG-Baghdad
  - Protect population
  - Reduce violence
  - Interdict accelerants
  - Balanced targeting approach
  - Expand MiTT, NPTT
- Enhance capability/legitimacy of ISF
- Exploit success in MNF-W
- Exploit transition to ISF in MND-N
- Transition to ISSR in the South
- Disrupt border infiltration (Iran/Syria)
- Transition to Iraqi self-reliance

Political
- GoI & USG similar goals and endstates
- Local and Provincial Elections
- Reconciliation policy
- Reasonable de-Baathification Policy
- Consistent and balanced Rule of Law
- Declared/enforced State of Emergency

Economic
- Expand Oil & Electricity sectors
- Release funds to Provinces
- Budget expended
- Synch with mil control of secure areas
- GoI/US synch economic devel effort
- Investment in SOEs & Other industries
- Expand PRTs-link to mil success

Opportunities
- Door for Sunnis to participate in GoI
- Split between Sunni tribes and AQI
- Splits between Shia factions
- Population weary of conflict

Risks
- ISF not capable of "retain"
- GoI unwilling to put Iraq ahead of political/sectarian impulses
- GoI unable to provide political/economic follow-up to security

UNCLASSIFIED//FOUO

UNCLASSIFIED//FOUO

The Threats and Their Objectives

The term AIF is not adequate to describe:

1. Shia vs. Sunni Sectarian Violence
2. AQ and AQI
3. Sunni Insurgency
4. Kurdish expansionism
5. Shia on Shia Violence
6. External influences (Iranian, Syrian and Turkish)

UNCLASSIFIED//FOUO

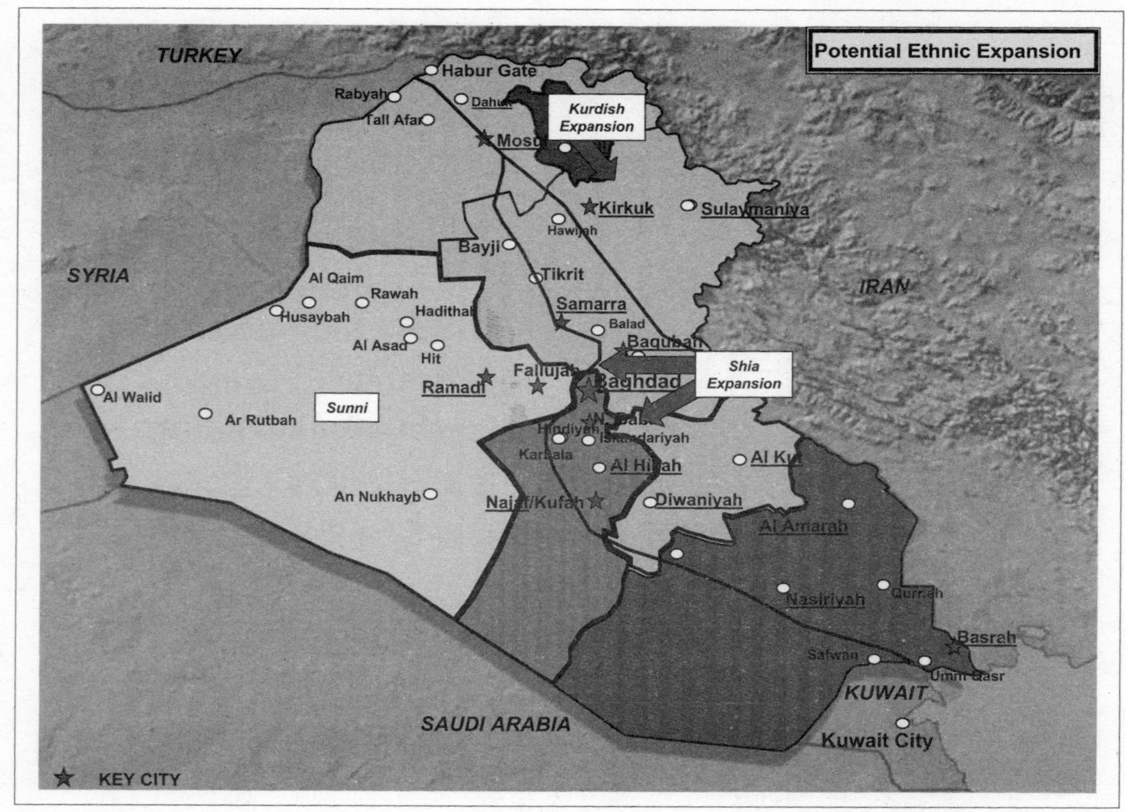
Potential Ethnic Expansion
TURKEY
SYRIA
IRAN
KUWAIT
SAUDI ARABIA
Kurdish Expansion
Shia Expansion
Sunni
Habur Gate
Rabyah
Tall Afar
Kirkuk
Sulaymaniya
Hawijah
Bayji
Tikrit
Samarra
Balad
Al Qaim
Rawah
Husaybah
Haditha
Al Asad
Hit
Ramadi
Baghdad
Al Walid
Ar Rutbah
Karbala
Al Hillah
Diwaniyah
An Nukhayb
Najaf/Kufah
Al Amarah
Nasiriyah
Basrah
Safwan
Kuwait City
KEY CITY

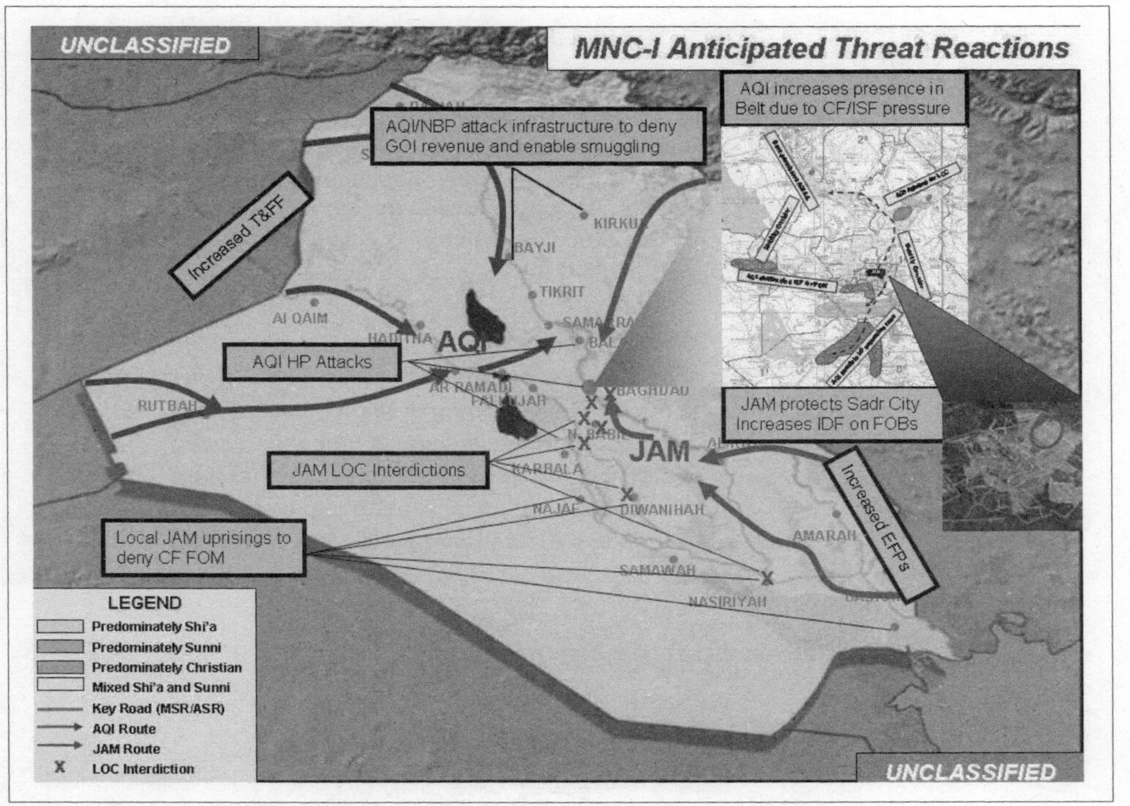
UNCLASSIFIED
MNC-I Anticipated Threat Reactions
AQI increases presence in Belt due to CF/ISF pressure
AQI/NBP attack infrastructure to deny GOI revenue and enable smuggling
Increased T&FF
KIRKU
BAYJI
TIKRIT
AI QAIM
AQI
AQI HP Attacks
AR RAMADI
BAGHDAD
RUTBAH
JAM protects Sadr City Increases IDF on FOBs
JAM
JAM LOC Interdictions
KARBALA
Increased EFPs
NAJAF
DIWANIHAH
Local JAM uprisings to deny CF FOM
AMARAH
SAMAWAH
NASIRIYAH
LEGEND
Predominately Shi'a
Predominately Sunni
Predominately Christian
Mixed Shi'a and Sunni
Key Road (MSR/ASR)
AQI Route
JAM Route
X LOC Interdiction
UNCLASSIFIED

UNCLASSIFIED//FOUO

The Operational Concept

<u>The Goal</u>: A stable Iraq (peaceful, united, representative, secure)

Key reads:

- Recognize there are different threats in different areas
- Realization that there is an ethnic problem
- Understanding sub-agendas of multiple groups/actors
- Each area requires multiple approaches based on multiple threats
- The Greatest Threat to Stability is escalating Sectarian Violence
- The Greatest Sectarian Violence is occurring in Baghdad, Baghdad Belts

Key requirements:

- Can not let Sectarian Violence continue at current rate, or increase
- Stop displacement of population, particularly in Baghdad
- Main effort-establish security in mixed Sunni and Shia areas-protect against Shia intimidation/displacement/violence against Sunni
- Supporting efforts-maintain security in Shia areas-protect against AQ accelerants and Sunni reprisals

UNCLASSIFIED//FOUO

UNCLASSIFIED//FOUO

The Operational Concept

Approach to different Threats:

Threat	Approach
Sectarian Violence	**-Establish combined CF-ISF security**
	-Ensure even-handed CF-ISF actions in the streets
	-Replace militias as the recognized security element
	-Promote political/national reconciliation
	-Separate factions
	-Broker cease fires
	-Counter extremists and accelerators to violence
AQ and AQI	**-Seek out and Destroy**
Sunni Insurgency	**-Bring them into the Political process**
	-Defeat those not reconcilable with a legitimate GoI
Kurdish expansion	**-Persuade Kurds not to over-reach (issues with Turks and Sunni Arabs)**
External Influences	**-Cut LOCs and improve border security**
	-Diplomatic pressure is necessary

UNCLASSIFIED//FOUO

UNCLASSIFIED//FOUO

Different Fights, Different Areas, Different Approaches

The Threat	Objectives	Manifestation/ Indicators	Locations	Approach
Sectarian Violence	Shia-Expand/Consolidate Power Sunni-Regain Power Control resources Fear/revenge cycle	Intimidation Murders Population moves	Baghdad and Baghdad Belts N. Babil Baqubah	Facilitate reconciliation Act as third party Broker cease-fires Counter accelerants Peace enforcement
AQ and AQI	Establish safe haven in Iraq Establish caliphate for Mid-East	High Profile attacks (VBIED, SVIED) Sectarian catalyst or accelerants	Baghdad N. Babil Fallujah Ramadi Baqubah Samarra Kirkuk Mosul	DESTROY AQ and AQI Classic COIN
Sunni Insurgency	Weaken & subvert the GoI Delegitimize GoI	Attacks on CF Retaliatory atks on Shia	Baghdad N. Babil Fallujah Ramadi Samarra Baqubah Kirkuk	Bring into Political process Legislation for reconciliation; de-Ba'ath; Economic incentives, Provincial elections Defeat those not reconcilable-COIN
Kurdish expansionism	Physical, Political and Economic Autonomy	Take over Kirkuk Sunni Arab DPs Peshmerga in area Violent Arab reprisal	Kirkuk Mosul	Art 140 resolution Even-handed exec. of resolution Hydrocarbon law Intl facilitation Peace enforcement
Shia on Shia Violence	Consolidation of Power primarily in the South	Attacks on each other, primarily in the South	Baghdad Najaf Basrah	Low priority Monitor, broker deals Opportunity to split Shia at political level
External influence (Iran, Syria, Turkey)	Iran-Keep US mired down Syria-Survival Turkey-Control Kurds	Training, Funds, Weapons and Technology (EFPs), Terrorists and Foreign Fighters	Iran-Baghdad, Baqubah, Najaf, N. Babil, Basrah Syria-Baghdad, Fallujah, Mosul, Ramadi Turkey-Kirkuk, Mosul	Diplomatic Pressure Deterrence by threat of force Improved POE security IO illustrating interference

UNCLASSIFIED//FOUO

Different Fights, Different Areas, Different Approaches

The Threat	Objectives	Manifestation/ Indicators	Locations	Approach
Corruption	Individual Wealth Individual Power Other Political/Personal Agendas	Collusion of GoI officials and insurgent leaders/militia Lack of trust in GoI and ISF Lack of services/infrastructure maintenance De facto sectarian policy	In key geographic locations In key governmental functions associated with critical resources Iraqi Security Formations	Internal Controls, intelligence, leveraged pressure Application of Rule of Law and transparency
Lack of Capacity and inexperience	Bureaucratic and Political resistance to change	Slow political action on legislation Lack of budget execution Lack of confidence in GoI	Ministries In key geographic locations In key governmental functions	MNF-I and USG support/pressure
Violent Criminals	Local Individual wealth Local power Subvert the local, provincial, and national GoI Intimidate population and ISF	Intimidation and Murder Extortion Kidnappings for ransom Black-marketing Collusion with GoI officials and insurgent leaders	Major urban centers	Empower/support the police Enforce the rule of law Arrest, Prosecute, Convict Improve judicial process Phased removal of price controls Publicize conviction of criminals Increase GOI detention capability

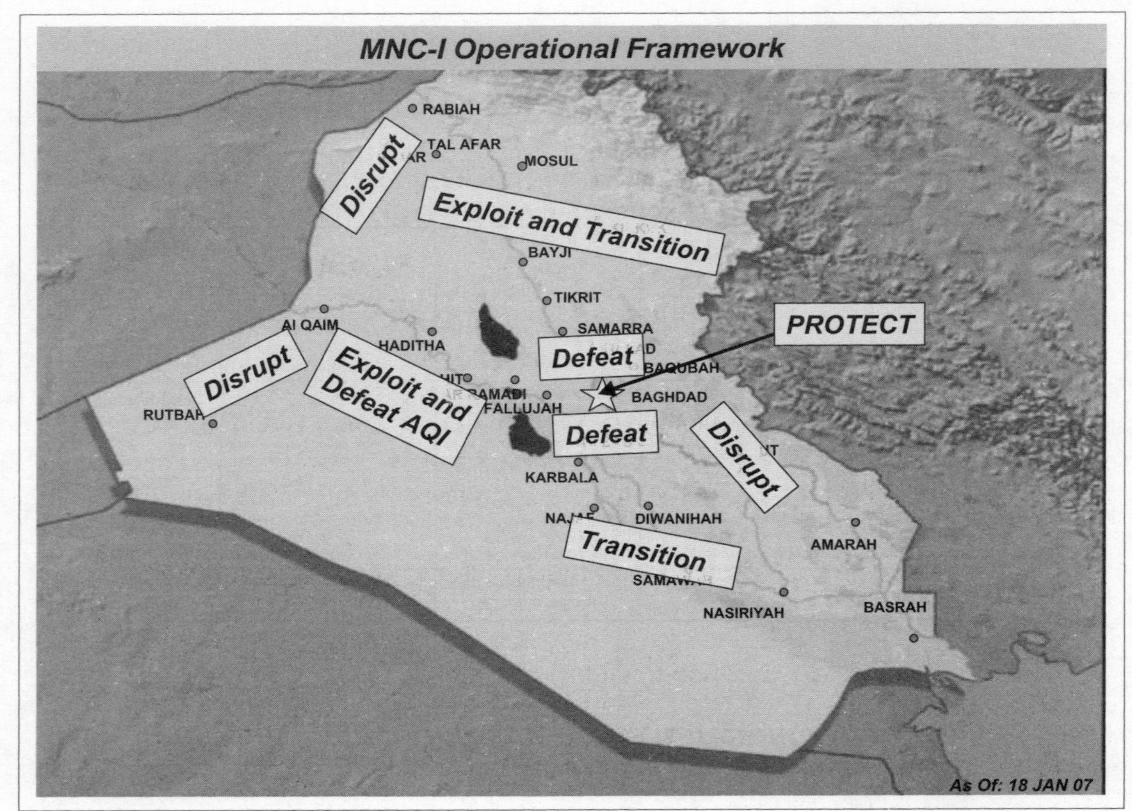
MNC-I Operational Framework
RABIAH
TAL AFAR
MOSUL
Disrupt
Exploit and Transition
BAYJI
TIKRIT
SAMARRA
PROTECT
AI QAIM
HADITHA
Disrupt
Exploit and Defeat AQI
Defeat
BAQUBAH
BAGHDAD
FALLUJAH
RUTBAH
Defeat
Disrupt
KARBALA
DIWANIHAH
Transition
AMARAH
NASIRIYAH
BASRAH
As Of: 18 JAN 07

UNCLASSIFIED//FOUO

Considerations

- Recognize that there are different fights in different areas and there are multiple fights in each area
- The greatest threat to stability is Sectarian Violence
- Improved security is job one
- The ISF is the visible arm of the GoI, manifested in legitimacy when Rule of Law derived from GoI policy/legislation is fairly enforced by the ISF
- Security not followed with visible political, economic actions by GoI can not be decisive
- Sunni inclusion in the GoI through reconciliation will reduce Sunni insurgency and make AQ more vulnerable
- Sustained security and united population can lead to further rejection of external influences (AQ, Iran, Syria, Turkey)

UNCLASSIFIED//FOUO

UNCLASSIFIED//FOUO

MNC-I Mission Statement

MNC-I Mission MNC-I conducts combat, stability, and support operations in coordination with the Iraqi Security Forces to secure the population, defeat terrorists and irreconcilable extremists, neutralize insurgent and militia groups, and transition responsibilities to the ISF in order to reduce violence, gain the support of the people, stabilize Iraq, and enable GoI security self-reliance. NLT December 2007, we will establish stability and create irreversible momentum with the Iraqi population, the GoI and ISF toward the ultimate goal of self-reliance.

UNCLASSIFIED//FOUO

UNCLASSIFIED//FOUO

Commander's Intent
(1 of 3)

- **Purpose**

In order to break the current cycle of sectarian violence, we must set the conditions for the ISF to emerge as the dominant security force, able to protect the population and provide security in a fair and impartial manner. This operation will be Iraqi-led with Coalition support. Much more than a military operation alone, it must include a combination of military, economic, and political actions.

Militarily, we must interdict accelerants of Baghdad sectarian violence emerging from Southern Salah ad Din, Eastern Diyala, and Western Anbar, exploiting recent successes in these areas to continue the transition to Iraqi security self-reliance and enhance the prospects for reconciliation. A key will be our ability to neutralize VBIED and EFP networks.

Within Baghdad, we must move deliberately and maintain a robust, combined presence in each administrative district until we have firmly established Joint Security Stations manned by CF alongside ISF that are loyal to the GOI and can provide adequate protection for the population. Our operations must be deliberate, our goals achievable and sustainable. We will only be decisive when security is sustained over time with Iraqis fully in charge.

Economically, we must create a combination of near-term and long-term employment opportunities and improve basic services in order to generate economic growth in poor neighborhoods.

Politically, we must set benchmarks to address the dismantling of Shia militias, deal with de-Baathification, and move towards provincial and local elections.

UNCLASSIFIED//FOUO

UNCLASSIFIED//FOUO

Commander's Intent

(2 of 3)

- Key Tasks
  - – In conjunction with the ISF, secure the Iraqi people, with a focus on Baghdad; as a minimum:
    - Maintain consistent forward presence – 24/7 CF coverage in clear, control, and retain areas until CF shift to the periphery
    - Be deliberate – resist the urge to surge; as the operation progresses, give priority to the retention and control of cleared areas; ensure the right amount of security forces are controlling the districts
    - Achievable – demonstrate real and perceived success, early-on and throughout the operation
    - Sustainable – as ISF and CF control expands, avoid overstretch and prevent re-infiltration; carefully consider the risks of committing to new clearing operations
  - – Interdict accelerants of Baghdad sectarian violence
  - – Neutralize VBIED networks
  - – Neutralize Sunni and Shia extremists that conduct EJKs, IED and IDF attacks – balanced operations targeting groups on both sides of the sectarian divide
  - – Improve security at Ports of Entry to reduce illegal cross-border activity, with a priority to stemming the flow of weapons and EFPs from Iran
  - – Enhance the capability and legitimacy of the ISF
  - – Transition to Iraqi security self-reliance
  - – Support PRTs and interagency partners in the implementation of economic development initiatives

UNCLASSIFIED//FOUO

UNCLASSIFIED//FOUO

Commander's Intent

(3 of 3)

- Endstate
  - Baghdad secure and considered so by Sunni and Shia alike; violence in Baghdad reduced to a manageable level
  - ISF viewed by Iraqis as the dominant security force in Baghdad
  - Iraqi-led C2 structure for Baghdad in place and functioning
  - GOI perceived as taking the issue of sectarian violence seriously and seen as acting to reduce it
  - Transition to Iraqi security self-reliance initiated IAW the Bridging Strategy and making steady progress throughout Iraq
  - Enhanced capacity of GOI to provide essential services and infrastructure maintenance
  - Foundation laid for self-sustaining economic growth
  - CF positioned on the periphery of urban areas; enhanced transition teams and dedicated strike forces in place

UNCLASSIFIED//FOUO

UNCLASSIFIED//FOUO

Critical Conditions

Beginning the Operation

- ✓ Concurrence from GOI on the concept of operations and the endstate
  - Start, stay, and finish together
  - GOI must publicly announce and display their support until endstate achieved
- ✓ GOI must give the proper support and authority to its security forces without undue interference and influence
- ✓ GOI must support a "balanced" targeting approach, allowing operations throughout the city – to include shia areas
- ✓ GOI extension of existing state of emergency, with measures including at a minimum:
  - Banning vehicles from selected locations
  - Controlling access into, and internal to, the city as required
  - Random searches of vehicles, people, businesses, and homes
  - Full enforcement of the weapons ban
- GOI must seriously consider declaring a cease fire, institute a mid-term amnesty program, and – with reconciliation in mind – determine a policy defining the endstate for all militias
- GOI must release all DFI funds to Anbar, Tal Afar, and Samarra to cultivate Sunni trust and confidence
- In coordination with the GOI, the Coalition must have a coordinated and synchronized reconstruction and beautification plan as it clears, controls, and retains districts in Baghdad
- GOI must pass legislation and announce a timeline for local and provincial elections as soon as possible
- GOI must develop, announce, and implement a reasonable de-Baathification program
- USG must engage GOI and encourage GOI to endorse and fund state-owned enterprise reinvigoration initiatives proposed by the Brinkley Group

UNCLASSIFIED//FOUO

UNCLASSIFIED//FOUO

Phasing Construct

Phase I: Setting the Conditions
- **GOI political conditions**
- **Organize forces**
- **Disrupt VBIED and EFP networks**
- **Develop Baghdad C2 structure**

Overlap between phases and within certain phases

Combined operations with the ISF

Phase II: Clear, Control, Retain

MND-B ***MAIN EFFORT:*** *Clear* / *Retain*
- **Secure Baghdad**

SUPPORTING EFFORTS:
- **Interdict accelerants to Baghdad sectarian violence**
- **Outlying MNDs exploit prior success**
- **Neutralize VBIED and EFP networks**
- **Deny extremist group sanctuaries**

Phase III tasks also support the main effort

Phase III: Retain and Renew
- **Transition to Iraqi security self-reliance**
- **Economic development initiatives**
- **Sustain PIC; continue transition to PIC**

Increasingly capable ISF throughout Iraq supports the effort to secure Baghdad

Phase IV: Exploitation
- **Conduct strike ops against AQI and Shia extremists**

Operational Overwatch

UNCLASSIFIED//FOUO

UNCLASSIFIED//FOUO

Clear, Control and Retain

1. Designated <u>clear</u> forces with specific objectives:
   - ❑ Combined IA/NP and CF Operation
     - Cordon and Search
     - Cordon and Knock
     - Deliberate, precise targeting (can be multiple targets)
   - ❑ Heavy combined presence established to protect the population
   - ❑ "Quick start" short term employment projects identified and resourced

<u>Clear</u>: remove all enemy forces and eliminate organized resistance within an assigned area. Security Forces (ISF and CF) and infrastructure required to protect the population identified and resourced.

2. Designated <u>control</u> forces with specific objectives:
   - ❑ IA/NP Brigade maintains heavy presence in District to protect the populace
   - ❑ Coalition Battalion supports IA/NP BDE operations to protect the populace (requires a 24/7 presence in sector)
   - ❑ Joint Security Stations established with IP/IA/NP and Coalition Forces
   - ❑ Coalition Force QRF prepared to support
   - ❑ Short term employment projects on-going, long term employment and reconstruction projects identified and funded

<u>Control</u>: maintain physical influence over a specified area to prevent its use by an enemy or to create conditions necessary for successful friendly operations. Security Forces (ISF and CF) in place to protect the population and security infrastructure improvement / construction ongoing.

3. Designated <u>retain</u> forces with specific objectives:
   - ❑ IPs conducting routine police actions
   - ❑ IA or NP BDE in tactical overwatch
   - ❑ Coalition Battalion in Operational Overwatch
   - ❑ Long term employment and reconstruction projects on-going or complete

<u>Retain</u>: ensure a terrain feature controlled by a friendly force remains free of enemy occupation or use. All required Security Forces (ISF and CF) are in place, fully functional, and sustainable.

UNCLASSIFIED//FOUO

UNCLASSIFIED//FOUO

Clear, Control, Retain and Transition

1. Begin Clearing Phase

1. Are sufficient ISF and CF on hand to clear the designated administrative district?
2. Are sufficient ISF and CF available to transition to the control phase?
3. Is target development sufficient to begin clearing phase?
4. Are sufficient adjacent forces available to conduct interdiction, control or block tasks in support of clearing operations?
5. Have "Quick start" short term employment projects been identified and resourced

YES

2. Begin Control Phase

1. Are ISF and CF partnerships establish and functional? (CF BN DS to ISF BDE)
2. Is there a CF TST unit available?
3. Are sufficient ISF and CF available to conduct control operations?
4. Are the required number of Joint Security Stations at initial operational capability?
5. Is sufficient barrier material available to begin establishing "vehicle free zones" and "gated communities"?
6. Are Neighborhood and District Councils formed or forming?
7. Are short term employment projects on-going and long term employment and reconstruction projects identified and funded?

YES

3. Begin Retain Phase

1. Are the required number of Joint Security Stations at full operational capability?
2. Is there a dedicated CF TST available?
3. Is the ISF Brigade and Joint Security Station adequately manned with ISF and CF?
4. Are the IA, NP an IP cooperating to provide security to the citizens of the district?
5. Has the GOI accepted responsibility for the management of ongoing reconstruction projects?
6. Are NACs and DACs functional?
7. Are long term employment and reconstruction projects on-going or complete?

YES

4. Begin Transition Phase

1. Are the IPs capable of conducting effective law and order operations with IA or NP overwatch?
2. Are local governance systems operational – local to provincial?
3. Are enhanced MiTTs in place and opeational?
4. Are CF in postion to provide a QRF or reinforce the ISF if required?

These criteria are to be viewed as the minimum standards to progress from one phase to the next. However, each area and Administrative District will be different - Commanders must view this criteria as "commander's intent" and be prepared to operate within it to achieve their mission.

UNCLASSIFIED//FOUO

UNCLASSIFIED//FOUO

Baghdad Security-The Way Ahead (1 of 2)

- MNC-I understands **time is not on our side—must have visible progress soon** and use time pressure to help GoI reach political accommodation now
- **Visible progress can create momentum and space** for economic/legislative action
- **Security provides momentum and sets the conditions** for GoI (Governance), ISF, economic success
- **Security synchronized with Governance and Economic development can work, but** it will take great internal political effort from the GoI in the short term

UNCLASSIFIED//FOUO

UNCLASSIFIED//FOUO

Baghdad Security-The Way Ahead (2 of 2)

- **How we see it going:**
  - **Main effort is growing political legitimacy and capacity** with supporting security, economic, information and overarching transition operations
  - **Main security effort will be on Baghdad and Baghdad Belts** (Enemy support zones/avenues of approach)
  - **Combined effort with ISF** partnered with CF
  - Supporting security efforts will be to **interdict accelerants/POE**
  - **Security actions will be deliberate**—designed to retain cleared areas
  - There will be no hurry to move to new areas, unless the situation dictates; and there will be no hurry to transition, unless ISF are really ready/capable of success
  - **May have to re-clear** areas if intel/situation warrants
  - **May need to take risk in other areas away from Baghdad** (MND-N and MNF-W) if required and based on opportunities for earlier transitions there
  - **Transition to ISF will also be deliberate**—designed to not regress/lose control of the population
  - Transition will encompass partnership and enhanced transition teams, from CF elements
  - Transition will also encompass a gradual reduction of CF footprint, first to tactical overwatch, then to operational overwatch once security is retained in designated areas
  - **CF will retain strike capability for TSTs and freedom of movement**
- **Timely and effective GoI economic actions, synchronized with and immediately behind successful clear, control, retain operations contributes to momentum of improved security**—this is where ISF/GoI legitimacy has the most potential for taking root in population centers—(Baghdad first)
- **Legislation and effective application of policy** on de-Ba'athification/ reconciliation, provincial election plans, and release of funds for economic development, **simultaneously with fully established security allows GoI to gain nation-wide legitimacy** in eyes of all of the Iraqis

UNCLASSIFIED//FOUO

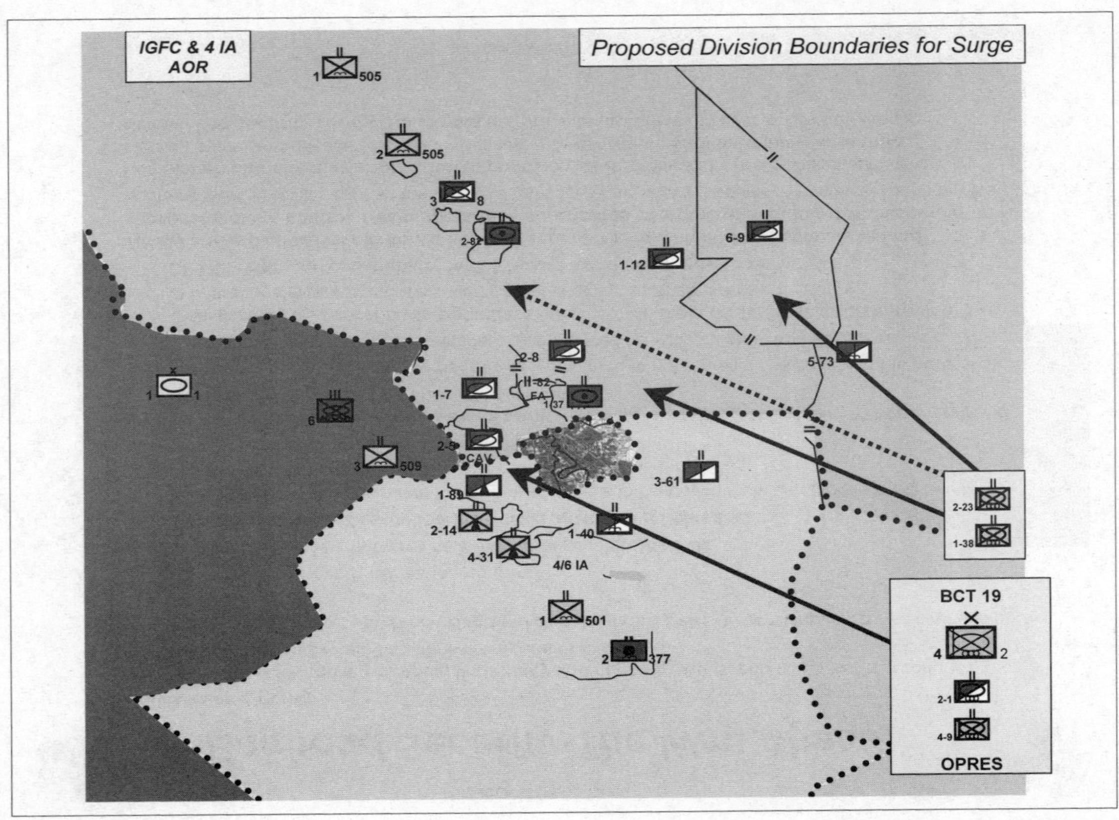

IGFC & 4 IA
AOR
Proposed Division Boundaries for Surge
1 505
2 505
3 8
6-9
1-12
5-73
2-8
1-7
1-37
6
3 509
3-61
2-23
1-38
2-14
1-40
4-31
4/6 IA
1 501
2 377
BCT 19
4 2
2-1
4-9
OPRES

UNCLASSIFIED//FOUO

MNF-I Issues for Consideration

Political:

- Focus Main Effort ⇨ Political reconciliation and GOI capacity
- Engage with Tribes and Imams
- Manage the "blame game" – Iraqis will blame us for everything that goes wrong
- Create seamless relationship between MNF-I and Embassy
- Put pressure on approval of critical legislation:
  - Hydrocarbon legislation
  - Provincial Powers Law and related laws for provincial elections
  - Amnesty Amendment
  - Approval of article 140/Relations with Kirkuk
  - De-Ba'athification legislation
  - Reconciliation process for militias (DDR is a GOI not a CF task)
- With USM-I, Apply diplomatic pressure on Syria, Iran, and Turkey

UNCLASSIFIED//FOUO

UNCLASSIFIED//FOUO

MNF-I Issues for Consideration

Security:

- Identify and agree on command and control relationships post 1st March
- Emphasize MNC-I, MNDs, & BCTs joint planning with the Iraqis (Re-shape MNSTC-I umbilical cord)
- Achieve and effectively publicize quick wins
- Expand rule of law detention capacity and facilities
- Redo MNF-I strategic guidance and plan for bridging strategy and transition

Economics:

- Move mindset from <u>reconstruction</u> to <u>economic development</u>
- Help Iraqi's spend their money
- Push for continuing US Reconstruction Budgets ($1.2 billion FY 2007 supplemental critical to partners (USAID))
- Leverage PRTs – Deployed, empowered, resourced, energized

UNCLASSIFIED//FOUO

UNCLASSIFIED//FOUO

Things that could go wrong

- Perception of continued violence in Baghdad despite the security surge
- GoI fails to put Iraq ahead of sectarian political agenda. Sectarian violence continues, possibly increases
- Significant Shia on Shia fight in the South with Iranian involvement, spills into Baghdad
- Death of Sistani
- Significant move by Kurds causes major incursion of Turkish forces in the North

UNCLASSIFIED//FOUO

UNCLASSIFIED//FOUO

Comments/Questions

UNCLASSIFIED//FOUO

D. GEN. PETRAEUS SUMMARIZES HOW TO OPERATE IN IRAQ

HEADQUARTERS
MULTI-NATIONAL FORCE – IRAQ
BAGHDAD, IRAQ
APO AE 09342-1400

21 June 2008

Multi-National Force-Iraq Commander's Counterinsurgency Guidance

- **Secure and serve the population.** The Iraqi people are the decisive "terrain." Together with our Iraqi partners, work to provide the people security, to give them respect, to gain their support, and to facilitate establishment of local governance, restoration of basic services, and revival of local economies.
- **Live among the people.** You can't commute to this fight. Position Joint Security Stations, Combat Outposts, and Patrol Bases in the neighborhoods we intend to secure. Living among the people is essential to securing them and defeating the insurgents.
- **Hold areas that have been secured**. Once we clear an area, we must retain it. Develop the plan for holding an area before starting to clear it. The people need to know that we and our Iraqi partners will not abandon their neighborhoods. When reducing forces and presence, gradually thin the line rather than handing off or withdrawing completely. Ensure situational awareness even after transfer of responsibility to Iraqi forces.
- **Pursue the enemy relentlessly.** Identify and pursue AQI and other extremist elements tenaciously. Do not let them retain support areas or sanctuaries. Force the enemy to respond to us. Deny the enemy the ability to plan and conduct deliberate operations.
- **Generate unity of effort**. Coordinate operations and initiatives with our embassy and interagency partners, our Iraqi counterparts, local governmental leaders, and non-governmental organizations to ensure all are working to achieve a common purpose.
- **Promote reconciliation.** We cannot kill our way out of this endeavor. We and our Iraqi partners must identify and separate the "reconcilables" from the "irreconcilables" through engagement, population control measures, information operations, kinetic operations, and political activities. We must strive to make the reconcilables a part of the solution, even as we identify, pursue, and kill, capture, or drive out the irreconcilables.
- **Defeat the network, not just the attack**. Defeat the insurgent networks to the "left" of the explosion. Focus intelligence assets to identify the network behind an attack, and go after its leaders, financiers, suppliers, and operators.
- **Foster Iraqi legitimacy**. Encourage Iraqi leadership and initiative; recognize that their success is our success. Partner in all that we do and support local involvement in security, governance, economic revival, and provision of basic services. Find the right balance between Coalition Forces leading and the Iraqis exercising their leadership and initiative, and encourage the latter. Legitimacy in the eyes of the Iraqi people is essential to overall success.
- **Employ all assets to isolate and defeat the terrorists and insurgents**. Counter-terrorist forces alone cannot defeat Al-Qaeda and the other extremists; success requires all forces and all means at our disposal—non-kinetic as well as kinetic. Employ Coalition and Iraqi conventional and special operations forces, Sons of Iraq, and all other available multipliers.

Integrate civilian and military efforts to cement security gains. Resource and fight decentralized. Push assets down to those who most need them and can actually use them.

- **Employ money as a weapon system.** Use a targeting board process to ensure the greatest effect for each "round" expended, and to ensure that each engagement using money contributes to the achievement of the unit's overall objectives. Ensure contracting activities support the security effort, employing locals wherever possible. Employ a "matching fund" concept when feasible in order to ensure Iraqi involvement and commitment.
- **Fight for intelligence.** A nuanced understanding of the situation is everything. Analyze the intelligence that is gathered, share it, and fight for more. Every patrol should have tasks designed to augment understanding of the area of operations and the enemy. Operate on a "need to share" rather than a "need to know" basis; disseminate intelligence as soon as possible to all who can benefit from it.
- **Walk.** Move mounted, work dismounted. Stop by, don't drive by. Patrol on foot and engage the population. Situational awareness can only be gained by interacting with the people face-to-face, not separated by ballistic glass.
- **Understand the neighborhood.** Map the human terrain and study it in detail. Understand local culture and history. Learn about the tribes, formal and informal leaders, governmental structures, and local security forces. Understand how local systems are supposed to work—including governance, basic services, maintenance of infrastructure, and the economy—and how they really work.
- **Build relationships.** Relationships are a critical component of counter-insurgency operations. Together with our Iraqi counterparts, strive to establish productive links with local leaders, tribal sheikhs, governmental officials, religious leaders, and interagency partners.
- **Look for Sustainable Solutions.** Build mechanisms by which the Iraqi Security Forces, Iraqi community leaders, and local Iraqis under the control of governmental institutions can continue to secure local areas and sustain governance and economic gains in their communities as the Coalition Force presence is reduced. Figure out the Iraqi systems and help Iraqis make them work.
- **Maintain continuity and tempo through transitions**. Start to build the information you'll provide to your successors on the day you take over. Allow those who will follow you to virtually "look over your shoulder" while they're still at home station by giving them access to your daily updates and other items on SIPRNET. Encourage extra time on the ground during transition periods, and strive to maintain operational tempo and local relationships to avoid giving the enemy respite.
- **Manage expectations.** Be cautious and measured in announcing progress. Note what has been accomplished, but also acknowledge what still needs to be done. Avoid premature declarations of success. Ensure our troopers and our partners are aware of our assessments and recognize that any counterinsurgency operation has innumerable challenges, that enemies get a vote, and that progress is likely to be slow.
- **Be first with the truth.** Get accurate information of significant activities to your chain of command, to Iraqi leaders, and to the press as soon as is possible. Beat the insurgents, extremists, and criminals to the headlines, and pre-empt rumors. Integrity is critical to this fight. Don't put lipstick on pigs. Acknowledge setbacks and failures, and then state what we've learned and how we'll respond. Hold the press (and ourselves) accountable for

accuracy, characterization, and context. Avoid spin and let facts speak for themselves. Challenge enemy disinformation. Turn our enemies' bankrupt messages, extremist ideologies, oppressive practices, and indiscriminate violence against them.

- **Fight the information war relentlessly.** Realize that we are in a struggle for legitimacy that in the end will be won or lost in the perception of the Iraqi people. Every action taken by the enemy and United States has implications in the public arena. Develop and sustain a narrative that works and continually drive the themes home through all forms of media.
- **Live our values**. Do not hesitate to kill or capture the enemy, but stay true to the values we hold dear. This is what distinguishes us from our enemies. There is no tougher endeavor than the one in which we are engaged. It is often brutal, physically demanding, and frustrating. All of us experience moments of anger, but we can neither give in to dark impulses nor tolerate unacceptable actions by others.
- **Exercise initiative.** In the absence of guidance or orders, determine what they should be and execute aggressively. Higher level leaders will provide broad vision and paint "white lines on the road," but it will be up to those at tactical levels to turn "big ideas" into specific actions.
- **Prepare for and exploit opportunities.** "Luck is what happens when preparation meets opportunity" (Seneca the Younger). Develop concepts (such as that of "reconcilables" and "irreconcilables") in anticipation of possible opportunities, and be prepared to take risk as necessary to take advantage of them.
- **Learn and adapt.** Continually assess the situation and adjust tactics, policies, and programs as required. Share good ideas (none of us is smarter than all of us together). Avoid mental or physical complacency. Never forget that what works in an area today may not work there tomorrow, and may or may not be transferable to another part of Iraq.

NOTES

The foundation for this book, and the source of most of the quotations that appear in it, is a series of interviews I did in Baghdad and Washington, D.C., over the course of 2007 and 2008 with Gen. Petraeus, Gen. Odierno, and scores of their key staffers and commanders. I also interviewed many officers at the ends of their tours after they returned home. Where quotations are not cited below, they are either from public hearings, press conferences, and briefings or from those hundreds of hours of interviews and subsequent e-mail exchanges.

I also benefited from reading recent books on Iraq by Francis West, Kimberly Kagan, and Peter Mansoor. As is evident in the notes below, I also have relied on work by colleagues at the *Washington Post,* as well as reporters at other news organizations.

Epigraph

vii The quotation is from book 6, chapter 3, of Clausewitz, *On War* (edited and translated by Michael Howard and Peter Paret, Princeton Univ. Press, 1976).

Chapter 1: Things Fall Apart

3 **"It was a mediocre morning":** Lance Cpl. Sharratt's comments were made in a transcript posted by *Frontline,* the Public Broadcasting System's invaluable documentary series.

4 **"They didn't even try to run away":** Sgt. Mashoot's comment to investigators was reported in a *Washington Post* article that appeared 6 January 2007.

4 **"The American fired":** The comments by Salem are quoted in the *Washington Post,* 9 May 2007.

4 **"While in the house which I identified as House #2":** Lance Cpl. Tatum's comment is contained in a signed statement given to the Naval Criminal Investigative Service on 3 April 2006, correcting a statement he had given on 19 March 2006.

4 **"I heard Younis speaking":** Fahmi's recollection is an article in the *Washington Post,* of 27 May 2006.

5 **"'Hey, where are the bad guys?'":** Lt. Kallop's testimony is quoted in the *Washington Post,* 9 May 2007.

5 **"Even though there was no investigation at the time":** Lance Cpl. Wright's comment to investigators was quoted in the *Washington Post,* 7 January 2007.

6 **"I thought it was very sad":** Lt. Col. Chessani's recollection is contained in a transcript of an investigatory interview conducted on 19 March 2006.

6 **"There was nothing out of the ordinary":** The comments by Col. Davis are quoted in the *Washington Post,* 9 May 2007.

6 **"no bells and whistles went off":** Maj. Gen. Huck's comment is in a transcript of an investigatory interview conducted on 4 April 2006.

7 **"You are not going to like this":** Lt. Gen. Chiarelli's exchange with Gen. Huck is related in a signed statement given by Huck to the Naval Criminal Investigative Service, 18 August 2006.

7 **"indiscriminately":** This and subsequent quotations from Bargewell are from his eighty-eight-page report marked "15 June 2006 (Final)."

7 **Underscoring Bargewell's findings:** The data cited in this paragraph are from a document titled "Mental Health Advisory Team (MHAT) IV, Operation Iraqi Freedom 05-07, FINAL REPORT, 17 November 2006, Office of the Surgeon General, Multinational Force-Iraq, and Office of the Surgeon General, United States Army Medical Command."

8 **"God damn, 15 civilians dead":** Col. Ewer's exclamation is in a transcript of an investigatory interview conducted on 19 March 2006.

9 **"There's an undeniable sense":** Senator McCain's comment was made in a speech at the American Enterprise Institute, 10 November 2005.

10 **"It sucks":** Spec. Ivey was quoted in the *Washington Post,* 27 July 2006.

10 **"corrupt, . . . tied to being involved in extra-judicial killings":** Maj. Williams's comment is in an interview conducted by the Army's Combat Studies Institute at Fort Leavenworth, Kansas, for its studies of "Operational Leadership Experiences."

10 **"The truth is that many commands":** Capt. Martin's assertion is made in his article "Tempo, Technology and Hubris," *Marine Corps Gazette,* May 2007.

11 **"I'd never seen it at this level before":** Maj. Mendelson's observation is in his interview for the Leavenworth series "Operational Leadership Experiences."

12 **"By and large, the battalions continued to do what they knew best":** West's comment is in his book *The Strongest Tribe* (Random House, 2008).

13 **"The costs of failure are likely to be high":** This appears in "The War in Iraq: An Interim Assessment," by Andrew Krepinevich, prepared for OSD/Net Assessment, November 2005.

14 **"Haziness about ends and means":** Cohen's comment is in "No Way to Win a War," the *Wall Street Journal,* 7 December 2006.

15 **the United States needs a real strategy:** Krepinevich's article "How to Win in Iraq" appeared in the September/October 2005 edition of *Foreign Affairs.*

16 **"To be effective, the so-called pacification program":** Kissinger's article was "The Viet Nam Negotiations," *Foreign Affairs,* January 1969.

19 **"to be a good average is safer":** Lloyd George's comment is quoted in *The Rules of the Game: Jutland and British Naval Command,* by Andrew Gordon (John Murray, 1996).

22 **"a combination of being the president and the pope":** This Petraeus comment appeared in the *Washington Post,* 16 May 2003.

22 **"If others found him hard to love":** Rick Atkinson's comment is in his book *In the Company of Soldiers* (Henry Holt, 2004), as is Gen. Freakley's comment about Atkinson being "probably closer to him."

Chapter 2: How to Fight This War

25 **"cultural insensitivity":** Brig. Aylwin-Foster's article, titled "Changing the Army for Counterinsurgency Operations," was carried in *Military Review,* November-December 2005.

26 **"The population . . . becomes the objective":** This appears in Galula's seminal work, *Counterinsurgency Warfare: Theory and Practice* (Praeger, 1964).

27 **"paradoxes of counterinsurgency":** This and the subsequent series of quotations are from "Principles, Imperatives and Paradoxes of Counterinsurgency," *Military Review,* March–April 2006.

27 **playing with paradox:** This aspect of Abbasid literature is discussed by Hugh Kennedy in *When Baghdad Ruled the Muslim World: The Rise and Fall of Islam's Greatest Dynasty* (Da Capo, 2004).

28 **"In counterinsurgency, killing the enemy is easy":** Several months after Petraeus read Kilcullen's essay, which circulated first by e-mail, it was carried in *Military Review,* May–June 2006.

29 **"An operation that kills five insurgents is counterproductive":** The manual was published as *FM 3-24: Counterinsurgency,* Headquarters, Department of the Army, December 2006.

31 "We needed elections": This is in the essay by Gen. Fastabend titled "How This All Ends: It's fourth and long, go deep," unpublished document given to Gen. Petraeus, late April 2007.

31 the leading Shiite party, the United Iraqi Alliance, won 70 of 81 seats: The data in this paragraph is from "Iraq's Year of Voting Dangerously," by A. I. Dawisha and Larry Diamond, *Journal of Democracy,* April 2006.

32 "we heard an explosion": From Maj. Lewis's interview for Leavenworth's "Operational Leadership Experiences" archives.

33 violence had increased at a steady pace since March 2005: This is from the Pentagon's report to Congress "Measuring Security and Stability in Iraq," December 2007.

33 "The situation in the last six months": Kubasi was quoted in the *Washington Post,* 23 January 2006.

34 "We have become reactive": This is from Capt. Martin's article "Tempo, Technology and Hubris," *Marine Corps Gazette,* May 2007.

37 "Every time you left the gate": From Maj. Williamson's interview, "Operational Leadership Experiences," Fort Leavenworth.

41 "We live in darkness": Jasim was quoted in the *Washington Post,* of 29 May 2006.

46 "rose considerably": Capt. Comstock's study "The Battle for Saydia: An Ongoing Case Study in Militia Based Insurgency" was carried on the website Small Wars Journal, April 2008.

46 "JAM/Shia militia group kidnaps a Sunni male": Capt. Haas was quoted in Comstock's study, see previous note.

46 "People are killed here every day": Capt. Showman's observation is in the *Washington Post,* of 27 October 2007.

47 "Leave, join or die": Capt. Francis is quoted in Comstock's study cited earlier in this chapter.

47 "I don't think this place": Sgt. Alarcon is quoted in same *Washington Post* article of 27 October 2007 that quoted Showman earlier in this chapter.

47 "When we got there, it was mixed Sunni and Shia": Maj. Gilmore's interview, "Operational Leadership Experiences," Fort Leavenworth.

47 "The social and political situation": Col. Devlin's analysis "State of the Insurgency in al Anbar," 17 August 2006, bears his title ("II MEF G-2") but not his name.

48 "Using a small, localized cell": Capt. Few's study "The Break Point: AQIZ Establishes the ISI in Zaganiyah" was carried on the website Small Wars Journal, also in April 2008.

50 "They ordered these Kurdish units": From Maj. Matt Whitney's interview, "Operational Leadership Experiences."

51 "kiss of death": Kilcullen's comment was made in a briefing titled "Counterinsurgency in Iraq: Theory and Practice, 2007."

54 "deeply flawed in timing and resources": Cordesman's comment appears in his essay "Iraqi Force Development," distributed 27 November 2006.

54 "The strategy was a hope": From West's book *Strongest Tribe,* (Random House, 2008).

57 "You'd find dumped bodies": From Maj. Voorhies's interview "Operational Leadership Experiences."

57 "We may need more resources": West and Cohen, "Our Only Hope," *Wall Street Journal,* 8 January 2007.

58 "We had two bites of this apple": Most of the quotations from Gen. Keane in this book are from the hours of interviews I did with him, but this one is from the transcript of an interview he did with *Frontline.*

59 "I don't believe we can continue": Senator Snowe was quoted in the *Washington Post,* 20 October 2006.

59 A light in Ramadi: Much of this section is based on an interview with Col. MacFarland, as well as follow-up exchanges by e-mail, but a few of the quotations from him are from his official interview with the Contemporary Operations Study Team at the Army's Combat Studies Institute, Fort Leavenworth, Kansas.

62 "It was actually a very small number": Lt. Col. Negard was quoted in the *Washington Post,* 2 May 2006.

62 But Carter Malkasian: His observation is in his article "A Thin Blue Line in the Sand," DemocracyJournal.org, Summer 2007.

63 **"Today, there is no tribal sheikh":** Qadir, as quoted in the *Washington Post,* 20 May 2006.

67 **"For all intents and purposes":** Malkasian, "Thin Blue Line," quoted earlier in this chapter.

70 **"Part of me died along":** Gibbs's mother, Debbie Halstead, was quoted in the *Winston-Salem Journal,* 9 December 2006.

70 **"He was one of those people":** Ivan Ryndych's comment appeared in *Newsday,* 8 December 2006.

70 **"Please don't portray this as a tragedy":** Re McClung was quoted in the *Los Angeles Times,* 13 December 2006.

71 **"Well, Grant, we've had the devil's own day":** This anecdote, which appears in many histories of the Civil War, was originally told to by Gen. Sherman to a reporter for the *Washington Post* and then quoted in the *Army and Navy Journal,* 30 December 1893, according to Jean Edward Smith's *Grant* (Simon & Schuster, 2001).

72 **"Sean had obviously done something extraordinarily important":** The data in this paragraph, and earlier in this chapter, about the cooperation of Ramadi-area tribes is from a briefing, "Tribal Cooperation Jan 07," that was given to Petraeus when he visited Ramadi in February 2007.

Chapter 3: Keane Takes Command

75 **"one of the nastiest campaigns":** This appears in Sen. Webb's book A Time to Fight (Broadway, 2008).

76 **"How's your boy?":** The exchange between President Bush and Webb is based partly on an interview with Webb but mainly on an accounts in the *Washington Post,* 29 November 2006, and an article in *The Washingtonian,* February 2008.

91 **"We don't easily jump":** Martin's comment is in his interview with the Contemporary Operations Studies Team, Combat Studies Institute, Fort Leavenworth, Kansas.

92 **"It's important to trust the judgment of the military":** President Bush's interview with the Washington Post was quoted in the newspaper on 20 December 2006.

93 **"I am not persuaded":** Powell appeared on *Face the Nation,* 17 December 2006.

94 **"Without additional combat forces":** Senator McCain's comment was quoted in the *Washington Post,* 17 November 2006.

98 **President Bush hit a new low in his ratings:** The data here is from the *Washington Post*–ABC News Poll, posted by the *Post,* 12 December 2006.

99 **"there was not enough civilian participation":** From Kinnard's *The War Managers: American Generals Reflect on Vietnam* (Da Capo, 1991).

103 **"We are losing":** The conclusions of the "council of colonels" are summarized in the briefing "Strategy for the Long War, 2006-2016: 'Where we are going,' 27 October 2006."

Chapter 4: A Strategy Is Born

121 **"Producing Victory":** Lt. Col. Ollivant's article appeared in the July–August 2006 issue of *Military Review.*

Chapter 5: If You're So Smart . . .

139 **"sense of reality":** Ambassador Carney's comment appeared in the *Washington Post,* 14 January 2007.

Chapter 6: Gambling on a "Shitty Hand"

155 **"We redefined success":** Sky said this first to me in an interview about her work in the winter of 2006–7, then repeated it in her essay "Iraq 2007—Moving Beyond Counter-Insurgency Doctrine: A First-Hand Perspective," published by the Royal United Services Institute, London, April 2008.

156 **"to settle for far less":** Fastabend's essay "How This All Ends: It's Fourth and Long, Go Deep," unpublished document given to Gen. Petraeus, late April 2007.

160 **"rapid decisive operations":** For example, see "A Concept for Rapid Decisive Operations," by the J-9 Joint Futures Lab, Joint Forces Command, August 2001.

160 **"dominant maneuver, precision engagement and information operations":** The study done at

the School of Advanced Military Studies is "To Fight and Win America's Wars . . . and Then What?: A critical analysis of rapid decisive operations in a post-Saddam Iraq," by Army Lt. Col. John Metz, May 2003.

161 "We need rapidly deployable": Secretary Rumsfeld's comments were made in a speech at the National Defense University, Washington, D.C., 31 January 2002.

161 "Our mindset was not to kill": Lt. Burns's discussion appeared in his article on "Iraq and the Young Maneuver Leader," *Armor* magazine, July–August 2008.

163 "reaching terminal velocity": Maj. Gillespie's quotation is in his "Operational Leadership Experiences" interview with the Combat Studies Institute at Fort Leavenworth.

163 "We refer not so much to the single outstandingly significant report": Clausewitz's insight on intelligence is made in his discussion of "The People," book 6, chapter 6, of *On War.*

166 "Get out of your Humvees": This is from Maj. Halloran's interview with the Combat Studies Institute at Fort Leavenworth.

166 an average of more than one car bomb attack a day: The data in this paragraph on bombings and downings of helicopters was carried in "Iraq's Sectarian and Ethnic Violence and Its Evolving Insurgency," by Anthony Cordesman, with the assistance of Emma Davies, Center for Strategic and International Studies, 3 April 2007.

166 "It's getting worse": Partlow's article ran in the *Washington Post,* 6 February 2007.

166 "When we first moved into the AO": The operations officer is quoted in the report of the "Theater Operations Detachment" for the Center for Army Lessons Learned at Fort Leavenworth," 13 January 2008.

167 "Our first two weeks": Lt. Carlisle's recollection is in the same CALL report.

167 "My platoon sergeant came to Iraq": Lt. Williamson's comment was made on the Army website Platoon Leader.

167 "We did not know": Lt. Col. Crider's quotations are from "Operation Close Encounters," an unpublished essay that circulated by e-mail.

167 "constant enemy small-arms fire": Lt. Gross's comments are from the website Platoon Leader.

167 "We don't need any more information": Capt. Keirsey recounted his bluff in "Reflections of a Counterinsurgency Company Commander," which appeared first on the Army website Company Commander and was reprinted in the June and July 2008 issues of *Army* magazine. Keirsey also was interviewed in the CALL report.

171 "qualified optimist" and "hardest that I have ever experienced": Except for this paragraph, and for the first paragraph in chapter 10, the quotations from Gen. Petraeus in this book are from interviews I did with him or from documents. In this paragraph, "qualified optimist" was a comment he made in an interview on *Charlie Rose,* 26 April 2007. The other quotation appeared in the *Times* of London, 21 February 2008, in an online posting of the transcript of an interview by Deborah Hayes.

171 "I never thought I was going to see": Staff Sgt. Nunez's quotation appeared in *Stars & Stripes,* 24 April 2008.

173 "dividing neighbor from neighbor": Professor Niva made this assertion in "The New Walls of Baghdad," *Foreign Policy in Focus Report,* 21 April 2008.

174 "The insurgency is like a shark": This appears in "13 Bullets on the Insurgency in Anbar," issued by the Marine intelligence staff in Iraq in March 2008.

174 "The Defense of Jisr al-Doreaa": This was carried on the Small Wars Journal website in June 2008. I am told it will be published as a book by the University of Chicago Press.

176 "First people weren't working with us": Lt. Col. Michael is quoted in the CALL report.

176 "When we first came over": Col. Grigsby made this comment during a briefing with reporters at the Pentagon, 13 December 2007.

178 "hopeless": Lt. Freeze's memoir, "Notes from Down Range," was carried on the Army website Platoon Leader.

180 "They were carrying bodies": The Iraqi's comment appeared in the *Washington Post,* 4 February 2007.

180 "These guys are real smart": Lt. Von Plinsky was quoted in the *Washington Post,* 22 April 2007.

181 "the insurgents assassinated him": Spec. Hollopeter was quoted in *Stars & Stripes,* 19 June 2007.

181 The battle of Tarmiyah: Most of this section is based on interviews with soldiers involved in this action and with documents provided by their commanders. I first learned of this fight from an account by Greg Jaffe that appeared in the *Wall Street Journal* on 3 May 2007. Among the documents I used were "Memorandum for Commander, 1st Brigade Combat Team, 1st Cavalry Division/ Subject: 15-6 Investigation Concerning the Suicide Vehicle Borne Improvised (SBVIED) attack on the Tarmiyah Combat Outpost," by Lt. Col. Scott Efflandt, 2 March 2007; "Patrol Base Tarmiyah: Critical Event Lessons Learned," undated PowerPoint briefing; "Demon Co. Update," 1st Sgt. William Tramel, 25 February 2007; "The Battle for AO North," a history of the operations in Iraq in 2006–7 of the 2nd Battalion, 8th Cavalry Regiment.

181 "The explosion threw me": Lt. Jokinen's memory is in "Sworn Statement of 1LT Jokinen, Shawn R, 19 Feb 07."

182 "Everything was black": Staff Sgt. Copeland's recollection is from "Sworn statement of the events of 19 Feb 2007, Tarmiyah, Iraq, D C 2-8 Cav, Statement of SSG Copeland."

185 "The very fundamental issue": Gen. Sheehan's criticism appeared in the *Washington Post,* 11 April 2007.

185 "It flat out sucks": Pvt. Perkins's complaint was quoted in the *Washington Post,* 13 April 2007.

185 "I believe myself . . . that this war is lost": Senator Reid's assessment was quoted in the *Washington Post,* 20 April 2007.

186 "a brief exchange of fire": That characterization appeared in *Stars & Stripes,* 1 September 2008, as did the quotations from the testimony of Pfc. Hartson and of Sgt. Leahy.

188 "admit defeat": Gen. Rose's conclusion was reported in the London Daily Telegraph, 4 May 2007.

188 "The war in Iraq is approaching": Kissinger's warning was offered in an opinion article that ran in the *Washington Post,* 10 July 2007.

188 "Today, the wind—by grace of Allah": Al Qaeda's boast was quoted in the U.S. government's digest of *Jihadist Websites* on OpenSource.gov, 5 July 2007.

188 "We're tired of being lost": Sgt. 1st Class Eaglin's gloomy comment appeared in the *Washington Post,* 8 May 2007.

189 "I don't see any progress": Spec. Tertulien's comment was quoted in the *Los Angeles Times,* 25 August 2007.

189 "We passed the top half of a HMMWV": Lt. Weber's recollection is in his untitled interview on the Army's Platoon Leader website.

189 "I can't take it anymore": This suicide is recounted in a remarkable series of articles that appeared in *Army Times* in December 2007.

189 "We see that a vast majority": The opinion piece by the seven soldiers from the 82nd Airborne (Spec. Buddhika Jaymaha, Sgt. Wesley Smith, Sgt. Jeremy Roebuck, Sgt. Omar Mara, Sgt. Edward Sandmeier, Staff Sgt. Yance Gray, and Staff Sgt. Jeremy Murphy) appeared in the *New York Times,* 19 August 2007.

190 "cautious, very cautious, optimism": Senator McCain's assessment and Senator Graham's assertion about "We're doing now what we should have done three years ago" were offered at the Combined Press Information Center, Baghdad, 1 April 2007.

191 "He rolled over on the supplier": Maj. Allen's comment is in his interview in the Fort Leavenworth's Operational Leadership series.

191 "They feel as long as the Americans are there": Sgt. Maj. Clemens's comment is in his interview with the Operational Leadership series.

192 "The quality of life in Jisr Diuala": Grigsby's comment was made in a briefing with Pentagon reporters, 14 May 2008.

193 "synchronization of ISR/HUMINT/SIGINT": This is from "Ironhorse OIF 06-08," an undated operations report by the 1st Brigade Combat Team, 1st Cavalry Division.

195 "by not emphasizing population protection": Maj. Gen. Stone's analysis was offered in his undated memorandum "Task Force 134: From Strategic Risk to Strategic Advantage." The survey data in this and the following paragraph are from an untitled Task Force 134 PowerPoint briefing on the demographics and views of the detainee population.

197 "Of the twenty-seven hundred Iraqi security forces": Lt. Col. Miska was quoted in the *Washington Post,* 4 September 2007.

Chapter 7: Signs of Life in Baghdad

200 **"Now that the Sunnis are all gone":** Capt. Wink was quoted in the *Washington Post,* 16 July 2007.

202 **"Use minimum force":** Lt. Coppock's "Counterinsurgency Cliff Notes: Techniques for the Conventional Rifle Platoon, in Layman's Terms" was posted on the Small Wars Journal website in April 2008.

206 **"It's like raising a crocodile":** Al-Muttalibi's simile appeared in the *Washington Times,* 23 July 2007.

206 **"those terrorist elements":** The United Iraqi Alliance's statement was quoted in the *Washington Post,* 3 October 2007.

206 **"a coalition of gangsters, tribal leaders and opportunists":** Professor Porter's characterization was posted on the "Kings of War" blog, 16 July 2008.

207 **"If Jack Bauer doesn't negotiate with terrorists":** Spec. Horton posed this question on his blog, "Army of Dude," 24 July 2007.

207 **"We're going after al Qaeda":** Lt. Col. Kuehl recounted this statement by an Iraqi fighter in the *Washington Post,* 9 June 2007.

207 **"These guys looked like a military unit":** Capt. Wilbraham's comment is in the same Post article cited above.

209 **"Iraq obeys only force":** Col. al-Zobaie's assertions were quoted in the *Washington Post,* 24 March 2008.

210 **"There were almost 600 fighters in our sector":** The diary entries were quoted in the *Washington Post,* 10 February 2008. Some additional quotes are from documents released the same day by the U.S. military in Iraq under the title "Daily Diary of al Qaeda Sector Leader Called Abu Tariq."

210 **The insurgent who loved *Titanic:*** Most of the information in this section came from interviews conducted by e-mail with Capt. Cook, but it also relies on his written "Patrol Debriefs" and some other material.

213 **"You know that your jihad":** This and subsequent quotations from Col. Ismael and Sarhan are from a transcript of a recording of their meeting in January 2008.

215 **"knew where the [arms] caches were":** Capt. Galvach was quoted in the *Washington Post,* 9 August 2007.

215 **"one more step toward the fragmentation":** Malkasian expresses this concern in his article "A Thin Blue Line in the Sand," DemocracyJournal.org, Summer 2007.

216 **"embraced auxiliary tribalism":** Long's observation is in "The Anbar Awakening," *Survival* magazine, April 2008.

216 **"several ministries are so controlled":** The untitled study, written in September 2007 by the staff of the U.S. embassy in Baghdad, to my knowledge has never been released.

217 **"We did not fail":** Col. Gentile's article, "Our troops did not fail in 2006," was carried in the *International Herald Tribune,* 24 January 2008.

219 **"Just let them drive through":** This is quoted in the report of the "Theater Operations Detachment" for the Center for Army Lessons Learned at Fort Leavenworth," 13 January 2008.

219 **"a potential disaster":** Capt. Press's comment is in his article "After Action Report: Working with the Awakening in Central Anbar," *CTC Sentinel,* September 2008, published by the Combating Terrorism Center, U.S. Military Academy, West Point, N.Y.

224 **"The tribal strategy":** Long's comments are in "The Anbar Awakening," *Survival* magazine, April 2008.

225 **"fragmenting at a remarkable rate":** Professor Lynch made this comment on his website, AbuAardvaark.typepad.com.

Chapter 8: The Domestic Opposition Collapses

232 **Barbero, who had been thinking about the Middle East:** Barbero's monograph, titled "Iran-Iraq War of Exhaustion: The result of the paradoxical trinity," was published by the School of Advanced Military Studies, Fort Leavenworth, 15 May 1989.

240 **"By the end of 2007, less sophisticated forms of IEDs":** The report by Catherine Dale of the Congressional Research Service is "Operation Iraqi Freedom: Strategies, Approaches, Results, and Issues for Congress," 22 February 2008.

241 **"The surge hammered us at first":** The soldier's quote, subsequent quotes from other soldiers, and the data here are all from "Mental Health Advisory Team (MHAT) V/Operation Iraqi Freedom 06-08: Iraq/Operation Enduring Freedom 8: Afghanistan," 14 February 2008, Office of the Surgon, Multi-National Force-Iraq, and Office of the Command Surgeon—[deleted], and Office of the Surgeon General, United States Army Medical Command.

242 **"the systematic misuse of official institutions":** The study by the International Crisis Group is "Where Is Iraq Heading? Lessons from Basra," 25 June 2007.

244 **"the handwriting is on the wall":** Senator McConnell's comment appeared in the *Washington Post,* 27 May 2007.

244 **"By the time we get to September":** Representative Boehner's prediction was made on *Fox News Sunday,* 6 May 2007, and quoted the following day in the *Washington Post.*

245 **"Many of us had hoped this summer":** This is from Gen. Petraeus's letter to the troops, issued 7 September 2007.

249 **Between June and December:** The data in this paragraph are from a briefing I attended at Camp Liberty, Iraq, on 31 January 2008, and from accompanying slides titled "MND-B Operations & Intelligence Briefing."

254 **The best evidence for that new hands-off attitude:** The data on television news coverage of the war in this paragraph appear in "Iraq war disappears as TV story," by David Bauder, the *Miami Herald,* 17 March 2008.

254 **"It seems like a bad dream":** George's comment was quoted in the *American Journalism Review,* April/May 2008.

Chapter 9: The Twilight Zone

259 **"progress":** Lt. Freeze's comment is from his online memoir, "Notes from Down Range," carried on the Army website Platoon Leader.

261 **"I don't think there is something":** Salih's comment appeared in the *Washington Post,* 10 August 2007.

263 **"The longer the Iraqi government":** White's comment appeared in the *Pocono Record,* 4 May 2008.

263 **"a good guy":** This is quoted in the report of the "Theater Operations Detachment" for the Center for Army Lessons Learned at Fort Leavenworth," 13 January 2008.

265 **"They are like mercenaries":** The Associated Press report was carried by the wire service on 29 June 2008.

265 **"Despite the repeated assurances":** Professor Hanna's article ran on the website of World Politics Review, 10 July 2008.

266 **"Oh people of Iraq":** *Guardian,* 10 November 2007.

266 **"Many times he had":** Capt. Cosper was quoted in the *Los Angeles Times,* 29 June 2008.

266 **"they've grown into a much more organized":** This is from Horton's blog, "Army of Dude," 24 July 2007.

267 **"deeply troubled":** Moore's article ran in the *New York Times,* 23 February 2008.

269 **"Our mission is to protect":** Starr was quoted in the *Washington Post,* 20 September 2007.

269 **"The Iraqis despised them":** Degn was quoted in the same *Washington Post,* article above.

270 **"It had every indication":** Lt. Col. Tarsa's observation is in the *Washington Post,* 12 October 2007, as is Capt. Cherry's comment that, "This was uncalled for."

Chapter 10: Big Wasta

This chapter relies in part on "The Battle for Basra," by Marisa Cochrane, *Institute for the Study of War,* 23 June 2008.

273 **"You know, we all feel much older":** Petraeus said this on CNN, 19 March 2008.

274 **"brazenly challenging":** Barnett's article, in the April 2008 issue of *Esquire,* was titled "The Man Between War and Peace."

275 **"General Odierno has experienced":** Herrington was quoted in the *Washington Post,* 16 February 2008.

277 **"By late 2007, the British position":** Cordesman's comment is in his study "Iraqi Force Development 2008," published by the Center for Strategic and International Studies, Washington, D.C.

277 "I'm not going to go into details": Marston's comments on the frustration of British officers were made at a symposium on counterinsurgency at the National Press Club, Washington, D.C., 22 July 2008.

287 "Nothing succeeds with the American public like success": Petraeus's dissertation is titled "The American military and the lessons of Vietnam: A study of military influence and the use of force in the post-Vietnam era" (Princeton University, 1987).

290 "Iraq is a badge of honor": This quote appeared in the *Washington Post,* 12 June 2006.

Chapter 11: After the Surge

297 "As Nouri al-Maliki has become more capable": Kahl's comment was made in a press briefing on Iraq given by the Center for New American Security, 13 August 2008.

297 "a totalitarian regime": Barzani's comment appeared in "Kurd-Arab Tensions May Threaten Iraq Calm," Reuters, 13 November 2008.

297 "the land the surge forgot": This is the title of a report by Michael Knights issued by the Washington Institute for Near East Policy, 30 October 2008.

297 "the war waiting": McCaffrey's assertion is in an After Action Report on his visit to Iraq and Kuwait in October and November 2008.

297 provoking the Kurds' Barzani to issue an ultimatum: In an interview with *Ashard Alawsat,* available at http://www.asharq-e.com, 3 September 2008, Barzani stated that "never, we will not relinquish Kirkuk whatever the circumstances are."

297 "The Iraqi army's campaign in Diyala": Hilterman's analysis appeared on the website Abu Aardvark under the title "Kurds See the Future and Don't Like It," 1 September 2008.

298 "The surge may have bought transitory successes": Simon's analysis is in "The Price of the Surge: How U.S. Strategy Is Hastening Iraq's Demise," *Foreign Affairs,* May/June 2008.

299 "rubber-stamping": Obama made his remarks to Terry Moran of ABC's *Nightline,* 21 July 2008.

304 Some 50,000 soldiers now have prescriptions: This was reported by Gregg Zoroya in *USA Today,* 21 October 2008, as was the information about the 509th Engineer Company.

304 The quality of recruits: The information in this paragraph about recruiting problems is from an article by Josh White in the *Washington Post,* 23 January 2008.

305 The military also has been admitting more recruits with criminal records: This and the other data in this paragraph about conduct waivers are from an article by Ann Scott Tyson that ran in the *Washington Post,* 22 April 2008.

305 "incredible stress": This and the other statements by Gen. Cody appeared in an article by Tyson in the *Washington Post,* 2 April 2008.

Chapter 12: Obama's War

307 "We're not looking at doing things fast": Col. Johnson's comment was made during a Pentagon roundtable with defense bloggers, 12 August 2008.

307 "The Vietnam War had drawn to a close when I was fairly young": Sen. Obama made this observation on the CNN television show *Fareed Zakaria GPS,* 13 July 2008. During that same interview he also made the comments about not abandoning Iraq that are quoted at the end of this paragraph.

309 "My 16-month time line, if you examine everything I've said": Obama's statement was reported widely, including in the *Washington Post,* 4 July 2008.

310 "a unified democratic country or to a fractured sectarian one": Janabi's analysis, "The Importance of Iraq's Provincial Elections," was published by the Washington Institute for Near East Policy on 26 September 2008.

311 "One particularly ominous aspect of Anbari politics": Lt. Cdr. Lindsay's observation in his essay "Does the 'Surge' Explain Iraq's Improved Security?," carried in the MIT Center for International Studies' "Audit of the Conventional Wisdom," September 2008.

Epilogue: The Long War

314 On the phrase Wolfowitz used, see for example my book *Fiasco,* p. 98, where he is quoted as saying, "it is hard to conceive that it would take more forces to provide stability in post–Saddam

Iraq than it would take to conduct the war itself and to secure the surrender of Saddam's security forces and his army—hard to imagine."

314 **See, for example, Klein's discussion** of the failures of imagination by both sides in the 1973 downing of a Libyan airliner by Israeli fighter jets, in chapter 5 of *Sources of Power: How People Make Decisions* (Boston: MIT Press, 2001).

315 **"History provides countless warnings":** Cordesman's observation in his essay "Grand Strategy and Iraq's Uncertain Future," published by the Center for Strategic and International Studies, 31 October 2008.

315 **"there has never been a successful counterinsurgency that took less than 10 years":** Kilcullen said this on the *Charlie Rose* television show, 5 October 2007.

316 **"This mission will be long":** Biddle's estimate is in his article "Patient Stabilized?," *National Interest,* March–April 2008.

317 **"only a decades-long American occupation":** Col. Gentile's prediction is in "A (Slightly) Better War: A Narrative and Its Defects," *World Affairs,* Summer 2008.

317 **"power sharing is always a prelude to violence":** McCreary's analysis appeared in his *NightWatch* e-mail report of 11 September 2008.

318 **"If the Americans leave":** Staff Sgt. Benavides was quoted in an article by Sam Dagher in the *Christian Science Monitor,* 3 July 2008.

318 **"a colossus with feet of clay":** Visser's description is in his essay "The Sadrists of Basra and the Far South of Iraq," published by the Norwegian Institute of International Affairs, May 2008.

319 **"the Sadrists are Tehran's historical main enemy":** Visser noted this in "The Sadrists, the Bush Administration's Narrative on Iraq, and the Maysan Operations," posted on www.historiae.org on 3 July 2008.

320 **"it is our friends who will come to power":** Khatami said this to Nasr, who included it in a draft of a study on "The Implications of Military Confrontation with Iran" and permitted me to quote it here.

322 **"The Iraqi army is a predominantly Shia institution":** This is from the same "Operational Leadership Experiences" interview with Sgt. Maj. Clemens that is quoted in Chapter 6.

323 **"watching *The Sopranos* or watching *The Godfather*":** This is from the "Operational Leadership Experiences" interview with Maj. Voorhies cited in Chapter 2.

323 **"they wanted to go back to the old way underneath Saddam":** Maj. Arnold stated this in his official "Operational Leadership Experiences" interview, Combat Studies Institute, Fort Leavenworth, Kansas, 16 January 2008.

323 **"Saddam Hussein taught them how to do that":** This is from Maj. Whitney's "Operational Leadership Experiences" interview, quoted in Chapter 2.

323 **"They're going to be ruthless":** Maj. Burr's prediction appears in his official "Operational Leadership Experiences" interview, Combat Studies Institute, Fort Leavenworth, Kansas, 13 April 2007.

324 **"the whole notion of democracy and representative government in Iraq was absolutely ludicrous":** Maj. Quayle states this in his official "Operational Leadership Experiences" interview, Combat Studies Institute, Fort Leavenworth, Kansas, 19 September 2008.

324 **the story of a Turkmen Shia police chief:** Capt. Gorkowski recounted this episode in "After Action Report: Assessing Acceptable Corruption in Iraq," CTC *Sentinel,* published by the Combating Terrorism Center, U.S. Military Academy, West Point, N.Y., August 2008.

325 **"America will have bequeathed a highly unstable state":** Dodge's warning is in "Iraq and the Next American President," *Survival,* October–November 2008.

ACKNOWLEDGMENTS

First, I want to thank my wife, inspiration and fellow writer, Mary Kay Ricks.

I also am endebted to my children, who are always interesting.

Scott Moyers, who has guided my writing career, even went so far as to suggest the title of this book. I am grateful also to my new editor, Ann Godoff. Also at Penguin Press, Lindsay Whalen and Abigail Cleaves were a pleasure to work with.

I particularly want to thank my editors at the *Washington Post* who supported this project: Susan Glasser, Len Downie, Carlos Lozada, Rajiv Chandrasekaran, and Bill Hamilton. Many colleagues at the *Post* also helped me: Steve Fainaru, Karen Deyoung, Walter Pincus, Dana Priest, Robin Wright, Joby Warrick, Ann Scott Tyson, Amit Paley, Josh Partlow, and, most notably, Josh White and Sudarsan Raghavan.

I am indebted to Kurt Campbell and Michèle Flournoy, and everyone at the Center for a New American Security, the wonderful think tank Kurt and Michele founded. This is the second book I have done under Kurt's auspices, and I have come to believe that in another life he was a very successful publisher. My researcher at CNAS, Michael Zubrow, helped every day to increase both the accuracy and scope of the book. I deeply appreciate his tireless work.

I want to thank Gen. David Petraeus, Gen. Raymond Odierno, and their staffs and subordinate units for their openness and tolerance on a series of trips I made to Iraq in 2007 and 2008. I appreciate the work of Lt. Col. Joe Yoswa and Col. Steve Boylan in facilitating my visits. I also want to thank Lt. Col. James

Hutton, Maj. Joseph Edstrom, and Maj. Brian Tribus for their help on my last trip to Baghdad for this book.

I also appreciate the help provided by dozens of soldiers who shared everything from letters and personal e-mails to PowerPoint summaries of their operations. I also am especially obliged to several officers who went out of their way to help me understand key phases of the war or important aspects of it: Col. Sean MacFarland, Lt. Col. Pete Kilner, Lt. Col. Joe Rice, Capt. Samuel Cook, and several members of the 1st Cavalry Division.

To my mind, the heroes of the Iraq war are the everyday soldier and the average Iraqi trying to get by. I am in awe of the Iraqi staff of the Washington Post's Baghdad bureau, who through death, kidnappings, and bombings have not only held together but produced superb journalism.

I am obliged to the Sandy Spring Friends School of Sandy Spring, Maryland, which responded with swift generosity when one Iraqi family associated with the *Post* was forced to flee Iraq. The school took two Iraqi students into its warm and tolerant environment. Those wishing to support its efforts should make out their checks to "Contribution to Financial Aid—Iraqi Refugee Fund" and send them to:

Karl Gedge
Sandy Spring Friends School
16923 Norwood Rd.
Sandy Spring, MD 20860

I am endebted to Greg Jaffe of the *Wall Street Journal,* who wrote the first account of the battle of Tarmiyah and who was generous in connecting me to members of the unit that fought there.

I appreciate the help given me by Sandy Ain, Ellie Rider, and Anne Russell Ricks.

I also want to thank my critical readers: Kurt Campbell, Shawn Brimley, retired Col. Robert Killebrew, retired Lt. Col. Terry Daly, Lt. Col. Joe Rice, Tom Donnelly, Mary Kay Ricks, and, especially, Vernon Loeb, once a great colleague and still a true friend.

The mistakes are my own.

INDEX